Profits in Buying & Renovating Homes

by

Lawrence Dworin

Craftsman Book Company
6058 Corte del Cedro/ P.O. Box 6500 / Carlsbad, CA 92018

To my wife, ***Mary****, without whose help none of this would have been possible.*

Library of Congress Cataloging-in-Publication Data

Dworin, Lawrence, 1953-
Profits in buying & renovating homes / by Lawrence Dworin.
p. c.m.
Includes index.
ISBN 0-934041-57-1
1. House buying. 2. House selling. 3. Dwellings--Remodeling--Economic aspects. 4. Real estate investment. I. Title.
II. Title: Profits in buying and renovating homes.
HD1390.5.D96 1990
643'.12--dc20 98-15011
CIP

Sixth printing 2002

Cover credits:
Dawn Shears: Design and Color Photography
Marilyn Cornell: Black and White Photography
Ed Bowers*, Home Detailing:* Home Restoration Work

Contents

CHAPTER ONE

Remodeling for Profit

There are probably as many ways to make money in real estate as there are people in the business. It's an enormous field, with many occupations and hundreds of specialties. All offer opportunities for those who know how to take advantage of them.

Your local library probably has a shelf of books on the subject. Some are good, some aren't. Many emphasize the financial side of real estate: making complicated deals to buy low and sell high, without doing any improvement work on the property. That isn't how I make a living in this business.

So what could I possibly offer that's new, that you haven't heard before?

I'll tell you. I'm an *investor/remodeler*. Notice that "investor" comes first. I'm in the business of making money from homes that I buy, fix up, and sell. Not just any home, not just any fix up, and not just any sale, mind you. It has to be done exactly right to make the right kind of money. And I *do* make money, plenty of it. I have to, it's my job. It's all I do. If I don't make money on my sales, I don't eat.

If you're interested in remodeling homes that you've bought for resale, this book is for you. My approach is simple, it works, it's low-risk, and it pays well. It's even fun — most of the time.

I'm going to explain, in detail, exactly how I make a good living in this business. I've learned a few things in the last 12 years. I've made some mistakes, taken a few wrong turns and stumbled more than once. But I've got most of the kinks out now and I see opportunities almost everywhere, in every part of the country, in hundreds, maybe thousands of communities.

What I do isn't unique. I think almost anyone could do it. Of course, it helps to know something about building and construction trades. I worked as a tradesman before quitting to do the work I do now. But if you've got some background in construction, a little cash, and are willing to get your hands dirty, this may be a good-paying career for you. On the chance that I'm right, I hope you'll stick with me long enough to consider my approach.

My Approach to Remodeling

Residential remodeling is very big. The home remodeling business is an enormous industry — not quite as big as new home construction, but much more steady and growing much faster. Many communities are passing no growth or slow growth initiatives to limit new housing. This is bad news for new home builders, but great for remodelers. These initiatives will force people to buy older homes and remodel them, and builders to look carefully at remodeling for their future. As the housing stock in this country grows older, the remodeling industry will grow with it. I'm told that in Europe, home remodeling is a much bigger industry than new home construction. We may see the same thing happen here during your lifetime.

Most homes are remodeled either by professional builders working for the owner, or by an owner who has the time and talent to do the work. Both the talented amateur and the professional remodeler have the same goal in mind — creating the nicest home possible for the owners' use. And there's nothing wrong with that — an owner with the desire and money to pay deserves as much.

If you're like most people, you're willing to spend more when it's you that gets the benefit. You want to please yourself and your family. The little extras in your life are worth the cost. "Who cares if the sink costs $2,000," you say. "It's exactly the one my wife wants."

My approach is different. As I said, I'm an *investor/remodeler*. My focus is minimizing the inputs to maximize the output. I've discovered that doing more work doesn't guarantee that I'll make more money. On each home I fix up, there's a point beyond which the cost of additional work can't be recovered on sale. Knowing how much to spend and where to spend it is one of the secrets I'm going to share with you.

Knowing what I know makes me less work-oriented than most remodelers, whether professional or amateur. It also affects the focus of this book. Most of the remodeling books I've seen approach the subject from the point of view of the work to be done. The authors assume that you have to work more to make more money or make the home more attractive and functional. The harder you work, the better you've done. That isn't what I've learned.

My Teacher Is Experience

Another reason you may want to try my approach is that I'm writing from experience. Many books are written by people who don't actually do the work they write about. They just like to talk about it, or maybe they just like to write books. They sit at their word-processing terminals and write about the way they figure it ought to be, or the way they imagine it is. There's little first-hand information in books like that. It's possible to write a book from what you learn in books or magazines. I haven't done that.

What you find between the covers of this book is all original and all based on my own experience. With very few exceptions, I'm only going to tell you what works for me — and sometimes about what didn't work for me. I'm not going to recommend anything unless I've tried it and know it works. And for good reason. Even some of my best ideas turned out to be flops.

There are a couple of exceptions that I couldn't resist. But I'll clearly identify them as possibilities you might want to consider — not what I'm recommending.

Buying, Remodeling, and Selling

Buying, remodeling, and selling homes is a big subject. To help you understand all the details, I'll go through the entire process with you step-by-step. We'll cover each subject in logical order, the same order you'll follow when you try it.

The first subject we'll cover is how to select the right property. This is probably the most important part of the entire process. I'll suggest a procedure for evaluating the properties available and the criteria you'll use when making the final choice.

Then we'll go into financing. How are you going to pay for the property? This can be a real problem. Many people who would like to buy and remodel houses can't because they don't have enough cash. I'll suggest some available options if your cash is limited.

Once you have the property, what should you fix and how should you fix it? I'll go through most of the common repair problems you can expect to run into, and suggest some good ways to deal with them.

What about improvements? How can you bring your run-down, out-of-date house up to the standards we've come to expect in a modern home? Improvements can be very expensive. Some are worthwhile and some are a waste of money. I'll help you decide which is which.

Nobody likes an ugly house! How can you make your house beautiful and desirable, so it brings top dollar, and yet not spend a fortune doing it? I'll explain inexpensive ways to turn a sow's ear into a silk purse.

We'll finish up with a section on selling your house. You won't get your profit until you find a buyer. I'll go into the options available to you for finding one, and closing the deal.

Now that you know what's ahead, let's get started. I hope you're ready to charge into the world of real estate and find that diamond in the rough just waiting for you to come along.

Pick Your Specialty

I believe the surest way to make money in real estate is to pick one type of property and specialize in it. There isn't one real estate industry in America. There's a million of them, one in each neighborhood and within neighborhoods, one for each type of home. It's impossible to know about every kind of property available on the market in every community. There are just too many. My specialty is single-family homes located near the community where I live. I don't do commercial property, I don't do multi-family, and I don't do construction contracting. I work in big-city suburbs, not small towns or resort areas.

I've chosen my specialty for several reasons, which I'll discuss a little later. I concentrate on single-family homes in a limited area. I've come to know my market. I know what buyers want in their homes. I know the best price range for maximum resale value. I know which streets and what neighborhoods are a good choice and which are a bad choice. I don't experiment with different types of property. I'd rather do a good job in a limited area with a certain type of home than run the risk of getting wiped out in unfamiliar territory.

Why Buy?

Many people, especially tradespeople, ask me why I buy the homes I remodel. Why risk my own money? Why take on the aggravation of being totally responsible for a major project? Is it really worth it?

My answer is a resounding *"YES!"* and for a number of reasons. I'll explain them one at a time.

Big Profits

First of all, as you might guess, there's good money to be made from buying and remodeling homes. Doing most of your own work compounds your profits. I'll explain.

You probably know of at least one investor who buys houses and hires contractors to remodel them. The contractors hire tradesmen to do the actual work. The tradesmen are paid a wage for their time, the contractor earns a share for his part of the job, and the investor makes a profit on the sale of the house, less expenses.

If investor/remodelers are active in your community, most are working this way. Many real estate investors make a good living like this. If you don't have the time and don't know anything about construction, maybe that's all you can do. Projects are being done this way every day

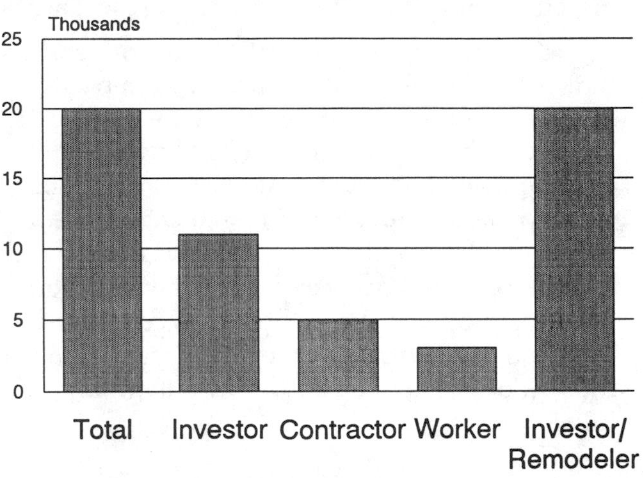

Figure 1-1

Investor/remodeler keeps it all!

and in every part of the country. I guess that proves there's plenty of profit in it.

William Nickerson, the famous author of real-estate books, suggests exactly this approach. He hires everything out. His book, *How I Turned $1,000 into $1,000,000 in Real Estate*, is a classic. The information in the book is as valuable today as it was when it was written in 1959. It's one of the few real-estate books that I recommend.

But what if you do some or most of the work yourself? If you buy the house, you're the investor. If you organize the work, you're the contractor. If you do some or all the work yourself, you're the tradesman. Therefore, you're entitled to the wages paid to the contractor and the tradesman, as well as the investor's profit. You're paid triple for every hour of work you put in on your project! Figure 1-1 shows the difference in profit margin between an investor and an investor/remodeler.

I've said that there's good money to be made in this business. So why don't I hire tradesmen to do all the work? Here's my answer: Absentee investor/remodelers lose control. They aren't there to make the thousands of decisions that are required for every job. They pay too much for supervision, for materials and for labor when they rely on someone else to do the work for them. My advice is to do what you can and what you enjoy. You'll end up putting far more profit in your pocket.

Steady Income

If you're a contractor or a tradesman, you'll have slow periods. There won't be enough work to keep you busy. If you've ever watched your bills pile up while you wait for work that doesn't come in, you know what an uneasy feeling that is. Remodeling your own houses can put an end to that feeling. You create your own job and you're your own boss. You can plan your work to stay busy for weeks or even months at a time.

What if you're too busy to have time for your project? No problem. Your own house can wait a week or so. Of course, it isn't a good idea to leave it unfinished for too long. After all, you have monthly payments. But a week lost now or then won't make much difference.

This flexibility is important, especially if you work at another job. You can buy and remodel homes at your convenience. If the work load varies during the year at your regular job, plan work on your remodeling project when you have time. You control the work. The work doesn't control you.

Rental Income

Another way to guarantee a steady income from your investments is to plan on renting out some of your completed houses. If you've selected a good property, the monthly mortgage payment and expenses will be less than the potential rent on the property. Rent it instead of selling. This can benefit you in several ways. You'll have a steady flow of money coming in every month, year after year, and rental property offers you a good tax break. Believe me, it isn't difficult to accumulate enough rental income to cover all your basic living expenses.

That's exactly what I do. My rental property provides the income I need to cover my monthly bills. I use the profits from the properties I fix up and sell for spending money and new investments. Even if I don't do any work one month, my expenses are paid and I'll still be able to eat. When you're self-employed you don't get sick days, vacation days, unemployment compensation, or any of the other fringe benefits that make life more secure. However, rental income goes a long way towards solving that problem. If you don't work you'll make less money, but you won't starve.

Work When You Want To

Here's another advantage you have as an investor/remodeler. You get in, do your work and get out. You buy a house, fix it up, sell it, and then you're done. If you want, you can then go on and buy another property; or you can take some time off for a vacation; or you can go back to your regular job. It's your choice.

Buying and remodeling houses isn't a continuing commitment. You're only committed to one house at a time. It gives you a more flexible work schedule than anyone working for wages.

Be Your Own Boss

If you're a remodeling contractor, you're already your own boss, at least in a sense. Of course, you work for yourself. But in fact, your customers are your boss. They determine when you work, and how you work, and what has to be done over. Let's face it, you won't be in business very long if you don't do what your customers want. Unfortunately, some customers can be very difficult — nit-picking, unreasonable, and fault-finding. You know what I mean. They can take all the fun out of your work.

When you're remodeling your own property, you're the customer. You can do anything you want, and do it your way. You don't have to justify your costs, or have your best ideas rejected, or good work ruined by someone else's whims. What you want is what you get. You're responsible only to the future buyer. And you may not meet that buyer until the project is finished. For me, this alone makes buying and remodeling houses worthwhile.

Of course, sooner or later you're going to have to deal with customers. That is, if you want to sell the house. But all your customers ever see is the finished product. They won't know what the house looked like before you started or how you managed to make it as nice as it is. Better yet, they won't care. You're offering them a good house for a good price. They're happy, and you're happy. You're making a good profit.

Other professions— If you're a tradesmen or handyman, you may never have been your own boss before. It's a rewarding experience. I spent several years of my life working for other people. I know what it's like to do seemingly pointless tasks because someone higher up has a crazy idea. I also know what it's like to have valuable, creative projects rejected. Well, as your own boss, you don't ever have to put up with that.

Sure, being the boss can be a headache at times. You have the final responsibility for everything, and sometimes it won't be pleasant. If there's a job that's so nasty and disgusting that I can't even *pay* someone else to do it, guess who gets stuck with it? And if I don't make as much on a project as I expected, there's no one to blame except myself. However, just being able to say, "We're going to do it my way, because I'm the boss," makes it all worthwhile. Maybe you feel the same way.

Owners Have Privileges

While the building code and zoning ordinances vary from city to city, property owners have less restrictions than hired contractors. Most laws, after all, are made to protect the property owners. You only have to worry about the codes which will protect you from yourself!

As an owner, you won't need a contractor's licence to work on your own property. You *will* need to get permits for major work, and your work *will* still have to pass inspection. But many cities issue "owner permits," which are usually very easy to get. A lot of the work you'll be doing may not involve any paperwork at all! As a contractor, you'd need a briefcase full of plans and permits to do any work at all.

Many cities require general contractors to use subcontracts for trades like plumbing and electrical work. But many of those same cities will issue you an "owner permit" to do the work yourself. That can save you a lot of money. Of course, you'd better know what you're doing (for your own safety, and to pass inspection). Subcontract anything that's over your head. You're not going to lose anything. You'd have had to do that as a contractor anyway.

Work Preference

Another advantage to being both the boss and the owner is that you can organize the work to suit yourself. For instance, you can hire out jobs you don't particularly like, and just do what you enjoy (most of the time). You can do the work in any order you like, although you have to be practical. Some jobs *have* to be done before others. You wouldn't want to lay carpet before painting, for example. But in most cases you can do what you want, when you want and the way you want.

Tax Advantages

Many tax advantages are available to investor/remodelers. Although the 1986 Tax Reform Act eliminated some of them, enough remain to make buying and remodeling homes worthwhile. In fact, since the Tax Reform Act eliminated so many deductions in other areas, my line of work may actually have come out better by comparison.

The profits you make from buying and reselling houses are now taxed as ordinary income, but all your job-related expenses are deductible. This includes mileage and gasoline for the time you spent driving around looking at property; your closing costs, mortgage interest and property taxes; and the cost of the tools and supplies used to fix up the property. Your accountant can probably suggest other deductions you're legally entitled to claim.

You'll probably pay less tax on profits from the sale of a house than you would on equivalent income as an employee. See Figure 1-2.

The tax benefits are even better with rental property. If you rent a house out, your profit is distributed over many years. If you're on the border of a higher tax bracket, this can be very helpful. Even more helpful is your depreciation allowance on the property. You can deduct a percentage of the cost of your property as depreciation, even if the property's value is going up!

The maximum allowable depreciation on rental property at the time of this writing is

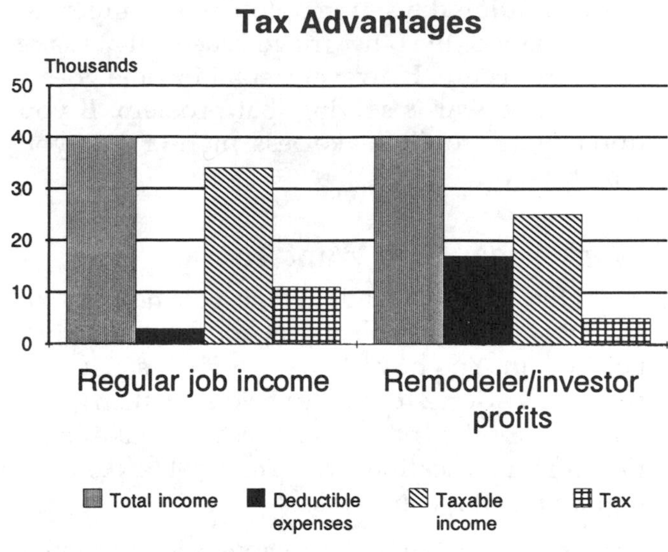

Figure 1-2

Investor/remodeler pays less tax on income

roughly 3.4 percent per year. The cost of the building can be depreciated over no less than 29.5 years. But I have properties that are increasing in value about 20 percent a year. Yet I can still depreciate them by 3.4 percent a year! You won't be taxed on the appreciation (which is your profit) until you sell the property. That's a good deal. Not as good as it was before the Tax Reform Act, but still good. With rental property you can make a very good income year after year and pay little or no tax at all! You get to keep your money, instead of giving it all to Uncle Sam. There are very few businesses where you can do that . . . legally. I'll go over this in much greater detail in the section on "Rental."

Sound Interesting?

I hope by this time you're beginning to see the possibilities. The purpose of this chapter is to whet your appetite for more. And, of course, there's plenty more — more to learn, more opportunities to recognize, and more pitfalls to avoid.

If you're ready to dive in and begin at the beginning, go on to Chapter 2.

CHAPTER TWO

Selecting the Right House

Nothing is more important than buying the right property in the first place. If you select a good property, it's hard to avoid making money. You can just sit on it while it appreciates in value. If you select the wrong property, breaking even may be the best that can happen. What's the worst that can happen? You have to sell the property at a loss to salvage your credit rating.

The real estate section of my local newspaper has had several articles about people who've bought houses, fixed them up, and gone broke trying to sell them. You may have heard similar horror stories from friends. If you've been in the real estate business very long, you know people who've taken a beating speculating in property values.

It's true. I've seen it happen. Make a few mistakes and you can lose your shirt. But I've heard many more stories about people who make a good living fixing up houses for resale. And because there are far more successes than failures, I think you've got a good chance of being successful in this business.

How do you know the right house when you see it — the house where a minimum of work and money offers the maximum return? Well, keep reading. That's the subject of this chapter.

Successful investors do their homework. They study the homes for sale and pick the right property in the right community at the right time. They know their home prices, they know the market, and they know what they can afford to get into. They also know how to estimate their expenses and their potential profit . . . *before they buy!*

Of course, no one hits a home run every time at bat. Even successful investors have an occasional failure, just as a novice can stumble onto success. But to succeed in this business you have to pick winners most of the time. That's what this chapter is intended to teach.

What Property Is Best for You?

What do I mean by *best*? Best is a relative term. What's best for me may not be best for you. How much money do you have? How much time do you have? What skills do you have? All of these have a bearing on what kind of property is best for you.

Where do you start looking for something to buy? My suggestion is that you start by organizing or classifying the available property.

What's Your Price Range?

Price is a pretty obvious way to classify property. It will help you narrow the field. There's no point in looking at expensive property if it's out of your price range. So let's decide what price range is right for you.

There are three very broad price ranges when you're looking for property: cheap, moderate- to middle-priced, and expensive. Again, these terms are relative. Expensive, for instance, can be anything from $200,000 to $10,000,000. And moderate to one person may be cheap to another. In many parts of the U.S., any home over $250,000 would be considered expensive, average is about $130,000, and cheap is anything under $80,000. Of course, these figures vary with the area and can be expected to increase in the future. In New York, for example, the average price for a used home is about $200,000. In California and Hawaii, the average resale price is above that. On the other end of the scale, the going rate for the average home in many small midwestern towns is well under $80,000.

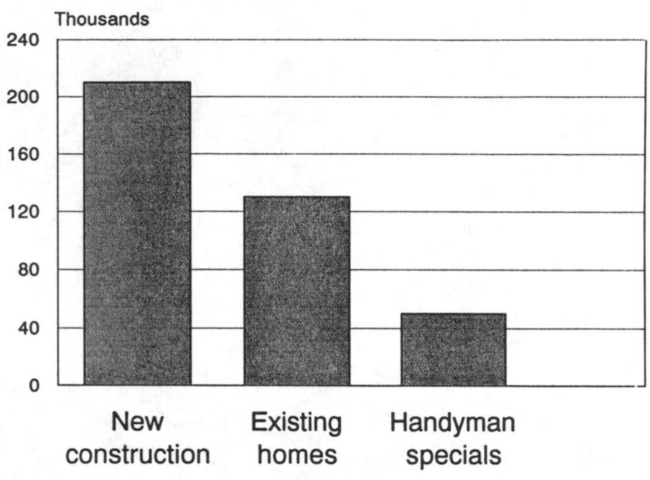

Figure 2-1

Handyman specials are a bargain in today's housing market

Keep in mind that these prices are for existing homes, not new construction. The homes that you'll be considering as remodeling projects are far from new, but the price of new homes will affect you. The more expensive new homes become, the more appealing your remodeled home will seem by comparison. The graph in Figure 2-1 clearly shows the advantage of buying an existing home, particularly one that needs a little work.

Generally you'll find the largest selection of homes in the moderate- or middle-priced housing range. That's the price range that I deal with most often, and the one I recommend. There are more advantages and fewer risks for me than in low- or high-end housing.

Let's look at the advantages and disadvantages of dealing with each price range. Your circumstances may be a little different from mine. Maybe you could do better with lower cost or higher cost homes. Each price range has its advantages. But listing advantages and disadvantages is a lot like telling "good news and bad news" jokes. Don't get too excited about the good news until you've heard the bad news. Let's start by looking at high-end property.

Figure 2-2
Big houses can bring big profits

Expensive Property

What you'll find in this price range, and even what is considered expensive, varies from area to area. If you're not sure how the prices in your area compare to the national averages, a good real estate agent will be able to help you.

Advantages— When you work with expensive property, everything is big. Houses are big, lots are big, *and profits are big.*

You'll be dealing with upscale buyers who have borrowing power and down payments — usually from the sale of another home. They aren't afraid of large price tags. If they like your house, they'll cheerfully pay a *lot* of money for it. People who have big incomes are more concerned with getting the features they want than how much they have to pay for them. They want a nice home with quality that shows. If you can remodel larger homes in good neighborhoods, like the home in Figure 2-2, you can make good money in this business.

What's the difference between a $5,000 kitchen and a $25,000 kitchen? Some of the difference is in the materials, but most of it is time, skill, and design. A $25,000 kitchen requires highly skilled labor. You can't do Chevy work and expect to get a Mercedes Benz price for it. But if you create a Mercedes-quality home, you can get Mercedes-type money for it. If you have good sources for materials, and the talents required for the job, you can make as much as $20,000 by remodeling the kitchen alone. Remodel the rest of the house and you're talking *good* money!

Here's another big advantage to dealing in high-end property. Homes in expensive neighborhoods are often drastically underpriced if they've fallen into disrepair. Why? Because most upscale buyers don't have the time or the patience to redo an out-of-date or rundown home. Their time is valuable, probably a lot more than either yours or mine. As a rule, they'll pass up a house that needs work. They just don't want the headaches involved in redoing it. They aren't bargain hunting, they're house hunting.

That's where you come in. You don't care how it looks — you're going to remodel it anyway. You *do* care that it's a bargain. It's an opportunity for you to make a lot of money. Simple cosmetic work can knock as much as $50,000 off the price of an expensive house. If it needs serious work, a new roof for instance, the price can drop by $100,000. You bring the house up to the neighborhood standards and you can pocket the difference. I don't consider $100,000 bad wages for a couple of months' work.

This sounds great, doesn't it? But stop a minute. If it's such a good deal, why isn't everybody doing it? Well, here's the bad news.

Disadvantages— Cost! First of all, luxury homes, even when in bad shape, are still luxury homes. Sure, it may be $100,000 underpriced. But we're talking about a $300,000 house that you can maybe get for $200,000. At 20 percent down plus closing costs, you'll need to come up with about $50,000 cash, plus about $1,600 a month for payments. Do you have good credit? Maybe you can buy with only 10 percent down. Then you'll only need $30,000 cash. Of course, your payments will be higher. Can you cover a $1,800 payment? Keep in mind that you'll be kissing $1,800 dollars goodbye every month the house is vacant. You'll have to work fast!

What about a zero down payment loan? Though you may find deals like this for cheap property, they're rarely available on expensive property. And even if they were, no down payment means higher monthly payments, maybe $2,000 a month. How many months can you afford to pay that?

The second disadvantage is the amount of work involved in redoing a large house. Remember, everything is big in expensive properties, and big houses simply take more work than small ones. Even if the house *only* needs paint, you may be looking at weeks of work and thousands of dollars in materials. Why? Because there are so many square feet to cover! If you hired a paint contractor to do a complete exterior paint job for a large house, it could easily run $10,000 or more.

Now you understand why the upscale buyers pass these homes by. They didn't get rich by being stupid. They think, "Hmm — $10,000 for paint, $25,000 for a new kitchen, $15,000 for roof work. That's $50,000 in repairs plus all those headaches . . . No, it's not worth it." Of course, it will only cost you a fraction of this amount if you can do the work yourself. But you're still talking about thousands of dollars for materials, months of work, and mortgage payments all the while. Do you have this kind of time and money in your budget?

And what about the quality of the work? Remember, upscale buyers are very finicky. Most refuse to tolerate second-rate work. Are you a skilled finish carpenter? If not, don't touch that kitchen! You're better off leaving it alone than doing a second-rate job. A poor quality job will cost you, not make you money. Even if you managed to sell the house with a second-rate kitchen, your buyers would simply have the kitchen torn out and redone correctly. They aren't going to pay you extra for work that has to be redone!

Deluxe homes are not for the "do-it-yourselfer." If you're not a highly skilled craftsman, hire the work out. Of course, every penny you pay for wages comes out of your profit. Fine craftsmen don't work cheap, and they're not likely to wait until you sell the house to get their money. You need to have enough in your budget to pay them as the job progresses. Do you have a few thousand dollars available for this purpose?

The same thing goes for that exterior paint job. Don't think you can just slap on some discount brand latex and get $10,000 for it. It's not uncommon for a buyer to hire professional inspectors to check out a home before they buy. After all, they're paying a lot of money for the property. You can't slip a shoddy paint job past an inspector. You'll have to scrape and caulk the wood siding, repair any damage, and paint with at least two coats of top-quality paint. Nothing short of this will be acceptable. If you've ever done it, you know how much work that is. Of course, you'll be well paid for your time, but don't make the mistake of thinking it's easy.

And here's my last point: In all property investments there's an element of risk. Nothing in life is 100 percent certain. If you buy a house way under market value and complete it quickly, you'll probably be able to sell it quickly, too. But what if you can't? Can you afford to keep up $1,600 payments for, say, six months? If you can't, you'll have to sell low in order to get rid of it. If you sell low, you won't make very much money, will you?

The value of high-end homes fluctuates with changes in the economy. An expensive house is a major financial burden. Buyers aren't likely to commit themselves to a $2,500 monthly payment if their jobs or the economy are uncertain.

Upscale housing is "trade up" housing. You're not selling to first time buyers. Your buyers already own a nice home. They just want a *nicer* one. In a good economy, they'll buy up, and be willing to pay top dollar for it. In a weak economy, people stay where they are. If prospects improve, they'll consider buying something really nice the following year. Can you afford to wait until next year to sell the house?

Even under ideal circumstances, the time span between making a purchase offer on a house, taking possession, doing your repairs, selling and actually closing escrow on the sale will be at *least* three months, and probably six or more. Real estate sales take time, and the work takes time as well. You may begin the process in a sunny economy and watch it slide into a recession before you're ready to sell. Then what are you going to do with your expensive house?

If these questions leave you feeling a little uneasy, consider less expensive property. You can buy several moderate-priced houses for the price of one expensive one.

Expensive vs. less expensive— What about less expensive housing in a bad economy? Isn't it also difficult to sell? No. People have to live somewhere. Those who already have nice homes will stay where they are. But people who don't have homes will buy what they can afford. The cheaper the housing is, the less a downturn in the economy will affect it. (See Figure 2-3.) I try to buy property cheap enough so that I can make out even if there's a recession. This may be overly cautious, and I may have lost some good opportunities by following this principle — but then I've never lost a penny in real estate. Not many investors can make that statement.

The Effect of Economic Conditions on Home Sales

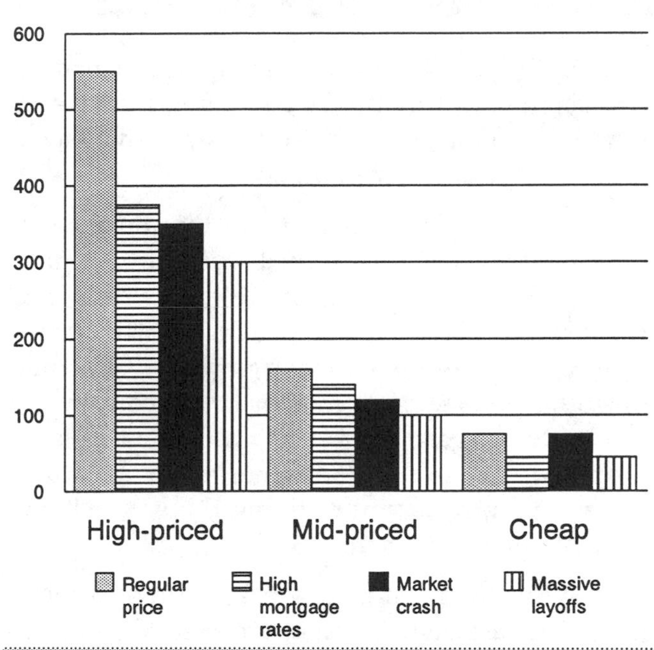

Figure 2-3
Risk increases with price in bad times

By now you probably have the impression that I don't believe in buying expensive property. That isn't exactly true. I simply don't recommend buying expensive property unless you can afford to live in it yourself. That's the only way I know of to protect yourself from all the problems we just covered.

Buy the most expensive property you can comfortably afford. Select a home with a down payment that you can handle, and a monthly payment that's suitable for your income. You don't have to worry about finding a buyer for the property, because you're the buyer of last resort. You don't need to worry about the quality of the work because you already know what you'll accept. Plan your work with the thought that eventually you'll want to sell the house, and of course, make a tidy profit. However, if it takes a while, it isn't a problem. You simply live there, and enjoy your luxury home.

You may have to work in this business a while before you can afford your first luxury home. However, the principle is the same for whatever level of property you can afford. *Always keep the most expensive property for yourself.* If someone offers you a good price for it, you can always sell it. But, in case they don't, you don't have to worry about making payments on a vacant house. As long as you're living there, you'll get some value for your money.

While the benefits of working on expensive properties are high, the risks are even higher. I do *not* recommend this kind of property to the beginner. One bad deal on expensive property can quickly wipe out your working capital.

After you've successfully completed a few properties, and you're confident about your skills and abilities in this area, you might go after an expensive property. But make sure you've got enough cash to work with. There's simply too much that can go wrong. And like everything else when you're dealing with expensive property, if it goes wrong, it goes wrong *big*!

Cheap Property

What do I mean by *cheap property*? I mean property that's just about the cheapest single-family home available — or at least in the bottom 10 percent of all homes offered. In many areas that's in the $80,000 range, with your completed renovation. Sometimes you can get middle-range property so heavily discounted that it slips down into the cheap range. In fact, my favorite kind of property is the house in a middle-income neighborhood that's such a disaster it's been discounted down to the value of the bare land! That's where I make my best money. But that's not what I'm referring to here. When I say cheap, I mean property that's never going to be worth very much, no matter what you do with it. There are definite advantages and disadvantages to cheap property.

Advantages— Price is obviously the biggest advantage of cheap property. How much money will you need to get started on cheap property? Sometimes nothing. This is where you find the zero down payment deals.

There are people who feel that their property is worth less than the amount owed. If the property hasn't been maintained, they may be right! It's just a liability. The seller may literally give the property away just to get out from under the mortgage payments.

I've bought a number of houses where the sellers walked away with no money at all. When all the outstanding debts, fees, and commissions were paid, there was nothing left. I've even seen cases where the former owners had to pay money out of their own pocket to get rid of the house. They took less than nothing for their property to avoid foreclosure. It was worth it to them to pay a few hundred dollars and save their credit rating.

In this business, someone's financial problems can become your opportunities. Sometimes homeowners have nothing to fall back on in times of trouble. When a layoff or divorce results in a distress sale, some people have to sell homes quickly for whatever a quick sale can bring. I've seen some incredible deals that fall into this category. There's nothing wrong with the property. The owners have the problems, not the house.

The death of the owner prompted the sale of the house in Figure 2-4. It had obviously been neglected, inside and out, for some time. The former owner's son just didn't want the responsibility. He sold it under market price, which made it a good deal for me. Not a great deal though. The neighborhood was old, and not improving. All I did was make minor repairs, paint, and clean the yard up a bit. A small investment of time and money made a modest profit.

A big advantage of cheap property is that you don't have to worry about finicky buyers. In

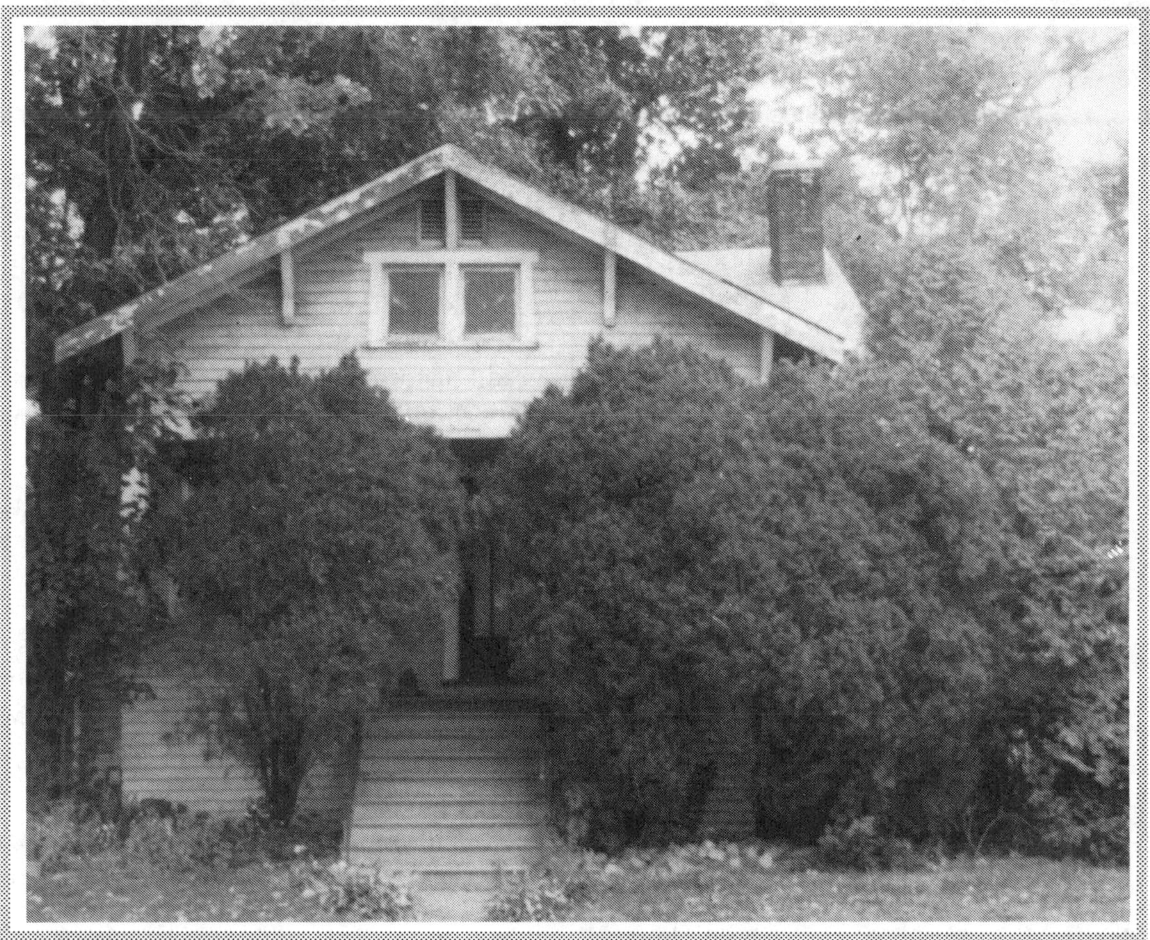

Figure 2-4
Neglected older home in older neighborhood

this price range, your remodeling should result in a clean, decent, functional house that's up to code, but nothing more. It doesn't need to be fancy, and your buyers won't care if it isn't perfect. As long as it's clean and everything works, you'll have no trouble selling a home in the cheap range.

Since most cheap houses are fairly small, the amount of work you have to do is considerably less. It doesn't take as long to paint a little house as it does to paint a big one. You could complete a dozen plain, small houses in the time it would take you to do one expensive house. If you don't have a lot of time to spare for a project, a cheap house might be a good buy for you.

Also, cheap property isn't affected very much by changes in the economy . . . unless there are massive local layoffs. Changes in the stock market won't affect the buyers of houses in this price range. If the owners lose their jobs, that could be serious. But they'll probably be able to cover their house payments with unemployment compensation.

There's very little risk involved with cheap property. With little or no money down, you won't have much of your own money tied up. If it takes a while to sell the house, the mortgage payments are reasonable. You can probably afford to carry the house for a short time.

There's one more advantage I should mention. If you make a mistake, you've lost less. Until you have confidence in your ability to do this kind of work, learn your lessons on cheap houses.

They offer you the benefit of on-the-job training without the threat of a huge financial loss.

Disadvantages— The most obvious disadvantage of cheap property is that it's just never going to make you rich. Most cheap property is located in lower-middle-class or lower-income neighborhoods. The people who buy houses in these neighborhoods don't have a whole lot of money to spend.

So even if you turn this old, run-down house into a palace, your buyer won't be able to pay very much for it. It may sell quickly because it's the nicest home in the neighborhood, but it won't sell for much more. If you're very lucky, you can make a $10,000 profit on a cheap property. But you're not likely to make a $75,000 profit on a house that sells for $80,000.

Here's another disadvantage: You'll probably have to do a lot of work to bring the house up to standard. Unlike expensive property, chances are you'll be facing more than just cosmetic repairs. Expect to find massive damage on cheap property: rotten roofs, demolished walls, and ruined plumbing and electrical are common. While the quality of work on a cheap house doesn't have to be as good as on a better house, the *quantity* may be staggering.

Someone made the mistake of buying the home in Figure 2-5 as a fixer. Soon it was back on the market for almost the same price it had originally sold for. Why? The roof had been leaking for so long that there was extensive interior damage throughout the house. The repairs would have cost more than the house could ever sell for. So the buyers put on a fresh coat of paint and hoped somebody else would be foolish enough to take it off their hands. Be extra careful when buying cheap property!

Cheap houses aren't heavily discounted if they're just ugly or dirty. That won't lower the price as much as it would on an expensive house. People shopping in this price range don't have such high expectations. In cheap housing, you have to take what you can get. You won't get a big discount on these houses unless they're practically unlivable. You can make money on cheap houses, but you're going to earn every penny of it!

When it comes time to sell the property, you may face another problem. Your prospective buyers aren't always A-1 credit risks. Many people in this income bracket don't have credit cards or bank accounts. Even though they may be very responsible about paying their bills, they have no credit history. They pay for everything with cash. They might not understand credit and finance, or they just prefer to avoid it.

Others may have a lot of black marks on their credit report, such as defaulted loans, evictions, and bankruptcies. They may love your house, but they aren't going to be able to get the loan. Well then, how are you going to sell your house? You may have to do some creative financing. The buyer's problems are now your problems.

What if your buyers quit making their payments? It's much more difficult to take possession under a deed of trust or mortgage than it is to evict a rental tenant. Laws vary from state to state, but in many states, the process can take up to a year. Beware of buyers of cheap property who use the law to their advantage. There are such people. They have no intention of ever making any payments. They only buy property to get a year's free rent. During that year, they're likely to take out their bad humor on your property. By the time you get it back, it may be in a lot worse condition than it was when you first bought it.

You can avoid getting involved in situations like this by insisting on a down payment equal to one year's rent. Usually that's only $6,000 to $8,000. If your buyers don't make their payments, you'll at least break even on the rent during the eviction process. It may make your house a little more difficult to sell, but the added financial safety is worth it.

If you have very little money to work with, or your credit isn't very good, cheap property is a good place for you to start. But if you can manage to come up with a little extra, I strongly

Figure 2-5
New paint job, but rotten roof

recommend moving up to moderate-priced property instead. While the risks in cheap property are less, the benefits are much less as well.

Moderate-Priced Property

Now we come to my specialty: moderate or middle-income houses. Almost all the property I buy falls into this category. Let me tell you why.

Advantages— Good profits. While moderate-priced property can't yield as much as expensive property, it's still possible to make a good return. A $25,000-$50,000 profit is not unusual, and in most cases you don't have to work too hard for the money.

One important feature about moderate-priced property is that the discounting phenomenon that occurs in expensive property occurs here, too. It's often possible to get a mid-priced house cheap, simply because it's dirty and needs paint. Middle-class buyers don't like dirty, ugly houses any more than more prosperous people do. Of course, they're not as finicky as the wealthy, but they still don't buy houses that badly need repairs.

That's exactly what got me started in this business. I wanted to buy a house for myself, but I didn't have very much money. I couldn't afford a nice house in good condition. After looking at many depressingly unaffordable houses, I came across one that was substantially cheaper than all the rest. It needed exterior paint, and the yard was piled with mountains of trash. The real estate agent who showed me the property said that most people wouldn't even look at the inside of the house. They took one look at the exterior and said "Forget it!" This was lucky for me because the interior was in absolutely perfect condition.

Since I was the only prospective buyer, I made a low offer on the house, and the owners accepted. I spent $100 on paint and minor repairs, got rid of the trash, and sold the house for a

Figure 2-6
There is good profit potential in this mid-priced home

$10,000 profit. "Not bad for a week's work," I said. So I found another property and did it again . . . and then again . . . and again.

The important difference between dealing in mid-priced property and cheap property is that you can buy low and sell high when your work is complete. Unlike cheap property, which will never sell for very much, there's a good potential profit to be made on a $130,000 home (especially if you can buy it for under $80,000). The house in Figure 2-6 is the only run-down house in a nice neighborhood. This house could be a real money-maker. Buyers in the mid-price range have more financial leeway. If they really like your house, they might be willing to spend a little more, say $140,000. Lower-priced homes "ceiling out" much sooner. No matter how much they like it, lower-income buyers simply can't pay any more.

Often you can buy a mid-priced home for just a little more than a cheap home, and with similar terms. Distress sales are almost as common in moderate-priced areas as they are in cheap areas. Zero-down deals or assumptions of existing loans are harder to find, but they do turn up occasionally. And even if you have to get a new loan to buy the property, you only need to come up with a moderate amount of cash. With $10,000 to $15,000 down you can find plenty of good properties that will resell in the mid-price range. This is a far cry from the $25,000 to $50,000 you might need to get into more expensive property.

Less risk— Probably the most convincing reason to buy a mid-priced home is that they are, overall, less risky than either expensive or cheap houses. Your purchasers are likely to be middle-class people, with good jobs and good credit. And since the middle-class makes up the largest share of people in the home-buying market, you'll have a large number of potential buyers. You can easily sell to someone who'll qualify for a new mortgage, and this makes a tremendous difference to you.

A new mortgage (for you as the seller) is the same as cash. You can pay off whatever mortgage you had on the house and walk away with a cash profit. If the purchaser should quit making payments, it's the new lender's problem, not yours. Selling to someone who's able to get a new loan eliminates the risk to you.

What if you can't sell right away and you have to make payments on the property? The payments won't be so high, not that much more than you'd have to pay for cheap property. Your risk, in terms of the monthly payments, is close to the cheap property. But your profit potential is much higher. Therefore, the overall risk vs. benefit ratio is much better for mid-priced than for cheap property.

The return ratio— Another good comparison is how much return you'll get on your labor and expenses. It costs roughly the same to paint a cheap house as it does a moderate-priced house. Yet the paint job will raise the value of a mid-priced house more than the value of a cheap house. Why? Because repairs like this usually increase the value of a house in proportion to its potential selling price. The higher the potential value of a house, the greater the percentage of profit you'll get on your improvements.

Let's say we're choosing among three houses, each one in a different price range. If they're all dirty and in need of paint, the prices of all three would be driven down. But how much? In the case of the expensive house, the price would probably drop by something like 20 percent. High-income people have very little tolerance for dirty, unpainted, peeling houses. The mid-priced house would drop less, but still quite a bit, probably something like 15 percent. The cheap house, on the other hand, would only decline about 5 to 10 percent. It can't go down too much because the price of the house is already low. Also, the lower the price range of the house, the more tolerant buyers are of its defects.

How does this translate into dollars and cents? In the case of a $400,000 house, the price may go down to around $320,000, an $80,000 drop in value. The mid-priced house would drop from $130,000 to $110,000, still a substantial amount. The cheap house, whose maximum value is $80,000 to begin with, would decline in value only $4,000 to $8,000 at the most. It's interesting to note that the expensive house would drop as much in dollar value as the total cost of the cheap house.

Looking at these figures, you can see that the expensive house obviously has the greatest profit potential — *if* you can afford the $320,000 price tag. The cheap house, at the opposite extreme, has an attractive price but little profit potential. In fact, by the time you consider the cost of buying and selling, it could leave you with a net loss.

The mid-priced house, on the other hand, is a possibility. Its price is affordable, and the $20,000 potential profit (less expenses) makes it almost worth buying, though you could probably find something better. You want to *clear* at least $20,000 on the deal.

Let me make a quick point here about profits. If you're going to make a living in this business, you really have to restrict yourself to good profit properties. There are lots and lots of easy fixers like my first house that are discounted 10 to 20 percent below market. You can do dozens of these, but not make much money because of the time and cost involved in buying and selling the property. So when I say you want to clear at least $20,000 on a deal, I'm not being optimistic, I'm being realistic.

Disadvantages— The only disadvantages of mid-priced houses are comparative: it doesn't offer the profit potential of expensive property, and it costs a little more to buy than cheap

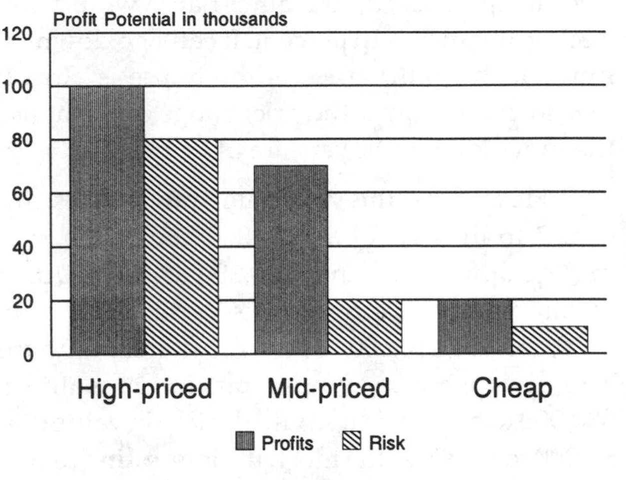

Figure 2-7

Mid-priced houses offer best profit to risk ratio

property. However, the relative disadvantages are more than offset by the advantages that mid-priced housing offers.

Which Should You Buy?

Obviously, I recommend buying mid-priced housing if you can possibly afford it. Since there are good profits to be made in this range, the reduced risk gives moderate-priced properties the best benefit vs. risk ratio. (See Figure 2-7.) The risk is less in terms of selling potential, and only slightly higher than cheap properties in terms of the cost per month. However, if you have little or no money to work with, cheap property is better than nothing. You can still make money on it, but you have to be very careful. It's important to choose *good* cheap property. I'll talk about the differences between good cheap property and bad cheap property later on in the book.

But price range is only one factor you have to look at in purchasing a piece of property. There are other factors to consider. Evaluate the location — the entire neighborhood.

Choosing a Neighborhood

Now that you've tentatively decided what price range you're interested in, where are you going to look for a house? I'd start by considering the neighborhood. I'm sure you've heard of the "First Rule of Real Estate." It states that the three most important things to look for in a piece of property are:

1) location

2) *location*

3) location

It's hard to overemphasize this point. Remember, you can change anything about a piece of property except its location. Wherever you find it, that's where it's going to stay. You can *never* make up for an undesirable location.

Most buyers pick their houses, not by size, color or shape, but by neighborhood. They pick a neighborhood they're interested in, and look there. Then, they look at the prices of houses within that neighborhood. It's not just coincidence that the property listing books in real estate offices are organized by neighborhood. Potential buyers usually have both a price range and neighborhood in mind when they start looking for a home.

Prospective customers rarely need directions to the neighborhood. Most of my buyers know exactly where my houses are. Why? Because they'd been looking for a house in that exact area. Many of my customers had friends or relatives in the neighborhood. Some even grew up there. They knew the area was desirable and had their hearts set on getting a house there. In situations like this, you have very little trouble selling a house.

So, if there are a lot of nice neighborhoods in your city with homes in your price range, which one should you start looking in? The obvious answer? The one closest to home.

Staying close to home minimizes travel and commuting time while you're working on the property. You'll appreciate this convenience when you have to drive there every day. But there are other reasons why you should stick close to home. The most important one is that you're familiar with your neighborhood.

Start With What You Know

Start with what you know. That's good advice for doing almost anything, but it's imperative to the investor. It's part of doing your homework, and all successful real estate investors *must* do their homework.

For most of us, the areas we know best are where we live and work. Start there. Study the neighborhoods around your home. Learn as much about the neighborhood as possible. You might also consider neighborhoods where you grew up or where you have close friends or relatives. If you already know some of the people in the neighborhoods you're thinking about, you have a head start.

If you're considering a home in an unfamiliar neighborhood, do some looking and checking before you buy. Start by driving up and down all the streets. Look at all the houses, the yards, the commercial areas and the people.

If you're comfortable in the area (and you shouldn't consider any area unless you are), get out of your car and take a walk. You'll be amazed at how much you can see just in the course of a pleasant stroll. You'll notice all sorts of things you wouldn't see while driving. Does the neighborhood look fresh? Do you detect pleasant aromas such as flowers or home cooking? Or does the neighborhood smell like garbage or chemicals? Find these things out now.

Smells and noise are both important things to notice. Are you close to a freeway, railroad or noisy factory? There are a lot of exterior elements that affect property values, not only of a single house, but a whole neighborhood. Figure 2-8 shows how proximity can be either a negative or positive influence. Again, the higher priced the neighborhood, the more particular your buyers will be. When you buy a house, make sure it's in an area where *you'd* enjoy spending time. If it isn't, maybe you should buy somewhere else.

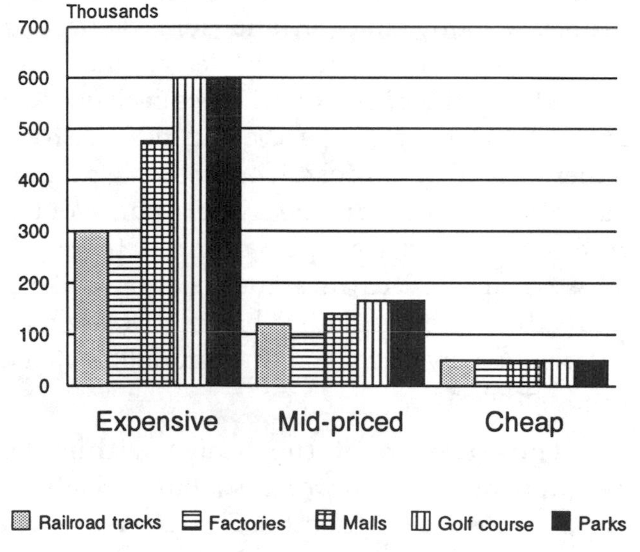

Figure 2-8

Negative and positive factors affect expensive homes more

Consider Your Buyer

If you've ever tried to buy and sell anything, you know that it's a lot easier to buy things than it is to sell them. So begin thinking about the person who'll purchase your remodeled house before you buy it. Selling your house is the key to making good money in this business. If you can sell your house for a good price, you've got it made. If not, you're out of business. Always keep your eventual buyer in mind while you're looking.

As you consider a neighborhood, think about who lives there. Is it a young family neighborhood, mostly singles, or older people? What would you guess is the average household income?

Then evaluate the areas within the neighborhood. Are some locations better for people without children and some better for those with young children? Which are the better streets to consider? Do some homes back up to an open space, or perhaps the business district, rather than other houses? Are some streets busier than others? Where are the schools, parks, or the access to public transportation? If there are negative influences in some locations, like a railroad track or unsightly businesses, are they outweighed by the general desirability of the neighborhood?

The location of the house within the neighborhood is important, but it isn't as important as the neighborhood itself. People will accept a bad location in their chosen neighborhood over a good location in a different neighborhood. They'll even accept a smaller house with fewer luxuries and amenities if they can live in a particular neighborhood.

That's why getting to know the neighborhood is so important. You need to be sure that you buy in an area where people want to live. You may be able to get a great deal in a bad neighborhood. But if everyone's selling there and no one's buying, your great deal may turn out to be a white elephant. If you choose the right neighborhood, you'll never have any problems selling.

Read All About It

I always buy a neighborhood newspaper, if there is one. If there isn't, try to get copies of local newsletters, church bulletins, or any printed matter about the neighborhood. Subscribe to any of these that you can. I have subscriptions to several local newspapers. I don't always get a chance to read them, but just leafing through them helps me keep on top of what's happening in the neighborhoods I'm monitoring.

You want to know what kind of problems you may be facing if you buy in an area. Is crime up? Are soaring property values causing tax increases? Are new developments and improvements being planned? Are businesses closing down or new ones moving in? Is this an active community? If so, what issues are local citizen groups involved in?

Look in the local want ads. Are many homes and businesses for sale? Or are properties in short supply and going for top dollar? Check the "Houses for Rent" column. This will give you a good idea about how people feel about the area. If rents are high, and properties are in short supply, the area is desirable. There usually won't be many homes for rent in the very best areas. If many homes are available and if rent is cheap, that's a bad sign.

Read the classified ads. Note the asking prices. What prices do you see most often, and what size house do you get for that price? You can also estimate the ratio of owner to non-owner homes in the area by watching the number of rentals listed. Look for signals that indicate changes taking place in the neighborhood. More important, determine whether the changes are for better or worse.

You may think that doing all this research is an unnecessary nuisance. It isn't. It's probably the most necessary nuisance you'll have to do. Don't bypass it.

Neighborhoods in Transition

One indicator of change in a neighborhood is the type, condition and number of cars you see around. You can learn a lot about the people living in the houses by their cars. Houses change slowly, but cars change quickly. It takes a few years of neglect before a really well-built home begins to look bad. But watch out if there are a couple of rusted-out junkers parked on the street. You can be pretty sure things aren't going well there. If you see several old cars around a house, there may be several tenants living there — a good sign of probable neglect.

On the other hand, an improving neighborhood is likely to have a lot of very nice cars in front of modest houses. Stylish cars tell you that couples with good incomes are living in the homes.

One problem with changing neighborhoods is that they don't always change at the same rate. Some change fast, some change slowly. Some start to change, and then stop. Look for signs of continuing progression. Are people making improvements to their homes? Are they painting, putting in new landscaping, or adding a room or second story? Do you see more and more improvements each time you go through the neighborhood? It's hard to second guess the future. That's why you have to make a safe choice. Pick a few neighborhoods that you know really well, and watch them closely. That way, you won't have any nasty surprises.

Good vs. Bad Neighborhoods

I've spent a lot of time talking about good property versus bad property. But until now I haven't given you any solid criteria for distinguishing between the two. What is a good neighborhood? It's a pleasant, safe place to live. But, more important, it's a desirable place to live. People want to be there. Ideally, more people want to live there than there are houses available. This creates rising prices, and opportunities for you and me.

The very best neighborhoods are not only good, they're constantly getting better. People are adding improvements to their homes. Property values are going up. New businesses and developments are moving in. New municipal facilities are being built and the schools attract the best teachers. These are the kinds of neighborhoods everybody wants to live in. You'll never have a problem selling a house in a neighborhood like this.

A bad neighborhood, on the other hand, is exactly the opposite. It's deteriorating, both physically and socially. More people are moving out than moving in. As the neighborhood changes from predominantly owner-occupied to tenant-occupied, people quit taking care of their homes. The property values drop. The people living there are unhappy about the condition of the neighborhood, which makes them unfriendly. They don't know their neighbors or care about what's going on in the neighborhood. The crime rate goes up. Businesses begin closing down and stores move out. This isn't the kind of neighborhood people want to move into. It's very hard to sell a house in an area like this.

Bargains to Avoid

Since a declining neighborhood isn't very desirable, there are usually houses available that appear to be great bargains. Sometimes you'll find a terrific home, in perfect condition, going for a fraction of the price of a modest home in a better neighborhood. This may be a very tempting buy, especially if you've been looking for a while and haven't come up with anything else in your price range. All you've seen is a bunch of tiny, poor-quality houses selling for outrageous prices . . . and then you come across this one great bargain!

It's the house of your dreams, at half the price you expected to pay. Sure, the neighborhood isn't all that great, but what a bargain, how can you lose? You'll be able to make a huge profit, right?

Real estate agents who aren't very good — or very ethical — will encourage you in this line of thinking. You'll hear "Right! You'll never find a deal like this in another neighborhood. If you want property to make a profit with, this house is it. If you can't make money here, you'll never make money in real estate." Of course, they're dead wrong. Why would they say these things to you? Either they're fools or they think *you* are. Perhaps they suspect that if they don't sell this albatross to you, they'll never sell it.

Don't believe everything you're told. Even real estate agents may be a bad judge of value. Follow your own good sense. How long has the property been on the market? If it's such a good deal, why hasn't it sold before? Check it out carefully. If it appears to be too good to be true, there's probably something very wrong.

What Is It Worth?

As a matter of fact, most houses are not worth more *as is* than the asking price. (Not if you're looking at them in terms of a quick resale.) Most homes are priced at fair market value. If a great house, in perfect condition, hasn't sold after being listed a while, then it probably isn't even worth the asking price. The agent may say, "Make an offer. I bet the sellers will take a lot less!" And they might. But if you offered them half what they're asking, you might still be paying too much for the property!

Why isn't a big, beautiful house in a deteriorating neighborhood worth as much as, if not more than, a little cottage in a stylish area? The house may be four times the size of the cottage. It may be loaded with quality craftsmanship and luxury features that the other one lacks, but no one wants it. The cottage will sell for a higher price than the beautiful home. Does that make sense?

A home's price is what people are willing to pay for it. Nothing more and nothing less. Consider clothes, for example. People pay a lot of money for the latest designer fashions. But you couldn't *give* those same people outdated clothes to wear, even if they were of exceptional quality. Are the stylish clothes any better than outdated clothes? Not really. But function alone doesn't dictate our choices. Other factors, especially peer pressure, ego and family demands, influence our buying decisions. And all these factors are enhanced by our exposure to the media and advertising.

No matter how you analyze it, the issue comes down to this: People will pay a great deal to get what they want, no matter how unreasonable it may seem. And if what you've got isn't in the area they want, they won't take it — not for any price. No matter what you do, *you* can't control what people want. But if you know what it is they *do* want and you're able to provide it, they'll pay you well for it.

The Concept of Worth in Real Estate

The little cottage in the stylish neighborhood is worth more than the big home in the bad area simply because *people believe it is*. If people believe that it's better to live north of the river, or west of the railroad tracks, or south of the highway, *then it is*. It's that simple. When all the vacant lots are sold and there's no more available building space, home prices will go up and up and up. That's supply and demand.

The shorter the supply and the greater the demand, the more a home in the right area is worth. People will even outbid each other and pay *more* than the asking price for a home, just to live there. Is it worth it? For the buyer who wants to live in a particular area, yes, it's worth it. They could get more home for their money elsewhere, but they won't be happy. The housing market in a good area works like an auction, with prices going as high as the market will bear.

Even though it may seem crazy, you'll actually be better off buying a shack in a stylish neighborhood, regardless of how outrageous the price, than a beautiful home in a bad area. If the demand is high enough in the stylish area, the shack will sell for even more tomorrow than it did today. But the beautiful home may sell for less than the bargain price you paid for it, even if you add improvements. If there are plenty of homes to choose from and no demand, you're stuck!

Changes Over Time

What if you wait a while? Won't that bad area eventually improve? It may, but then it may not. Or it may take ten to fifteen years to turn around. That's a pretty long-term investment. Your best bet would be to wait until the neighborhood improves, and *then* buy property there.

Of course, the stylish area may someday become unstylish, and the property values drop. The overpriced shack will sell for the price a shack ought to sell for. But when? Ten years from now? Twenty? A hundred? There's just no way to tell. You have to work with the situation that exists now. You can safely assume that a solid, stylish, desirable and improving neighborhood will stay that way for at least a year and probably many years. That's long enough for you to buy a house, fix it up, sell it and make your profit. Then it's not your problem anymore.

There's always good property available, but it isn't always easy to find. It's important to be patient, and have confidence in your own judgment. The knowledge you acquire while looking will greatly improve your ability to make decisions. The more you know, the fewer mistakes you'll make. Never rush into a purchase without a thorough investigation of what you're getting.

Now that you know how to choose a fixer-upper to remodel and resell for profit, let me end this chapter with an entirely different creature — what I call the *professional* handyman special.

Can You Handle a Professional Handyman Special?

I talked earlier about fixer-uppers that sell for 20 percent below market. A *real* handyman special isn't priced 20 percent below market, it's priced 20 percent *above the cost of the land.* Or maybe *at* the cost of the land alone. That's because these houses just aren't livable. They're full of serious health and safety violations that make them dangerous. They smell bad and they look worse. In fact, every time I look at one with my real estate agent, he says "How can anyone live like this!" Of course, most people can't. Most people don't even want to walk into these places, much less buy them.

Many of them are just this side of condemnation. If you don't buy it for renovation, it's likely to be an empty lot next time you drive by. But why would you even want to bother with a place this bad? I'll tell you why. Because their prices are ridiculously cheap. After all, they're literally worthless to the average person.

And they'll be worthless to you if you don't have the advanced construction skills and know-how to make them livable — even desirable. Don't misunderstand what I'm talking about here. These houses need *major* work, full-time work. I've often put 400 to 600 manhours into one of these. That's about four to eight weeks of full-time work for me and a helper or two. If you could only work evenings and weekends, it would take you years to renovate one. I'd say $25,000 is the average cost to turn one of these places into a house you can sell.

Obviously, you can't make money on a handyman special like this unless you buy it dirt cheap. And you have to follow the same rules I've outlined in this chapter for buying investment property. Choose a house in a good area that will be desirable after it's renovated. Stay within the limits of your skills and your capital. If you follow these guidelines, you can make a career of renovating and selling handyman specials. I know. I've done it for years.

In fact, I've made money buying places from the people who bought them to fix up. People who underestimated the job and overestimated their abilities. In one case, the buyers lovingly refinished the woodwork and installed beautiful ceramic floors. Meanwhile, the walls and ceilings were collapsing all around them. They put in hundreds of hours and thousands of dollars, then sold it to me for less than they paid for it. I made money on it because I know what to do and how to do it. *Never take one of these on if you don't have the qualifications!*

CHAPTER THREE

Using Real Estate Agents

Every serious real estate investor needs a good real estate agent. The agent you select can save you hours or days of valuable time that might be wasted looking at unsuitable property. They can help you negotiate the deal and then steer you to the financing you need. Real estate agents can be especially helpful in finding the type of property you want. But it's important that you understand how real estate agents operate, what they do and what they don't do. That's the purpose of this chapter.

Visiting a Real Estate Office

Begin by visiting a real estate office in the neighborhood where you're shopping. Don't go to a real estate agent in the neighborhood *where you live* just because it's convenient. Unless you have established a good working relationship with an agent, find one that specializes in the area where you want to buy. Most real estate agents specialize in the areas close to their offices. Use a local agent who knows the neighborhood well. If you have a choice, pick a larger office that's doing a lot of business in the area.

Better agents work hard to become well known in a limited area. They go from door to door, leaving their business cards and talking to people about their plans. That's one way they get property listings. Good agents are active in the community and know about everything bought and sold in the area they serve. They can be a valuable source of information and may be able to steer you to exactly the property you want.

As soon as you walk into the office, you'll discover why I emphasized the material in the last chapter. The first questions any real estate salesperson will ask you are: "What neighborhood are you interested in?" and "What price range do you want?" Since you've read the last chapter, you'll be able to answer these questions quickly and intelligently.

Look at the Listings

Tell the sales agent what you want and ask if you can look through their book of listings. Most offices will have a multiple listing book with pictures and brief descriptions of all the homes for sale in that area. It's a valuable reference and one you'll use a great deal in this business. Real estate agents are very possessive of these books, but they're also very eager to help you find something to buy.

Ask the agent if there's a quiet place or an empty office where you can sit and go through the book. (You won't be allowed to take the current book out of the office.) Look through the listings carefully. Consider each one, even if you're not interested in it. This will take some time, but it's worth it. Don't let the agent rush you. It's very important to look over the listings carefully.

Using the MLS Book

The multiple listing service book (often called the *MLS*) will introduce you to what's available in the area. These books are generally organized first by area, then by type of property: single-family homes, followed by attached homes (duplexes, townhomes, and condominiums). Within these types the listings are by price, from the least to the most expensive.

Figure 3-1 shows a typical listing. Every real estate board uses a slightly different format, so the listings you look at may not be the same. All listings will include the same general information: number of bedrooms and bathrooms, lot size, number of stories, price, etc. Some of this information is abbreviated, but unraveling the code is easy once you've done it a few times.

What the agent may neglect to explain, unless you ask, is the information on the listing. This information is very helpful, so it's good to know what it means. The real estate books themselves don't clearly explain all the details and abbreviations used. I learned how to read listings by asking questions. To save you some time, I'll go through the listing in Figure 3-1, starting from the top.

The picture— Most people look at the picture first. That's a good place to start. Unfortunately, pictures in most listing books are very poor. Some listings, usually those created by computer, don't have pictures at all.

What can you tell from the picture in Figure 3-1? You can see that this is a two-story bungalow. It's fairly attractive, with no obvious exterior modifications. You can't tell much about its condition or features. It's even hard to tell the size of the house from the picture. Big houses sometimes look small in MLS books and small houses can look big.

But look carefully. You can save yourself a lot of time. Try to spot evidence of neglect, such as broken windows, or rusted-out gutters. Pay particular attention to the condition of the landscaping. If the yard is badly overgrown and weedy, chances are that the house is in poor condition as well.

One interesting thing I discovered looking at this picture: the trees are full of leaves, meaning this picture was taken in the summer. It was January when I first saw the listing, so I knew that the house had been on the market for several months. This is very important information! Sellers who have been trying to sell a house for a long time are much more likely to take a lower offer than sellers who have just put the house up for sale. This is a point I'll emphasize often. Knowing the "listing date" of a house — the date it was first offered for sale — can be worth several thousand dollars to you. *Always ask about the listing date if you don't see it!* The real estate agent can find it out for you.

Under the picture in Figure 3-1 are five boxes. Let's look at them one at a time.

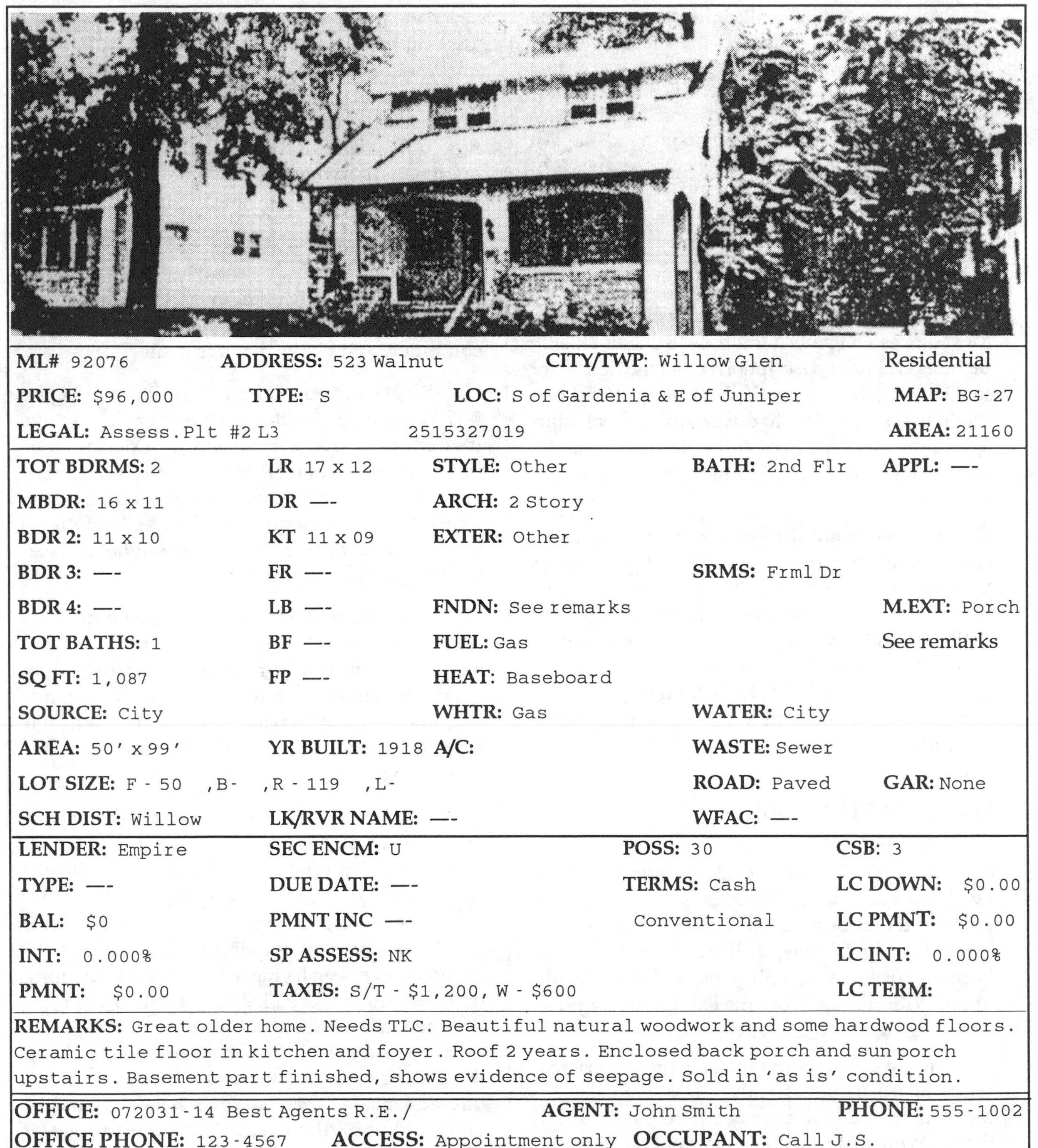

ML# 92076	**ADDRESS:** 523 Walnut	**CITY/TWP:** Willow Glen		Residential
PRICE: $96,000	**TYPE:** S	**LOC:** S of Gardenia & E of Juniper		**MAP:** BG-27
LEGAL: Assess.Plt #2 L3		2515327019		**AREA:** 21160

TOT BDRMS: 2	**LR** 17 x 12	**STYLE:** Other	**BATH:** 2nd Flr	**APPL:** —
MBDR: 16 x 11	**DR** —	**ARCH:** 2 Story		
BDR 2: 11 x 10	**KT** 11 x 09	**EXTER:** Other		
BDR 3: —	**FR** —		**SRMS:** Frml Dr	
BDR 4: —	**LB** —	**FNDN:** See remarks		**M.EXT:** Porch
TOT BATHS: 1	**BF** —	**FUEL:** Gas		See remarks
SQ FT: 1,087	**FP** —	**HEAT:** Baseboard		
SOURCE: City		**WHTR:** Gas	**WATER:** City	
AREA: 50′ x 99′	**YR BUILT:** 1918	**A/C:**	**WASTE:** Sewer	
LOT SIZE: F - 50 ,B- ,R - 119 ,L-			**ROAD:** Paved	**GAR:** None
SCH DIST: Willow	**LK/RVR NAME:** —		**WFAC:** —	

LENDER: Empire	**SEC ENCM:** U	**POSS:** 30	**CSB:** 3
TYPE: —	**DUE DATE:** —	**TERMS:** Cash	**LC DOWN:** $0.00
BAL: $0	**PMNT INC** —	Conventional	**LC PMNT:** $0.00
INT: 0.000%	**SP ASSESS:** NK		**LC INT:** 0.000%
PMNT: $0.00	**TAXES:** S/T - $1,200, W - $600		**LC TERM:**

REMARKS: Great older home. Needs TLC. Beautiful natural woodwork and some hardwood floors. Ceramic tile floor in kitchen and foyer. Roof 2 years. Enclosed back porch and sun porch upstairs. Basement part finished, shows evidence of seepage. Sold in 'as is' condition.

OFFICE: 072031-14 Best Agents R.E./ **AGENT:** John Smith **PHONE:** 555-1002
OFFICE PHONE: 123-4567 **ACCESS:** Appointment only **OCCUPANT:** Call J.S.

Figure 3-1
Typical multiple listing

Box one: Listing information— The first box describes the property by number, location and price.

- **ML#:** The listing number. Some real estate listings include a listing date. Others don't. But all listings have a chronological listing number. In Figure 3-1 it's in the upper-left corner, called the "ML#." If you know the highest listing number in use and you know roughly how many listings come in a month, you can figure out approximately how many months the house has been on the market. If you ask the agent for this information, they'll usually tell you. If there is a listing date noted, it'll usually be at the very top, near the ML#.

- **ADDRESS:** Street address of the property.

- **CITY/TWP:** This tells you the city, suburb, or subdivision name and the type of area (residential) where the home is located. Our home is in the city of Willow Glen. If it was a township it would say "T-Willow Glen."

Check the address on your map. Is the 500 block of Walnut a good area of Willow Glen? You better know this before you invest any more time or money in this listing. Is Walnut busy, running alongside a superhighway, or is it a quiet side street?

Consider the location very carefully. Think about the price of other homes in the neighborhood. As we said earlier, there are good and bad locations even in good neighborhoods. How does the location fit the price of the house? Luxury homes, for example, should be on quiet, tree-lined streets where the lots are big and there's plenty of privacy. It's hard to sell an expensive home on a busy street near a business district. Even good homes sell at a discount in poor locations.

Another thing to consider is whether the house is located right in the middle of the neighborhood or at the border. If it's at the border, what's on the other side: a better neighborhood, or a worse one? Proximity to a better neighborhood will increase the value of your house, while being right next to a bad area will decrease it.

- **PRICE:** If you'd been looking through the listing book with me, you'd know that 523 Walnut was the first listing in the Willow Glen section. Since the houses in each section are arranged in order of price, you'd know that this was the cheapest house in Willow Glen at that time.

Obviously, the price of a house is going to be very important. But it's not the only consideration. Remember, a bargain is only a bargain if you can sell it for more than you're paying. It's more important to find the house that will yield the maximum return for your time and effort. That's probably not the cheapest house in the book.

In this case, the asking price of $96,000 tells you a lot. If you had been looking through the listings for Willow Glen, you'd know that a house of this description, in this area, should be selling for at least $40,000 more. You'd want to look into this house and find out why it's so cheap.

One thing to keep in mind — you rarely have to pay the full asking price for any property. You can usually count on getting it for about 10 percent below the listing price, even if the house is cheap in the first place. If the market is hot, or the price has been lowered several times, you may not get as much of a discount, but you can almost always get it for a little less.

- **TYPE:** The *S* stands for "single-family" home.

- **LOC:** If you weren't sure where this house was located, you'll find the cross streets listed here.

- **MAP:** These are map co-ordinates. If you aren't familiar with the location, you can check the map in the front of the book.

- **LEGAL:** Here you find the legal description of the property. That's essential information if you want to go to the County Recorder's Office to check on easements or title to the property. If you're buying through an agent, you shouldn't have to worry about this. Your agent's job is make sure you have all the information you need about the property. But if you want to double-check any information or buy without an agent, you may need to go to the County Recorder's Office. Real estate agents *work* for their money. If you don't hire one, then *you* have to do their work.

- **AREA:** 21160. This is the realty board area. A real estate agent could tell by this number which realty board the listing falls under. It's another way of pinpointing the location of the property.

Box two: Property information— The next box has detailed information about the house itself. It shows the number of rooms and room sizes, house size, lot size, age, type of heating, and city services available.

- **TOT BDRMS:** 2, There are only two bedrooms in this house.

- **MBDR:** Master bedroom size is 16 feet by 11 feet, a pretty good size.

- **BDR 2:** The second bedroom is 11 feet by 10 feet, also a fairly good size for a second bedroom.

- **BDR 3 and BDR 4** are blank. This is a major drawback for this house. I generally prefer three-bedroom houses. However, this points out one of the limitations of these listings. I discovered later that this home has an enclosed, heated, upstairs porch which could easily be turned into a third bedroom. It even has its own hallway entrance (unlike many porches, which are entered through other bedrooms). Turning a two-bedroom house into a three-bedroom house is an excellent way to increase its value.

- **TOT BATHS:** 1. The top of the fourth column across indicates that the only "BATH" in the house is on the second floor. However, there was also an unenclosed toilet in the basement that isn't noted in the listing.

- **LR:** Living room size is 17 feet by 12 feet.

- **DR:** Dining room. This area is blank. However, if you look under SRMS (special rooms) in the fourth column, you'll see that there's a formal dining room (Frml DR) noted. This should probably be listed under the DR. with the room dimensions included.

- **KT:** Kitchen, 11 feet by 9 feet.

- **FR:** Family room, none.

- **B:** Library/study/den, none.

- **BF:** Breakfast area, none.

- **FP:** Fireplace, none.

- **STYLE:** Other. When in doubt, real estate agents always list the house as "Other." You'll probably find as many other-style houses as special styles listed in these books. This style of house is correctly known as a California Craftsman-style bungalow.

- **ARCH:** Architecture, 2 story.

- **EXTER:** Other. This house is stucco, which is rare in my area. Most houses are brick or have aluminum siding, which is why the agent put "other."

- **FNDN:** Foundation, See remarks. The remark tells you that there is a partially-finished basement and some hardwood floors.

- **FUEL:** Gas.

- **HEAT:** Baseboard. The listing agent was a little careless here. Figure 3-1 shows baseboard heating with gas fuel. What's gas-fueled baseboard heat? It turned out to be gas-fired circulating hot water with baseboard radiators. That's a deluxe heating system.

  Of course, the listing isn't exactly wrong. The home does have baseboard radiators and the system is gas-fired. But "gas-fired hot water" would have been a lot more informative.

- **WHTR:** Water heater. Gas.

- **A/C:** Air conditioning, none.

- **SQFT:** 1,087, is the total square feet of living area. Bigger is usually better. This house is about as small as I would consider. I don't want to add living area. That's too expensive. Extra expense increases my cost and my risk. But I would consider converting less-used space into an extra bedroom. That's why this home attracted me. It had that potential third bedroom upstairs.

- **SOURCE:** City. The source for most of the information in this listing was the City of Willow Glen.

- **AREA:** 50′ x 99′. Usable land area, 4,950 square feet.

- **LOT SIZE:** F-50 (front), R-119 (right). The lot is 50 feet across by 119 feet deep. The lot is rectangular, so just two measurements are needed to give you the size. Only 99 feet of the 119 foot depth is considered usable. The remaining 20 feet of lot depth is probably a utility easement, slope or setback.

- **SCH DIST:** Willow Glen. School districts are important to buyers with children. Some school districts, like Willow Glen, are very desirable. The only legitimate way to get your kids in a school district may be to live there. It's important to know which schools in which districts are considered desirable. Many states administer standardized tests to all children throughout the state and publish average scores for each school and school district. The local newspaper probably publishes results for neighborhood schools. That's valuable information in your search for the most desirable property.

- **YR. BUILT:** 1918. Often the age of the house appears near the top of the listing.

- **LK/RVR NAME:** Lake/river name, none. Property with water frontage is always worth a great deal more. As a rule, even a view of the water raises the value.

- **WATER:** City. This line and the two lines that follow can be very important. Most urban homes will have water and sewer connection and be on a paved road. But rural homes may not. A home without piped water, or that isn't connected to a sewer line, or doesn't have a paved road access is worth far less than a home with these conveniences.

- **WASTE:** Sewer.

- **ROAD:** Paved.

- **WFAC:** Blank. This home has no waterfront access.

- **GAR:** Garage, none. Here's another problem with this house. Many buyers won't even consider a house without a garage.

- **APPL:** Appliances (last column). There are no special appliances noted in the listing. Some homes include the stove or dishwasher which are often built in. Occasionally you may even get a refrigerator.

- **M.EXT:** Miscellaneous Exterior, Porch, See remarks. This notation tells the reader to check the remarks section for more information about the exterior improvements. This house has an enclosed back porch and a sun porch upstairs. Look for improvements such as swimming pools, patios, or decks listed under M.EXT.

Box three: Financial information— The next section summarizes important financial information. The listing agent for this house didn't bother to fill in all the information. That's too bad. We need to know about financing. The property is more valuable to you if you can assume an existing loan, buy on a land contract, or use an FHA or VA loan. In this case, the seller would accept only cash or a new conventional loan.

Note carefully the terms on the listing. Most houses are worth more if alternative types of financing are offered. Later in this book I'll explain what you need to know about financing.

- **LENDER:** Empire. Empire Savings holds the first mortgage on this property.

- **TYPE:** Here you should find the type of loan on the property, such as conventional, VA, FHA or LC (land contract).

- **BAL:** The balance due on this home was $89,000. That figure should have been listed in this space. It's important to know what the payoff is on the current loan. It's pointless to offer the sellers less than they owe. The balance due tells you how much room the seller has to negotiate. You'll usually pay less than the asking price. But you'll almost always pay the owner at least the loan balance plus the selling costs.

- **INT:** Interest rate on current loan. If you want to assume the seller's loan, the current interest rate will be important. If the loan is assumable and if the interest rate is lower than the current going rate, the existing loan is very attractive. Unfortunately, most loans today are not assumable unless the terms are very favorable to the lender. And usually the lender will have to qualify you just like a new borrower, even though you're taking over an old loan.

- **PMNT:** The current loan payment is important if you plan to assume the loan.

- **SEC ENCM:** Secondary encumbrance. If there are second or third mortgages on the property, they'll show up here. Add this amount to the first mortgage to know the total loan on the property. "U" means unknown, not very helpful of this agent.

- **DUE DATE:** This tells you how old the loan is. Most loans run 30 years.

- **PMNT INC:** Payment includes. All payments include principal and interest, but they can also include taxes and insurance as well.

- **SP ASSESS:** Special assessments. *NK* means *none known.* Special assessments might include a water or sewer bond that will be added onto your property tax bill for several years. Pay attention to these details. They all increase your monthly payments.

- **TAXES:** S/T- $1,200, W- $600. Here you have a separate listing for summer tax (S/T) and winter (W) tax. In some states the taxes are shown as an annual figure, $1,800, even though two tax bills, usually of $900 each, may be sent out.

  Always note the taxes due on any piece of property. This figure, divided by twelve, will be added to your monthly principal and interest payment if your lender insists on tax impounds. All lenders figure taxes as part of your monthly carrying cost, even if you pay property taxes biannually.

- **POSS:** Possession, 30. You can take possession of the property 30 days after closing.

- **TERMS:** Cash or conventional loan. These are the purchase terms acceptable to the seller. They will not accept FHA, VA, LC or an assumption.

- **LC DOWN, PMNT, INT, TERM:** If a land contract is offered, this area will show down payment, monthly payment, interest rate, and the term of the loan. All zeros indicate no land contract offers are acceptable.

- **CSB:** 3. Commission to the selling broker is three percent of the selling price. This information is important to the agent showing the property. They want to know how much they'll make on the sale before they put any effort into selling it. The total real estate commission is usually six or seven percent of the selling price, split between the listing and selling brokers. The commission comes out of the seller's proceeds.

Box four: Remarks— This may be the most informative section of the listing. Unfortunately, it's often left blank by listing agents.

In this case, the remarks section tells you almost the whole story about this house. "Needs TLC." This is a polite way of saying that the house is a mess. Other ways of saying the same thing are "fixer-upper," and "handyman special." Listing agents always try to make the best of a bad situation.

Notice the comment, "shows evidence of seepage." Seepage? When you see something like that, you can expect to find the basement under a foot of water. This time I was surprised to discover that the basement was completely dry. The problem was a leak in the second-floor bathroom. It had rotted out the floor, causing the ceilings in the dining room and kitchen to fall down. That's seepage all right!

Finally, the agent added "Sold in 'as is' condition." That's interesting — every existing home is sold that way. The comment is just the agent's fair warning: This home is in bad condition. Don't expect much.

Fortunately, I wasn't scared away. The note "Enclosed back porch and sun porch upstairs" turned out to be very valuable to me. The upstairs sun porch wasn't noted in the top part of the listing where it should have been. I ended up buying this house and turning the porch into a third bedroom. With three bedrooms, the value of this house increased considerably. If the upstairs porch hadn't been listed, I would have passed this listing by.

Sometimes you have to read between the lines to find good investment possibilities. The bedrooms were good-sized. There was a nice, large living room, and a formal dining room. It seemed to have potential — a diamond in the rough (really rough) — and certainly worth further consideration. I put it on my list of houses to visit.

Listing books can show you the alternatives. It narrows down the number of houses you need to visit. But the most important step in the process is the on-site inspection.

Box five: Real estate agent information— The last section of the listing shows the name of the listing real estate agent, their company name, realty board number and telephone number. It also shows if the house is occupied. If it is, your agent must call for an appointment. Under Occupant: this listing says "Call JS." This means the agent must call the listing broker for an appointment. The last phone number is usually for the occupant, but in this case it's the broker's home number. After making an appointment, my agent showed me the house pictured in Figure 3-2. In spite of the problems, I decided to buy it.

Read All the Listings

On the first pass at an MLS book you may not find anything of interest. Don't give up. New books are issued regularly. You'll have another opportunity later. But you should have learned something about the market for homes in your chosen neighborhood. You'll know the listing price of the cheapest and most expensive houses in the neighborhood. You won't be able to buy a house cheaper than the cheapest house, or sell one for more than the most expensive.

As you read through the listing book, think about the value of homes, even those that aren't in your price range. What do you get for your money? What do buyers expect in each price range? What's the difference between a house selling for $150,000 and one selling for $200,000? What do you get in a $100,000 or $150,000 house? What makes the cheap homes cheap and the expensive houses expensive?

By answering these questions, you should begin to see a pattern in the neighborhood. The average-priced house has features that most potential buyers expect to find in a home in that neighborhood. Try to find a house that's priced well below average because it doesn't have those features. Then see if adding those features will increase the value more than the cost of the changes. For example, I converted the upstairs porch on the house in Figure 3-2. That increased the resale price far more than the cost of conversion.

Try to estimate how much value you can add and how much it will cost to add that value. Here's where your experience in the construction industry comes in handy. You'll probably know about how much time and material will be needed to improve the house. After studying the listings and looking at the homes for sale, you should be able to estimate the resale price. The house is going to be worth more. How much more? Look at the price ranges. What do other houses with those features sell for? The MLS book should help you answer that question.

Studying the MLS is the best way I know to educate yourself on the value and prices of homes being sold in your community. The MLS book

Figure 3-2
An ideal fixer found through the MLS

tells you what your house will be worth when it's done, and what the competition will be when you're ready to sell. *The time to consider these issues is before you buy,* not when you get ready to sell.

There's another advantage to estimating the value of the completed house. You'll discover the maximum amount you can invest and still make a profit. Of course, a lot depends on how much you pay for the property. But calculating the maximum sales price will help you decide whether a particular property is worth considering.

What to Look For

By now you should have a feel for the type of property you want. You're looking for a cheap house, possibly in bad shape but with lots of potential and in a good neighborhood. Actually, you'd settle for a house in good condition, in a good neighborhood, as long as it was still cheap. That's usually too much to hope for, although it can happen. Tight money or personal problems sometimes force people to sacrifice their homes for whatever price they can get. If you happen to be at the right place at the right time, and you have the money (or can get it fast), you may get a bargain. Don't count on this happening too often. I've stumbled on maybe two real bargains in the 12 years I've been in this business. Usually, I have to work for my money. Probably you will too.

The perfect fixer-upper is a quality home in a quality neighborhood. It's selling for less than other homes in the neighborhood because it has problems. Ideally these problems are cosmetic defects you can remedy without spending too much money or too many weeks of work. Always look for a house that comes as close as possible to having nothing major wrong with it. It's cheap mostly because it looks bad and scares buyers off, not because it has serious problems no one can remedy at reasonable cost.

Don't buy a house in good condition selling for a few thousand dollars under market price. A house like that is worthless to you. If it's already in good condition, there's little you can do to raise its value enough to make a profit. The exception might be a house that could be expanded easily. I'll cover that a little later.

To make a profit, the house has to be heavily discounted — 30 to 50 percent below market value. Here's why. Your transaction cost (the cost of buying, holding for a few months, and then selling) will probably be about 15 percent of the price. This is how I came up with that percentage. The cost of getting a new loan will be 3 to 6 percent, depending on interest rates and points. If you need a broker to sell the house, add in another 6 percent. Plus, you have payments, taxes and insurance to pay until the home is sold. The longer it takes you to make the repairs and sell the house, the higher your expenses will be. But the average will usually be about 15 percent. That means you have to sell a $100,000 home for at least $115,000 just to break even — and that's if you don't invest a dime on improvements!

Transaction costs stack the deck against you. You have to buy a home that's marked way down below the value of the others in the neighborhood, or you can't make any profit. But that isn't the only problem. You must be very careful about the improvements you make in the property. You *have* to make the repairs that make the house livable, but beyond that, watch out. Most home improvements are worth only a fraction of their cost in resale value. Even though you do the work yourself, the costs still add up. That's why I don't recommend making major improvements.

Of course, there are exceptions. You can probably guess several. For example, it's harder to sell a two-bedroom house than a three-bedroom house. Finding a way to add that third bedroom at minimum cost can bring the resale price of that home way up. A second bathroom is also cost effective if it can be done easily and cheaply.

Homes badly in need of cosmetic repairs are sometimes sacrificed up to 50 percent of their potential value. These represent the best financial opportunities for you, but they're not easy to find. It takes a lot of looking to find the right investment.

Keep in mind also that every house in bad shape isn't necessarily a bargain. Many sellers think their run-down house is worth every bit as much as one in good condition. In fact, many sellers don't think there's anything wrong with their homes. They've lived with the peeling paint and falling plaster so long they no longer notice it!

Don't Give Up

Don't get discouraged after your first look at the listings. There may not appear to be anything with decent potential in your price range. The agent may not offer any encouragement. After all, real estate agents make the most on higher-priced homes. There's more commission for them and probably little or no extra work. I've had them tell me, "You're crazy. You'll never find a house in Willow Glen for under $100,000!" I had just bought one for $96,000 a few days earlier, so I knew better. Eventually I found another one for $98,000. If you run into an agent with an attitude like that, just ignore them and keep on looking through the listings. Something will turn up.

Take Your Time and Look

In this line of work, you learn something from every house you inspect. There's no substitute for seeing for yourself first-hand. You can even learn a lot from houses you don't want to buy. How much do they cost? What do you get for your money? Do they have any profit potential for you? If so, why? If not, why not? There's as much to be learned from the rejects as from houses you decide to buy. Looking at properties is the way you get to know your market. It's how you learn precisely the value of homes in your selected neighborhood. It's the *only* way I know to identify bargains.

Try driving around the neighborhood on a Sunday afternoon. Look at all the houses that are open for inspection. If you've been interested in real estate for any length of time, you may already have made a habit of doing this. It's a quick and easy way to see a large number of houses in a short period of time, without having to bother with appointments. It's a great way to get a feel for the price and value of homes in your area.

My wife and I have a house shopping game we like to play when checking new homes offered for sale. Without looking at the listing, we guess how much the owner is asking. The closest guess is the winner. If we both guess much more than the asking price, we may have stumbled on a bargain. Guessing about the price is a valuable exercise. When you can guess prices accurately, you're a good judge of real estate values in your area. This is exactly the knowledge you need to succeed in this business!

FSBO vs. Real Estate Agent

FSBO stands for "For Sale By Owner." Some books on real estate claim that this is a great way to make money. They say that you'll find many "For Sale By Owner" houses ridiculously underpriced. Or, at the very least, the houses will be selling for thousands of dollars less, because the seller doesn't have to pay a real estate commission. These houses aren't in the agent's listing book. They're usually advertised in the newspaper or sometimes only by a sign in front of the house. Are these houses worth looking into?

My experience has been that most FSBO's are not a bargain. Usually owners who sell their homes themselves are trying to maximize their profits, not save you money. They don't want to pay an agent a commission because they want to pocket every dollar they can possibly squeeze out of the deal. Will they sell the house for thousands less because they aren't paying a commission? Not likely, at least not until the house has been on the market for a *very* long time!

Consider Your Seller

What kind of person is the ideal seller in this business? Someone who cares more about getting

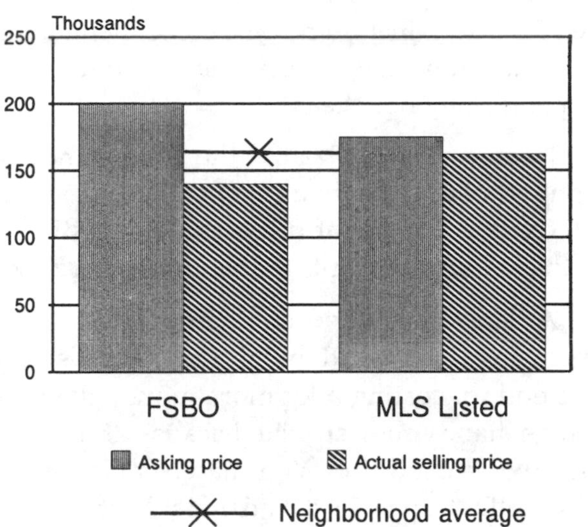

Figure 3-3
Asking and selling prices

rid of the house than how much they can get for it. They have the type of property that Robert Allen, the well-known real estate author, refers to as "no-wants." People are likely to take any reasonable offer for a no-want. This is the kind of seller and property you should look for.

The desperate seller will always list with a real estate agent because the property will sell faster. To them, speed is more important than price. These are the people I like dealing with. If they'll let me have their property cheap, I'll buy it quickly!

FSBO's rarely fall into this category. Usually, they aren't even very reasonable. The sellers often take their homes a little too personally. To them, the house holds a million dollars' worth of fond, family memories. Therefore, they'd like a million dollars for it. They'll settle for less, of course, but they think they're doing you a favor by asking only $250,000 for their $100,000 castle. If you offer them less, they'll be mortally offended. They simply can't be objective and business-like about their property.

This is one of the advantages of working with an agent. You don't even have to talk to the owners — your agent has to. If the owners are unreasonable, the agent's the one who has to tell them. Sometimes real estate agents really earn their commissions. Some sellers can be very abusive.

Many FSBO's will eventually wind up being listed by agents. After sitting on the market for months and months without any offers, the sellers begin to get a little more practical. At this point, you might even be able to get a good deal on the property. I've bought several houses in this way. As you can see in Figure 3-3, what people want for a home when they sell it themselves and what they get is very different. The asking and selling prices of homes sold through an agent are much closer because the agent sets a more realistic value on the property.

What about those "ridiculously underpriced" houses that the real estate books talk about? Their advice is obsolete. In the mid-1970's, when home prices were increasing very quickly, many sellers weren't aware of actual market prices. They probably bought their house in 1950 for $12,000, and thought they were making a killing selling it for $40,000 in 1976. After all, they more than tripled their money. They didn't realize their house was worth $70,000.

Today you're not likely to find anyone who's that ill-informed. There's been too much publicity on the skyrocketing cost of housing. People are much more likely to *over*estimate their property values than underestimate them.

That doesn't mean that you'll *never* find any FSBO bargains. It never hurts to read the want ads, or call the number on the "For Sale" signs to find out the price. If it seems like a bargain, it certainly won't hurt to make an appointment and take a look. Just don't restrict yourself to For Sale By Owner's. You may find a bargain there, but your chances are much better looking in the MLS listings.

Repossessions

If you live in a big city, you may occasionally see ads in the newspapers listing houses in foreclosure. Some real-estate authors tout repossessed houses as the way to make a fortune. According to them, these houses can be bought very cheaply, and resold for huge profits. I've found that this is rarely the case. You may sometimes be able to buy them cheap, but you're not going to make big profits. In fact, you may not make any profit. Let's consider why.

First of all, foreclosures don't just "happen." It can take from four months to more than a year to foreclose on a piece of property. The owners are repeatedly notified that they are in arrears, and given every opportunity to do something about it. Regardless of what you may have heard, no lender wants to take back a home. Neither government agencies nor private lenders want the house; they simply want their money. They're in the lending business, not the real estate business.

Everyone loses in a foreclosure. It's a very costly business, and usually a last resort after every other option has been exhausted. So why hasn't the former owner of the house been able to either sell the house or renegotiate the mortgage over the course of a full year? There may be other reasons, but in at least 90 percent of the cases, the owner's interest is worthless. The house can't be sold for enough to cover the loan. And no one will loan any more money on it. The owner's best option is to walk away from it.

Few homeowners are happy about losing their home. They're likely to take their bad humor out on the house, leaving it both worthless and unlivable.

How does a house become worthless? Most of the time, it's because of a deteriorating neighborhood. No one wants to live there, so the houses just sit empty, deteriorating more. There are hundreds of houses like this for sale in many older urban areas. Newspapers will occasionally have page after page of HUD or bank repossessions listed for sale. Ninety-nine percent of them are in very undesirable neighborhoods. The remaining one percent are not cheap!

I can't overemphasize the importance of neighborhood. If you bought one of these houses and fixed it up beautifully, it would still be worthless! No one wants to live in a battle zone.

As I just mentioned, sometimes you'll find a foreclosure in a good neighborhood. Usually these end up costing a lot more money than the average handyman special because they're in much worse condition. You may be able to pick up a HUD "repo" in a bad neighborhood for $5,000 to $10,000. But in a good neighborhood the bids will go up almost to market price very quickly. It's fine to pay market price for a repossession if you're going to live in it, but not if you're looking for something you can turn over for a profit.

You must also understand that the law in many states is very favorable to a former owner who has been evicted. The owner may have up to a year to cure the default and claim possession. You may not get clear title to a foreclosed house for many months after the sale. Be very careful about this. You don't want to fix a house up and then have the former owner reclaim it, no matter how nicely he thanks you.

If you decide to bid on VA or HUD repossessions, get advice from a real estate pro who knows the business. The government has some very particular requirements.

Slum Lords

So, who buys the cheap "repos?" Investors who plan to become slum lords. They buy the house for as little as possible, generally $5,000 to $10,000. They put as little money into it as they can get away with, and then rent it out. I've heard of homes that sold for $5,000 renting for $500 a month. That's a 120 percent a year return on investment! But I wouldn't try it.

These landlords put no money into maintenance. They ignore complaints from the tenants and citations from the city. Eventually, when the house becomes unlivable, the landlords abandon it. They usually use an out-of-state corporation as a front for this kind of activity, so they can't be traced. The city winds up getting stuck with the bill for demolition. This is a nasty business. It victimizes poor people, contributes to urban decay, and adds to the burden of taxpayers.

Legal Repossessions

Another class of repossessions are houses impounded by the government for legal infractions by the owners. Most commonly, these are Internal Revenue Service impoundments for nonpayment of income tax. But another type of government impoundment is becoming more and more common: homes purchased with drug money. These homes, impounded by the Drug Enforcement Administration, are auctioned off in government sales. The owners may be in jail or they may have left town to avoid jail. The homes are often very valuable, in perfect condition, and in nice neighborhoods. While these houses are not all that easy to find, they may offer good profit potential. I've heard of several great deals on houses like these, although I've never been able to get one myself. If you're interested in them, check at your county courthouse. They sometimes have lists of properties that are going to be sold at auction.

As I said in the beginning of the book, there are hundreds of ways to make money in real estate. My experience has shown me that the most reliable and consistent way to find properties with investment potential is to work with a good real estate agent. Not all houses are listed with agents, of course. But those that aren't are harder to find. Multiple listing books provide a steady source of houses, conveniently organized by area and price. You'll be able to find a good property more quickly and more easily by using a real estate agent.

Selecting an Agent to Help You

How do you find the right agent? My advice is not to commit yourself to the first agent you contact. Make sure you feel comfortable with the agent and have confidence in their ability. And remember, just because you go out looking with an agent doesn't mean you're committed to buy through him. Be careful. An incompetent agent will almost certainly waste your time and may waste a lot of your money as well.

A Little Background in Real Estate

The laws governing real estate agents vary from state to state. But most agents are licensed by the state and are independent contractors working out of a real estate office. These offices can be either independently owned by a broker, or part of a national chain, such as Century 21 or Real Estate One, and managed by a broker. State licensed real estate brokers supervise the sales agents, whether it's a franchise or an independent office. All real estate sales agents must work under a broker. Everyone in the office works on a commission basis.

Sales agents and brokers belong to a local real estate board. The location of their office usually dictates which board they belong to, but they can belong to more than one. Each real estate board has rules their members should follow.

Real estate boards are usually served by a multiple listing service which publishes the listing books we discussed earlier. Today, most offices are linked by computer to the local multiple listing service. When a sales agent or broker signs a contract to sell a house for the owner, the agent types the listing into the computer and it's distributed to all the other real estate offices in the area. They also enter information on houses that are in the process of being sold or have been sold. That way all the sales agents know which houses are available, which have sold, and how much the houses sold for. Any agent from any office is entitled to sell any house listed in the multiple listing book. Once or twice a month (depending on the area), all the information is re-compiled and re-published in a new MLS book.

Real Estate Commissions

When an agent sells a house that was listed by another office, the listing agent and the selling agent usually split the commission. Both agents generally have to split their share of the commission with the broker in charge of the office where they work. The exact split between the brokers and sales agents is negotiated when the agents begin working in an office. Part of this commission split goes to pay for office overhead and expenses. The rest is the broker's commission for overseeing the work of the agents.

If agents sell one of their own office's listings, then the whole commission stays within the office. That increases the agent's share. This is important to know, because it's obvious that sales agents prefer to sell their own listings so they get larger commissions. The split varies, of course. But some sales agents can keep up to 80 percent of the commission. This fact can work either for you, or against you, as we'll see in a bit.

Since real estate agents work entirely on commission, it's to an office's advantage to have as many sales agents as possible. The more listings the office can get and the more sales they make, the more money the brokers make. It doesn't matter if an agent only sells one house a year, that's one more commission that the broker or office gets. Since the agents work entirely on commission, they only get what they earn. But everything they earn, they have to share.

As a result of this system, there are hundreds of part-time real estate agents in the business. Some are good, and some are terrible. If you're unfortunate enough to run into one of the less competent agents, you'll wonder how they could possibly make any money. The answer is, they don't make very much. They don't usually last very long in the business either. They manage to sell a house to a friend or relative and that's about it.

This kind of agent has only the foggiest idea how to handle their paperwork or close a deal. Fortunately for those they sell to, the managing broker has to go over all the paperwork. But even then, if you get a bad agent, it can take months to straighten out the mistakes. I've learned to avoid the amateurs in this business. But sometimes I end up buying a property that was listed with an incompetent agent. This can be a real headache!

Testing an Agent

How can you spot an incompetent, unprofessional real estate agent? It's not too hard. Here's a simple test.

Personality— Does the agent have a pleasant, professional, business-like manner? Anyone who's boastful or arrogant or who seems to be doing you a favor by answering your questions, fails the test, in my opinion. There are thousands of agents around. Find one who wants to work for you.

Competence— One good way to assess the competence of an agent is to tell them right off that you're an investor looking for houses to buy, fix up, and sell. If the agent is competent, intelligent and experienced, their eyes will light up at the mention of the word *investor.* A good agent will have worked with investors before (you're not the only one in the world), and will be anxious to work with you.

Most people only buy a few homes in their entire lives. I buy as many as five houses in one year! The houses investors buy may not be very expensive, but when you consider the number, the commissions add up. A good agent can work both ends of the deal for you. That is, they can help you buy one while they help you sell another, and get commissions off both. Over several years, your business could add millions of dollars in sales volume to an office. A competent agent will realize the value of your business and give you the red-carpet treatment.

On the other hand, incompetent agents think you're a small fish because you buy cheap houses. Since you're looking at cheap houses, not the expensive ones they prefer to sell, they won't want to waste much time on you. They don't understand that buying and selling houses is your business.

A good agent will understand that you're looking for a specialized item: a house that you can make money on. Because you're planning to remodel, you'll accept a house that's run down, but it must be a bargain. A bad agent will continue to try to steer you toward a nicer, more expensive house. They have a hard time catching on to what you want. It's better not to waste your time explaining it over and over. Just find another agent.

Industriousness— Good agents work hard to find property for their customers. If they know what you're looking for, they'll call you when something comes up that may have possibilities for you. They'll check all the new listings every day, looking for bargains. They'll keep plugging away until they find a house for you.

I have very little patience with agents that say, "You'll never get a property in this neighborhood for that price! That's ridiculous! You'll have to pay much, much more!" I can't tell you how many times an agent has said this to me. They were all wrong. I always find the property I want for what I want to pay (more or less). Why do agents say this? Because real bargains are hard to find and many agents are too lazy to look.

Trustworthiness— Real estate agents have an obligation to act in the best interest of their clients. They also have, quite naturally, their own interests at heart. You need to find an agent who feels these two interests aren't in conflict. In fact, they're one and the same. In other words, get an agent that has your best interest at heart.

Here are some unethical actions to watch for:

- Avoid agents who try to stuff their own listings down your throat. As I said earlier, agents earn bigger commissions if they sell property that they've listed themselves. It's only natural that they would want to emphasize their own listings. However, if they insist on showing you nothing but their own listings, find another agent.

- Incompetent agents pressure their clients. I can't tell you how many times an agent has said to me, "Offer full price, or believe me, you won't get the house." This is an insult to your intelligence. If the house has been on the market for several months, what makes this agent think it will be snapped up in the next hour or so? The agent wants you to pay the asking price so he doesn't have to negotiate with the seller. You're asked to spend a couple of extra thousand dollars to save a few minutes of the agent's time. Don't tolerate this kind of treatment!

- One trick unscrupulous agents use is to pocket a listing. They'll hold off putting it into the multiple listings until they've shown it to all their clients. That's an easy way to increase the chance of selling their own listing. This is a breach of the agent/client relationship. It's also illegal, but some agents do it anyway.

- Agents acting solely in their own interest will want you to buy anything, regardless of price. And the more you spend, of course, the bigger their commission and the happier they are. Often they'll try to talk you into looking at property that's more expensive than you can afford. They'll give you a big sales pitch and try to fast talk you into a bad deal. They'll say "I know it's a little out of your price range, but it's such a wonderful house!"

These agents are not only devious, they're foolish. They want you to buy a house you can't make any money on. That wastes everyone's time. You're not looking for a mansion to impress your friends, you're looking for a money-maker.

You can sometimes use unscrupulous agents to your advantage. If you're interested in one of their properties, try making a low offer on it. The agent will pressure you to raise the offer, but don't do it. If you won't raise your offer, they'll turn the pressure on the seller to come down. If they really want to sell the house, maybe they'll even cut their commission a little. You may be able to negotiate a better deal with such an eager sales agent.

Even though there are occasional advantages, I recommend avoiding inexperienced and unprofessional real estate agents. Sooner or later one of them is going to make a major mistake at your expense.

What Your Agent Can Do for You

A good agent can be your best resource. Let's consider some of the valuable services they can perform for you.

Provide Background Information on Property

An agent's job is to get the information you need. An agent may be able to discover information about a property that you would find difficult or impossible to uncover by yourself. For example, here's some information an agent developed for me:

"The house is being sold by a married couple who are getting a divorce. It's been on the market almost a year. The price has been dropped from $150,000 to $110,000. The sellers are desperate to sell, but they need a cash offer." This tells you that you can offer less than $110,000 and they'll probably take it. But don't bother asking for terms. They need cash. The couple wants to cash out now so they don't have to continue to deal with each other.

Another agent told me, "This property is being sold by an investor. It's just gone on the market. But he's in no hurry to sell. He won't budge on the price, but he's willing to offer good terms." This is also valuable information. If you're short on cash, this information might make the house very attractive to you. In any case, knowing your seller's motivation can save you time and trouble. There's no sense in making a low offer the owner will never accept.

Another agent once told me, "The house belongs to an older lady with four grown children still living at home. It's ideal for them — a big house with four bedrooms. But I think she's selling the house just to get away from the kids. She wants some peace and quiet in her old age. It's been on the market for seven months, and she's anxious to sell. She just wants enough out of the sale to pay off all her loans and buy a smaller place for herself." You know immediately that you can't go too low on this offer. The owner needs some cash out of the sale. But the chances are she has an old loan that may be assumable. If you have enough cash, this could work out nicely for you.

Information like this can save you time and money. Like the "remarks" section of the listings, the background your agent offers can make the difference between a good deal and no deal.

Watch for Bargains

A good real estate agent spends a lot of time in the office, looking over new listings and keeping track of what's available. They're right there when the bargains pop up. As I mentioned before, it's sometimes possible to get a nice house, in good condition, in a nice neighborhood and for less than market value. However, you have to be in the right place at the right time, or have an agent who is.

Where is the "right place?" For a real estate agent, it's in the office every day checking the "hot sheet," the new listings that come off the computer every morning. If an agent spots one of these bargains and knows you're anxious to buy, you should be the first one they call. These bargains don't turn up all that often, but when they do, make sure you have someone who will call you *first*.

Financial Help

Finally, your agent can help you get financing. A good agent knows which lenders are offering the best financing at the moment. Since interest rates and lending programs change constantly, you need a sharp, professional agent who keeps up with this information. Also, because they deal with lenders all the time, they usually know which ones are reliable and which ones to avoid. If you're having a hard time getting financing for one reason or another, a good agent's advice can make the difference between closing a deal or having it slip through your fingers.

How to Work with Your Agent

Assuming that you've found a good real estate agent, what's the best way to work with your agent?

Explain clearly and exactly what you're looking for. Identify which neighborhoods you want to buy in and how much you're willing to pay. Be candid about what you do and how much you're willing to invest in repairs and alterations. Make sure the agent understands that the houses you buy have to be potentially good houses in good neighborhoods. They have to be cheap so that you'll be able to make a profit on them.

If you're short on cash or expect to have trouble getting the loan, tell your agent. Real estate agents are good at solving problems like these. Conversely, if you have plenty of ready cash, let them know that as well. More bargains are available to cash buyers.

If you're like me, you may be a little hesitant to tell people your business. Some people are very negative about this type of work. They insist that no one can make a full-time job out of redoing houses. But let me assure you, they're wrong. I've done it.

Tell your agent all about your work. A good agent will be very enthusiastic. In fact most agents know several other people, including other real estate agents, who remodel houses as a sideline. Your agent may have contacts that will help you find investment-grade properties. People in my business often come to know about more good properties than they can handle. They may turn over their excess to you in hopes that you'll return the favor if you ever find yourself in the same position.

One nice thing about this business is that you don't need to worry much about competition. For every person who buys and fixes up run-down houses, there are at least ten people out there messing them up. Believe me, handyman specials are being created much faster than we can renovate them. You'll never have to worry about running out of work!

CHAPTER FOUR

Buying the House

Let's suppose you've selected eight or ten homes as good prospects and have found a real estate agent who's able and willing to work with you. What next? Well, obviously the next step is seeing the houses — and the problems that come with them. Here's what can you expect to find.

Nearly every house you look at will be dirty and in need of paint. That's the starting point. Some will be dirtier than others. I usually haul at least thirty bags of trash out of every new property, and occasionally I've had up to a hundred bags. Figure 4-1 shows a small portion of the trash left in the back yard of one of my houses. Don't get too upset about the volume. You can easily hire someone to clean out the trash.

Most handyman specials are poorly decorated. The decor will be very dated, in bad taste, or both. Again, don't worry about how it looks now. The uglier the house is, the better it is for you. Ugly decor drives away most buyers. You'll be able to buy the house for less. Since you're going to redo the interior anyway, it doesn't matter to you how ugly it is.

The front and back yards are usually overgrown and the grass dead. Depending on the size of the property, you may have another thirty bags of weeds and leaves to haul away.

Learn to recognize a diamond in the rough. Look past what's there now and visualize what *could* be there. This is one of the most valuable skills you can have in this business. The more you develop the ability to visualize, the more effective you'll be at choosing good properties.

Conduct a Thorough Examination

On your first visit, examine the property thoroughly. If you're seriously interested in it, look in, under, and around everything. Be sure you bring a flashlight, a small pocket level, a tape measure, and something to write on. I have a checklist that I designed for my convenience — and to make sure I don't forget anything — and I always carry several copies with me. I fill one out for each house I inspect. Since I'm usually in a hurry, it makes this first examination easier. There's a copy of it at the end of this book. Feel free to print as many copies as you need. You'll find that it will save you a lot of time. Just check off everything as you go along. Be sure you make complete notes of all the defects and damage. You have to know exactly what's wrong with the house before you can decide what it's worth to you.

Examine the exterior structure of the house. Does it have a pleasing look, or is it a hodgepodge of poorly-done additions and modifications? It's difficult to beautify a house with a poor design. Look at the outline of the frame. Does it sag anywhere? Is it perfectly straight, or crooked? Does the foundation appear even and level? Structural repairs are nearly always expensive — and seldom increase the value in proportion to their cost.

Are the roof and siding in good repair? You can see certain defects from the street. For instance, the streaks of discoloration on the roof of the house in Figure 4-2 indicate a serious rot problem. You should be able to spot problems like this quickly. Do the windows and doors appear to be OK? Don't overlook the sidewalks

Figure 4-1
Typical trash at a handyman special

Figure 4-2
Streaks on roof indicate a rot problem

and driveway. Are they in good condition? Replacing concrete is expensive. Does the house have a garage? If so, what's the condition?

How much land comes with the property? Are there any problems with the lot? What about the neighboring lots? Is there anything offensive about them, such as piles of rubbish or a noisy business in the neighborhood? I thought the house in Figure 4-3 was an ideal prospect for me. It was a good house on a nice residential street. But the price was too low. There had to be a reason. I couldn't see any until I checked on the vacant lot next door. Records at City Hall showed that a hotel was going to be built close by. Its parking lot would extend to the lot line of this house. No one wants to live by a busy parking lot. It's noisy and will be lighted at night. I learned my lesson in time. When there's vacant property nearby, check for planned construction on that lot.

How large is the house? This is one of the most important considerations. Does it have a pleasant entry? How is the interior laid out? Do the rooms flow easily from one to the other, or are they clustered together in an inconvenient way? Do they offer space and privacy? Does the house have undesirable elements, such as a bathroom that opens onto the kitchen? Problems like this are hard to remedy.

Are the ceiling, walls, and floor in good condition? Watch for cracked plaster — that may be a sign of water leaking somewhere — "seepage" as it was described in Chapter 3.

The kitchen and bathroom are rarely in good condition in a handyman-special, and they're the most important rooms in the house. How big are they? Do they need complete renovation or just minor repair? If these rooms require a great deal of work, the cost of remodeling may be too high to make the project worthwhile.

Figure 4-3
A nice house that will be next to a hotel parking lot

Check the plumbing, heating and electrical systems. Major repairs here can be very expensive. Turn on all the taps, flush all the toilets, turn on all the lights, open and close all the doors, turn the furnace thermostat up to max and see what happens.

Don't forget to inspect the basement, attic and crawl spaces. That's where you discover secrets about a home. Has the floor been braced up from below? It's sometimes possible to spot serious defects by checking above and below the living areas. Discover these things before, not after, you buy a house.

Check with your city or county building department. Are any uncorrected code violations on record for this house? Are any building permits still pending final inspection on this house? If you buy the property, you'll have to correct violations or get the final inspection. That can run up your expenses fast.

You can expect any house you're considering to have some problems. Otherwise it wouldn't be for sale at less than market price. However, if a house fails in too many ways, then repairing it won't be economical. Your best bet would be to keep looking.

Evaluate the Property

Finding houses selling at the right price may be the most important step in making money in this business. But evaluating a prospective house is nearly as important. Don't let anyone rush you. There's a lot of money riding on your decision.

When you sign the Offer to Purchase, you've made a commitment. If your offer is accepted, you're obligated to buy. Otherwise you lose your deposit and may end up in court. Be absolutely sure you know what you're going to do with a house before you make an offer.

Think about the repairs, modifications, and improvements you would like to make. Which are essential? Which are optional? Which will add more to the home value than the cost of improvement? Would something else work better? Are you planning to do enough? Make these decisions now, not after you're stuck with the property.

Once I've examined a house, I usually go home and think about everything that I could do with it. Some things may be impractical because they're too expensive or too difficult. However, if you don't stretch your imagination, sometimes you overlook the best opportunities. Consider carefully. You don't want regrets later. Also, you may find that your ideas are good and practical, but the property itself isn't. There are some things you can't change, like the neighborhood.

Things to Think About

I almost never see a house that can't be renovated, *but I see a lot of houses that shouldn't be renovated.* What's the difference? The renovation *must* be worth more than it costs. If it isn't, it's like throwing your money down the drain. Put all your facts on paper. Be certain the property is a money maker. You can use a simple formula to determine your potential profit margin:

Find your projected selling price (value after the completed renovation). Be hard-headed and realistic. This is no time for unbounded optimism. Next, estimate your costs (property, plus improvements, plus buying and selling costs). Again, be realistic, not optimistic. Finally, subtract your cost from your selling price. What's left is your margin. Is that margin worth your time and trouble? Is it worth the risk you're taking?

Let's see how this formula works in practice:

Determining your selling price— Using the house on Walnut Street that I discussed in Chapter 3 as an example, here's how I use this formula.

When I first examined that house I noticed quite a bit of water damage. Because of a leak in the porch roof, one corner of the porch was rotted out and needed rebuilding. The kitchen, dining room and downstairs bedroom ceilings were all ruined by a plumbing leak in the bathroom above. All these ceilings had to be replaced. The bathroom floor needed reinforcing with new wood and replacement tile. There was no insulation in the attic. The house needed to be completely repainted, inside and out, and new carpeting installed.

All of this work I considered basic repairs. It absolutely needed to be done. The house was unlivable without it. If I wanted to, I could have done the repairs and stopped there. The house would then be livable and I could sell it for a fair price. But why settle for a few thousand dollars profit when much more was possible? It would be worth a lot more money if I made some easy improvements in addition to the repairs.

I proposed to convert the enclosed upstairs porch into a bedroom, turn the basement toilet into a half bath, complete the recreation room in the basement, and update the kitchen. Instead of a two-bedroom, one-bath home with a dingy basement, I would have a three-bedroom, one and one-half bath home with a brand new kitchen and an attractive basement recreation room. I knew the cost of these changes and how long they would take. But that's not enough information.

How did I decide the extra work and expense would pay off? By studying the listings and knowing what improvements would add to the value of the house. First I had to decide how much a house in that neighborhood would sell for if it had all the features that I intended to add to this one.

I studied similar houses in the multiple listing book. You can rarely find one that's exactly comparable. Some will have a few more features, a better location, or be in better condition. Others will be a little less valuable because they lack some quality. What you want to do is come up with a range of value for your finished house. The cheapest house I could find that would resemble my remodeled house was for sale at $150,000, around 50 percent more than the asking price for this house. That was my bottom figure.

I estimated my top resale price at $180,000, just under double the asking price. Houses selling above that price range generally had features that mine wouldn't. They had more square footage, or fireplaces, or a deck, or other conveniences. My house couldn't compete in that category. So it was clear that the range of value for my renovated house would be 50 to almost 100 percent more than the asking price.

Remember that listing prices are just asking prices. Few houses listed in the MLS book sell at the asking price. Anyone can ask anything they want for their home, but that doesn't mean anyone will pay it. You need to check actual *selling* prices. Your agent can help you there. All real estate offices have lists of recently-sold properties with their actual selling prices. Be sure to check this list.

Comparing asking prices and selling prices will show you how active the real estate market is in your area. Houses usually sell for about five percent below the asking price. If houses are selling substantially below the asking prices, the market is slow. People just aren't getting as much as they, or their agents, think the property is worth. There can be several reasons for a slow market: an economic downturn, high interest rates, or a local problem, such as a plant closing.

If houses are selling for very close to the asking price or even above the asking price, it means that the market is hot! The demand is so great that competitive bidders are forcing the prices up. This is a very good sign. If prices are rising, then time is on your side. The longer it takes to complete your project, the more your house will be worth. You may even be able to list and sell it above the range you originally estimated.

Determining your costs— When you've found the potential value of a house, it's time to estimate your repair and remodeling costs. I listed all the work that I wanted to do on the Walnut Street house. Then I estimated the cost of doing that work.

You may need to use a remodeling cost-estimating book to help you calculate your costs. I know what most jobs cost, but occasionally I come across something I'm not familiar with, so I keep an estimating book handy. There are a few on the market designed to help contractors make fair and accurate job quotes. I've been using the *National Repair & Remodeling Estimator*, which gives the manhours and costs for removing and replacing most items I have to deal with, and sometimes I turn to the *National Construction Estimator*. Although written for new construction, its coverage is so complete that I can get prices for things I've never had to install before. Both are published by Craftsman, are very reasonably priced, and come with a free computer estimating program and database.

You may need to modify the figures a bit. If you do all the work on a particular task yourself, your labor costs will be zero. You want to keep track of your time though, so you'll know if your time was well spent. Not only do you want to know how much your time is worth, but you also want to know how much it would cost someone else to hire the work done by a contractor.

Most people won't buy a home that needs $10,000 to $20,000 in repairs. I do. But only if the cost of repairs (including my time) is less than the value added by the repairs.

I estimated that the repairs and improvements on the Walnut Street house would cost approximately $6,000. Then I had to add in my purchase costs. If you need a new mortgage to buy a house, you'll need to figure in at least $3,000 to $6,000 for closing costs on your loan. (We'll analyze these expenses in detail when we get into the section on finance). You also have to remember to include payments on the house while you're working on it and selling it. Finally, include a couple of thousand for miscellaneous expenses. I've discovered that there are always some expenses that are hard to anticipate.

My balance sheet for the house on Walnut looked like this:

- Cost of work $6,000
- Closing costs $6,000
- Payments (about $1,000/month for 4 months) $4,000
- Miscellaneous expenses $3,000
- Total $19,000

This added up to a substantial amount of money. Figure 4-4 shows that over half of my expense is finance cost: getting a new loan and servicing that loan until the house is sold. And note that I haven't included a commission on sale as part of my transaction cost. I'll explain that later.

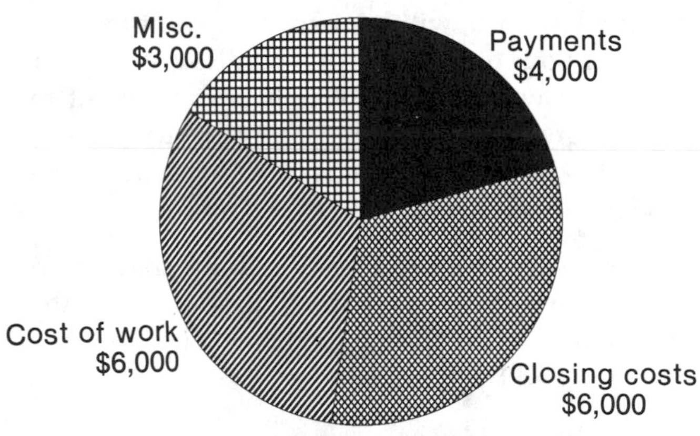

Figure 4-4

Estimated renovation costs

Sometimes I find I've estimated a bit high, but usually my estimate is pretty close to the actual cost. Avoid fooling yourself with a low estimate. It's better to be off on the high side than find you don't have the money to complete the job. That's a sure way to go broke.

If this house will be worth between $150,000 and $180,000, and if I paid the full price of $96,000, I'll make $54,000 to $84,000. My transaction cost and the cost of repairs will be $19,000. So my net will be between $35,000 and $65,000. That's not too bad. But that isn't all profit. The cost of my time isn't figured in yet. Let's see how much I'll be making for my time.

Determining your wage— To determine my hourly wage, let's go back to the labor figures excluded from the cost breakdown above. We need to know how much work is involved in the job and how much I'll be doing myself. A minimum profit of $35,000 may look good, but if it's going to take me 4,000 hours of work, I'd do better working for wages.

Of course, I'm not going to take on a project that would take 4,000 hours, but it's surprising how much time you can spend fixing up a home.

For the house on Walnut, I estimated the work at 400 hours (10 weeks at 40 hours a week). Dividing the $54,000 to $84,000 by 400 hours gives me a wage of between $135.00 and $210.00 per hour. That's not too bad. Of course, this assumes I do all the work myself. I don't. I hire out the simple work, like clean up and painting, and do the complex or skilled jobs myself (plus the management and financial work). I figured that my actual time on this project would be about 200 hours. The balance of the labor costs was included in the $6,000 estimate for repairs. My actual wage on this project was well over $300 per hour. That's more like it! I know some lawyers who would like to do that well.

If I did all the work myself, I could keep another $2,000 or so. But I'd be working for $10 per hour, which is what I generally pay my help.

I don't take on any project that doesn't pencil out at $75 an hour or better. Less than that, and I won't even consider it. Of course, I prefer to make more. I often make over $300 per hour on a good project, like the house on Walnut Street. But when there aren't any great properties available, I sometimes settle for less. Everyone has to eat. But I've never taken on a house where I expected to earn less than $75 an hour for my time.

Your profit margin— On this job I have to make $49,000. That's $19,000 for expenses (work, financing, loan payments, and miscellaneous) and another $30,000 for my time (my minimum wage of $75 per hour times the estimated 400 hours of work). Can I make $49,000 on the sale? Remember that my lowest estimated selling price was $150,000 and my highest price was $180,000. Subtracting $49,000 from $150,000, I find that I could pay $101,000 for this house and still clear $75 per hour for my time. The asking price is only $96,000!

If I can sell the house at my highest estimate, $180,000, I could pay $131,000 for the house and still make my minimum $75 per hour. There's no need to do that, of course.

What offer should I make on the house? The asking price is $96,000. I could have paid full asking price and still made a profit, but every dollar cut from the purchase price raises my profit by a dollar.

Negotiating a Deal

I've lost a few deals because I wouldn't meet the owner's demands. But I've also made some good money through sharp bargaining. Negotiating requires special skills, just like carpentry or plumbing. Some people aren't good at it. Others take real pride in their negotiating skills. Let me summarize what I've learned about negotiating the most attractive deal on old houses.

Let's say you've found a house that shows good potential. You've figured your costs and know how much you can afford to offer. *It's very important to keep these figures in mind.* Don't let anyone talk you into offering more than your top figure. If you do, you'll find yourself working for peanuts.

Sometimes you may find yourself in a situation where there are competing bids on a property. A house may be worth more to someone who's planning to buy it and renovate it for their own use. They can pay a lot more than you can because they're not looking for a profit. They may love the house. To them, it's a dream come true. To you, it's just a job. My advice is to let them have it. There are other houses and other neighborhoods. There is no house you *simply have to have.* Never try to outbid someone who plans to occupy a house. You simply can't afford to compete with them.

Making an Offer

Your first step in negotiating a purchase is to make an offer. Your real estate agent will write up the offer. This is a legal document. Once you sign it, you've obligated yourself to buy the house for the offered price if the owner accepts. Don't sign an offer lightly. If the sellers accept your offer, you've got the house at that price. If someone offers $10,000 more tomorrow, that's just too bad. The house is yours at the price in your offer. And if you find that you miscalculated and the $10,000 extra you thought you could come up with isn't there, the house is still yours at the price in your offer.

The purchase terms are an important part of every offer. Often they're even more important than the actual price. For instance, I'd gladly pay you a million dollars for your house, if you'll let me pay it off at the rate of $1 a year for a million years. That's an extreme example. But you should get the idea. Terms can make a big difference to both the buyer and the seller. We'll discuss various terms in detail when we discuss finances. Let's just assume that your first offer will be a purchase with a new conventional loan. To the owner, that's almost as good as cash.

Making your first offer can be tricky. You don't want to offer too much and miss out on some of your potential profit. You don't want to waste everyone's time by offering too little. One way to help determine what to offer is to find out how much the seller owes on the house. The information should be in the real estate listing. You know that the sellers won't take less for the house than they owe on their loan, plus their selling costs. This information is extremely important to your negotiations.

Sometimes the deal falls through right here. I've looked at some properties where the seller owed more than the maximum amount I was prepared to pay. For example, what if the sellers of the Walnut Street property were asking $110,000 and owed a total of $100,000 on their loan? They couldn't possibly accept less than $107,000. And I wouldn't want to pay more than $101,000. In a case like this, it isn't likely that we'd be able to work out any deal acceptable to both buyer and seller.

The actual loan amount due on the Walnut Street house was $89,175. They also had to pay the real estate commission of $5,350, $150.50 for the title policy, $35.75 for revenue stamps on the deed, and $4 for recording fees. All this together gave them an absolute bottom line of $94,714.75. They couldn't sell below this figure and pay off their obligations. As you can see, this doesn't leave a whole lot of room for negotiation on a house with an asking price of $96,000.

Should you offer them their bottom line figure? That isn't usually a good idea. Sellers will rarely accept it. If they do, they get nothing for their house at all. Only a desperate seller would accept an offer this low. Be prepared to pay a little more than what you think their bottom line is.

I figured the owners of the house on Walnut Street were pretty desperate. If I could shave the price a little, it was time well spent. The house had been on the market for a year with no takers. It was in bad shape, and getting worse all the time because of the roof and plumbing leaks. I offered them $95,000, just above their minimum, knowing that they'd make a counteroffer.

Sellers rarely accept your first offer, even if it's a good one. They'll usually come back with a counter price of $500 more. It's like a game, and I admit I do this myself sometimes. Sellers (or their agents) think they can wheedle another $500 out of almost anybody. Always offer a little over minimum but less than you expect to pay. You'll probably end up getting the property for close to the price you wanted to pay in the first place. You'll be happy, and the sellers will be happy too, because they'll think they got something extra.

The owners of the Walnut Street house made a counteroffer of $95,500, just as I knew they would, and I agreed to the deal. I bought the house for $5,500 less than the least amount I had calculated it was worth to me. The extra money translated into that much more profit on my work. The sellers were also happy. They were out from under a burden they couldn't afford to handle much longer. And the neighbors were happiest of all. Something was finally going to be done about that old eyesore on Walnut Street!

I think my experience on the Walnut Street house will be typical of the experiences you'll have in this business, no matter where you buy and sell homes. Many old homes badly in need of repair don't sell for much more than the value of the existing loan.

Once in a while you'll find an old fixer-upper that's owned "free and clear." Handyman specials are usually the result of many years of neglect. Some of the houses I've worked on haven't had any basic maintenance (or cleaning!) for twenty years. The owners continued to make their payments, but did little else. Either they lost their ability to care for their home due to illness or old age, or they simply didn't care how they lived . . . I've found some very odd people living in handyman specials. Let's face it. Most people wouldn't let a valuable piece of property fall down around them if they were capable of doing something about it.

Seasonal Price Variations

There was another reason why the owners of the Walnut Street house were happy to sell. Negotiations were taking place in the dead of winter, in some of the worst weather we've had in years. This was an added advantage for me. There are very few shoppers out at that time of year. It wasn't likely that someone would come along and offer full price for the house while I was in the middle of negotiating my deal. Time was on my side, and I could afford to take my time. I might have been hesitant to do this in the spring.

The volume of home sales varies quite a bit over the year. Homes always sell better (and for

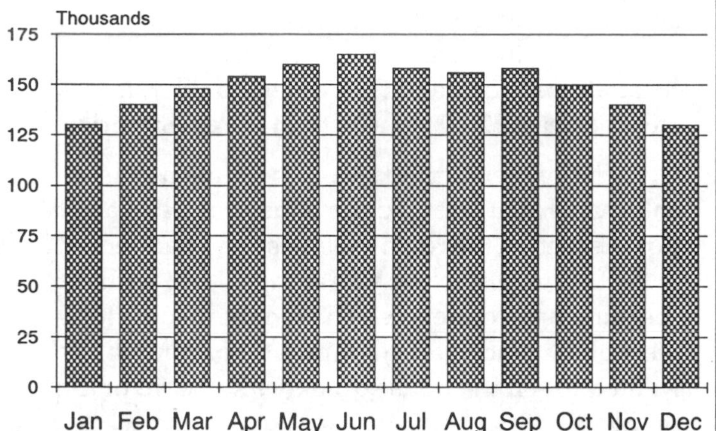

Figure 4-5
Average home sales

higher prices) in the spring and for lower prices in the winter, especially in the north where the winters are severe. Fewer people are shopping for homes in the winter. I hear that the market is also weak in the high heat of summer in the south and southwest. For most people, buying a house isn't urgent. If it's too hot or too cold, they'll wait until the weather improves to go out looking.

The demand for real estate is highest in the spring. Families prefer to buy in the spring so they can move during summer when their children are out of school. Figure 4-5 shows my estimate of the monthly variations in housing prices during the year. You can see that prices for an average home rise during the spring, peak in June, and quickly drop in October. When you're buying, take advantage of the seasonal slack periods to find the best deals. When you're selling, you want to put your house on the market when you can demand the highest price.

Tough Negotiations

You won't run into easy negotiations for bottom-of-the-line property too often. Most people want to get some money out of their house. One thing you can be sure of, you won't get the house if you offer less than the loan payoff value. You may have to negotiate back and forth a while. You may even end up paying the asking price, if it's worth it to you.

Another house I bought recently illustrates an important point. The owners weren't highly motivated or under pressure to sell. I was interested in a house that was listed for $119,700. My calculations showed that the most I could pay for it was $114,000. I asked the agent about the house. He told me that it belonged to a real estate company that had bought it only a few months before. They had paid a low price and wanted to resell it for a profit. But they weren't in a hurry to sell because it was rented and the rent income covered the carrying cost.

Checking the listing, I discovered that the real estate company owed $98,700 on the house. That was just about what they paid for it, since they bought it with zero-down by assuming a loan that was in default. I figured their bottom line at about $99,000, since they didn't have to pay a real estate commission to themselves. I offered them $102,000, giving them an easy $3,000 profit. Their counteroffer was "$109,500, take it or leave it."

I considered this. They were in no hurry to sell and I was sure at this point that they probably wouldn't take any less for the property. Was the house worth this much to me? It wasn't an incredible bargain, but yes, I could still make a good profit on it. The deciding factor was the market. At another time, I might have skipped this house and looked for something better. But it was early spring and I hadn't found anything else. Prices were beginning to rise and it could have been several months before I found another house to buy. Rather than wait for the spring rush to be over, I bought the house.

The real estate company made about $10,000 on a house they owned for three months. They hadn't done any repairs or improvements on the property and had turned it over for a quick profit. If you're in the right place at the right time, you can make quite a bit of money with deals like this.

Even though the real estate company made a good profit on this house, I made even more. Of course, I had to work for my money. But I got an attractive offer on the property before I had finished my repairs and made a reasonable profit. Sometimes, that's the best you can do.

Unsuccessful negotiations— Hard nosed negotiating will sink some deals. Sellers can be just as unreasonable as buyers. Some set a floor price and won't accept a penny less. Some are offended if you make a low offer and refuse to negotiate at all. Some agents will try to talk you out of making low offers. "Don't offer them that little," they'll say. "The sellers will be offended and won't deal with you."

Well, I'm sorry. I'm going to continue to make low offers because I've had many low offers accepted. If the sellers are offended by my offer, then they don't really want to sell. I've only had sellers really offended twice. And in neither case were they so offended that they stopped negotiating. Remember, you're not trying to make friends, you want to buy their house. Even a seller that doesn't like you will take your money.

FSBOs— The most difficult people to deal with, as I mentioned before, are those selling their own homes. You're much more likely to have negotiations go bad when you're dealing directly with the owner than when you're going through an agent. Often, people who own handyman specials — and those are the kind we're dealing with here — can be a little weird. Your normal, run-of-the-mill people don't own and live in run-down houses.

In many cases, negotiations with FSBOs can become a very personal matter. Talk to these people for a while and you'll begin to see their problem. Your success or failure may be based as much on their personality as anything else. If you can get past that hurdle, you might be able to make a good deal.

If the property is a real bargain, you may decide not to do too much negotiating. For instance, a couple of years ago I looked at an FSBO in a good suburb. It was quite a nice house, without much wrong with it except for being dirty and in need of paint inside and out. Doing some quick calculations, I came to the conclusion that it was worth at least $30,000 more than the asking price.

The owner turned out to be quite a reasonable man. He had rented the house out. He wasn't experienced in the rental business and had rented to the first tenant who came along — and without checking any references. The tenant made a total mess of the place, causing him a lot of trouble. He wanted to sell the house quickly and be rid of the problem.

As far as he was concerned, when it came to selling houses, it was first come, first served. (He hadn't learned much from his experience with the tenants.) His ad in the paper had read "Open House, 6:00 p.m. to 9:00 p.m." It was 6:05 p.m. and we were the first ones there. The house was a real bargain. Rather than risk losing it to the next people to arrive, we decided that the best negotiation was no negotiation at all. We agreed to pay the asking price.

If the seller really wants to sell an FSBO, the price will be low to begin with. If it looks like it's overpriced, chances are you aren't going to be able to negotiate a bargain.

Experience Is the Best Teacher

I can introduce you to the subject of negotiation, but I can't make you an expert negotiator. There have been whole books written on the subject. In my opinion, the only good way to learn how to negotiate on houses is to do it. No two deals are alike because no two owners are alike. However, if you follow my suggestions, you won't go very far wrong. You may not always get the best price possible, but you'll always get an acceptable deal with room for a reasonable profit. If your negotiations are successful, what lies ahead? Unless you have unlimited cash, it's time to dive into the wonderful world of finance.

CHAPTER FIVE

Getting the Financing You Need

I've read a shelf of books that explain how to make money buying and selling real estate. Maybe you have too. Most include at least a few gems of wisdom. But I find major flaws with all. Many seem to me to be too simplistic to be useful. They're good at explaining the basics of financing, but they don't give you any practical advice. Others assume you can get loans on terms that would stretch even the First National Bank of Generosity. I don't see much value in information like that.

Another group of real estate books is much more sophisticated. They offer complex, detailed advice for structuring incredibly complicated deals. Whole books are devoted to a single type of investment strategy, such as buying with no money down. Authors Robert Allen and Albert Lowry have made names for themselves by offering this kind of advice. These books include some useful suggestions. But overall I can't take them too seriously. Most of the lenders and sellers I know would turn up their noses at complex deals like these authors recommend.

My experience is that homeowners rarely agree to complicated deals. If they don't understand your offer completely, they think you're trying to cheat them. They won't wait to hear your clever explanation; they'll just say "No!"

Even if you were able to get a seller to agree to an unorthodox financing deal, chances are the bank won't accept it. In the early 1970s, loan officers fell for some of these deals. They hadn't read the books their wheeler-dealer customers were reading. They have now. I find a lot more sophistication today among lenders. They've been burned too often. Some require their borrowers to sign documents swearing that they haven't entered into any undisclosed contractual obligation on the subject property.

I don't recommend complicated financial deals. This isn't a book about "creative" financing of real estate deals. It's about buying, remodeling and selling homes profitably. Finance is just one part. The more working capital you have, the easier it is to make a good living doing what I recommend. Even if your capital is limited, this book should help you steer clear of the most likely financial mistakes.

Believe me, it's hard enough to cobble together a good deal using simple, straightforward financing. Leave the fancy stuff to the manipulators. I'll explain plain vanilla financing, the type used on over 95 percent of all home loans.

A Little Background on the Lending Industry

First let me give you a little background on the home loan industry. It's changed a great deal in the last 20 years. And these changes affect every home buyer and seller. At one time all you had to do was apply for a loan at your local savings and loan association. They checked your credit history, appraised the property, and either turned you down or made a fixed interest rate loan. Loan fees were low, usually only a few hundred dollars. Lenders expected to make money on the interest their borrowers paid over the life of the loan, not on fees.

All this changed in the late 1970s and early 1980s. Growth of the secondary money market and deregulation in the banking industry made the home loan industry a highly competitive business. Savings and loan associations no longer dominate the market. Borrowers have more choices: banks, mortgage companies, even credit unions are now competing for your business. Fees vary, interest rates vary, and terms vary.

Variable interest rate loans became common in the 1970s when inflation was high and interest rates were volatile. Although variable rate loans were promoted as a great benefit to the consumer, their main advantage was to lenders. They helped shift the risk of rising interest rates from the lender to the borrower. Lenders didn't want to get stuck with billions in long term loans under 10 percent when they were paying more than 10 percent on deposits.

Enforcing "Due On Sale" clauses also helped lenders. Most home loans are written for 30 years. But the average home is sold every eight years. Forcing new buyers to get new loans at prevailing rates helped lenders reduce the number of low-rate loans on their books.

Most loan documents give lenders the right to assign (sell) the loan to some other company. The borrower just goes on making payments as usual, but to the new holder of the loan. During the 1970s a large secondary market developed for home loans. Many primary lenders decided the profits were better in selling off their loans than in holding them to maturity. This gave them a continuing source of funds for new lending, but it also cut into their long-term profits. To counter their losses, they began charging higher fees for originating loans. They also began tailoring their loan terms to suit the requirements of secondary lenders that bought loans.

Who buys these mortgages? A few are bought by private investors and insurance companies, but most are bought by organizations that were created by the federal government to stabilize the mortgage market. The one you hear the most about is the Federal National Mortgage Association (FNMA), also known as Fannie Mae. Ginnie Mae and Freddie Mac are two other federally-sponsored secondary lenders.

These mortgage agencies were set up to make it easier for people to buy homes. When mortgage money is in short supply, they buy the mortgages that the lenders have on hand, freeing up the lender's assets so they can issue more loans. The idea is to encourage lenders to write loans. That helps the average American buy a home.

How This Affects You

What difference does this make to you, the loan applicant? It makes a *big* difference. In the old days, you dealt with a loan officer one-on-one. You had to convince that officer that you were a good risk. Now, you deal with a primary lender that's acting as an agent for one of the national mortgage associations. What that lender thinks of you is no longer of great importance. What matters most is that you meet the national mortgage association's lending standards. If you don't fit the profile, you won't get a loan.

This is a particularly serious problem for investors. The federal mortgage associations were set up to help individuals finance the purchase of a home, not to help investors make money. As a result, there's a ceiling on the number of home loans a person can have at one time. It changes frequently, but at the moment it's five. Once you have loans on five homes, you're out of the game as far as the national mortgage associations are concerned. It doesn't matter how reliable or wealthy you may be.

There are still a few banks around that hold onto some or all of the loans they originate. These are called *portfolio* lenders. These tend to be smaller, family-owned, small town or suburban banks. If you do business with one of these banks, you're in luck. They'll give you the kind of old-fashioned, personal service that used to be a part of banking. However, these smaller institutions are disappearing fast. They're being bought up by the big banking conglomerates. Occasionally a large institution will grant you a portfolio loan, but you'll pay for this special service in higher interest rates and fees.

Lenders and Real Estate Investors

In most businesses, once you've established a good relationship with the manager, you can expect continued good service. This isn't true of lenders. The fact is, they really don't want too much repeat business.

I know what you're thinking. You don't believe what I just said. You may say "I do business over and over with my bank. They want *my* business!" True, but let me explain.

First of all, understand this. I'm not talking about day-to-day banking business — making deposits and writing checks. With that business you'll never see anything but smiles. Banks want all of that business they can get, especially if the balances are large. However, if they've written a loan on one house and you ask for a loan on *another*, you're a second-class customer. And, the more loans you ask for, the lower you sink. If you don't believe me, try it!

Why Banks Don't Want Repeat Business

Chasing away repeat customers may seem crazy, but in banking it makes sense, sort of. Here's why:

The risk of multiple loans— First of all, when the bank loans you money, they're taking a chance on you. There's always the risk that you might not pay the money back. The more money they loan you, the bigger their risk is. If you pay off one loan and then apply for another, fine. But, if they grant you another loan while the first is still outstanding, their risk doubles. Those aren't great odds, and banks are traditionally very conservative. Their idea of a good deal is one with no risk at all. So even if you can qualify financially for a second loan, they aren't particularly inclined to give it to you.

What if you apply for the second loan from a different bank? Your chances of getting it are much better because neither bank has too much money riding on you. Each bank risks losing money on only one loan, rather than one bank losing on *two* loans.

What about an old-fashioned portfolio lender that knows you're a good guy? Wouldn't they give you a loan on a second or third home? Sure they can, but usually they won't. Even if you've made every payment on every loan on time for the last ten years, they don't want to bet too much on one customer. Better to spread the risk. And even portfolio lenders often use Fannie Mae guidelines in approving loans. If you have too many loans on the books, too bad. You have to conform to the guidelines in case they need to sell some loans in the future. Loans that can't be resold create problems for them.

The risk of business loans— There's another reason why lenders prefer to avoid making multiple home loans to a single person. Anyone who wants several home loans on several properties is in the business of buying and selling houses. Have you ever tried to apply for a business loan from a bank? If you have, you know what a nightmare it can be. Every detail of your life is scrutinized. The rules are so tight that you're lucky to borrow enough money for lunch.

On the other hand, if your personal credit is halfway decent, you can cruise into a bank and walk out with a $10,000 or $20,000 personal loan. This is "any purpose" money. If you tell the bank that you plan to spend it on a vacation to Europe, they'll say "Fine." But if you even hint that the money is going to be used for business, they'll start asking penetrating questions.

I know that doesn't seem reasonable. You'd think that a bank would want you to do something productive with the money. After all, if you're successful, you'll have more money and can pay back the loan easily. That's just common sense, isn't it?

There's just one hitch. Banks don't use common sense, they use statistics! Statistically, the rate of default on personal loans nationwide is very small. Only about 2 percent are not paid back. But the default rate on small business loans is about 20 percent. So if you want to use money for business instead of pleasure, you move from a very low-risk category to a very high-risk category. The bank doesn't care what your business is. All they know is that it's a business, and therefore, a risk.

Past loan abuses— Unfortunately, many of the present lending policies in the home loan industry are the result of past abuses. The small minority who used the loopholes in the mortgage-lending system to their own advantage have spoiled it for the rest of us. Banks, mortgage associations, and individual investors have all been cheated out of billions of dollars in shady real estate schemes. As a result, lenders — and especially the mortgage associations — have become very cautious. They're just trying to limit their losses.

Policies Towards Investors

The mortgage associations didn't set out to dictate policies or discourage banks from dealing with people who wanted to invest in residential real estate. But here's the result: Lenders now charge investors much higher rates for non-owner-occupied home loans. The investors must also make a larger down payment, usually 30 percent minimum. And the number of loans held by any individual is limited. It's much safer and easier for the banks to loan money to individual homeowners. They don't really want to deal with people investing in homes.

Of course, intense competition in a weak economy may force lenders to change their policies and lower some of their charges. Investors have a much easier time getting loans when they're the only ones buying. It's always better to be buying when the market is cold, and selling when the market is hot. The only problem is anticipating the market and being ready when the time is right.

When I applied for my first mortgage, in 1978, I paid a total of $250 in service fees. Today, the situation is quite different. Earlier this year I bought a house and paid service fees totaling $2,723, or about 10 times the fees I paid ten years ago . . . and this was one of my least expensive mortgages! In exchange for this, I got a few hours worth of service in the form of paperwork. The rest was profit for the lender.

Working with Lenders

Unless you have the full purchase price of a house in cash, you'll have to get some type of financing. That means you'll have to learn how to deal with lenders. There are several ways to finance a home purchase. All have advantages and disadvantages. Advantages to the seller may be disadvantages to the buyer, and vice versa. It's important to know how the various types of financing affect you as the buyer or the seller. You always want to use a method that will work *for* you, not *against* you.

Financial terms, like price, are an important part of every negotiation. Make sure you're thoroughly familiar with all the options. When you submit an offer, be very careful to identify the terms you're offering. If you don't understand them, your risk multiplies.

A new conventional loan from a bank or other lending institution is by far the most common method of financing. While most homes are bought this way, not everyone understands exactly how it works. Knowing what lenders look for in a borrower can mean the difference between getting the loan and being rejected.

Qualifying for a Loan

When you take out a loan, the house you're buying secures repayment of the amount owed. If you stop making payments on the loan, the lender can foreclose your interest in the house and sell it to pay off what you owe. The loan contract is usually called a *note*. In most states the security interest or *lien* on the house is created by a mortgage. In some states, the lender is secured by a *deed of trust*. In practice, there isn't much difference between a mortgage and a deed of trust. Both give lenders the right to sell the security (the home) if the borrower stops making payments.

Mortgages and deeds of trust work well enough. But lenders would much rather get paid on time than take over homes owned by their borrowers. Lenders don't want to be in the real estate business. *They don't want to repossess houses.* Not only is it a lot of trouble, but they almost always lose money. Most people don't default on home loans unless they can't sell the home for enough to pay off the loan. Foreclosure usually nets lenders less than the amount owed and far more headaches than they expected.

Your good credit works for you— Lenders protect themselves from foreclosure by checking the credit standing of all loan applicants. They want to make sure that applicants have both the ability and the desire to repay the loan. They check your personal financial profile. They want to know how consistent you are at paying your bills, how stable your job is, and how much money you have in savings. You have to fill out a long, detailed application form and agree to a credit check and employment verification.

Having a good credit history is important when you apply for a loan. If you've repaid loans in the past, they feel you can probably be trusted to do it again. Your employment record also tells the lender about you. If you've had a good job for a long time, chances are you'll continue to have a good job. That means you have a stable income.

If you're self employed, like me, your lender may want to document your income. They may require a balance sheet and income statement and copies of your tax returns for the last two or three years. I've been asked to provide copies of my rental agreements and copies of my tenants' cancelled rent checks. One lender even wanted signed letters from all my tenants stating how long they had lived in my property and how much rent they paid.

Your down payment— Lenders also protect themselves by requiring large down payments. The down payment lowers the amount you have to borrow and increases your commitment to the loan. If you have a considerable amount of money invested in your property, you're much less likely to let it go into default. This makes the lender more secure. The more money you put down, the more willing the bank will be to grant you a loan.

For instance, if you want to buy a $150,000 house and you can put 20 percent ($30,000) down, the loan will be for $120,000. If the loan goes into default, the bank will repossess a $150,000 house to cover the $120,000 loan. Even in a quick sale, the home should go for more than enough to cover the loan. Even if the borrower lets the house deteriorate, as most people in foreclosure do, it will probably still be worth at least $120,000. The down payment is the bank's margin of safety. The larger the down payment, the safer the loan.

Borrowers with good credit records and a steady income may be able to get loans for as much as 95 percent of the purchase price. If your credit record isn't as good, if you've changed jobs several times, you may still get the loan, but only for 60 or 75 percent of the purchase price. The greater the credit risk, the greater the down payment the lender will demand. Your good credit could mean the difference between coming up with $7,500 or $60,000 on a $150,000 purchase. The number of houses any investor can afford to buy depends on the down payments required.

Lenders also want to know where the money for your down payment is coming from. They'll ask to verify your bank account to make sure you've had the money in your possession for a long time. They want to make sure you're not borrowing the down payment. If you are, that's one more liability that you have to pay back, and less equity you have in the property.

Owner or non-owner occupied loans— Lenders always ask whether or not you intend to live in the home. It's much easier to get a loan on an owner-occupied home than on a non-owner occupied home. Loans on non-owner occupied homes have a higher risk to the lender. Tenants rarely take the same interest in property that owners do. If you request a non-owner occupied loan, you'll probably have to come up with 20 to 30 percent down, and pay a higher interest rate for the loan. Some people lie when asked this question (some real estate books even recommend lying), and some banks don't check. Some banks do, though. If you already own several houses, and you tell the bank you want to move from your $200,000 home to a $90,000 fixer, they probably will check.

Managing Your Payments

Lenders are also concerned about your ability to make monthly payments. The bigger your payment in relation to disposable income, the more likely a default. Lenders uses ratios of payments-to-income to decide how high your payment can be. There are three ways to adjust the size of your payments when you're working with a set loan amount. Let's consider each:

Extending the loan term— The bank can extend the length of your loan. The payment on a 30-year loan will be less than on a 15- or 20-year loan. However, lenders rarely make loans for more than 30 years.

Lower interest rates— You can shop around for lower interest rates. Lenders are competitive. A lender short on business may lower rates to lure customers away from competitors. Find a lender that offers an interest rate one-half or one percent lower than the others and you've cut the monthly payment 5 to 10 percent.

If you don't plan on keeping the property, consider an adjustable rate loan. It doesn't matter how high the interest rate can go as long as it's low for the first six or twelve months. Lenders often offer loans with low initial rates as an incentive to bring in customers.

Use a calculator or computer to check how various interest rates affect the size of your payments. You can get a financial calculator like the Texas Instruments "Personal Banker" for about $30. It's a good investment. Lenders will give you all the figures needed if you ask, but won't say anything if you don't ask. They prefer customers who accept the interest rate offered without asking.

Interest	Principal					
	92,000	96,000	100,000	104,000	108,000	112,000
	Payment					
8.0	675.07	704.42	733.77	763.13	792.48	821.83
8.5	707.41	738.17	768.92	799.68	830.44	861.19
9.0	740.26	772.45	804.63	836.82	869.00	901.19
9.5	773.60	807.23	840.86	874.50	908.13	941.77
10.0	807.38	842.48	877.58	912.68	947.79	982.89
10.5	841.57	878.16	914.75	951.34	987.93	1024.52
11.0	876.15	914.24	952.33	990.43	1028.52	1066.61
11.5	911.08	950.69	990.30	1029.91	1069.52	1109.14
12.0	946.33	987.48	1028.62	1069.77	1110.91	1152.06
12.5	981.89	1024.58	1067.27	1109.96	1152.65	1195.34
13.0	1017.71	1061.96	1106.21	1150.46	1194.71	1238.95
13.5	1053.79	1099.61	1145.42	1191.24	1237.06	1282.87

Figure 5-1
Mortgage comparison table

The interest rate quoted may determine whether you can qualify for the loan. For instance, checking the table in Figure 5-1 you can see that a $100,000 mortgage at 11.5 percent would give you a monthly principal-and-interest payment of $990.30. At 9.5 percent, the same loan would cost you $840.86 a month, a savings of almost $150 a month. If you could get a loan starting at 8 percent interest, your monthly payments would be only $733.77, a savings of $256.53! You can see how much the higher interest rates cost you.

Most conventional mortgages are fully amortized over the life of the loan. That means that they are figured so you have a zero balance at the end of the loan term. On a 30-year loan you make 360 equal payments. With each payment you pay a portion of the principal, and the interest on the remaining balance. Nearly the whole monthly payment goes to cover interest during the first few years of repayment. But as the unpaid balance declines, the amount of interest you pay declines, and the amount applied to principal grows. Figure 5-2 shows the rate of declining interest over the life of the loan.

As you can see, the first few payments are almost entirely interest, while the last are almost entirely principal. You don't reach a 50-50 split between principal and interest for about 22 years. The top of the loan amortization table (Figure 5-3) shows how much you actually repay the bank on a $100,000 loan at 9 percent for 30 years. It's a whopping $289,664.14. You pay a total of $189,664.14 in interest! If you have a computer, you can generate an amortization table like this for any set of terms. It takes only a few minutes.

Sometimes people talk about buying property to hold as an investment. That's a good idea as long as you buy in an area where homes are steadily rising in value. Never plan on gaining equity in property simply by making payments. Check an amortization table. During the first few years, you accumulate only a few hundred dollars in equity. It takes years and years to build up

Fully amortized loan

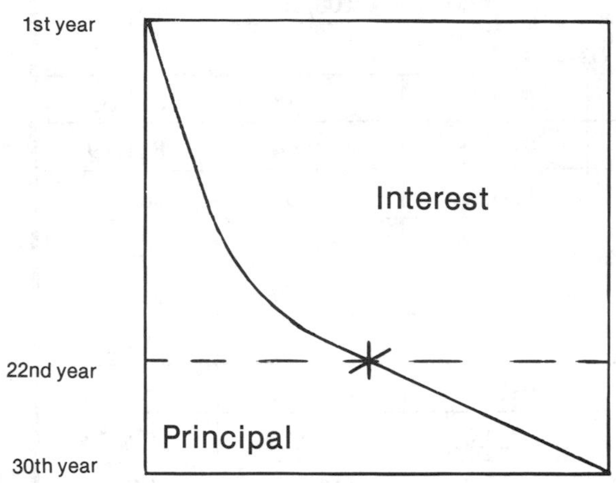

Figure 5-2
You pay mostly interest for the first 22 years!

any significant equity through payments alone. The best way to build equity quickly is to buy wisely and remodel to add value.

Increase down payment— The third way to decrease your monthly payments is to increase the amount of your down payment and make your loan amount smaller. Lenders like this, but it takes more cash. A bigger down payment means more money out of your pocket. That leaves less available to meet operating expenses. This should be your second to the last option for lowering your payments. Your last option is finding a different property; one that you can buy with a smaller loan.

Taxes and Insurance

Your monthly payments include more than just payment on the principle and interest. It also includes insurance and property taxes, even if you choose to pay these once a year in lump sums. Some lenders prefer that you have an impound account for insurance and taxes so that they can make the payments for you. If you skip insurance or tax payments, you put the lender at risk. That may be grounds for foreclosure.

Lenders insist that you carry enough hazard insurance to cover their investment. If the house burns down, proceeds from insurance should cover the cost of rebuilding the home or paying off the loan. Few people would keep making loan payments on a home that's no longer standing.

Property taxes vary from area to area. In my state, I pay about $200 a month on a $100,000 property. That's a major expense. Be sure you know what the taxes are on a property before you think of buying it. The tax information should be clearly shown on the listing at the real estate agent's office. *If it isn't, ask!*

Of course, cities and counties (usually with the consent of the voters in those cities and counties) have the authority to raise taxes. You may find that property taxes in one city are two to three times higher than in another city. Don't guess on the tax rate. You may find yourself stuck with a monthly tax bill neither you nor any potential buyer is willing to pay. Be particularly careful if you see a beautiful house, in perfect condition, for a surprisingly low price. The price may be low because the taxes are too high. If you think the taxes will go down in a few years and you can afford to wait it out, you may end up with a great bargain. But that's gambling at high stakes. You're better off looking at property with a more favorable tax rate. Don't take a chance of losing your investment because you can't pay the taxes.

Loan Fees and Other Costs of Buying

Loan fees and closing costs will be a major expense. They're part of every real estate transaction. But few people know exactly what they're getting for the money. And these charges have skyrocketed in the last few years. You can now expect to pay $3,000 to $5,000 in closing costs. Usually this money has to be paid in cash before escrow closes.

Amount Financed	$100,000.00		
Annual interest (%)	9.00		
Term in years	30		
Monthly loan payment	$804.62		
Annual loan payment	$9,655.47		
Total interest paid	$189,664.14		
Total loan payment	$289,664.14		
End of month	**Interest paid**	**Principal paid**	**Principal remaining**
1	750.00	54.62	99,945.38
2	749.59	55.03	99,890.35
3	749.18	55.45	99,834.90
4	748.76	55.86	99,779.04
5	748.34	56.28	99,722.76
6	747.92	56.70	99,666.06
7	747.50	57.13	99,608.93
8	747.07	57.56	99,551.37
9	746.64	57.99	99,493.39
10	746.20	58.42	99,434.97
261	423.48	381.14	56,082.95
262	420.62	384.00	55,698.95
263	417.74	386.88	55,312.07
264	414.84	389.78	54,922.28
265	411.92	392.71	54,529.58
266	408.97	395.65	54,133.93
267	406.00	398.62	53,735.31
268	403.01	401.61	53,333.70
269	400.00	404.62	52,929.08
270	396.97	407.65	52,521.43
351	57.93	746.69	6,977.35
352	52.33	752.29	6,225.05
353	46.69	757.93	5,467.12
354	41.00	763.62	4,703.50
355	35.28	769.35	3,934.15
356	29.51	775.12	3,159.04
357	23.69	780.93	2,378.11
358	17.84	786.79	1,591.32
359	11.93	792.69	798.63
360	5.99	798.63	0.00

Figure 5-3
Loan amortization table

I like to know what I'm getting for my money. You should too. Here's what that $3,000 to $5,000 covers:

The Lender's Fees

When you're looking for a loan, check with a few lenders and compare rates. A loan broker will shop rates for you for a small fee. Loan brokers will also do a quick check on your credit history and financial condition. This is called prequalifying. They'll ask about your income, your job, how much money you can put down, and about the property you're buying. If they think you'll qualify for a loan, they'll ask you to fill out an application . . . and that's when you begin to pay.

Application fee, credit report and appraisal fee— The application fee, which also includes a credit report from a company like TRW, will cost you between $50 and $250. You'll have to pay for this when you fill out the application, whether you actually get the loan or not. It's the lender's charge for determining your credit worthiness. If for any reason they decide not to loan you the money or if you decide not to go through with the transaction, you don't get the money back.

The appraisal fee is another nonrefundable charge. Lenders won't consider your application until they have an estimate of the property's value. The lender will hire an appraiser to prepare a report on the property. The appraiser visits the property, checks for problems or defects and compares it to other homes in the area that have been sold recently. The appraiser also evaluates the neighborhood, determining whether prices are stable, declining or increasing.

The appraisal should show that you're paying a reasonable price for the home. If the appraisal comes in well below the proposed purchase price or below average for the neighborhood, you may have problems getting a loan.

Lenders are very cautious about making loans on houses in bad condition. They don't want to get stuck with an eyesore. That can be an expensive mistake. Last year I bought a house that needed a lot of work. To my surprise, the lender refused to approve a loan until some key repairs had been completed. I was supposed to complete repairs on a property I didn't own yet! The seller refused to pay for any repairs. He was selling the house because he couldn't afford to maintain it. What could I do?

My real estate agent saved the deal. She made sure that the seller was bound by the purchase contract to sell the house to me once those repairs were completed and the house was reinspected. But I still felt there was a lot of risk. If the deal fell through for some reason, I would have repaired someone else's house for free.

I made sure there was nothing else in the way of my mortgage approval, and my agent carefully worded the agreement so that the seller couldn't back out of the deal. I was afraid he'd say, "My, what a nicely repaired house. I think I'll keep it." He didn't — or couldn't, and it worked out well for both of us. I did the repairs and got the loan.

Because of the many savings and loan failures in the last few years, lenders are tightening up on their loan policies. It's harder and harder to get loans on property where the values are uncertain. I may have to make another deal like this in the future. Be very careful if you find yourself in a similar situation.

Appraisal fees run between $100 and $300, plus an additional $50 to $100 for a follow-up inspection if you have to make repairs as I did. If you apply for a loan on rental property, the lender may request a rent appraisal too. That will cost about $75 extra. These fees are paid to the appraiser, but the lender collects from you.

Loan origination fee, loan discount and underwriting fee— The next group of fees are part of the closing costs you pay the lender after the mortgage is approved and the sale goes through.

The *loan origination fee* covers the cost of processing the paperwork for your loan. It can be a flat fee, usually around $400, or one percent of the loan, which is considerably more. If it's a percentage of the loan, then it covers the lender's costs as well as their profit on your loan. You may be charged one or the other, or both.

Whenever you hear people talking about loans, you'll also hear the term *points*. That's the loan discount. One point is 1 percent of the total loan amount. The origination fee can be quoted in points: "You can get the loan at 10-3/4 percent plus 3 points." If you're getting a $100,000 loan, that's the same as saying: "You can get the loan at 10-3/4 percent plus $3,000." Quoting the cost in points must make it easier to slip the charge past an unsuspecting borrower. *Three points* sounds like a lot less than $3,000.

Either way, these points are part of the lender's immediate profit. If your lender pays 9 percent for money and lends it to you at 11 percent, the 2 percent spread has to cover overhead and profit. But if the lender sells your loan in the secondary market, they don't make that spread for very long. Loan fees help make up the difference.

I'm sure you understand the trade-off between interest rates and loan fees. A lender can raise or lower interest rates and still come out with the same profit margin by adjusting the points charged. They can also cut their profit margin for good customers by lowering the points charged. You can *buy up* or *buy down* interest rates with points. If the going rate for loans is 10 percent plus 2 points, you may be able to get the same effective rate by paying 11-3/4 percent and no points. That's a buy up, but not all lenders will allow this.

Discount points are buy downs. This is more common than buying up, but it works just the same. If the going rate is 11-3/4 percent, you can buy the interest down to 10 percent by paying 2 points. Lenders like to attract customers by advertising lower interest rates than their competitors. You may not actually pay less for the loan. The difference is usually made up in higher points. Pay close attention to the ads. The points are generally mentioned in the small print.

Whenever you deal in VA loans, you'll have to consider the points. The VA sets the interest rates that lenders are allowed to charge. Rather than lose money on these loans, the *seller* has to pay points to make up the difference between the going interest rate and the lower VA rate on the loan. That can be a considerable chunk of the seller's profit. Be careful about selling under these circumstances.

The lender may also charge you an *underwriting fee*. The underwriter reviews all the information that has been compiled about you and the property and determines if you're a good risk. The underwriter's information and recommendation is then passed on to the loan committee that decides whether or not to write the loan. Underwriting fees may be included in the loan origination fee or charged separately. The fee is usually between $50 and $100.

Always ask about fees when you ask about a loan. You need to know not only what the interest rate is, but also what fees and points you'll have to pay. Be sure to ask what each fee covers, and the cost of each. Not all lenders use the same names for their fees. They may tell you that they don't charge an origination fee. And they don't. But they neglect to mention that they charge *another* fee for the same purpose. And it could be just as high, or higher.

What does a buyer get in exchange for his thousands of dollars in fees? A few hours of paperwork and a big debt. How can lenders get away with all these charges? They have borrowers over a barrel. If you don't like it, you can just pay cash for your house!

Pass-Through Expenses and Escrow Fees

Figure 5-4 summarizes closing costs for one of the properties I bought recently. These are fairly typical costs for the buyer. This one totaled $6,905. Many of the items shown are called *pass throughs*. These are expenses collected on behalf of others (by your lender or escrow processor) that you pay at the close of escrow.

City and county property taxes are among the pass-through fees. The seller is entitled to reimbursement for taxes paid beyond the date of close of escrow. Taxes and insurance are always paid in advance, usually six or twelve months in advance.

If the lender will be making tax and insurance payments for you, they'll collect money in advance for the payments. These are often called *escrow reserves*. After title passes, the lender will put a portion of your monthly payment in a special account and draw on this account to make tax and insurance payments.

You'll pay interest on your loan from the day the loan is funded, which may be a few days before escrow closes. Monthly interest should be prorated so you pay interest only for the rest of the month after the sale closes. Loan payments are always figured from the first day of the month.

You also pay a fee of about $75 for tax service, so your mortgage holder will be notified if the taxes on the property aren't paid. Other minor fees will include the county transfer tax, recording fee and the actual cost of messengers, if any are required. These miscellaneous fees shouldn't total more than about $50.

If the lender wants a survey of the property, you'll have to pay for that as well. Lenders tell me

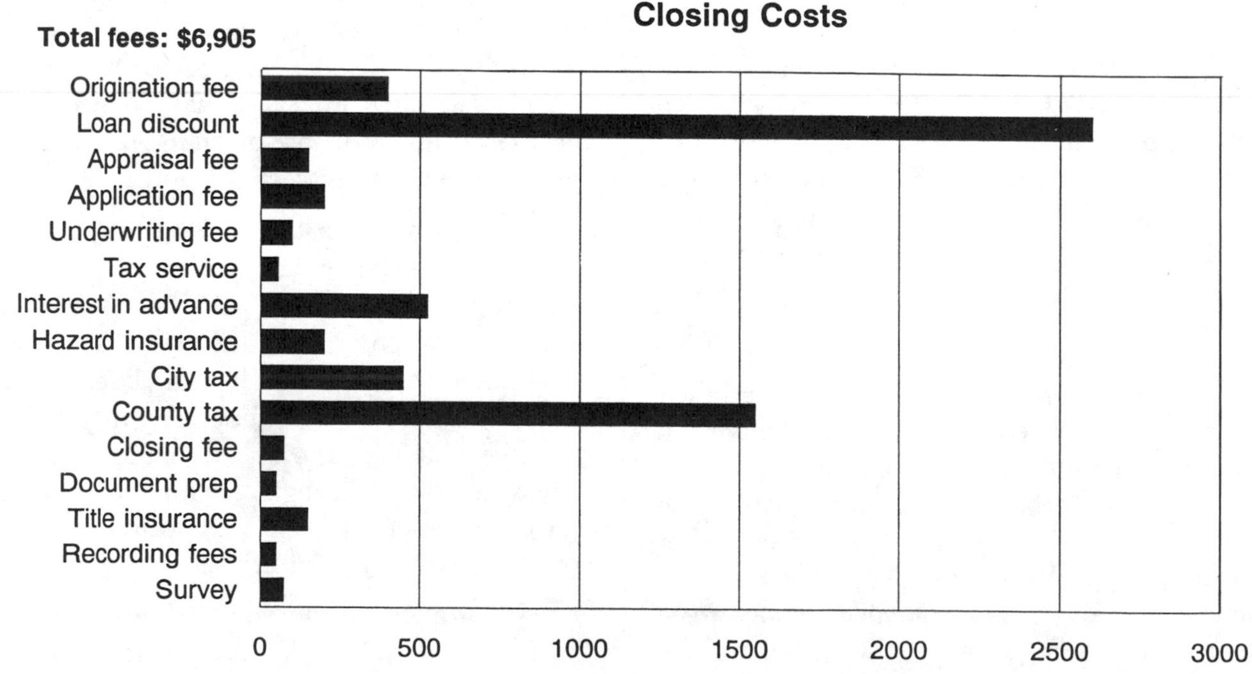

Figure 5-4
Be sure you know what you're paying for

that getting a current survey is their only way of being sure the house is built on the right lot. Survey fees are usually based on the hours required. A typical cost for a residential lot is about $100.

You'll also pay about $125 for a title insurance policy. The seller should provide a policy that guarantees you're getting clear title to the property. That protects both you and the lender.

If you live in a state where the paperwork is handled by an escrow company, a title company, or a lawyer instead of your lender, you'll pay for these services as well: a document preparation fee, a loan tie-in fee, and an escrow or closing fee. These should total $300 to $400. All of these fees are customary. They're just part of the cost of transferring title to real estate. To me, only the loan fees seem excessive.

Advantages and Disadvantages of Sales Transactions

As I said at the beginning of this section, every type of financing has both advantages and disadvantages — for both the buyer and the seller. You need to understand these transactions from both sides because you'll be both a buyer and a seller.

From the seller's point of view, the most desirable financing is (in order of decreasing desirability):

- Cash
- Loan assumption (if possible)
- New loan
- Land contract, or other private deal

Cash

Everybody knows you can't beat cash. From the seller's point of view, cash is the best choice. The problem is, hardly anyone has enough money on hand to buy a house for cash.

As a buyer, even if you had the cash to buy outright, you wouldn't want to tie up all your money in a single property. If you ever find yourself in a position where you could pay cash, however, it can be a valuable negotiating point. You can always offer less money if you can pay cash, and you can usually beat any other offers that the seller may be considering.

Simple Assumption

To this point I haven't talked much about assumable mortgages, for a good reason: they're very hard to find. Let's take a moment to consider what an *assumption* is.

At one time most loans were assumable. That meant that the seller could turn over his house, mortgage and all, to someone else. The new owner would pay the seller enough to cover the seller's equity in the house and then make payments on the existing loan. It was all very simple. In many cases, the buyer didn't even need to qualify through the bank. The seller could turn the house over to anybody he chose. And, most important, the buyer paid no closing costs, just a $40 transfer fee. Under the right circumstances, this is an ideal way to buy or sell a house (see Figure 5-5).

Unfortunately there are two big problems with assumptions. First, the seller's house may be worth a lot more than the amount of the mortgage. In that case, the buyer has to make up the difference to the seller in the form of a very large down payment. This is the *amount needed to assume*. And it could be a lot. Not every new buyer has $40,000 or $50,000 dollars for a down payment. That makes many assumptions impractical.

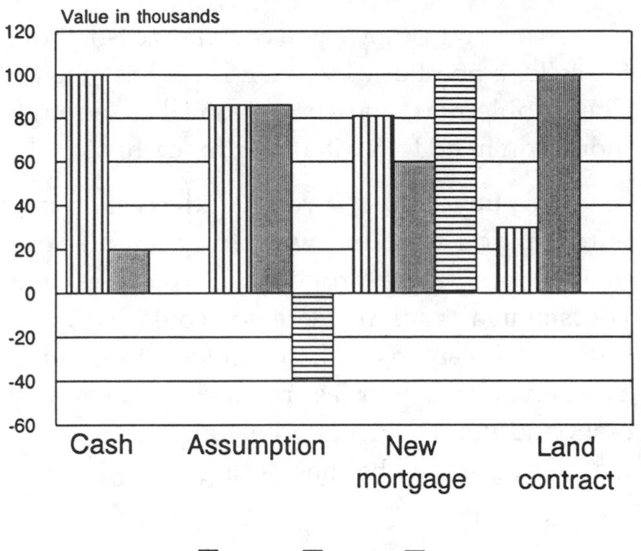

Figure 5-5
Advantages to parties involved

Second, since the late 1970s, most lenders have a *Due on Sale* clause in their notes. A loan can't be assumed unless the note allows it, and most lenders changed their loan documents to avoid assumptions. Lenders don't want to be trapped in old, low-interest mortgages with 30 years to run.

An assumable low-interest loan makes a house very easy to sell, but from the bank's point of view, assumptions are a disaster. Now almost all lenders insist that the loan be paid off in full when the house is sold. As a result, almost all assumable loans are over ten years old and the owner's equity is usually very high.

An exception to the rule— Lenders sometimes permit assumption of a low-interest loan when the borrower is delinquent. As I mentioned before, banks hate to repossess a house. They will do almost anything to avoid it. If the current owner of the house is in default and trying to sell, it might be worth talking to the lender. Explain that you'll buy the house if you can assume the loan, but not otherwise. They might let you take over the payments — even on a non-assumable loan. It is, after all, only non-assumable if they say it is. They won't be too happy about it, but for them it may be a good alternative to foreclosure.

Obsolete advice— Due on Sale clauses have made some of the tricks advocated by get-rich-quick-in-real-estate authors obsolete. Here's what they recommended: Find property with an assumable loan. Get the seller to take a note secured by the house for most of the remaining purchase price. This would bring the amount owed to 90 percent, or sometimes even 100 percent of the value of the property. You could literally get a house for no money down!

As I said before, loan officers read these books too. Due on Sale clauses helped protect the lender's interest and eliminate the little or no-money-down buyers. With a 100 percent loan, the first trust deed or first mortgage holder is more at risk, even though the holder of the second is more likely to be wiped out.

You can't find homes with large assumable loans any more. Of all the homes I've bought, only one had an assumable loan. If you're lucky enough to find another, it's an ideal way to buy, and certainly worth asking about. Just don't hold your breath waiting for one to come along.

New Loan

From the seller's standpoint, the next best form of financing is to get cash from the proceeds of a new loan. That's the most common form of financing today. A new loan, while not as good as cash, is still very desirable. It's almost the same as cash to a seller. The buyer borrows to pay the seller who gets a lump sum payment when the deal closes.

You can get new loans through banks, savings and loans, some credit unions, private lenders, or mortgage companies. By far, most loans are made through major lending institutions and mortgage companies. We've discussed banks and savings and loans as lenders. Let me explain a few things about mortgage companies.

Mortgage companies— I try to avoid dealing with mortgage companies. I only use them as a last resort. There are a few good ones around, but they're hard to find. Banks are a lot more reliable than mortgage companies because they're big institutions with a lot of assets. They're much more heavily regulated than mortgage companies. I like to work with established lenders who will be there next year too.

Many mortgage companies are small fly-by-night operations. It's very difficult to find an "old" mortgage company. Almost all of them are just starting out and eager for your business — or so they say. The reason so many are new is that few stay in business very long. A few bad apples have given the entire industry a black eye. Unfortunately, there are few laws to protect consumers from mortgage company abuses.

Why deal with mortgage companies at all? Because they really *do* want your business, unlike some banks. If there's anything in your application that suggests you might have a problem or present some risk, many banks won't even talk to you. Mortgage companies, on the other hand, will work hard to get your mortgage loan through. Why? Because they'll make a lot of money on it. Mortgage companies generally charge higher interest rates, and higher fees, than banks. That, coupled with their low overhead, helps them make a better margin on their deals.

Mortgage companies are really loan brokers. They try to resell all their notes before you sign the papers. They work hard to find an investor who wants to buy your note. Banks usually won't do that. As a result, mortgage companies will find ways to make loans that banks and savings associations wouldn't even consider. That's why you may someday have to deal with one. When no bank will take your business, a mortgage company may.

Here's something peculiar about the loan brokering business. Sometimes a mortgage company can sell your note to a bank that wouldn't do business with you directly. This actually happened to me recently. I applied for a loan with a bank and was informed that I didn't meet their lending guidelines. I already had too many home loans. So I took my business to a local mortgage company that I had dealt with before. They cheerfully took my business, and placed the mortgage with the same bank that had just rejected my application.

Mortgage companies have better connections in the mortgage market than most investors. They're the primary channel for tapping money from private investors. These investors don't have the strict loan policies that the big lending institutions have. They'll loan money to anybody they consider a fair risk — for a price.

Problems with mortgage companies— First I warned you to stay away from mortgage companies unless you had no choice, and then I told you how they can get you money when other lenders can't. So, what's the problem?

Some mortgage companies aren't as ethical and reputable as they could be. They may promise one thing and deliver another. For instance, there's the practice of *lowballing*. They quote one rate, but when it comes time to buy, the rate turns out to be much higher.

I had an experience with mortgage company lowballing a few years ago. I applied for a mortgage at 7-1/2 percent interest, with 20 percent down. The loan originator told me there would be no problem. I waited. Weeks went by. I called the mortgage company repeatedly, but the loan officer was always out. He never returned my phone calls, or my agent's, or the seller's.

Finally, just a few days before the offer to purchase was to expire, I received an acceptance letter. Only now, the deal was 9-7/8 percent interest, with 30 percent down. The mortgage company had waited until the last minute to quote me the new figures. They knew I'd go elsewhere if I had the chance. They assumed at that point it was too late for me to shop around for a better loan and still keep the sale together. They were wrong. I took a chance and managed to get another loan.

Another trick mortgage companies sometimes pull is to delay ordering an appraisal until they see if your credit clears. They're supposed to order the appraisal as soon as you apply. That's why you pay for it with your application fee. If you don't qualify, however, the appraisal is wasted. If they hold it up and you don't qualify for the loan, they pocket the appraisal money. That's an extra $125 to $250 easy profit. They get away with it because nobody checks up on them.

If you know you'll qualify easily, what difference will it make if the appraisal is delayed? Just this: You may have to wait weeks until an appraiser can come out and make a report on the property. Appraisers are often backlogged with work. This can delay the close of the purchase. At best, it's an annoyance; at worst, the delay can extend beyond the expiration of your offer to purchase, and you may lose the property.

These are the risks you take when you deal with mortgage companies. Of course, there are mortgage companies that are ethical and value their reputations for honesty and reliability. But the ones that don't are the ones you hear the most about. I've had good experiences with some companies, and bad experiences with others.

How do you know which ones are good to deal with? Discuss the matter with your real estate agent. A good agent will know which mortgage companies can be trusted, and which ones to avoid. That's part of their business. If your deal falls through, your agent won't get a commission. They work hard to get lenders and buyers together.

Government-backed mortgages: FHA and VA— You may occasionally run into government-backed mortgages, such as FHA and VA. You can apply for an FHA or VA loan through any authorized lending institution or mortgage company. These loans are also sold on the secondary money market, so all borrowers must qualify under Ginnie Mae (Government National Mortgage Corporation) guidelines. The government doesn't provide the money for these loans, it only guarantees the lender against loss in the case of a foreclosure. The loans are offered with low interest and small down payments, or in the case of VA, no money down at all. The object is to help people buy a home who might otherwise not be able to qualify for a loan.

For the buyer, there are three problems with these kinds of loans. First, for a VA loan, you need to be a veteran or currently active in the armed forces, and you must have served a minimum number of days on active duty during a specific period of time. Widows of veterans who died of service-related injuries are also eligible unless they remarry. With a VA loan, the owner must intend to occupy the property as a principal residence. There are no eligibility requirements for FHA except your ability to repay the loan.

Secondly, FHA and VA loans have maximum limits. Depending on the area you live in, this may or may not be a problem. At this writing, FHA loans are limited to 97 percent of the first $25,000 and 95 percent of the balance, not to exceed a total of $101,250 for a single unit dwelling. You may not use secondary financing for the purchase. VA loans are limited to a maximum of $144,000. FHA and VA loans can't exceed the appraised value of the home. If a home is appraised for less than the selling price, either the buyer has to pay the difference in cash or the seller must lower the price.

The third problem for the buyer is that the house you intend to buy must meet government guidelines. Most of the houses I'm interested in won't pass. You won't be allowed to buy with a VA loan unless the seller repairs the defects. That isn't too likely.

FHA and VA loans often take longer to process than conventional loans, especially if you use a lender who isn't thoroughly familiar with government regulations. If the paperwork isn't just right, it can take months to straighten out. This is one reason FHA and VA mortgages aren't popular with sellers.

Another problem for sellers is the additional cost. The seller must pay discount points for the buyer's loan as well as the major portion of the processing and closing costs. That takes a big chunk of your profits right there. If you can buy VA or FHA, then do it. But be sure you deal with a lender who *specializes* in government-backed loans. There are many around, and they can process them just as quickly as a conventional mortgage. When selling, try not to get involved in anything that may get complicated or cost you more than you want to pay. Remember, terms are a big part of the negotiations. You don't have to consider VA or FHA offers if you don't want to.

Disadvantages of new mortgages— The main problem with a new loan is that the seller can't be sure the buyer will qualify. You may wait 60 to 90 days only to discover that your buyer can't get a loan anywhere. Then you're right back where you started, having wasted several months. By then, you may have missed the best selling season.

To protect myself from this, I like to know the terms of the loan for which the buyer is applying. I'm not being nosey, just prudent. I have the right to know if the buyer is a good risk.

If a buyer is applying for an 80 percent loan and is putting 20 percent down, there's a very good chance the loan will be approved — much better than with only 5 percent down. Only people with credit ratings as good as gold can get a home loan with 5 percent down, unless it's an FHA or VA loan. As a seller, you'd be foolish to take your house off the market for someone with only a remote chance of getting a mortgage. It would be wiser to wait for an offer that includes a 20 percent down payment, even if the offering price is a little less. Better to get a thousand dollars less on a sure sale, than grasp for straws. Holding property vacant is expensive. Don't waste time on unqualified buyers.

Consider getting the buyer prequalified through a third party. There's no better way to weed out the dreamers who couldn't possibly qualify for a loan. I know several loan brokers who are willing to prequalify buyers for me. They'll usually do this at no charge in hopes of getting some new business. You can request that your buyers be prequalified as part of your selling terms in the offer to purchase.

As long as you screen your buyers carefully, getting a new loan on the property is about the same as finding a buyer with all cash. The disadvantage for buyers is the expense of getting the loan. Well-qualified buyers can usually drive a harder bargain on price because the seller will get all cash. That's appealing to many sellers and makes it likely that they'll give a little on price.

Unfortunately the real winner in a new mortgage deal is the lender. As we discussed earlier, a borrower can expect to pay thousands of dollars for the simple privilege of getting a new mortgage. This money is gone forever — and chances are, the loan won't even be assumable. If you only own the house for three months, you may end up paying $4,000 in fees for the privilege of borrowing $80,000 for three months. This works out to about 5 percent a month, including payments. As an annual rate, that would be 60 percent a year! Obviously, you don't really want to put all this money out if there's another way to buy.

Occasionally I've had a seller willing to help with closing costs. Of course, there has to be a good reason. Usually it's because the house has been for sale for a long time. It may need work, or it's overpriced, or it's in a bad neighborhood. The seller thinks that this extra incentive might be enough to close a deal. It could be. A house that just needs work and has these incentives might be exactly what you're looking for. However, if the house is overpriced or in a bad neighborhood, you're better off passing it by, terms or no terms.

Land Contracts and Installment Sales

Many sellers are willing to finance a part of the sales themselves. Usually this is because the buyer can't qualify for a loan large enough to complete the sale. The buyer signs a note for the amount owed and the property sold secures payment on the note.

In some states these privately-arranged loans are called *land contracts.* In other areas they're called *installment sales contracts.* In either case, the seller becomes a secured lender on the property. The buyer pays off the loan, plus interest, to the seller under the terms of the note or contract. Let's consider the advantages or disadvantages of this type of sale.

The buyer— From the buyer's point of view, this is a great arrangement. You can save thousands of dollars in lender fees and closing costs, and there's no waiting. A privately-arranged and financed sale can usually close in just a few days.

In privately-arranged financing, all the purchase terms are negotiable. Interest rate, payments, loan term — everything can be negotiated. Your down payment can be as low as the seller will agree to, even zero. If you're buying a house for resale, this is a great way to make a deal. You may be able to arrange to have very little of your money tied up while you make improvements on the property. In exchange, the seller may want the loan balance paid off in six months or a year. Since you want to resell the house quickly anyway, a short term payoff isn't a problem for you. Of course, if you can't sell as soon as expected, you may have to scramble to find new financing on short notice. Be sure of your market before committing yourself to a deal like this.

There are two drawbacks for the buyer in this type of sale. One is the size of the down payment. Only a desperate seller would accept a zero-down land contract sale. Most sellers want as much cash as they can get and as soon as possible. This is particularly important if the seller is planning to buy another house. They'll need enough down on the sale to cover the down payment on the new house. Many sellers won't sell if they can't get enough cash to become a buyer again.

There's another problem with land contract sales: title to the property remains with the seller until terms in the contract are met. These conditions could be partial or total loan payoff. If the original owner leaves the area or dies before you take title, there may be problems clearing title so the property can be resold.

The seller— From the point of view of most sellers, installment sales are the least desirable. Let's consider why.

The main disadvantage is that the seller has to wait to get paid, usually several years. In fact, if the terms are like a conventional mortgage, it could be 30 years before the seller gets paid in full. Of course, they would be earning interest on it all that time. But very few people are willing to wait that long, unless they want to exchange their property for a long-term monthly income.

Most sellers who agree to land contract sales insist on a balloon payment after three to five years (or sooner, if possible). This means that the buyer is obligated to pay off the balance of the loan in one lump sum after the agreed-on term. Since these arrangements usually follow a standard 30-year mortgage amortization schedule, the buyer will have paid off almost none of the principle during this period. Under these circumstances, the buyer has simply managed to postpone the need for conventional financing for a few years.

This was very helpful in the early 1980s, when mortgage rates were soaring. It allowed the buyer to wait a few years to set up a long-term loan, and helped sellers who might otherwise not have been able to sell at all. When interest rates are moderate, a balloon-payment land contract sale isn't as popular.

The most serious drawback for the seller in a land contract sale is the risk. What if the buyer quits making payments? With a new conventional loan, this is no problem for the seller — it's the bank's problem. In a private financial arrangement, however, the seller has all the risk and the worries. As I said earlier, in many states it can take up to a year to evict a land contract buyer who stops making payments, even if the seller retains title to the property. And odds are, when the seller finally repossesses the house, the buyers will have torn out the furnace and sold it for scrap metal. Maybe that's why land contracts aren't popular with sellers.

If you decide to sell on a land contract, protect yourself. Check the credit of your buyer. You can request a credit report, just like a bank, as long as you get the buyer's permission. Go through an agency like TRW and get a payment and credit history run on any prospective buyer. A good credit report, plus a reasonable down payment, lowers your risks when selling through private financing. But there's always some risk. Avoid installment sales and you'll probably sleep better at night.

Reselling land contracts— Like loans, land contracts (or any other private financial agreements) can be resold. This has very little effect on the buyers, unless it changes the terms that they might be able to negotiate.

For the sellers, there are advantages to reselling a land contract. They get their money out of the deal in an immediate lump sum payment. They don't have to worry about collecting the monthly payments or what the condition of the property might be. The purchaser of the land contract assumes all the responsibility and all the risk. The sellers are out of the picture; they take their money and go. So, what's the catch? You know there has to be one.

Simple. Land contract buyers demand and get huge discounts from the face value. They pay only a portion of what the land contract is worth. When it comes time to collect, however, they get the whole amount. The difference is their profit. This is so profitable that some real estate authors, Robert Allen among them, recommend buying land contracts as a way to make money.

Here's an example of how this works. A few months ago I bought a property in a land contract sale. The seller was very reluctant to sell on a land contract because he wanted his money right away. However, the house had a leaky basement, and buyers couldn't get a new loan on the property. The seller had to either repair the damage, sell the property through private financing (land contract), or not sell at all. He didn't have any good choices available to him.

The total selling price of this house was $67,500. The seller still owed $30,000 on the property. I couldn't afford to give him that much down. The largest down payment I could come up with was $17,500. His real estate agent arranged the following deal: the seller would issue me a land contract for $50,000, with $17,500 down, at 11 percent interest, for a three year term. He would then immediately resell the contract to a land contract company.

From my point of view, as a buyer, this worked out fine. For the seller, it was a disaster. Why? Because the land contract company charged him a 30 percent discount! They only paid him $35,000 for the $50,000 land contract.

The seller wasn't very smart. He only owed $30,000. I had given him $17,500 as a down payment. If he could have borrowed another $12,500 from somewhere, he could have paid off the mortgage. Then, when the land contract came due in three years (or when I resold the property), he could have had $37,500. Instead, he only ended up with $22,500 . . . and, he paid the real estate agent a $4,000 commission out of his profits for setting this deal up. He lost money all the way around.

Of course, the seller may have had a very good reasons for doing this, even though it cost him a substantial loss of profits. I really don't know about his personal affairs. I only use this story to illustrate a point: you can resell land contracts, or any other type of debt, but you won't get a very good price for it. You can make a lot more money buying land contracts than you can selling them.

Personal Credit

We have already covered all the common ways used to finance property. There are also a few less common ways that may be worth considering in some situations.

You don't necessarily have to use mortgage money to buy a house. If your credit is good, you may be able to get 30 or 40 thousand dollars in personal loans that can be spent any way you want. In some cases, you may be able to get enough to buy a house.

Another source of funds is a home equity loan. These have become very popular recently. The security for this loan is the equity in your own personal home, the one you live in. If your personal home was a handyman special (like mine), or if you've lived in it a long time and its value has gone up, you may have quite a bit of equity. You can borrow up to 80 percent of the value and do whatever you want with the cash.

Finally, you can even charge a house on your MasterCard! Not literally, of course. But if you have a big line of credit, you can use your overdraft protection and write a check against it.

Charging a house on your MasterCard is a novel concept, but it isn't a very good idea. MasterCard charges 18 percent interest per year, and a large percentage of the balance has to be paid off each month. Use your credit cards for short-term purchases. If you charged $30,000 for a house, you'd have to make payments of about $3,000 per month!

The same is true of personal loans, and to a lesser degree, home-equity loans. These are supposed to be short-term loans, and they carry a fairly high rate of interest. If you run up huge balances on them, you'll have to make huge payments. You can go broke very quickly using short term credit for long term purposes.

I knew a couple who tried to build a real-estate empire using short term credit. They used their personal credit, including credit cards, to raise cash. Then they used the cash as down payments on property, lying to the bank about the source of the money. They bought houses and apartments, in good condition (not fixer-uppers), which they rented out. They were following the advice that was popular in real estate books in the mid-1970s. Some of these authors advised their readers to borrow everything they could, and buy all the property they could get their hands on. That's exactly what this couple did. In no time they owned property worth over a million dollars. They thought they were rich.

Unfortunately this story doesn't have a happy ending. The couple went bankrupt. Although they owned a million dollars worth of property, they *owed more than a million dollars on it.* Their equity was less than zero.

During much of the 1970s, inflation was eroding the value of the dollar 1 percent a month, and most land was appreciating much more than that. No matter how much you paid for property, it was worth more the following year. But in the early 1980s, when this couple bought, conditions had changed. Real estate prices leveled or even dropped. They had huge monthly payments and rental income that didn't even come close to meeting their monthly obligations. They made up the difference by borrowing as long as they could. Finally they couldn't borrow any more. Their real estate empire went down the drain, taking all their personal assets with it.

What the authors of these get-rich-quick books failed to mention was that their theories would only work during raging inflation. As the economy cooled, so did their schemes. My friends weren't the only people who lost heavily on real estate. They had good company.

When to use personal credit— I feel there are times when it's OK to use personal credit in real estate transactions. However, you need to be extremely careful. It can do you as much harm as it can good.

Use your personal credit in an emergency. For example, suppose it costs you a lot more than anticipated to fix up a house. This can happen very easily. If you find yourself short of money, you can't abandon the project half-finished. Borrow against your personal credit or use your MasterCard to get through the project. This is a legitimate use for your personal credit. You may run up a huge balance on your credit cards, but once the house is sold, pay it all off so you're ready for the next emergency.

Another good use for your personal credit is that "once-in-a-lifetime" opportunity. You may, on some rare occasion, find a house that's being sold very cheap because the owner desperately needs cash, right now! Assuming it's a wonderful and legitimate opportunity, it would be a shame to let it slip through your fingers. Of course, you have to be very careful about a deal like this. Use your personal line of credit only if the house is ridiculously cheap and you know you can resell it quickly.

Recognize that you're skating on thin ice when you use personal credit this way. It can be disastrous. You may have to sell the property cheap just to get rid of it fast. Make sure it's priced low enough that you can afford to resell it at less than market value and still make a good profit. Only then is this tactic worth the risk. It's far too dangerous to use for everyday financing.

Finally, it's a good idea to keep credit in reserve for bailouts. For instance, if you buy on a land contract that has a one-year balloon payment, and the house hasn't sold when it's due, you have a problem. You could refinance, but if you're about to put the house on the market, why go to all that expense? This is a good time to let your personal credit bail you out. Borrow enough money to pay off the land contract, and then pay off your credit line when the house sells. Again, this is a one-time emergency. Don't make a habit of relying on your personal credit line to bail yourself out.

I haven't tried to cram into this chapter everything there is to know about real estate finance. Instead, I've tried to give you a fairly good overview of what you need to know about finance in buying and selling houses. Remember, try to keep your finances simple. Avoid over-extending yourself. As long as you buy and sell conservatively, you won't lose money.

So, let's assume that you've picked out your house, negotiated a good deal, arranged financing, and taken possession. It's time for you to start working on your house. There are lots of books that explain carpentry and plumbing and roofing and all the construction trades. But how do you decide which jobs you should or shouldn't do? There are so many possibilities when you begin a project like this. Which jobs are worthwhile, and which are a waste of time? Which will cost the least but raise the value of your property the most? That's what the next section is all about.

CHAPTER SIX

What Work Should You Do?

Now that you've closed the deal and own the house, you're ready to get down to work. But what work are you going to get down to? Normally, if you're a contractor, customers tell you what they want done. You might offer advice, but *they* make the final decisions. If they want purple walls and a spa in the den, no problem. Get out your tools. The customer's the boss. You'll build anything they'll pay for, as long as the building code allows it.

But when you're in the business of buying, renovating and reselling for profit, it's a whole new ball game. You're the contractor *and* the customer, and you have to make all the decisions. Even if you've been working as a construction tradesman, you may never have been in quite this position before.

To make decisions that are reasonable and profitable, you need some basic guidelines. That's what this chapter's about. I'll cover the basic principles you should follow and then get down to specifics on exterior repairs. Later chapters will cover interior repairs and improvements.

There are three principles to keep in mind when you set out to renovate a house.

Principle #1: You Are in This Business to Make a Profit

It's easy to get carried away on a renovation project — wasting time and money on repairs that buyers won't pay extra for. I assume you like to do good work. We all do. And we'd like every finished project to be a showplace. But you can't make money that way. Your buyers have a limit on what they're willing to pay. That's why you've got to limit repair costs. I call that *cost control*. In this business, cost control means concentrating on fixing code violations and creating a clean, safe, livable house.

I know limiting your creativity spoils the fun. Most builders would rather build castles than warehouses. Every conscientious professional likes to do quality work, create something unique and make it the best he or she can. Dozens of times I've thought of something I would like to build into a house I own. But could I get anyone to pay for it? Of course, every buyer is thrilled to have a few extras *if I tossed them in for free*. But giving away my labor and materials isn't very profitable.

Now, I'm not saying that you can't add *any* extras. I often do. And you should too. But you have to select very carefully. Some extras can increase the attractiveness and marketability of your house far more than their cost. It's just that you have to choose wisely and set reasonable limits. Your projects *always* have to be cost effective. They can still be creative, as long as they're cost effective too.

Principle #2: You're Not Going to Live There

I'm indebted to Leigh Robinson, author of *Landlording*, for Principle #2. This is another concept to keep in mind. Just because you like something about a remodeled house doesn't mean anyone else will like it.

Your improvements should appeal to the potential buying public, not your personal taste. That's a simple matter of knowing your market — the people you expect sell to. Repair and improve homes to the level appropriate for the neighborhood, *not to your own personal standards*. Maybe you think every house needs an indoor spa and a skylight. That's fine for your home. But you're not going to live in this house! Let the standards of the neighborhood dictate what you do, not your personal taste. The people you're selling to aren't perfectionists. You shouldn't be either. This brings us to the third principle.

Principle #3: Don't Be Your Own Worst Customer

If you're in the construction business, you've probably had customers who demanded that everything be absolutely perfect. You already know that very few things in construction fall into the category of *absolutely perfect*. Cabinets and floor tile and paint jobs and woodwork are almost never perfect. There's always a little flaw somewhere. Little flaws aren't important. Don't try to make your houses perfect. Your buyers don't need it, probably won't notice it, and certainly won't pay for it.

Don't let pride of ownership drive you out of business. No house has to be flawless. Yours only have to fit in with the neighborhood.

Your buyer will be a lot more tolerant of small flaws than someone who hires you to do a remodeling project. Buyers don't scrutinize each item in a house. They look at the whole package. They evaluate the overall condition of the house and compare it to others they can afford. They won't notice little flaws in the cabinets, floor tile, paint job or woodwork. You're probably the only one who will notice defects like these.

Does this mean you should do sloppy work? Not at all. Remember, buyers will be comparing your house to the others that are for sale. They're not going to buy your house unless it's a better value than others they can afford. Your house has to be competitive; but it doesn't have to be perfect. As long as you're offering good value, you won't have any trouble selling.

Your buyers want value. You want maximum return on your renovating dollar. Between the two, there's plenty of room for compromise. Making the decisions is your job. Choose projects that give the best return on your investment because they create the most value for the lowest cost. This chapter will help you avoid impractical improvements that waste resources, and direct you to essential repairs that make good use of your assets.

Consider Your Buyer

The starting place is always your potential buyer. As I said, you're not going to live there. So who is? Let's focus on the type of person who'll be buying your house.

The Neighbors

What do you know about the people who will buy your house? Well, what kind of person would like to live in that neighborhood? To answer this question, just look around. The people who'll be interested in buying your house will probably be a lot like the people already living in the neighborhood. They'll have about the same income, need about the same number of bedrooms, expect the same conveniences, and demand the same quality as other owners in the neighborhood.

People like to live in a neighborhood where they feel comfortable, where they'll have something in common with the people around them. To find out what's appropriate for your buyer, take a walk or a drive around the neighborhood. You probably did this already before buying the property. But take another look now.

What kind of decorating do the neighbors seem to prefer? Are they high-style or more conservative? Are their houses well landscaped and improved, or are they simple and plain? Talk to the neighbors. Ask their opinions. Invite them in to see what you're doing. Believe me, ask a neighbor for an opinion and you'll probably get more than you know what to do with.

Portrait of the Buyer

Most potential buyers of low-cost houses aren't very sophisticated, either in their taste or their knowledge of home maintenance. Most will be first-time buyers. Their primary concern is finding a nice place to live. They want a home in a good neighborhood, big enough for their family, and in reasonably good condition. *Good condition* means everything has to look nice and work properly. They'd like some extra features if they don't cost too much. But, in most cases, the finer points of building are lost on them. They don't care what kind of siding they have, as long as it's solid. They don't care about the windows and doors, as long as they look nice and open properly. They don't care about the furnace, as long as it works.

Lack of sophistication comes from never having been responsible for a home before. If they've been living in apartments, they see everything from that point of view. They're excited about having more space, more privacy, and their own yard. They won't even notice the thermopane windows if they've never paid their own heating bills before. People who haven't paid large heating bills aren't sensitive to energy efficiency issues.

Neither will they be impressed by extra money spent on low-maintenance siding. Your buyers will be much more concerned about who's going to cut the grass next week than about the cost of painting the house in five years.

Affordability is your buyer's most important consideration, whether they're first-time buyers or not. All the time they're looking at your house, they're wondering if they can qualify for the loan and afford the payments. Cost is so important that they may not notice the wonderful features you've added. This is the bottom line for buyers: If they can't make the payments, they can't buy, no matter how nice the house is.

Here's something else to consider. Most buyers look at a dozen or more homes before making an offer on a house. Except for a few with very good memories, they aren't going to remember much about the details on each house. Which of the homes had a fireplace? Did they all have dishwashers? Did the home on Elm have two bathrooms or three? Is that the one with central air conditioning? Those are some very expensive questions. But most buyers won't remember which homes had which features. They're lucky if they remember how many bedrooms each had.

How, then, do home shoppers decide which house to buy? Having bought and sold dozens of homes in the last ten years, I can answer that question. They rely almost totally on first impressions. Some professionals call this *curb appeal*. But it goes deeper than that. If your house is in their price range, and if it makes an overall good impression in the first three minutes, they'll seriously consider it. Otherwise, most buyers will ignore it.

Consider Your Price Range

One of your considerations at the time you picked out the house was the price range. How much could the house be expected to sell for in this neighborhood? Ideally, you've bought well under the average selling price of most homes in the area. When you're finished, the home will sell for not much more than the average price of homes in the neighborhood. The difference is your investment margin and profit. That determines how much you can invest in the house and what you do to it.

Cheap Property

When you're dealing with cheap property, you can only afford to do what is absolutely necessary. Otherwise your profit disappears. You have very few options. My advice for cheap property is to do as little as possible, as inexpensively as possible.

In some cases, you may not be dealing directly with the consumer anyway. If you're working with FHA Section 8 housing, or any FHA or VA mortgages, the government will set the standards and you must follow them. Your decisions may be very limited. Sometimes the only thing that may be left up to you is the color of the paint.

In the middle and higher price ranges, where I assume you'll be most of the time, making the right renovation decisions makes a big difference in profit margin. Regardless of price range, you have to weigh the value of improvements to the buyer against your cost for those improvements. Naturally, you want the maximum benefit for the minimum cost.

High-Price Property

In upscale or high-price housing, the situation is just the reverse of low-price housing. Here you have much more flexibility. If you plan to sell a property for a million dollars, you can afford to put a great deal of money into it. In fact, you'll have to. Upscale consumers are sophisticated and demanding buyers.

In this price range, luxuries become necessities. These buyers want everything. They want the latest, most exciting features available on the market. They want quality construction and attention to detail. And why not? For the money they're willing to pay, they should get it.

I'm not going to talk much about renovating expensive property. Remember, I don't recommend this kind of project unless you really know the market. The big problem with high-end housing is that there are relatively few buyers. As the price rises, the pool of available purchasers shrinks. There are a lot more people who have $100,000 to spend on a house than there are people who have $1,000,000 to spend.

Another disadvantage of dealing in high-price housing is the competition with other builders. Everybody wants to get in on the million-dollar deals because the profits are bigger. When property values are rising, profits are staggering. But when the market turns cold, which it can do overnight, your luxury home can turn into a white elephant and a $100,000 loss. Can you afford a $100,000 loss? If not, stay out of expensive projects. Even if you *can* afford a $100,000 loss, don't try expensive projects unless you've had experience in the neighborhood.

The only exception to this rule is the one we discussed earlier: If you're renovating a house for your own use. This is the least risky way to approach any renovation project. If you're fixing up a house that you could live in for a while, take a few chances. In an emergency, make the house your home until a buyer comes along.

Be a little creative on a house you plan to occupy. If you're lucky, your dream home may be exactly the dream home someone else also wants. If they make the right offer, take the money and start on another dream.

That's how John F. Long, the well-known builder from Phoenix, Arizona, started out. He built a house for his own use. Somebody offered him a lot of money for it, so he sold it, took the money, and built an even better one. Somebody offered him even more money for that one. He sold it and built himself a fabulous house with the money. Someone offered him even *more* money for that one. Eventually, he caught on that this could be a good line of work. He went on to accumulate a fortune in residential construction.

Middle-Income Property

Most of this chapter will be about *mid-priced* property. By that, I mean what most middle-income buyers can afford. Middle-income buyers usually have proceeds from another home sale that will cover their down payment and transaction costs. "Mid-priced" covers a wide range of prices, usually more than 50 percent of all homes sold. You can easily be working in several price tiers and still be selling to middle-income buyers.

The relation between improvement cost and value of improvements to the buyer is especially important in mid-priced housing. Profits can be miniscule or they can be major. Every decision you make will carry a price tag. Do too little and you won't make much money. Do too much and you can actually lose money.

Cost Effectiveness

The key question on all improvements is "How much is this likely to raise the value of the house?" You always start with this limit: Turning the cheapest home on the block into the most expensive home on the block will nearly always be foolish. You can't put half a million dollars into a house that's in a $100,000 neighborhood and expect to sell it for over a million dollars. No matter how great your house is, millionaires don't want to live in a $100,000 neighborhood. You may sell your house for $150,000, but that's a disaster if you put half a million dollars into it.

If your house is in a neighborhood of $100,000 houses, you should be planning to sell it for about that price. Remember, it's always best to ask the average price but plan to sell a little less. That leaves room for bargaining and helps close the sale faster. Of course, if your house is nicer than others in the neighborhood, it might sell for a little more. But it has to be a *lot* nicer than the others to sell for just a *little* more.

Organizing Your Decisions

I've discussed the theory. Now let's get practical. Exactly what should you do and what should you skip? Of course, I can't talk about every possible improvement. There are thousands of them. But I'll suggest categories of improvements that are prudent and categories that are foolish. My object is not to give you answers that fit every situation. Instead, I'll suggest guidelines that apply to most projects.

My job would be easier if we were walking through an actual house that's about to be renovated. But we don't have that luxury. So I'll do the best I can with words and pictures. As we go through a typical job, I'll identify decisions we'll have to make and suggest what work should be done.

I've organized the material into two categories: repairs and improvements. Of course, you'll usually find that these overlap. Some repairs are improvements, and some improvements involve repairs. If we were both looking at the same house, we'd probably agree on what was an improvement and what was a repair. Generally, I feel that what absolutely has to be done, like a leaky roof, is a repair. Anything that can wait, like a fancy light fixture or a leaded-glass front door, is an improvement. The rest of this chapter will consider exterior repairs. I'll cover interior repairs and improvements in later chapters.

The Essentials

When you're in one of these fixer-uppers, dozens of repairs will be begging for your attention. Without making these essential repairs, the house will deteriorate further until it eventually becomes unlivable by today's standards. When it comes to necessary repairs, your decision isn't whether to proceed. It's how much to invest in each repair.

Should you simply repair what's damaged, or should you replace it? What should you replace it with? How does your choice fit in with your budget? Will replacing the damaged item greatly increase the value? Would repairing it give you the same value? These are the decisions we'll be making.

Exterior Repairs

Let's assume we're standing on the sidewalk in front of your new property. It's an average fixer-upper. What are we likely to notice? The first thing we see is that the house needs paint. I've never taken on a project that didn't need some exterior paint somewhere. This seems like an obvious decision. But wait. Are you sure you want to paint it? Maybe it would look better with new siding? And how about the color?

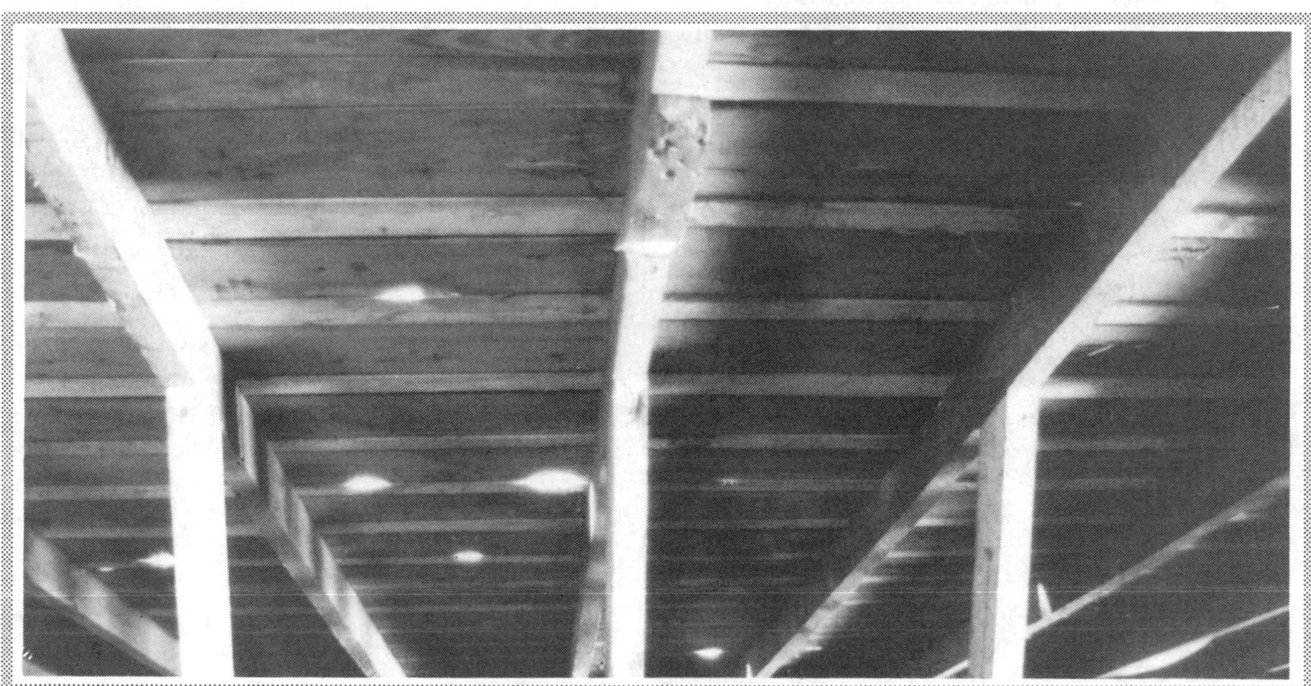

Figure 6-1
Holes in the roof — loads of them!

Figure 6-2
Part of this roof was completely rotted out

What seemed like an easy decision is usually more complicated. That's because paint isn't merely an essential repair, it's also *decorating*. And decorating falls under a different heading. The house not only has to be functional and weatherproof, it has to look good. People have to *like* it. This is one type of essential repair that takes some thought. We'll delay a decision on paint until later in this book.

What else do you notice about the property? Well, you want to make sure the house is secure against weather and vandalism. That's essential. If there are any broken windows or exterior doors, they get high priority on our repair list. Also, I always change the locks when I take over a house. There's no telling who has duplicate keys. A vacant house is a temptation, even in a nice neighborhood. If you're going to leave valuable tools or materials there, secure them with your own locks.

Once I made the mistake of saying "Oh, nobody would try to get into this old house. There's nothing here anyone would want." I don't know what the thieves did with fifteen gallons of 'Daring Indigo' house paint, but I had to replace them anyway. Let my mistake be your lesson.

Figure 6-3
Use dabs of tar to temporarily fix roof leaks

The Roof

What about the roof? Does it need repair? Should you patch it or replace it? If the roof is leaking in several places, it probably needs new shingles. It may even need more extensive work. Replacing a leaky or damaged roof is almost always a good investment. It won't cost all that much to replace, and buyers love to see "New Roof" in a real estate listings. Sales agents make it a big selling point.

Of course, not every old house needs a new roof. But if the roof was bad, the seller probably had to knock a few thousand dollars off the price you paid. So replacing a leaky roof will probably add at least as much value to the home as the repair costs. If you can do the work yourself, it will only cost you a few hundred dollars. That makes it an especially good investment.

Figure 6-1 is a picture I took from inside one of my houses. Can you tell what it is? You're looking up at the roof from the attic space. See those spots of light? Well, you shouldn't see them. If you see light through the ceiling, obviously you need a new roof — and probably repairs to walls and ceilings damaged by water.

Figure 6-2 is an exterior view of the same roof. The roof clearly needed replacing. My first concern was preventing more damage until I could get new shingles down. Filling the holes with tar (as in Figure 6-3) is a temporary fix. Beyond that you'll need to replace some shingles.

Figure 6-4
New, moderately-priced roof

I used Certainteed Sealdon 20 shingles on the house in Figure 6-4. These shingles are moderately priced and have an attractive pattern. I could have spent more, but I picked a type and style that suited the value of the house and the neighborhood. Before buying these shingles, I asked myself two questions:

1. Does the roof really need replacing?
2. Can I recover the cost of the repair?

The answer to both questions was "yes."

First, the roof was badly deteriorated. No reputable roofer would try to just repair it. I could see the damage clearly from the ground. If I didn't replace the roof, I'd have put my interior repairs in jeopardy. Why chance taking a lot of rain damage? It's just not worth the risk. It's better to do the repairs right.

Second, the cost of new shingles is always recoverable. Sellers usually have to discount a house thousands of dollars if it needs a new roof. Repairing the roof for a few hundred eliminates the need for you to offer a discount. So this repair *alone* guarantees to raise the value of the house by several thousand dollars — and that's all the more profit for you.

Concrete Flatwork

When you're buying a house, try to avoid any that need major repairs to a driveway, sidewalk, patio or concrete slab. Concrete flatwork repairs are expensive. And most of the time your buyers won't even notice the money you spent. They take concrete slabs for granted. You'll impress them more with a new $50 light fixture in the dining room than a new $2,000 driveway and walkway. How much will $2,000 invested in flatwork raise the value of your house? Next to nothing!

How much did a fractured driveway reduce the price of the house you bought? Probably very little. Why? Because it wasn't something anyone paid much attention to. Most buyers just want a

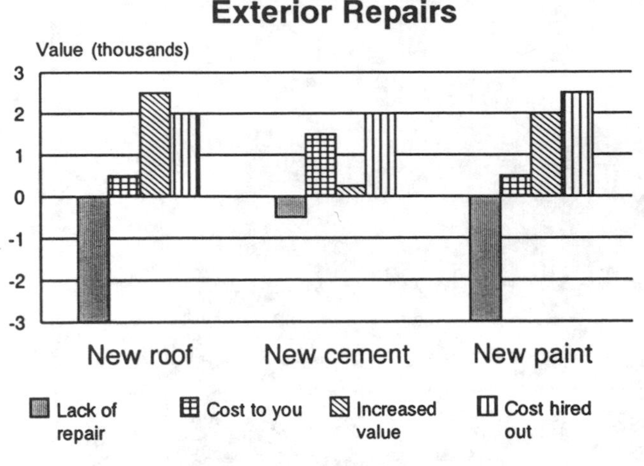

Figure 6-5
Value of various exterior repairs

hard, dry place to park their car. If the driveway is totally crumbled so they can't park on it safely, then they'll notice. Otherwise, leave it. Most people just don't care.

Buyers have no idea how expensive concrete flatwork is. If you remodel a kitchen or a bathroom, buyers will be impressed. They know that kitchen and bath renovations are expensive, and they appreciate them. Driveways and sidewalks, on the other hand, aren't glamor projects. Nobody impresses their friends with a beautiful new sidewalk.

Figure 6-5 shows my estimates of the cost and value of exterior repairs. I compare the cost of repairs with the reduced sales price if repairs aren't done. Notice how little concrete flatwork increases the value of a house. Compare that with the value of replacing the roof. Be wise. Put your money where it will do you the most good.

Some cities may force you to do certain repairs if you buy the property. This is something you should investigate before buying the house. If code-mandated repairs will be expensive and will add little to the resale value, don't buy the property (unless you can get it *really* cheap).

Siding or Paint?

The siding on most fixer-uppers is pretty ugly. That's why the house is cheap, right? If the siding is wood, it will need paint. If you're lucky, the house will have aluminum siding. But you're more likely to get asbestos shingle or asphalt fake-brick siding. There's nothing uglier than deteriorated fake-brick siding. It's guaranteed to drive away almost any prospective buyer, *except you*. You know you can get the house very cheap because of it.

How should you deal with deteriorating siding? Assuming the house isn't ready to collapse under it, you can always put on new siding. Vinyl or aluminum siding will cover up just about anything. But that's not always the best or easiest solution to the problem.

Consider what the buyers see when they first look at the house. A house with peeling or crumbling siding has a curb-appeal rating of zero. Nine out of ten buyers will turn on their heels and leave. But if the house seems to have a solid surface and a good color, buyers will be interested enough to come inside. Once you get them in the door, you can begin selling features of the home. The siding only has to be adequate. Perfection isn't necessary.

If you ask the buyers which they'd rather have, new vinyl siding or a new kitchen, they'll always choose the new kitchen. These two improvements can be about the same price. But the owners will use their kitchen every day. Kitchen improvements increase buyer satisfaction. New siding just looks better. If the existing siding keeps weather out, it's good enough.

Wood siding— If the siding is intact, a fresh coat of paint is probably your best choice. It's cheap, easy, and makes your house look better — fast. Covering wood siding with aluminum or vinyl siding will cost more, take a lot longer, and it will look almost the same when you're done. All you want to do is create a good first impression. Do it as easily and inexpensively as possible. Just put on a new coat of paint.

Wood is a very desirable and expensive siding material. Of course, few new houses have genuine wood siding. Panel materials, stucco and vinyl have nearly captured the market. If an old house has both wood siding and attractive interior woodwork, you've got a set of strong selling points. Don't think of your home as an old clap-

Figure 6-6
Asphalt "fake stone" siding

board relic. Instead, think of it as a quaint, charming, antique home. The age of the house then becomes a positive, rather than a negative selling point. The fact that wood requires a little more maintenance won't be that important to buyers looking for charm. People who collect antiques are willing to provide the extra care.

Asbestos or asphalt shingle siding— These are the least attractive sidings ever sold, in my opinion. They can be genuinely ugly even when in perfect condition. Back in the 1930s and 1940s asbestos and asphalt were popular because they were cheap, durable and relatively maintenance free. That's no excuse. They're still ugly. The home in Figure 6-6 is an example of asphalt "fake stone" siding. This home is in good condition. Too bad the siding (and the unattractive porch enclosure) make it look so bad.

There's one alternative that people rarely consider when dealing with siding: it comes off! If you remove a few pieces of this material, you may have a pleasant surprise. It might be covering perfectly good clapboard that only needs minor repairs and a new coat of paint.

A few years ago some friends of mine bought an old house covered with deteriorated fake-brick asphalt. Instead of covering it with siding, they tore off a few of the old shingles. Underneath they found Victorian woodwork in almost perfect condition. They painted the woodwork in authentic Victorian colors and turned the house into a showplace like the lovely Victorian home shown in Figure 6-7. A few blocks away there's a similar house that was renovated using aluminum siding. Modern aluminum siding completely destroyed the beauty of the original building. The result was a bastardized job with

Figure 6-7
Authentic Victorian house

no identifiable style, neither Victorian nor modern. The contrast between the two houses is striking.

Of course, there's no guarantee that you're going to find something good under the exposed siding. The old clapboards may be totally unusable. But have a look anyway. It only takes a few minutes to remove a few shingles. That time could save you thousands of dollars. Work carefully and you can replace the pieces you removed.

Another alternative to replacing the siding is to paint it. Ordinary latex house paint can be rolled on over asbestos shingles and it covers very well. The paint will actually last longer over this material than over wood. Asbestos shingles aren't porous and don't collect moisture. That makes it a good base for paint. Dark colors are the best choice when painting asbestos shingles.

Cement block— Here's another durable, low-maintenance but ugly material. No, I'm not going to tell you to paint it. You could, but it won't look any better. The best solution is to add an exterior coat of stucco. Many good products are available. Most are made with cement mortar mix. Some have fiberglass added. They can be sprayed or troweled on and produce surface textures from rough to completely smooth. Choose a texture that accents your decorating or landscaping scheme. Stucco comes in many different colors, so painting isn't necessary. It can be painted if you want, though. A new stucco surface will transform your house from a concrete box to an attractive and stylish home.

Brick siding— If you decide your house needs new siding, brick is one option. It can turn an ordinary home into a showplace. Of course,

Figure 6-8
Brick accents this Colonial-style house

real brick veneer is expensive. And if you want to use a full thickness of brick, a new foundation is needed. That much extra work won't be returned to you in resale value.

If your anticipated selling price doesn't allow an investment in real brick, check into brick slices. Dealers in your area probably offer brick siding panels mounted on a backing board. It's easy to install. I'm amazed at how authentic this looks. I'd swear it was real brick if I didn't know better. But even this type of brick is expensive, though much less than real brick.

When should you consider the expense of brick, or brick substitutes? If your project is in an upscale neighborhood where many of the other homes are brick, your buyers will pay extra for a brick house. This is particularly true if your house is one of the few non-brick homes in the neighborhood. A plain house surrounded by brick homes will look cheap by comparison. If you can't add brick siding, consider brick accents like the house in Figure 6-8.

If you decide to add brick siding, which should you choose? Real brick veneer or brick panels? Unless you're working in the no-compromise luxury range, brick panels offer advantages that are hard to pass up. They're less expensive to buy and less expensive to install. Brick panels can be installed easily by unskilled workers. This is important to me because all my helpers are unskilled, and I'm not much of a mason myself.

Brick panel siding looks good and may wear as long as the real thing. Some products, such as those manufactured by U.S. Brick Systems, come with a 50-year guarantee. Most buyers probably won't be able to tell the difference between the

Cost vs. Benefit of Paint or Siding

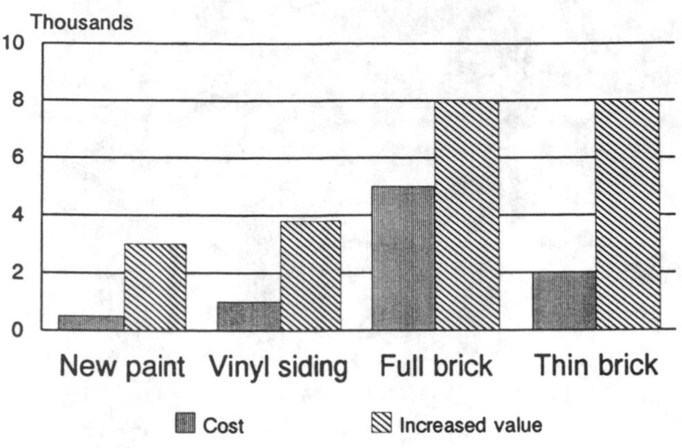

Figure 6-9
Exterior siding choices

Figure 6-10
Deteriorated, but repairable window

brick panels and real brick. Of course, if they ask you, admit that it's panel siding, not real brick veneer. More than likely, they won't care. After all, both products are real brick. The only difference is that the panels aren't a full brick thick.

Your siding choices— If you're forced to add siding, consider costs very carefully. Brick will be the most expensive choice. Paint is the cheapest. Vinyl and aluminum siding fall somewhere in between. Figure 6-9 compares the estimated cost and benefit range for several types of exterior treatment on a medium-priced home.

If your house is in a middle-income neighborhood of predominantly aluminum-sided houses, do what the neighbors have done. If aluminum siding is good enough for your neighbors, it's good enough for you. Most people would prefer brick or stucco, including the neighbors. But no one has it because no one wants to pay for it. That's good advice for you.

If necessary, you can paint over almost anything, even brick or aluminum siding. Of course, anything painted today will eventually have to be repainted. That eliminates its "maintenance free" benefit. Leaving siding unpainted may not be as attractive but certainly reduces upkeep expense.

Sometimes you may have to paint just to change the color. I've seen bright pink aluminum siding on a house, and on another, a pink brick addition to a yellow brick house. They looked so awful I got good deals on both houses. They each got a coat of paint, which cost me very little.

Houses with room additions, especially more than one addition, can present special problems. The addition may stand out like a sore thumb even if both the house and the addition are the same color. New siding is usually the best way to tie all of the parts together.

Windows

Be prepared to invest a little time and money in windows. The glass in most fixer-uppers will be intact. But beyond that you can't expect too much. Figure 6-10 is an example. Figure 6-11 is almost as bad. Even if the sash and sill are in fair condition, the screen and storm windows will usually be missing. I bought a house earlier this year that had eighteen windows — none of them with storms or screens. Most of the windows had loose panes. Years of aging had caused the putty to crack and fall out. There was nothing to stop

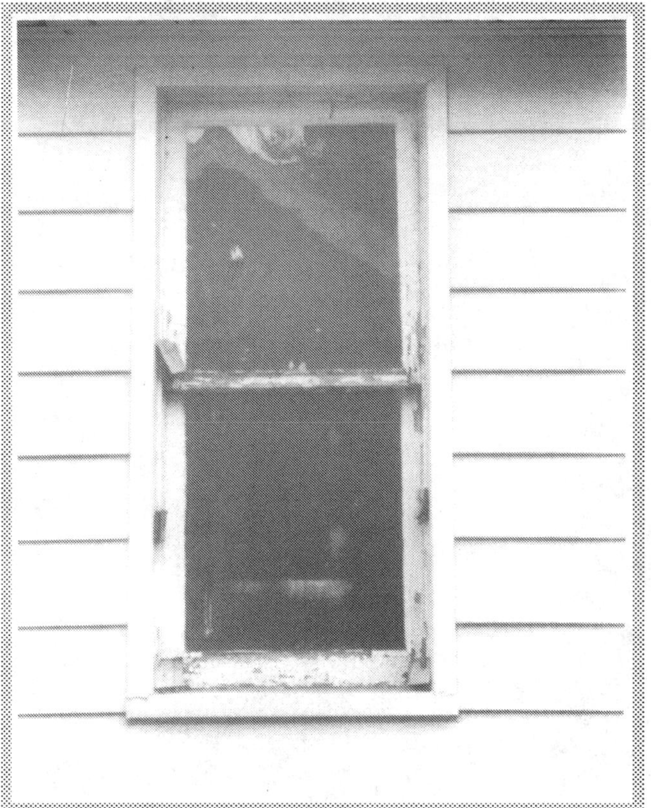

Figure 6-11
Cracked, peeling windows are typical on handyman specials

Figure 6-12
Cats can be very destructive

the cold winter air from blowing through the house. I got a good deal on the house. The sellers said they couldn't afford to pay the huge heating bills. I guess they never figured out why.

Storms and screens aren't expensive and are easy to put up. A house without good storms and screens is substandard. This is something people will notice. Buyers will assume the storms and screens are missing because you skimped on the basics (and probably cut corners on other essential too). You don't have to install the best storms and screens, but they need to be adequate.

What about the windows themselves? Should you tear them all out and replace them with modern windows? Probably not. I've found that almost all windows can be repaired. You might have to replace a sill here and there, but that's a lot easier and cheaper than replacing the whole window. The window in Figure 6-12 was badly shredded by a cat, but it was still repairable. Wood putty and paint are cheap and can work wonders on old windows. New replacement windows are expensive and installation takes time. You don't want to do anything that's difficult or expensive unless people are going to appreciate it. If windows open and close properly, and have storms and screens, that's enough.

The windows in Figure 6-13 appeared to be in bad shape. I could have replaced them. But look closer. Except for the lumpy and irregular putty around the panes, these windows are OK. They work just fine. All I did was add a fresh coat

Figure 6-13
The windows are old, but good

Before After

Figure 6-14
Improving the view

of paint and new screens. The new curtains (my wife's touch, far less expensive than new windows) drew the attention away from windows on the inside. New screens on the exterior caught the eye from outside. Buyers don't care if windows aren't perfect. They just glance at the windows before focusing on something more important to them.

Of course, I know that homeowners spend millions of dollars every year on replacement windows and replacement siding. These are very popular home improvement projects. Why, then, don't I think it's cost effective to replace them? Why would owners spend all that money on something I claim they don't care about?

There's a simple explanation. It applies to quite a few home improvement projects besides windows and siding. If you're like me, hardly a month passes without getting a sales pitch like this:

"Hello, Mr. uh, . . . Dorwin?"

"Yeah?" (I'm immediately suspicious of people who mispronounce my name.)

"I represent A-1 Home Improvements, and well, we're having a special on replacement windows . . . " or "We're installing aluminum siding in your neighborhood this month and we can give you a special deal . . . "

"No, thanks." I hang up . . . but many homeowners don't.

Windows and siding are high-profit items. It's easy to find a specialist who can do the work, often for no more than I would have to pay for

Figure 6-15
Beveled-glass oak doors

the same product. Do you have a buyer who really cares about siding or windows? No problem. That buyer won't have any trouble finding a someone to do the job — probably for about the same price as I'd have to charge. Since there's no profit in it for me, I'll let the buyer do it, *if the buyer is interested*. And remember, many aren't. That's why I avoid installing siding and replacing windows.

When to install new windows — You'll have to replace old windows that don't work any more. Last year I came across a good example of an unserviceable window. I bought a house with a kitchen window made from a single sheet of glass set in a frame made from used toe moldings. It didn't open, but it sure leaked freezing cold air in the winter. Obviously, something like this won't do. I replaced it with an inexpensive double-hung window.

On occasion I'll add a window in a room that obviously needs it. Builders sometimes economize by omitting windows, even where they're badly needed for light and ventilation. Of course, adding new windows is more of an improvement than a repair, so I'll save my discussion of this for the improvement section.

Occasionally you'll want to *remove* a window. Most homes need more windows, not less. But sometimes an amateurish addition will leave a window with a view of a wall, or worse, another room. Look at Figure 6-14. One of the windows in the bedroom opened into a garage addition. As you can see, removing the window was a big improvement. I'd call this a repair because the need is so obvious and the value added is far more than the cost.

Doors

What do you do about doors that have been kicked in or that are severely weathered? This is a common problem with fixer-uppers. Your decision should depend on which door you're dealing with. I usually divide exterior doors into two groups: first, the front entry door; and second, all the other doors.

The front door— The first thing your buyers will see when they come to look at your house is the front entry door. If it isn't clean, solid and attractive, it makes a bad first impression that turns buyers critical of everything they see.

Buyers look at the front door as the gateway to their home. This is the face they'll be showing to their friends and visitors. If they're embarrassed by it, they won't buy the house. You can't afford to have a shabby front door.

If the front door on your house is in bad shape, you'll have to do something about it. But don't spend too much. Let's look at some options other than buying an expensive new entry door.

First of all, can you repair the front door? Some older homes have beautiful front doors that would cost a fortune to replace at today's prices. Figure 6-15 shows the entry doors in one of my houses. These double French doors each have fifteen panes of beveled glass. I've seen doors not nearly as nice as these offered for over a thousand dollars. Of course, the doors in Figure 6-15

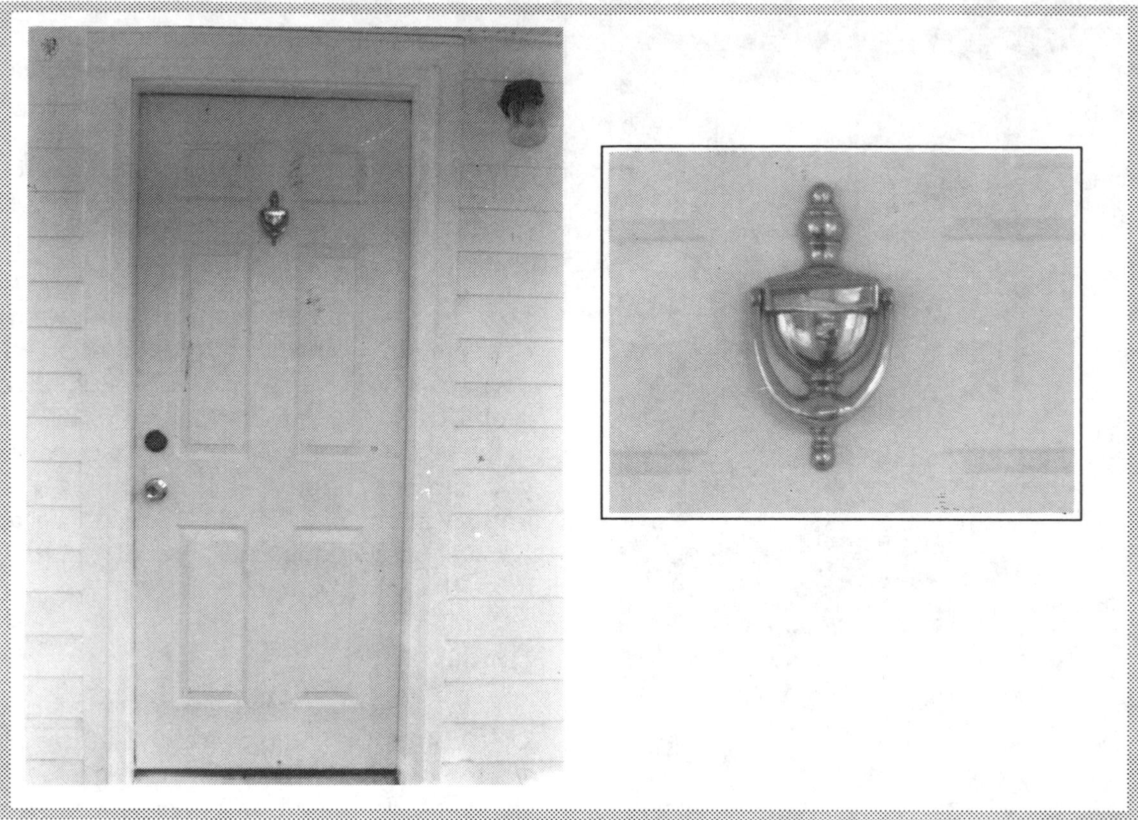

Figure 6-16
An attractive front door is important

needed new hardware, refinishing, and new veneer in spots. But the cost was modest. It would have been foolish to either replace the doors or leave them without repair. A few hours of finishing added thousands of dollars to the value of my house.

Another home I bought had a colonial entry door with a fan-shaped glass insert. Unfortunately, the door was cracked. A new door would have cost several hundred dollars plus an hour or more to hang it. I didn't want to lose the effect of a dramatic entryway, so I decided to repair the existing door. That's not always easy. Flimsy repairs won't last under constant opening and closing.

Here's how I did it. My favorite repair material is Bondo Auto Body Filler. I use it for all kinds of unusual jobs. Bondo both fills holes and acts as a glue to hold joined pieces together. It's strong, easy to work with, weatherproof, waterproof, and paintable. Anything designed to resist the shaking a car gets driving over potholes should hold up nicely on an entry door, even if it's slammed frequently.

To make the repair, I channelled out the cracks in the door, filled the channels with Bondo, sanded the surface smooth, and then repainted the door. It worked perfectly, has held up for four years, and should last for many more years. Bondo (or, I assume, nearly any metal filler) is great for small repairs. For making bigger repairs it's too expensive to be practical.

Sometimes the problem with an entry door is that it doesn't match the rest of the house. Usually this is because an owner replaced the original door with the cheapest door that would fit. Any entry door that doesn't match the style of the house creates an unpleasant, patched-together look. In this case, it's best to replace it. But don't spend more than necessary. Buy an attractive, solid, but ordinary wood door like the one in Figure 6-16. Don't bother with insulated steel

Figure 6-17
Reuse old doors

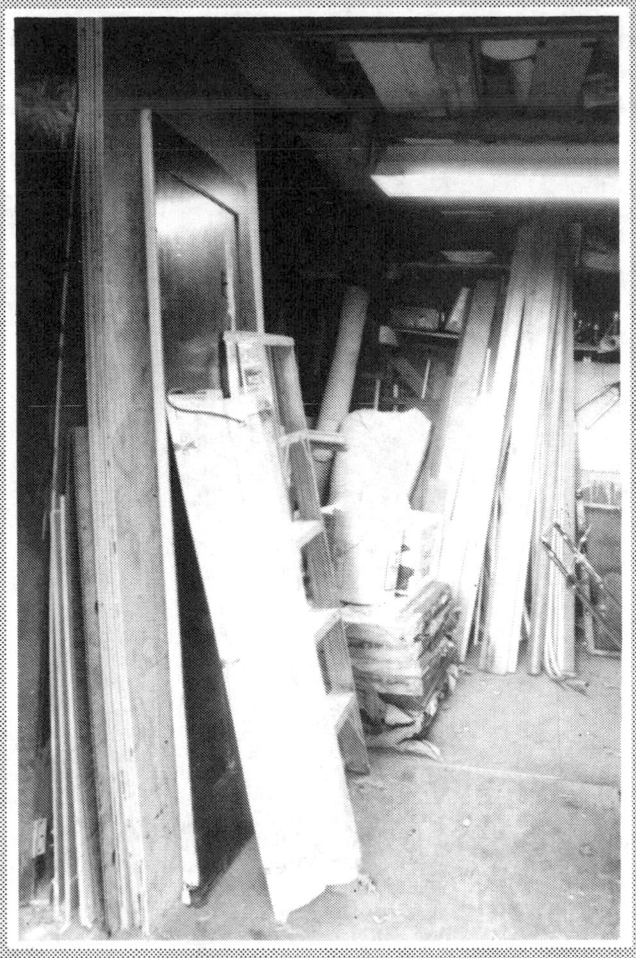

Figure 6-18
I always save usable building material

or fiberglass doors; your buyers won't notice the difference. You can dress it up with hardware, if that suits the style of the home. A brass-finished door knocker costs only a few dollars and adds a lot.

The other doors—The side doors and back doors are much less important than the front entry. Your buyers won't even notice them as long as they're solid and functional. Never replace a side or back door if the existing door can be saved. A fresh coat of paint is usually all that's required.

This is a good time to devote a few words to the joys of scavenging. I never throw away any useable building materials, especially doors. Every fixer-upper I've ever bought had at least one door missing or broken. When I work on an older home, I like to use old-fashioned doors as replacements. That way I can keep the style consistent. But it's not always easy to find the kind of door I need when I need it. So, whenever I run across an old-fashioned door, I save it. Sometimes I find extra doors in the homes I buy. Sometimes I have to buy from junk dealers.

Lately, several of my friends and neighbors have been modernizing their homes. I collected a pile of perfectly good old-fashioned doors they no longer wanted. Some of these were top-quality solid-wood doors and in excellent condition (Figure 6-17). They would have cost hundreds of dollars each, if you could get them at all. Yet, I got them free. I didn't know exactly what I was going to do with them, but I figured I'd find a use sooner or later. As it turned out, I used them all on recent projects.

Figure 6-19
Deteriorating storm doors create a poor impression

If you've been working on a contractor's payroll, you're probably not in the habit of saving used construction materials. Why should you? It's not your money. Who wants to bother going through piles of junk to find the right materials. You go to the lumberyard and order whatever you want. Right?

Believe me, you'll change your attitude fast when it's *your* materials and your own profit. Throw away something useful and you may regret it sooner than you know. It doesn't take many windows and doors to reach a thousand dollars in retail value. Get in the habit of saving even small items. For example, having a few scraps of wood needed for shims or a few drops of paint for touch-up on scratched molding can save you a trip to the lumberyard. An ugly but solid front door you take off one house might be just right for the back door on another.

Throw away anything rotted, rusty, or unserviceable. But save everything in good condition. I guarantee you'll find a use for it in this business. A good supply of spare parts will save both money and hundreds of trips to the lumberyard. Figure 6-18 shows my garage. If it looks like your local lumberyard or building supply dealer, you understand why?

There's another good reason to save spare parts. Nothing is standard on a fixer-upper. You may think it's too much trouble to cut an old door down to fit an opening. But you'll probably find that cutting an old door is only slightly more trouble than hanging a new door. Why? Because when you measure for that door you're going to get a nasty surprise. Odds are the width isn't 32,

Figure 6-20
Garages like these scare buyers away

or 36, or even 30 inches. It'll be something like 34-9/16 inches. New doors don't come in that size. You're going to have to cut the door, no matter what door you use, new or old.

Many of the houses I buy were built by the first owner, who may or may not have known anything about carpentry standards. The door frames are often odd sizes. You'll find situations like this in many old houses. Buy a new door and you'll still have to cut it down or build up the jamb to make it fit. When I need a weird-sized door to fit a weird-sized frame, there's probably just what I need somewhere in my garage.

If you must buy a new back or side door, get the cheapest you can find that's both decent and solid. It really doesn't matter what it looks like. Once you paint the door to match the house, it's practically invisible to your buyer. The same applies to storm doors. If you have one that detracts from the value of the house, replace it with a new one that's both sturdy and inexpensive (Figure 6-19). Again, don't bother with a deluxe storm door — your buyers won't even notice what kind it is as long as it looks good.

Garages

Garages on fixer-uppers are usually in terrible condition. Some people don't bother to fix roof leaks over a garage. Those leaks will cause the wood to rot. But the former owners probably didn't care. If they had cared about the property at all, it wouldn't have become a fixer-upper.

Sometimes your first impression in one of these garages is vertigo. No, you're not dizzy. The garage is leaning a little. What's causing the tilt? Check for rotted sills, loose boards, and cracked slabs. What's the best way to handle these problems? No, it isn't economical to tear it down! Anyway, homeowners like a garage, if just for the extra storage space. It's something they look for when they buy. But garages don't have to be

Before After

Figure 6-21
A little effort goes a long way!

perfect. Most garages, no matter how bad they look, can be repaired.

The garage in Figure 6-20 scared away most buyers. It looked terrible. But I knew it was structurally sound. All I did was add a new door and apply some paint.

Unless a garage is too far gone to work with at all, your best bet is to replace the rotted wood, add bracing and patches on the inside and paint the outside. Even a garage with serious problems can usually be pulled back together in a good day's work.

If the sills are bad, jack up the wall and replace the sills. If the studs are weak, add a few more. Put cross-bracing anyplace it will fit. Cross bracing always helps. Replace bad clapboards. Dig out any dirt that's piled above the level of the foundation. Soil piled against a stud wall is a major cause of rot. New shingles will dry up any leaks. If you can get the garage straight and sturdy and stop the rot, you'll have a usable building that can last for decades.

Figure 6-21 is a perfect example of what can be done with a garage in a very short time. This garage looked so bad (Before) that the real estate listing agent didn't even mention that there was a garage. She thought it just detracted from the value of the house. Taking the boards off the door and window was the first step. Once I could see what I had to work with, the job turned out to be

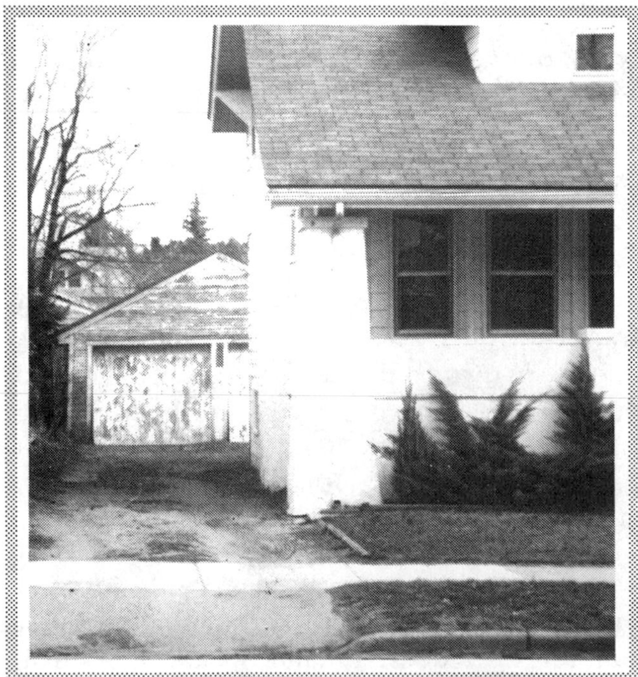

Figure 6-22
Nice house with a run-down garage and driveway

Figure 6-23
A typical handyman special garage

quite easy. I finished it in one day with one helper. We replaced the missing pane of glass, added a new door and new shingles, and finished up with a fresh coat of paint. At minimal cost, I had a garage that was ready for many more years of use (After).

A garage has to be solid and serviceable. But your buyers aren't going to live in it. They won't mind if it's a bit patched, so long as it doesn't detract from the general impression of the house. I'm amazed at how little care some people give to their garages. The home in Figure 6-22 was well maintained except for the garage and driveway. This little bit of deferred maintenance lowered the value of the home by thousands.

Remove all the rubbish around and in a garage. Make spot repairs to the driveway. Those simple steps go a long way toward improving the general appearance of the property. Figure 6-23 is typical of many of the garages I work with. The door, rain gutters and shingles needed repair. But the worst eyesore was the deteriorated driveway. See Figure 6-24 (Before). I freshened it up with some new gravel and added landscape timbers as a border. The finished driveway (After) makes an attractive but inexpensive addition to the exterior of the home.

Creative repairs— Occasionally I've run into some interesting garage repairs. Last year I bought a house with a garage that had suffered quite a bit of damage. The garage door had caved it. Someone had driven their car through it. (You come to expect that sort of thing in a fixer-upper.) I anticipated replacing the front door. But there was also a problem with the back wall. It seemed to be intact. But for some reason the sill had fallen

Before

After

Figure 6-24
Simple driveway repair

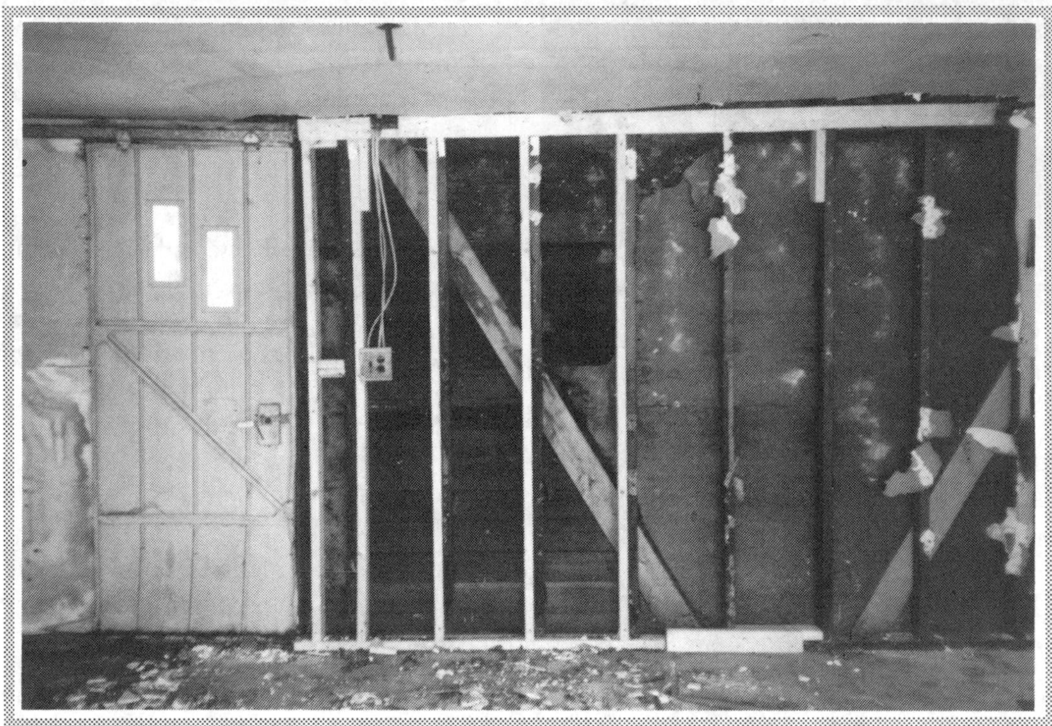

Figure 6-25
Garage repair in progress

off the cement slab. The whole garage sagged, listing to the rear where there was no support.

It seems that the former owner had a little trouble driving. I don't know if it was all the time, or just one very wild night. Apparently, he had forgotten to open the front garage door before driving in. Then, he kept on driving right through the garage until he hit the back wall, knocking the sill off the slab! I have to credit the neighbors for filling me in on these details. It's surprising how happy neighbors are to tell stories about former owners.

I spent some time figuring out how to fix this garage. I thought that if I jacked the garage roof up, the wall would swing into place. It didn't. Neither could it be shoved back, levered back, or knocked back with my sledgehammer. I was about to give up when I had a brainstorm. If the last owner had managed to knock the wall off the sill with his car, why shouldn't *this* owner, me, knock it back on the same way? I pulled my truck around to the back of the garage and drove into the wall! Amazing! It worked! Of course, I wouldn't recommend repairing walls this way on a regular basis. But sometimes unusual circumstances require creative solutions.

Once the wall was in place, I reinforced it with new bracing. Figure 6-25 shows the wall in the process of being repaired. This was one of my more memorable jobs. I just hope the neighbors didn't see me do it.

Garage doors— If you have to replace a garage door, think decorative as well a functional. Garage doors are highly visible. You might have to pay a little more for a nice door, but it's something that people notice. They have to open it every day. It's hard to say exactly how much a new garage door will increase the value of your house, but it will definitely increase its appeal. The garage door in Figure 6-26 changed the appearance of the house, from plain to pretty, adding character and style to an otherwise dull exterior.

Figure 6-26
Replace old garage doors with attractive new ones

Replace old-fashioned doors that open sideways with modern upward-acting doors. A replacement like this may be worthwhile even if the old doors are still functional. On a mid-priced house, install a garage-door opener.

A coat of paint will cover up all the repair work you do on the garage exterior. Why not do the same for the interior? Repainting the interior will disguise the patchwork. Some buyers would still notice the patches, of course, but you're not trying to hide them. You just want the garage to look nice. If you give the garage interior a fresh coat of white paint, people will be impressed by how bright and clean it looks. Figure 6-27 shows the value you can expect to get for work done on a garage.

Other Repairs

Other exterior repairs may be appropriate, regardless of price or neighborhood. Anything that's obviously broken (shingles, shutters, stairs, railings, porches, fences, rain gutters) should be repaired. But don't repair anything that will probably be replaced. There's not much point in fixing something and then throwing it out. I've made that mistake several times.

A few years ago I bought a house with a deteriorated privacy fence going across the middle of the back yard. The former owners had used it to keep their dog penned up. My first thought was, "What an eyesore. I've got to repair that fence." I spent several hours reinforcing it, straightening it up, and patching up the holes. Then I stood back to look at my handiwork. That was when I realized my mistake. "What a stupid place for a fence. It divides the yard in half. The house would be better without it!" I had wasted all that time repairing a fence that I ended up tearing down. If I had thought the situation through clearly, I could have saved myself a lot of work! So take my advice, think about everything you want to do before you do it. And if you're not sure whether to replace or repair an item, leave it until later, and think about it some more.

We've considered most of the exterior repairs you're likely to make on fixer-uppers. Remember, we've been talking only about exterior *repairs* so far, not improvements. Interior repairs are the subject of the next chapter. We'll talk about the exterior again when we discuss improvements, decorating, and landscaping. For the moment, however, we're ready to step through that beat-up front door and take a look at the interior.

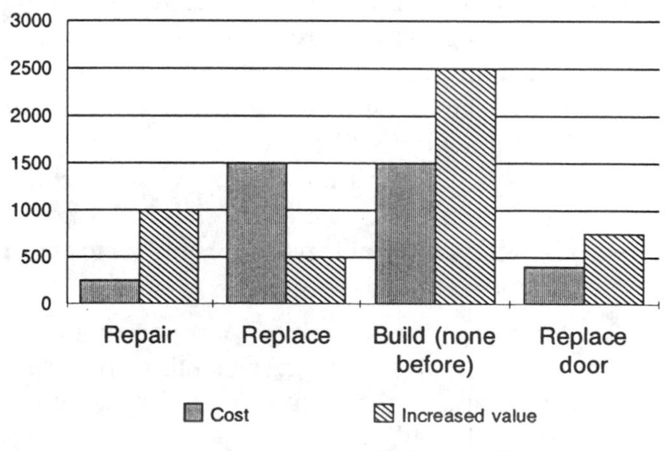

Figure 6-27
Cost vs. value on garage work done

CHAPTER SEVEN

Repairing Structural and Mechanical Problems

Repairs to the interior of a fixer-upper can be overwhelming. There are so many things that demand your immediate attention. Let's look first at the kinds of structural and mechanical problems that you're likely to find when you redo a house. I'll give you an idea of what I feel are manageable structural and mechanical repairs, and also tell you what types of problems to avoid getting yourself into.

First, organize your interior repair work into a logical sequence. I suggest tackling the structural problems right away. They're usually the most critical, and in some cases, delaying the repairs is dangerous! Begin with repairs to the floors, walls and ceilings or anything that operates inside the floors, walls and ceilings. This includes major plumbing, electrical, or heating problems. But reinforcing the structure of the house comes first. After all, there's no sense in fixing the leaky faucet in the bathroom if you can't safely walk on the floor. If the floor collapses, who cares if the faucet drips?

Sagging Floors

When you buy houses in bad condition, you'll probably notice some sections of floor that have too much bounce. Sometimes the floors visibly sag. I've been in houses where the floor bounces up and down so much that it feels like you're walking on a mattress. You go up and down hills and valleys as you walk through the house. It's enough to make you seasick.

A sagging floor may or may not be a serious problem. Whether it's a serious problem or not, a bouncing floor will nearly always scare off potential buyers and knock thousands off the purchase price. Floor problems are, after all, structural problems. The words *structural problems* usually send buyers flying out the door. They may not understand exactly what the structural problem is, but it sounds very bad and very expensive and they don't want anything to do with it.

Most people are afraid of these problems because they don't know how houses are built. What is the structure of the house? What does it do and how do you work with it? They think that since houses are big, heavy things, you'll need heavy equipment to make the repairs. This is a reasonable assumption, but it's wrong. You could actually lift an entire house right up off its foundation all by yourself. All you would need is enough inexpensive floor jacks. The fact that you know this, and other people don't, gives you a big advantage when you're looking at property. The more you know of course, the more advantages you have.

Common Causes of Floor Problems

I've found that improper modifications to the heating or plumbing systems are the most common causes of structural floor problems. Someone cut through the floor joists to install some new heating ducts or plumbing pipes without giving a thought to joist strength. I've seen houses with three floor joists in a row cut clean through. No wonder the house sagged in the middle!

Another cause of sagging or bouncing floors is poor construction. Many of the houses I deal with were, let's face it, cheaply built. The builders cut corners wherever they thought they could get away with it. The floor supports were never strong enough, and over the years the problem got worse. Even in well-built houses, sometimes the supporting floor members just lose strength as the years go by. You find this a lot in older homes. The wood dries out, becomes brittle, and the joists crack. If the crack is big enough, the joist loses its strength.

Recognizing Repairable Problems

I've said before that it isn't my intention to give detailed explanations of how to do any of the repairs I recommend. This isn't a "how to" book — it's a "what to" book. I tell you what to do, not how to do it.

There are several good books available which deal with the subject of structural repairs. The one I recommend is *Manual of Professional Remodeling* by Jack P. Jones, published by Craftsman Book Company. There's an order form in the back of this book. I like his simple approach to problems, rather than the "overkill" that you get in many other books. This is the right approach for the work you'll be doing.

Another good source for information is the February, 1987 issue of *Progressive Builder*. This magazine contains a group of articles, collectively entitled "Setting Floors Straight." These articles take much the same approach as Jones' book, but include more of the details you might need. Anyone fixing up older neglected homes should know these techniques. Understanding them will give you a much greater insight into the structure of your house.

I've used the advice in the book and the magazine, and I know it works. Knowing what to look for is half the work. Here are some examples.

A good example— A few years ago I bought a large house that was built in 1920. The floor seemed to have too much bounce under load. The problem was noticeable on the main floor and even worse on the second floor. I searched the first and second floors for signs of structural failure. There was nothing apparent. No cracked plaster or sagging ceilings. Everything looked fine. I couldn't see what could be causing the problem.

Then I remembered some good advice I'd read about older homes: When you suspect you're dealing with structural problems, go directly to the basement. Do not pass Go, do not collect $200. The basement is where you find out about the structure of the house — assuming the house doesn't have a finished basement with a

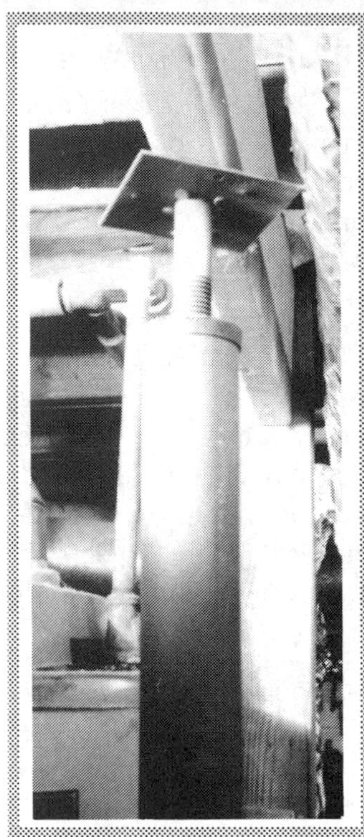

Figure 7-1
Floor jack provides temporary repair

ceiling in place. However, I've never seen a home in bad condition that had a completely finished basement.

This house had a large, elaborate staircase leading from the first floor to the second. It was directly over the stairway that led down to the basement. There's nothing odd about that. It's a common way to build staircases. But when I got to the basement I found that there didn't seem to be anything supporting the staircase! And because of the design of the house, these staircases supported a major portion of the weight of both the first and second floors. Obviously, something was holding it up; it wasn't floating in mid-air. The staircase was simply nailed into doubled floor joists. This gave it some support, but it wasn't strong enough to handle all that weight, particularly after many years.

Looking over the whole assembly, I decided that stress was concentrated on the left outside corner of the basement staircase. To test my theory, I put a floor jack under that corner and tightened the jack until it exerted enough force to lift the joist slightly. You could hear the house creak and move as I tightened it. I went upstairs to see how this was working. The problem had vanished. The floor was perfectly solid. The lack of support at this one point in the basement had been enough to cause the entire second floor to bounce.

Structurally, I could have solved the problem by just leaving the floor jack where it was. It was perfectly capable of supporting the load indefinitely. Floor jacks, however, give the impression of a temporary fix, and don't look nice. Potential buyers would ask embarrassing questions and I would have to tell the truth. Replacing the jack with a 4 x 4 post solved the problem and made explanations unnecessary. People don't ask about repairs they don't notice. And if they don't ask, I won't bring them up. Besides, 4 x 4s are cheaper than floor jacks.

The 4 x 4 freed up my floor jack for use somewhere else, and I soon found another place for it (Figure 7-1). The living room floor in this house still had some bounce in it after I had supported the stairs. Looking carefully, I found a cracked floor joist. The board had a big knothole near the middle of the span and had cracked at the weak spot beside the knot. A good carpenter would have found some other use for this piece.

In this case I patched the joist with a 2 x 12 and added another 4 x 4 post. You can see the finished job in Figure 7-2.

Avoid problem houses— Don't assume you can solve all structural problems. A house I didn't buy illustrates the point: most structural problems I won't touch with a 10-foot pole. This particular house had a large depression in the floor, about 8 feet around. It was in the center of the house just below the stairway to the second floor. What caused the depression? The second floor addition was built by an amateur carpenter who didn't support it properly. He'd simply added it on top of the first floor, without giving any thought to supporting the extra weight.

Figure 7-2
The 4 x 4 provides permanent support

As a result, the first floor was slowly sinking into the ground. It would have been pointless to try to repair this house. The foundation wasn't adequate for the weight. It was still actively sinking and would have to be reinforced from below. Unfortunately the house only had a crawl space — no basement.

I don't know about you, but I hate working in crawl spaces. Not only are they dirty, wet, and full of bugs, but, for some reason, animals like to go into crawl spaces and die. I tried making repairs on one house with a crawl space. That was enough for me! I won't touch a house with structural problems unless there's access from the basement. I suggest the same policy for you. Some inconveniences just aren't worth your efforts.

Working with Water Damage

Water can damage large areas. If you suspect water damage, you'll have to inspect practically every piece of wood in the house for rot. And every piece of rotten wood has to go. First, be sure to locate and repair the leak that caused the damage. Check out the extent of the rot before you begin to make any repairs. If the rot is bad enough, I recommend avoiding the project entirely.

I've repaired a lot of houses with leaky basements. Water in the basement may not affect the house structure at all. But you'd better check it out carefully, just in case.

Leaky Basements

In wet areas, like the Great Lakes region, a large percentage of basements have water problems. Nobody likes a leaky basement. They can be repaired, but it isn't an easy job. Plugging up the cracks in the basement walls doesn't usually do the job unless that's the only entry point for the water. If it is, and your repairs hold, you're done. Unfortunately, that's rarely the case.

Plugging up cracks doesn't solve leakage problems because most basement walls, particularly those built of cement block, are porous. You can fill all the visible cracks, but water will seep in through the block anyway. Basement "waterproofing" paint is another easy fix that's worth trying. You must understand, however, that this paint isn't really waterproof, it's just water *resistant*. It will help only if there's just a small amount of water seeping through a slightly porous surface.

Chances are, more than a small amount of water is seeping through. If there's a lot of water in the surrounding earth, there will be substantial hydrostatic pressure on the basement wall. Essentially, the basement wall is like a dam, holding back most of the water, but allowing some to enter.

Before After

Figure 7-3
Basement problems can be repaired

A few waterproofing paints have guarantees. But if you read the fine print on the guarantee, you'll see that it says "except where hydrostatic pressure exists." In the Great Lakes area, hydrostatic pressure exists everywhere, so this guarantee isn't a lot of help. Even if you apply the paint properly, hydrostatic pressure can cause water to leak around the paint, or even lift the paint right off the wall.

Now I'm not saying that you shouldn't try these measures. Cracks and holes in basement walls should be repaired just on general principles, even if that doesn't stop the leaking. Basement paint will make the walls bright and cheerful, even if they're still damp. Sometimes that's enough to make the house marketable.

The deteriorated, leaky basement in Figure 7-3 drove away most potential buyers. I decided to tackle the problem because I was sure it wasn't as bad as it looked. I reparged the basement walls with a thin layer of sand mix concrete with a latex strengthener. This creates a strong concrete mix that adheres very well even if the basement wall is moist. It's also water resistant. Look at the finished job. What a difference! Sealing and painting the basement made it look as good as new. If your basement problems aren't too severe, a layer of concrete may be enough.

Controlling Hydrostatic Pressure

But don't be too surprised if fixing cracks and painting are only cosmetic repairs. The basement may still leak badly. Hydrostatic pressure in the earth surrounding the house forces water into the basement. If the basement wasn't there, it would continue down to the natural water level in the soil. A basement interrupts this natural flow. The photo in Figure 7-4 shows a cement block basement wall full of leaks and water marks. There's enough water seeping in to create puddles on the floor.

The best way to deal with hydrostatic pressure is to reduce the flow of water around the home. Water leaking through basement walls begins as water saturating the earth around the building perimeter. Redirecting the drainage of rainwater away from the foundation is the first (and usually easiest) step in controlling basement moisture.

Figure 7-4
Cement block basement wall full of water leaks

Directing the water flow— Figure 7-5 shows the exterior of a house with a leaky concrete block basement. This is the same house as in Figure 7-4. The ground on this side of the house slopes toward the house instead of away from it. If you look closely, you can see water-borne debris that has settled next to the house. It appears to have flowed across the yard downhill from the trees. That tells me that water collects against the house.

My solution to the drainage problem was to regrade the yard, sloping the soil *away from the house*. See Figure 7-6. I also added a privacy fence to improve the look of the yard, and a "flying downspout" to carry the water away from the house. Rainwater from the roof now runs into a natural channel along the edge of the property. Figure 7-7 shows the strip of concrete I poured to fill the seam between the house and the sidewalk. It also encourages surface drainage away from the house and into the yard.

Improper drainage— Sometimes a driveway or patio slopes toward the house instead of away from it. If you come across this problem, it probably won't be practical to replace the slab or driveway. Instead, try sealing and waterproofing the area where the patio or driveway touches the house. This will keep water from seeping through the crack into the basement. Unfortunately, sealing water out of the basement may create long-lasting puddles along the exterior of the house. During the winter the water can freeze,

Figure 7-5
Water flow is toward house

Figure 7-6
Regraded side yard with "flying downspout"

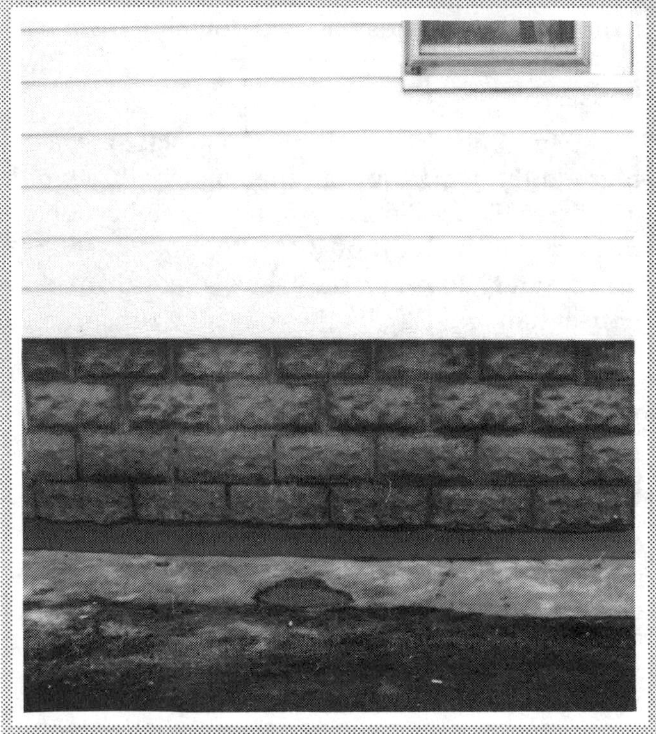

Figure 7-7

Concrete seal between sidewalk and house adds extra protection

creating a slick, icy path. But even this is an improvement over a wet basement, unless it creates a safety hazard.

Poor drainage from gutters and downspouts also contributes to standing water around a house. The gutters may be clogged with dirt, rusted out, or missing altogether. Check and repair the gutters, then properly direct the downspouts away from the house. The function of a downspout is to take rainwater and put it where you want it. Many people don't understand this. They just let the downspouts terminate on the ground. Then, instead of carrying rainwater away from the house, the downspouts direct it to exactly where it shouldn't be: the edge of the foundation. In a rainstorm, hundreds of gallons of water may collect at the building perimeter. A lot of this water will end up in the basement.

Arrange downspouts to carry water as far away from the house as possible, either by means of extensions or splashblocks. I always try to send direct runoff onto a driveway or some other concrete or asphalt surface that slopes to the street. One house I bought had gutters in place, but the downspout had fallen off. Rainwater poured off the roof and sat in huge puddles against the house. Gradually it seeped into the basement. I solved the problem by replacing the missing downspout, adding an extra long extension and then a splashblock at the end which emptied into the driveway (Figure 7-8). Don't allow runoff to puddle anywhere on the lot. It may take some creativity on your part to prevent this, but it's worth the effort.

All these methods will help to reduce the hydrostatic pressure forcing water into your basement. And there's one more idea that I've used on occasion. Look at Figure 7-9. Adding a simple, inexpensive patio like this also helps direct water away from the house. It keeps the basement dry while adding a useful and decorative feature.

Nice-quality patio blocks laid over plastic make a simple, easy-to-install patio. With a little bit of landscaping, it's an attractive addition to any house. Patios don't usually raise the value of a house enough to justify their expense, but if they solve a basement water problem, they're well worth the cost.

Figure 7-8

New downspout with extensions and splashblock carries water away from house

Figure 7-9
This inexpensive patio provides for water runoff near the house

You might need to use all, or just one or two of these remedies to solve your wet-basement problem. Even if you use them all, it won't be too expensive.

If all else fails— But what if you've done what I recommend and the basement *still* leaks? The problem is more than just local runoff. High ground water is probably creating hydrostatic pressure.

For instance, some homes in Southeast Michigan were built in what had been swampland. Well, you can't fool Mother Nature. She's trying to reclaim these suburbs as swamps. So far, she has been successful only with the basements. What can you do when you run into a problem like this?

It's almost impossible to stop the water from coming in, unless you waterproof the basement from the outside. That involves digging out the entire perimeter of the house and sealing the basement exterior with a waterproof coating. That's a huge job, and generally not worth the work. Even if you did it, there's no guarantee that the problem would disappear.

So if you can't stop the water from coming in, you have to deal with it once it's there. You can catch water as it seeps out of the walls and direct it away from the central area of the basement. You'll still have a humid basement, but it won't be wet.

There are a few basement waterproofing systems that apply this principle. The *B-Dry System* and the *Help! Basement De-watering System* are two that come to mind.

B-Dry System
13441 Copley Road
Akron, OH 44320
(216) 867-2576

Help! Basement De-watering System
162 E. Chestnut Street
Canton, IL 61520
(309) 674-4000

These systems use a barrier installed around the inside perimeter of the wall, or a trench dug around the wall to catch the water as it leaks in. Water goes from the trench into a drain or sump pump, and then out of the basement. So even though the water continues to leak in, it's removed before it can do any damage. This may not be the ideal answer to the problem, but it's the only practical, cost-effective way I know to handle very severe water problems.

Commercial water-control systems are expensive. You can build something similar yourself, but it's a lot of work. Don't go to all this effort or expense unless there's no other solution — and be sure the house is worth it. If a wet basement allowed you to buy a nice house at a bargain price, then a water-control system might be the key to a good profit.

Heating Systems

I love basements. Well, maybe that's overstating it a bit. Let's say I strongly prefer working on houses that have basements. They aren't just extra space. Basements give you easy access to the structural, heating, plumbing, and electrical systems of the house. That's important in a handyman-special, since there's usually a lot of work to do.

I also like basements because they're the best place for a heating system. Basement heating distributes heat evenly throughout the house. A good furnace is one item that buyers care very much about. So if you're lucky, your house may have a relatively new furnace located in the basement. Since heating systems usually have a long life, yours may only need a little cleaning.

If you're working on an older home, however, you may run into a furnace that's old and peculiar-looking. Don't let looks throw you. It's probably fully functional. Your buyers, of course, will scrutinize the furnace and also find it peculiar-looking. Does this mean you should replace it? This is one of those hard decisions you'll have to consider from time to time. Cost-effectiveness is the key. Furnaces are expensive. You don't want to replace anything expensive unless you're sure that you'll get an adequate return on your investment.

Buyers examine furnaces carefully because at some time during their house hunting they heard that furnaces (like roofs) are important. They usually don't know much about furnaces, and have little experience evaluating them. They'll generally divide furnaces into two categories: old and new. Their preference is, of course, for the new.

New vs. Old Furnaces

I've found furnaces to be amazingly durable. Some of my houses built in the 1920s have an original furnace that's working as good as a new furnace. They survive for decades in spite of abuse and lack of maintenance. Once in a while I might have to replace a fan motor or thermostat, but even that much is rare. Furnaces in most houses usually only need minor repair or adjustment, and they'll continue to work perfectly for decades.

Does this mean you should never replace a functional furnace? Well, not exactly. Buyers don't realize how durable furnaces are. The appearance of some of these old furnaces may upset them. If the furnace looks really bad, you may have to lower the price a little to attract buyers. Or, it might be better to replace the old furnace.

Figure 7-10
The "octopus"

What do I mean by old furnace? The actual age of the furnace doesn't matter. What matters is how it *looks*. Any furnace installed after 1950 will probably look reasonably modern to your buyers. That's good enough. Almost any forced-air furnace will be acceptable, except one that's oil-fired. It might pay you to convert these to gas.

Furnaces that have been converted from burning coal to other forms of fuel are marginal. The most common is the gas-gravity furnace. This is a very reliable furnace. Left alone, it will probably last longer than we will. However, it looks like an octopus, with tentacles of ductwork reaching out in all directions. (See Figure 7-10.) Some are so big they take up half the basement. That's a major drawback if a prospective buyer wants to convert the basement into a recreation room. If it comes between you and your sale, you have a decision to make.

Before you run out and buy a new unit, think about the basement itself. If you replace the furnace, would the basement be suitable as a recreation room? Would potential buyers consider the space a valuable extra feature? Would they be willing to pay full price for the house if you replaced the furnace? After exploring the possibilities, you may find that the basement is too small or the ceiling too low for practical use as a recreation room. Then you don't have to worry. A bulky, ugly furnace in an unusable area is best left alone.

These are decisions you have to handle on a case-by-case basis. A lot depends on your circumstances. How much are you planning to sell your house for? If you plan on selling a house below the average market price, then don't bother with discretionary items like replacing a perfectly good furnace. At low market price, people are getting a good deal already. They'll just have to take the house with the furnace as it is. You'll get buyers. Regardless of a few drawbacks, your newly-decorated, modernized house will still be nicer than anything else they can get for that price.

At the other extreme, if you're planning to sell a house on the high end of the market, replace the furnace. For that price, you have to be competitive. The buyers will be a little more picky, and they won't put up with things they don't like. You won't be able to get your price if the house has a major drawback like an undesirable furnace.

What if you plan to sell at an average price? Then there are more factors to consider. How hot is the resale market at the moment? If people are clamoring for houses, they'll overlook drawbacks that don't interfere with the function of the house. You don't need to worry about replacing a perfectly good furnace then.

Unfortunately, hot markets don't last forever. When the market is slow and houses are almost impossible to sell, buyers won't overlook anything. They'll disqualify a house for a minor drawback. Then you may want to replace the furnace, or if your finances permit, rent the house out for a while and wait for the market to improve. Once the market picks up, the house will sell for an even higher price, with or without replacing the furnace.

Finally, you need to consider how much a new furnace will cost. Will the house require a big furnace or a small furnace? How much new ductwork will you need? How much of the work will you be able to do yourself? Do you have a good source for heating equipment or labor (is your brother-in-law in the business)? The less it costs to install a new furnace, the more the balance tips towards replacing the old one. It won't be cheap, but it may cost you more not to do it.

When you decide to replace a furnace— If you decide to put in a new furnace, consider a high-efficiency model. They're a little more expensive, but they substantially lower your heating bills. You can turn a necessary repair into a selling feature — if you come across a buyer who'll appreciate it. Since it costs almost as much to install a cheap furnace as a good one, go with the higher-quality furnace.

If you decide to keep the house as a rental, a better-quality heating system should bring higher rent, especially in a cold climate. With lower heating bills your tenants can pay higher rent, but keep their monthly expenses the same.

Repairing Old Furnaces

Repairing old furnaces should be a subject in a "how to" book rather than my "what to" book. However, I've read dozens of "how to" books, and never found enough information on this subject to do me any good. Most people leave furnaces to the professionals, so there isn't much do-it-yourself information available. I've wasted a lot of time and effort learning to deal with heating problems. Most of the material I have to share with you comes from first-hand experience — taking furnaces apart and putting them back together again. Believe me, that's a difficult and tedious way to learn about heating systems! I've decided to devote a few pages to this subject, because if you don't hear it from me, you won't hear it at all.

If you're going to be working on many houses, sooner or later you'll run into a furnace that needs some kind of repair. You can't afford to call heating repair services for every minor problem. You need to know how to fix the common problems yourself.

People tend to blame their furnaces for all kinds problems. If they have cold, drafty rooms, or areas that don't heat well, they assume the furnace isn't doing its job. In my experience, the problem is rarely with the furnace or even the heating system. Leaky windows, ill-fitting doors, and lack of insulation are more likely to blame. Often there's more cold air leaking into a house than any heating system could possibly overcome. A little weatherstripping or glazing putty can solve these problems. But if the problem is in the heating system, you can usually trace it to the distribution network: the ductwork, pipes, or whatever delivery system the furnace uses. Let's consider the most common problems you'll find in heating systems.

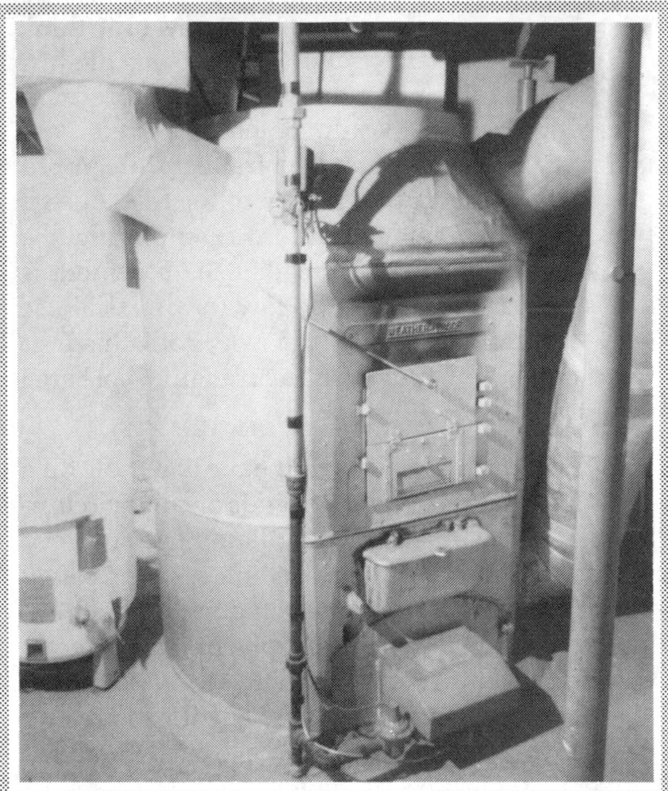

Figure 7-11
Gas gravity furnace

Forced-Air or Gas Gravity Systems

Most of the houses I've owned have had either gas forced-air or gas gravity heating. You probably know what a gas forced-air heater looks like. Figure 7-11 shows a picture of a gas gravity furnace. Both of these systems use ducts to carry hot air throughout the house and return cold air to the furnace for heating. Usually ductwork problems in these systems are fairly trivial and easy to correct.

Blocked hot air registers— Rooms are heated by hot air coming out of hot-air registers. If you block the registers by covering them with carpeting or paneling, the room will be cold. People don't seem to consider this. How is the hot air supposed to get through these obstacles? This is an easy problem to fix. Just cut away a piece of the carpeting or paneling.

Rubbish accumulating in the ducts is another common cause for blockage. Small children are often the culprits here. They like to hear things drop down into the registers. This is another easy problem to fix: just clean out the rubbish.

Sometimes you'll find hot air registers blocked by old remodeling jobs. If an added wall blocks off a register and you're planning to remove the wall, there's no problem. If you want to keep the wall, and it's a full, framed wall, then you have a serious problem. You may be able to install another register nearby without modifying the ducts. But if you can't, you may have to do some ductwork. This is a big, unpleasant job — one you want to avoid if possible.

Blocked cold air returns— The furnace also needs to have the cold air returned for heating and recirculating. It can't function properly if the cold air returns are blocked. These problems are usually caused by the same things as the blockages in hot air registers: carpet, rubbish, and bad modifications. Repair these the same way.

Uninsulated ductwork— I've often found long runs of uninsulated duct running through unheated areas of the house, such as attics or crawl spaces. Without insulation, much of the heat will be lost along the way. By the time the hot air reaches the more distant rooms, it'll be cold. This problem is more frequent in houses without basements, but it can happen in any home with poorly-installed ductwork. It's another easy problem to fix. Just wrap the ducts in insulation, and the problem will disappear.

Missing registers— In some houses you'll find rooms that don't have registers. This problem often occurs in houses where the heating system was installed long after a house was built. Either the owner or the furnace installer decided that it would be too difficult or too expensive to run ductwork to all rooms. Unfortunately, it isn't any easier or less expensive to run the duct now than it was then.

You have to decide how bad the problem is. Is it worth the amount of work involved? Which rooms are unheated, and how large are they? Are the rooms terribly cold and unpleasant, or do they get indirect heat from the adjacent rooms? If the problem isn't too bad, it might be best to ignore it. Or, in smaller rooms like a bathroom, you could add an auxiliary heating system that doesn't require ductwork, such as electric baseboard heat. Electric heat is expensive to operate, but if you only need it in one small room, it wouldn't be too bad.

Adding ductwork is a huge job. Not only is ductwork difficult to handle, but it takes up a lot of space. You have to find a place to put it. You may have to frame new walls around any duct you add. Of course, if you were planning extensive modifications anyway, tearing out a wall or two may not be a big problem. But that's not usually the case. Sometimes you can find a closet or some other convenient spot to run ductwork through. However, unless there's no other practical choice, avoid adding ductwork.

In a cold climate like Michigan, the lack of warm air ducting is a major drawback. If the house is in good condition, except for this one problem, I may decide to go ahead and tackle it. But if there's more than one problem like this, I'll usually look for a more attractive property.

Bad thermostats— Thermostats are very reliable devices, and would probably last hundreds of years if they weren't mishandled. Rough handling can break the delicate elements in them. This is the first thing I check when a furnace doesn't work. You can test it by shorting the wires that connect at the back of the thermostat. If the furnace comes on, you've found the problem. Thermostats are cheap and easy to replace.

Dirt— Furnaces need occasional cleaning. People who live in handyman specials rarely clean anything; certainly not their furnaces. Dirt collecting in a furnace can keep it from working properly. Cleaning a furnace isn't a big deal. Replace the filter, scrub the burners lightly with a wire brush, and vacuum up any debris. I've rarely found it necessary to do much more.

Fans— The fan is the only moving part in a gas forced-air furnace. Every 20 or 30 years, the fan motor may burn out. The furnace should have a switch labelled something like "Manual On," which turns the fan on. If you flip this switch, and the fan doesn't go on, you may have a bad motor (or a bad electrical connection). The motors cost a little more than thermostats, but they're not hard to replace.

Burner controls— Burner controls are in a little box mounted on the furnace. The box has wires coming out of two sides. The wires on one side lead to the thermostat, and on the other side they lead into the furnace. Once in a blue moon these controls will malfunction. You can test them by opening the box up and shorting the contacts for the wires leading into the furnace. These are the gas valve control wires. If this causes the burners to turn on, you've found the problem: the burner controls are bad. Usually you can't make repairs. Just replace the whole burner-control assembly.

Heat exchangers— If the heat exchanger burns out, you may have to replace the furnace. A bad heat exchanger will let toxic fumes into the house. This is the kind of thing unscrupulous furnace repair companies try to scare homeowners with. They'll say that you and your family may die unless you buy a new furnace (from them, naturally).

However, in all the houses I've ever owned, and many of them were over 60 years old, I've never had a heat exchanger go bad. I'm sure that sooner or later, somewhere, a heat exchanger may burn out. However, don't be too quick to assume that's the problem with your furnace. And, don't believe anyone who tells you that the heat exchanger is bad unless you're absolutely sure that they are competent and trustworthy.

Figure 7-12
Steam-heat radiator

Steam Heat

Steam heat is a very good heating system. When working right, it provides comfortable, even heat, without the drafts you can have with a gas forced-air system. It heats up more slowly, but stays hot longer, which keeps the temperature more constant than the off/on forced-air heaters. The only real drawback to the system is that it requires bulky radiators (like the one in Figure 7-12) in every room. Many people have problems with steam systems because they don't understand how to operate and maintain them. Most of the problems are simply caused by improper handling.

A couple of years ago I bought a house with a steam-heat system that needed minor repair. It was a problem because I didn't understand how the system worked, and I couldn't find any information on it. My wife finally found a couple of old books on the subject in the public library. The books were written around the turn of the century and were full of quaint Victorian engravings. They had the information I needed, however. I was able to tune up the system, and get it back in perfect working condition. I learned a lot on that particular job. Since steam heat is quite common in older homes, and information on it is hard to come by, I'll tell you what I discovered.

How steam heating works— Steam heating systems usually have a gas-fired boiler that heats water. The boiling water creates steam which rises (by gravity, like the warm air in a gas gravity furnace) up through the pipes and into the radiators. The radiators get hot and radiate heat into the room.

Most of the newer steam systems (installed after 1910) are one-pipe systems. I found this confusing at first. What happens to the old, used-up steam? How can it circulate if there's only one pipe?

The answer is that the steam, as it cools, condenses into water, and drips back into the boiler through the same pipe that it rose in. Steam goes up and at the same time water is dripping back down, the two passing each other in the same pipe. Clever, isn't it? Home heating technology was very advanced, even at the turn of the century.

Figure 7-13 shows a recent-model steam boiler. A gauge indicates the steam pressure and

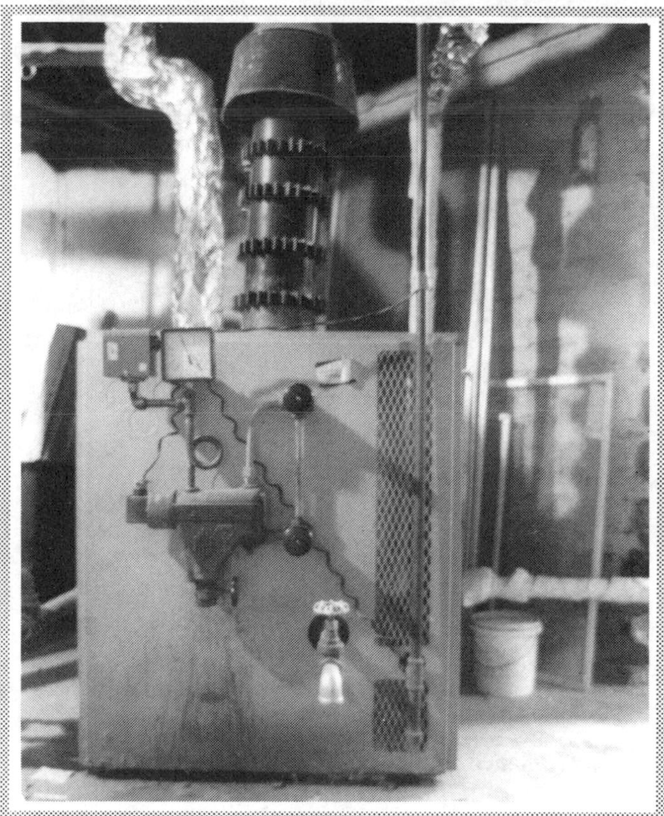

Figure 7-13
A recent-model steam boiler

a glass tube shows the water level. Valves release water when you need to flush the boiler.

Maintaining a steam system— To create steam, the boiler needs water. I was surprised to discover that in many systems the water intake isn't automatic. You need to check the water level in the boiler every couple of months during the heating season. If it's low, open a valve and add more water. Otherwise, the system will run out of water and shut itself down. A boiler that isn't working right may simply be low on water.

But don't add too much water. The boiler should be about three-quarters full. If you overfill the system, water will fill up the radiators and pour out all over the floor. You guessed it; I found this out the hard way! I spent an entire evening mopping up water and draining the system.

People don't often think of a steam-heat system as a type of plumbing system. But it is, and it can spring leaks just like any other type of plumbing. And, just like any other plumbing leaks, you need to repair them. Leaks in a steam system shouldn't occur any more often than leaks in toilets, sinks, or any other plumbing fixture.

Steam systems are often neglected. Some people think that leaks are part of the system and have to be tolerated. I found a good example of this attitude a few years ago. I bought a house from a couple who had become frustrated and disgusted with their leaky steam system. They sold their home cheap because of this problem. What was so wrong with their system? Loose fittings! After two turns of a wrench to each radiator, the system was fine. It hasn't leaked a drop since.

Valves— A valve controls the steam feed to each radiator. If you don't want any more heat, you simply close the valve and cut off the steam inlet to the radiator. Many people don't understand that you can turn off the heat to one room without turning off the whole system. They think the only way to deal with a room that gets too hot is to open a window. No wonder some people dislike steam heat. They simply don't know how to operate it. If you don't need heat, turn the radiator off!

Figure 7-14 shows the shut-off valve on a typical radiator. Like any plumbing valve, these steam shut-off valves will occasionally fail. You can buy replacement valves at any good plumbing-supply store. They screw in, like any other plumbing fitting.

The little silver device screwed into one end of a radiator (Figure 7-15) isn't an ornament. It's a cold-air release valve. In order for a radiator to heat up, something has to be done with the cold air that has been sitting in it. When the radiator is cold, this valve remains open. As steam rises in the radiator, it forces cold air out through the valve. When steam has displaced the cold air, heat expands a thermocouple in the valve which closes the outlet and keeps the steam in. If the valve is functioning properly, you'll hear it hiss as the steam fills the radiator and forces cold air

Figure 7-14
Radiator shut-off valve

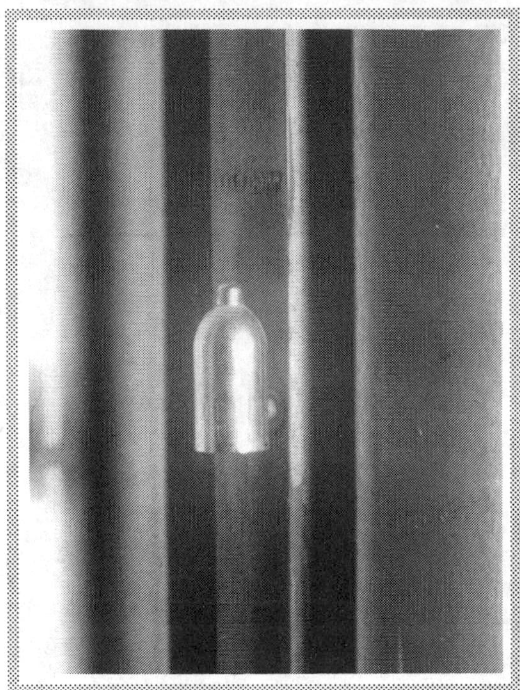

Figure 7-15
Radiator cold-air release valve

out. Then you'll hear a click as heat shuts the valve when the radiator is hot.

The valve looks like a bell with a knob at the top. It must be right side up (the little knob end always goes up) to work properly. If it's upside down or sideways, the radiator won't heat properly. You can solve a lot of radiator problems simply by making sure these valves are in their proper position.

Noises— The angles of the pipes in a steam system are critical. They must be either level, or angled slightly toward the boiler. Steam that condenses to water has to be able to return back to the boiler. If these angles change, maybe due to settling of the house, water may accumulate in the elbows and gurgle when steam passes through. You can repair this problem by restoring the original slope to the pipe.

You may also hear gurgling in the radiators. Make sure the radiator is either level or angled slightly toward the steam supply pipe. Radiators are very heavy. Sometimes the feet sink into the floor a bit. If the angle has shifted away from the pipe, water will accumulate in one corner and gurgle. You can easily restore the proper angle by sliding something (like pennies) under the radiator feet on the side opposite the supply pipe.

Replacing the steam boiler— These simple repairs have taken care of all the steam system problems that I've ever run into. However, it is possible that some day you may find a steam boiler that needs replacing. Fast-talking salesmen may try to talk you into replacing the whole system with something new and expensive. Don't buy it. New steam boilers are still available, including high-efficiency models. They're not hard to find. Even Sears carries them.

The only problem with keeping a steam heat system is that you can't add central air conditioning to it. Of course, I wouldn't recommend adding central air unless you're dealing with very expensive property, or your house is in an area where nearly every home has central air. Central air is very expensive. In most parts of the country, you won't even get your money back for an improvement of this type, much less make a profit on it.

If for some reason you decide to replace the boiler, your best replacement bet would be a hot water system. Or, if the reason you're replacing it is to add central air conditioning, get a hot-and-cold water system. Since this system uses pipes rather than ductwork, it will fit into the same spaces the old system occupied. You can't use the same pipes, but it will save ripping up the walls to put in new ducts.

Changing systems will still be very expensive. Even though you'll have fewer structural modification problems with a hot-and-cold water system, this is both the best and most expensive system available. This is OK if you're working on luxury property, where your buyers will expect this level of quality. On less expensive property, recovering your investment may be impossible.

Figure 7-16
This old hot water system works perfectly

Hot Water Systems

Many people consider hot water systems to be the best choice. They're used in many commercial buildings and luxury homes. You won't find this kind of heat in many fixer-uppers. But if you buy a house that has a deluxe system like this, you'll want to keep it. Figure 7-16 shows an old, but very high-quality, hot water system.

How it works— Hot water heating systems are very simple. Water is heated in a boiler, usually in the basement, and the hot water is pumped through baseboard heaters, which heat the rooms. Unlike steam, the water circulates through two pipes: an input pipe and an outlet pipe. One big advantage over steam heat is that the system uses small baseboard heaters, rather than radiators. Another advantage is that a good system may also have zoned temperature controls. There's a separate thermostat for each part of the house. You can regulate the temperature in each area. This is one of the few systems that has this kind of flexibility.

Problems— Unfortunately, hot water heat tends to have more problems than most of the other systems. The many moving parts could be the reason for this. It uses solenoid-operated flow valves to control the flow of hot water to the various parts of the house, and a pump to distribute the water throughout the system. These are in addition to all the parts that other heating systems have, such as a thermostat, burner controls, and burners. All the parts require occasional maintenance and require repairs just the same as any other heating system.

The two most frequent problems with hot water (hydronic) heating are with the flow control valves and the pump. The pump in the water system works a lot like the water pump in the cooling system of a car. It circulates water through the house. And like an auto cooling system, it can spring leaks. Solenoids in the control valve can also fail and leak.

Usually the leaks occur around the furnace, since that's where you find most of the fittings that screw together (the others are soldered). This is the best place to have a leak, if you must have one at all. These furnaces are generally located in a basement, where leaks are less likely to cause damage. The heaters in the upstairs rooms are usually made of soldered copper tubing. Since there are no openings in the tubing and copper doesn't rust, the upstairs plumbing should never leak unless it's physically damaged.

The most annoying thing about hot water heat is that everything has to be installed exactly right or there will be a leak. Replacing any part of the system involves plumbing. If you hate doing plumbing, this can be a major drawback.

Electric Heat

I live and work in Michigan. It gets cold here in the winter, very cold. That makes electric heat impractical. It's just too expensive. If the home you've bought is in a cold climate and has electric heat, you simply have to replace the system with something more affordable. That's a big, expensive job. It's only worthwhile if the house is extremely desirable.

The only practical use for electric heat in a cold climate would be in a super-insulated house. I once considered super-insulating a house for electric heat, but I came to the conclusion that it would cost more than replacing the system with a gas forced-air furnace. I decided not to buy the house.

In mild climates, electric heat isn't quite as impractical. Although it's still expensive to operate, you don't use it as often. The good news is that electric heaters are practically maintenance free. They're very simple devices. They have thermostats that turn them on and off. They heat up and they turn off. That's all there is to it. Once in a great while, a heater might burn out. If so, they're cheap and easy to replace. The only regular maintenance they need is cleaning. Dirt interferes with their operation, and leaves unsightly streaks on the walls.

Other Fuels

You may come across systems fired by other fuels. Let's consider some of them.

Oil— Although oil-fired furnaces are common in older homes, they do have some drawbacks. Most notable is that oil may not always be readily available. It also has an odor when it burns. Oil is used in both forced-air and steam systems.

An oil-fired forced air or steam system works almost the same as a gas-fired system of the same type. The only difference is the addition of a pump which forces the oil through a spray-nozzle burner, where it ignites and burns. The pump can fail (although it's usually quite reliable), so you'll need to check it when you're troubleshooting this type of furnace. Aside from that, all maintenance and repairs are the same as with a gas-fired forced air or steam system.

If you have an oil burning furnace, consider converting it to gas. Most home buyers dislike oil furnaces. Converting to gas will probably raise the value of your house enough to make the job worthwhile.

You only have to replace the burners, not the whole furnace, to convert to gas. The cost of the conversion will depend on how far the gas line has to be run. The farther your house is from the gas main, the more the gas company will charge for installation. If you already have a gas line to the house (for your water heater, for instance), converting the furnace to gas is easy and inexpensive. In a rural area, bottled propane may be the only gas available.

Coal— A few homes still use coal for heating, but not many. If you come across a coal-fired gravity furnace or a coal-fired steam furnace, don't repair it. Replace it. Nobody likes shoveling coal into their furnace. And don't bother trying to convert the system to gas. A coal furnace that's been converted to gas isn't very desirable. I wouldn't tear one out if it was already there and working, but I wouldn't spend money converting coal to gas fuel. A new, high-efficiency furnace would be a better investment.

Propane— You'll find propane fueled heating systems in rural areas where pipe-fed natural gas service isn't available. It works just like regular natural gas and you use it for the same heating systems. Propane is stored in pressurized tanks near the house, and fed through pipes into the appropriate appliances. It may not be as convenient as having your gas piped in, but it's the best you're going to get if your house isn't near a city. Maintenance and repair of propane-fired systems is the same as natural gas fired systems.

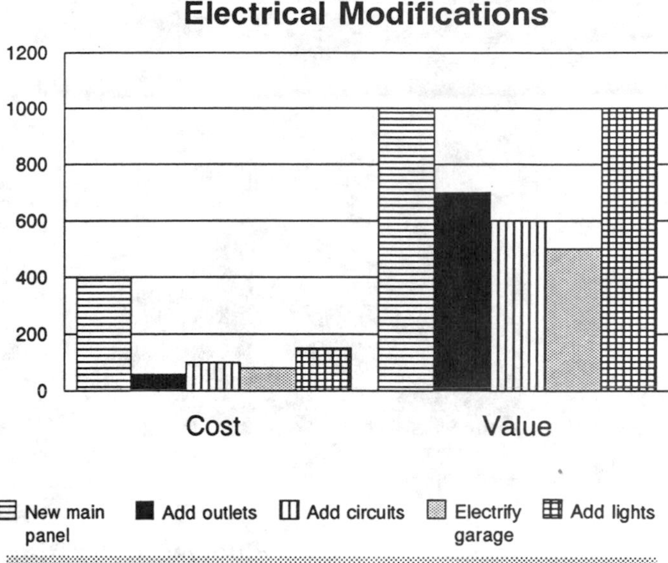

Figure 7-17
Electrical modifications add value

Electrical Modifications

Most older homes have limited electrical service — far less than we consider adequate in a modern home. I bought a large three-bedroom home a few years ago that had only four 15-amp circuits for the entire house! You can't live comfortably with so little power. You would blow fuses constantly just trying to use the modern appliances that families expect to have available. If you run into a situation like this, you'll have to replace the main service panel.

The Main Service Panel

Replacing the main service panel in a house may be expensive. But it's essential if you want to attract buyers not willing to live in the dark ages. This is one of those situations where you'll just have to shell out a few dollars.

Unfortunately, a new service panel doesn't have much sales appeal. Like many other functional modifications, people won't pay more for what they consider to be a basic necessity. But they won't buy at all without adequate electrical service. So, if you plan on selling, you'll have to modernize the system regardless of the expense.

Most buyers don't know too much about electricity. They know about safety however, and they don't like the idea of dealing with fuses. Given a choice, they will opt for a house with circuit breakers rather than fuses any day. So that's another reason to modernize the electrical system. People are afraid of fuses. They think they might get electrocuted trying to change them, or maybe the fuses will start a fire. They can deal much more comfortably with flipping the switch on a circuit breaker.

If you replace the service panel, be sure your prospective buyers know it. A new service panel indicates an updated and modernized house. Your real estate listing should say "New Electric." Most buyers won't know exactly what that involves, but they'll assume that if it's new, it must be good. Figure 7-17 shows the costs of various electrical improvements and the value each improvement should add to the resale price.

Lighting and Outlets

Unless your house is fairly modern, chances are it won't have enough electrical outlets in the kitchen. Electrical kitchen appliances such as microwave ovens, coffee makers, juicers, toaster ovens and popcorn poppers weren't even available when most of the houses I buy were built. Kitchens, and bathrooms too, are often short of outlets.

Before After

Figure 7-18
Fluorescent lighting brightens up basement

When you're evaluating the electrical needs of a house, be sure you think it through carefully. Organize the entire project in your mind before you start. Check each room to see if there's enough lighting and enough outlets. If you need to add overhead lighting or a lot of new plugs, you'll probably need some new circuits. Be sure your service panel can handle these new circuits. You may find that you have to add an auxiliary box to the existing panel to accommodate the needs of the house. Sometimes that may not be enough. You may be better off replacing the panel from the outset rather than trying to patch together a workable system from odds and ends.

A common electrical problem that I run into are outlets that don't work. Over time, the springs in the outlet wear out. When you plug something in, it falls right out. Buy a few dozen plugs and keep them on hand. That way, you'll always have one available when you need to make a replacement.

Basement lighting— Most building codes require a light for every 200 square feet of basement space. Handyman specials hardly ever have enough. I always try to bring my houses as close to code as possible, even in municipalities that don't require inspection. I don't like to sell substandard property.

Fluorescent utility lights brighten up a basement. They're especially nice for laundry and work areas. Fluorescent fixtures cost a little more than plain ceramic incandescent fixtures but they provide more light. They also give the basement a modern appearance that people seem to like. I think they add enough to the appeal of the basement to make the extra expenditure worthwhile. Look at the difference a new fluorescent light fixture makes in the dingy basement work area in Figure 7-18.

There's usually a shortage of electrical outlets in the basement as well. They don't cost much to add, and they greatly increase the utility of the basement, especially in a laundry area. Have enough outlets for a washing machine, dryer, iron, and maybe a radio all in use at the same time. The laundry area isn't very practical without plenty of outlets. People often check for things like this, and they're disappointed if they don't find them.

Weird Wiring

Do-it-yourselfers sometimes have strange ideas about electricity. You may find that some of the wiring in your house doesn't make any sense. One dangerous practice I've discovered is the use

Figure 7-19
Dangerous do-it-yourself electrical job

Figure 7-20
Live wire left hanging from wall

of ordinary lamp cord, instead of Romex cable, for running wiring through the walls. This could cause a fire, or at least blow a lot of fuses. If you find wiring of this kind, replace it. The overhead light in Figure 7-19 no longer worked. Instead of repairing it, someone ran a new wire from a wall plug to the light fixture. Not only is this messy and a violation of the electrical code, it's a safety hazard.

Another favorite practice of amateurs is leaving switches or light fixtures with exposed wiring dangling from the walls or ceiling. Apparently the former owners didn't mind having their fingers singed. Obviously, you have to remove them or redo them properly. The live wire hanging out of the wall in Figure 7-20 was intended for an outlet. The former owner just left it hanging. It only took a few minutes for me to finish this job correctly. The hard part, running the wire, was done.

Some unusual wiring practices are harmless. For instance, once I found that a do-it-yourselfer had added several outlets, each one wired on a separate circuit. That required a lot of extra cable. I hate to think of what all that expensive, unnecessary cable must have cost him. Still, there was nothing wrong with the wiring. I examined it carefully and made sure it was okay. Then I left it just as it was.

I always make a thorough check of the electrical system in every house I buy. This is especially important in older homes. You can leave two-wire wiring in place even though it's old, as long as it's still in good condition. However, you may need to replace old switches and fixtures. I take out anything that doesn't work correctly or that I think may be unsafe. Never leave anything that may be a safety hazard.

Plumbing Repairs

The basement is usually the heart of the home plumbing system (if you're fortunate and have a basement). Begin your plumbing inspection there. Check the hot water tank immediately. They have limited life spans. Next check the water pipes. Many older homes have a lot of crumbly, rusted pipes. If one is bad, they're probably all bad. You might as well start out knowing that you'll have to replace the whole pipe run if you find a bad section.

Many remodelers make the mistake of thinking they can just replace one deteriorated pipe or fitting. They buy a replacement for the bad part, but when they try to put it in, the connecting part crumbles. So they go back to the hardware store and buy a replacement for that part. But when they try to put the second part in, the part it connects to crumbles. This can go on all day. Save yourself some trouble. Buy enough pipe to replace the entire run. If you don't need it for this job, you'll soon find a use for it someplace else.

I like to use PVC pipe whenever possible. I recommend it highly. I used to do all my plumbing with galvanized steel pipe because that's how I was taught. I was suspicious of PVC at first, and not too eager to change. But I've found PVC to be great stuff. You simply glue the piping together. It's a lot like building model airplanes. The only problem I've found is that you can't unscrew it and do it over if you make a mistake. You have to cut out the bad piece and replace it. But it's easy to do. All you'll need is a little more pipe, a hacksaw and some glue. The parts are much cheaper than metal, so if you have a little waste, it's no tragedy.

I always keep PVC pipe and extra fittings on hand. Then if I have a plumbing system fall apart, I can quickly and easily replace the whole thing. This is a big help. I don't have to spend a lot of time running around collecting the pipes and fittings I need to make emergency repairs. Steel pipe is too bulky and expensive to keep around "just in case."

Emergency plumbing repairs can bring an entire project to a halt. Until you complete the repairs, you can't do anything that requires water. You can't even use the toilet! This becomes very inconvenient very fast. Even if you don't want to keep a large supply of pipe around, be sure to have some caps and plugs in various sizes. That way, if you can't rework the plumbing right then, you can at least cap off the damaged part and keep the water supply on.

Plumbing Modifications

I don't like plumbing work. PVC pipe makes it easier, but I still don't look forward to dealing with plumbing problems. So, I try to make as few plumbing modifications as possible. I repair or replace the fixtures that are in place, but only add new ones if it's obvious that they are needed. For instance, I had a house with a laundry tub and no faucet. I felt obligated to install a water supply since a laundry tub is useless without water.

Figure 7-21

Old cement laundry tub is a thing of the past

One plumbing modification is now required by many municipalities. You must replace old cement laundry tubs with fiberglass tubs. I think this is silly. However, code enforcement officers rarely ask my opinion, so I always go ahead and replace the tubs. It's hard to fight City Hall. Disposing of old cement laundry tubs like the one in Figure 7-21 can be a problem. I've found that they're much easier to get rid of when they're in small pieces. They break up quite nicely with a sledgehammer.

Problems to Avoid

There are some structural problems that are so difficult or expensive to fix that they eliminate a house from consideration. You simply can't make the repairs and still come out with a profit. Badly cracked plaster, walls way out of plumb, and sagging floors and ceilings are indications that a house may have severe structural problems. The following repairs are probably not worth your efforts:

Major Foundation Defects

It's possible to jack up a house and replace the foundation, but there's no inexpensive way to do this. Major foundation repairs are not a good place to invest your money. You may get thousands of dollars off the price when you buy the house, but it'll cost thousands of dollars to repair it. There's no profit there.

Fire Damage

I generally avoid buying houses with extensive fire damage. Fire does tricky things. It spreads and moves inside walls and pops out in unlikely places. It melts things, and it opens the house up to the weather. Most of the time water damage comes along with fire damage. First, there's damage from fire hoses. Then there's more damage from rain coming through broken windows or breaches in the roof. After a period of time, you'll also have rot problems associated with water. You can't assume that anything will be intact after this kind of treatment.

After a fire, you'll have to go over a house with a fine-tooth comb to find out what is salvageable and what you'll have to replace. Unless the house is very special for some reason, or you can buy it for almost nothing, it's not going to be worthwhile. I've seen repairs made on extensively fire-damaged houses. But these were mansions of historic value. In that case, the effort would be justified. People repair these houses as a labor of love.

Excessive Water Damage

Over a long period of time, water leakage can rot out the entire structure of a house. And it's not always immediately obvious. Sometimes water destroys sections of plaster. Sometimes it's invisible and you don't know what's been destroyed. Water running free inside a house can turn up in places you'd never even imagine. It flows over, under, around and through anything, and winds up in the most unlikely spots. Luckily, your nose will help find water leakage. A wet, musty, moldy smell gives you the first clue. Sometimes the smell is so strong it's sickening.

Every piece of wood in the entire house may be rot-damaged. I've seen houses like that. They seemed ready to collapse at any moment. I felt myself lucky to get out the front door alive. You can never assume anything with water damage. You have to check it out, carefully.

Excessive Termite Damage

Termite problems come with water damage because termites like to live in moist wood. If a house is infested with termites, you'll usually have two problems, termites and wood rot. If there's extensive termite damage to the main parts of the house, there will probably be extensive water damage as well.

Of the two, water is usually the greater problem. If you can eliminate the water, you can then exterminate and get rid of the termites. Of course, you'll still have to replace all the damaged wood. Termites tend to live in areas where wood comes into contact with the earth, but they'll spread throughout a house in time. Look for them in porches which were constructed without a proper foundation or in garages where the is dirt heaped up against the walls. You might also find them in leaky basements and attics.

In the northern parts of the country, termites aren't usually a big problem. I've found them most often limited to areas around the exterior of a house. In the South, however, particularly in the moist, humid regions, termites can be a serious menace. I recommend getting a copy of one of the U.S. Government publications on the subject. The U.S. Department of Agriculture sells several good, inexpensive booklets. For a current list of publications, write:

Publications Division/Office of Information
U.S. Department of Agriculture
Washington, DC 20250

If a termite inspection indicates serious infestation, don't go through with the deal.

Other Considerations

What I really dislike about serious structural problems is the uncertainty. When you're dealing with extensive fire, water, or termite damage, you won't know if the house is worth repairing until you've gone over every inch of it on your hands and knees. You can spend days checking for

Before

After

Figure 7-22

This lot is more valuable without the house

damage and still not be sure. Until you've done that, it's questionable whether the house should be repaired or demolished.

I usually don't like getting involved in a project that's speculative. I prefer buying houses with problems I can see and appreciate. You get enough surprises without inviting more. Before I begin on a house, I want to be sure my efforts aren't going to be a total loss. Of course, if you get one of these seriously damaged houses cheap enough, you might be able to make a good profit on it. But if you miscalculate the damage, you might end up working for free. I like jobs that are less risky. I'd rather be guaranteed a modest profit than go for a huge profit and lose.

Demolition

You should consider demolishing a house when the necessary repairs add up to more than 50 percent of its value. For example, if a house worth $100,000 needs more than $50,000 in repairs, you might as well just tear it down and build a new home. The house is essentially worthless. I don't recommend getting into a project like this unless the house is discounted almost to the cost of the land. Make this determination *before you buy*.

Sometimes a house will be priced at less than the value of the land alone. How can that be? Because the house is worthless as it is, but it will cost somebody to tear it down. If you do the tearing down, you make the profit. You can sometimes find good deals like this in areas that were zoned for single-family dwellings and have been rezoned for apartments or commercial use. The old house in Figure 7-22 was just such a deal. It was worthless standing, but the commercial zoning and its location on a main street made the lot all by itself quite valuable.

That's all I have to say about basic structural and mechanical system repairs for now. In the next chapter, we'll look at other interior repairs, including walls, ceilings and plumbing that don't involve the structure of the house. These problems will be a little easier to deal with, but you'll find that there's a lot more of them.

CHAPTER EIGHT

The Living Room, Dining Room and Bedrooms

The interior of the homes you buy will almost always be dirty. But that's just the beginning. You'll find holes in the plaster or wallboard, missing moldings, torn wallpaper, missing light fixtures, broken or missing switchplates and so on. These aren't major problems and require few decisions: clean out the garbage, patch the holes, replace what's missing, prepare the walls and ceiling for paint, apply paint or wallpaper. That's easy — and cheap. The biggest investment will be labor. And the time will nearly always be well invested. But doing that minor cosmetic work may be just the beginning.

How much more should you do? That's a very important question. Of course, the answer depends on the return you can expect for each extra dollar invested. This chapter is intended to help you make good decisions when considering repairs in the living room, dining room and bedrooms. I've grouped these rooms together in this chapter for one simple reason. All have one thing in common: no plumbing. For the same reason, you could include family rooms, dens and sunrooms in this chapter.

From a repair standpoint, these rooms are very similar. They're just boxes — walls, ceiling, floors, windows and doors. They're usually built of the same materials. Except for a little decoration in the living room or dining room, these rooms will be very plain. That makes it easier and reduces your cost.

Let's look at the repair decisions you'll face in these rooms, beginning with the ceiling.

Figure 8-1
Typical ceiling damage from a leaky upstairs bathroom

Figure 8-2
This ceiling looks terrible, but it's relatively easy to fix

The Ceiling

If you can make a ceiling smooth and white, you've done enough. I prefer a smooth plaster finish on the ceiling. It looks neat and it's easy to paint. You may find the ceilings that way, or they may just need a coat of paint to clean them up. Then you're lucky. If you're not so lucky, you'll have some water damage to repair. Most often, it will be water damage from a leak somewhere up above. Water tends to collect inside the ceiling and dissolve the plaster. Find the source of the problem and eliminate it, and then make the repair.

In a one-story house or on the top floor, the ceiling damage will probably be caused by a leak in the roof. If there's another floor above the damaged ceiling, chances are you'll find a plumbing leak in an upstairs bathroom. These can be pretty serious. Figure 8-1 shows typical ceiling damage caused by a plumbing leak.

With a badly damaged ceiling, your best bet is to rip out the whole thing and replace it with drywall. If the damage is limited to a small area, you might get by with a limited repair. But usually it's better to strip off the old plaster right back to the ceiling joists. Replacing the entire ceiling with new drywall is easier than trying to patch pieces of drywall into old plaster. It's very hard to make a good, invisible joint between plaster and drywall. Usually the seam is very obvious. Remember, it's hard to hide the ceiling. You can't hang a picture over it! Take the time to get a nice smooth finish.

Think of a damaged ceiling as an opportunity. It probably scared off all the other buyers. Recently I bought a very nice fixer-upper that had only one major problem — the ceiling. There was a huge whole in the dining room ceiling. You can see it in Figure 8-2. The rest of the ceiling sagged and looked like it was about to fall. I knew that this ceiling would be cheap and easy to fix. But because other prospective buyers didn't know that, they just turned and walked away. I bought the house way under market value and sold it for an attractive profit. Drywalling the ceiling was very little work for the money I made.

Another advantage to removing the ceiling is that it exposes the framing. You can see where the water is coming from and anything else that's likely to cause damage. If needed, you can repair and strengthen the floor joists for the second floor. If you're planning to install ceramic floor tile in the second-floor bathroom, it's important that the floor is absolutely solid. Any springiness to the floor will cause floor tiles to pop loose.

Ceilings are a problem for most do-it-yourselfers. The proper way to repair ceilings is with either plaster or drywall. But very few do-it-yourselfers know how to handle these materials. Instead, they try to make do with second-rate alternatives like ceiling tiles or even wood paneling. A lot of your work will be removing amateur repairs done by previous owners.

Alternatives to White Plaster or Drywall Ceilings

My usual goal is to create a smooth, white ceiling. But that's not always easy. I find a variety of ceiling treatments in the houses I buy. Some will be easier to deal with than others. For instance, some people paint their ceilings colors other than white. A colored ceiling is disturbing to some people. It makes them feel like there's something looming over their heads. Or, they may feel uncomfortable in the room, but not know why. A white ceiling visually disappears. It reflects light and makes a room feel open and airy. I always paint ceilings white.

Textures— I've owned several houses that had textured stucco ceilings. Certain architectural styles, particularly in homes built in the 1920s, favor stucco ceilings. It was an integral part of the design. But not all my houses were built in that era. Their stuccoed ceilings were the result of amateur repair jobs. Do-it-yourselfers often use stucco because it's a quick and easy way to deal with minor ceiling damage, such as cracks and small holes.

Here's my policy on stucco, or any other textured-plaster finish: I don't like them, but they don't bother me enough to make me redo a whole ceiling. If the finish is applied competently and it blends adequately with the style of the house, I'll leave it. In fact, if the ceiling was done well, but it's slightly damaged, I'll repair the stucco. But I would never put stucco on a ceiling myself.

A stuccoed ceiling has several drawbacks. To begin with, it accumulates cobwebs and is hard to clean. Once stucco gets dirty there isn't much you can do with it except give it a fresh coat of paint. It's also hard to paint. You need a special roller, a lot of time, and a huge amount of paint. I don't like modifications that create maintenance problems.

Finally, since stucco is often used to cover damaged plaster, people have come to associate it with hidden damage. Whenever they see a stuccoed ceiling they're likely to ask "Why did you cover that with stucco? Is there something wrong with it?" I can answer truthfully, "I didn't stucco the ceiling; the former owners did and I don't know why." This satisfies most people, but I'd rather they didn't have to ask about the ceiling. It's bad for sales.

One house I bought had a stuccoed ceiling in the kitchen and breakfast area. Whoever applied the stucco thinned the mixture too much. It dripped, and then hardened into long, sharp spikes which hung like stalactites from the ceiling. They were positively frightening. The spikes looked as though they might break off and fall like darts. In fact, one stabbed me in the head while I was trying to get a closer look. At first I wasn't sure what I could do with this ceiling. Fortunately, the spikes were easy to break off. I scraped a drywall knife across the ceiling to smooth the surface. The result was a texture that looked about like a normal stucco job, so I left it alone.

Acoustic ceiling tile— Another favorite of do-it-yourselfers' is acoustic ceiling tile. They either install it on a drop-ceiling framework or they attach it directly to the old plaster. Acoustic tile is an easy alternative for people who don't

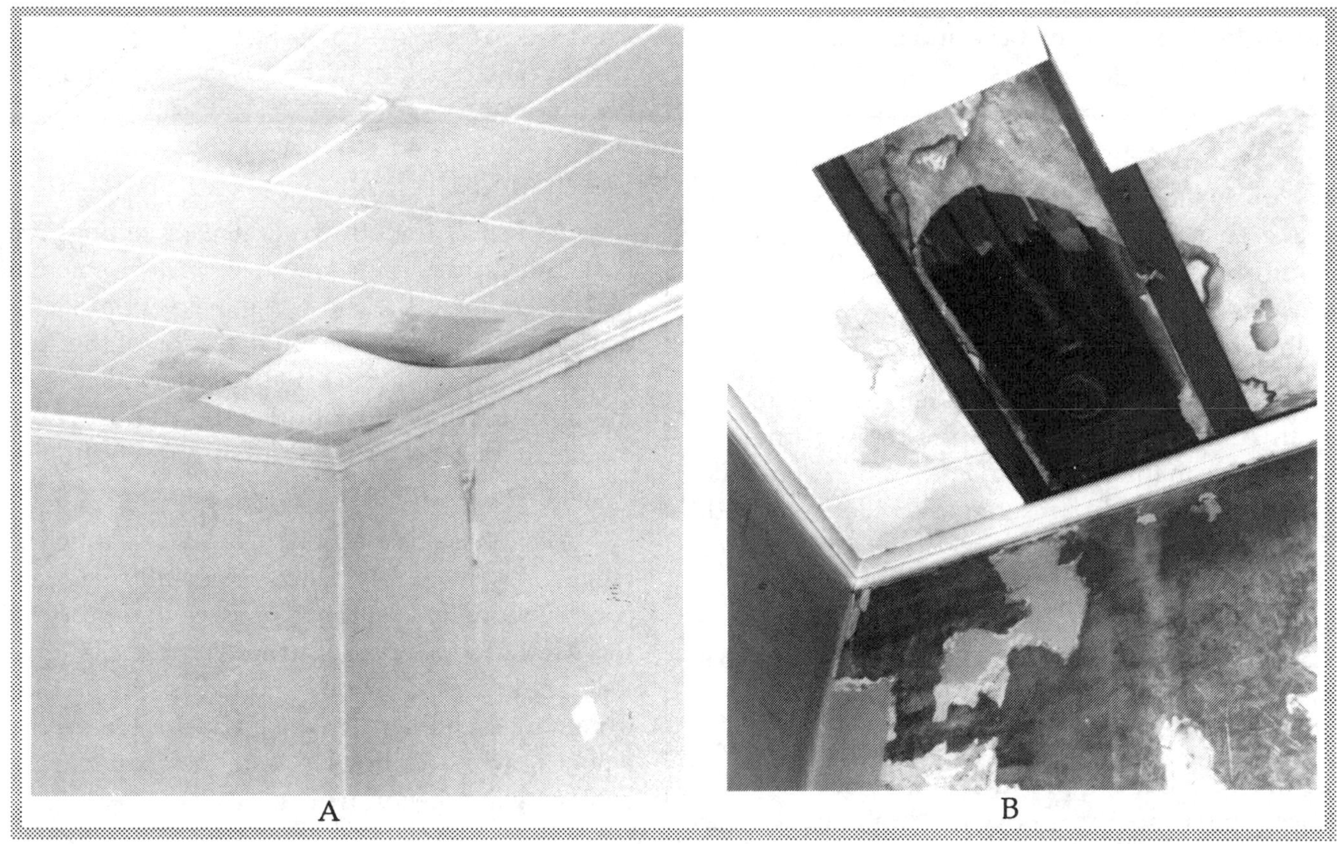

Figure 8-3
This ceiling repair failed because the original leak wasn't fixed

know how to handle drywall. But it isn't durable or, in my opinion, very attractive.

Ceiling tile in an upstairs room of the house indicates that there's been some kind of ceiling damage. Your first impression is that the repair was made by someone who didn't know how to fix ceilings properly. From there you begin to wonder what else they didn't do right. Amateur repairs can be scary.

I avoid using ceiling tile in any room except one, the basement. Some types of ceiling tile resist basement moisture very well. And nearly any type of ceiling tile will make a basement seem less like a concrete cave.

About half the houses I've worked on had ceiling tile installed somewhere in the living area. I find it most often in kitchens. That's because the second-floor bathroom is usually located over the kitchen. When the bathroom leaks, the kitchen ceiling falls in. Obviously, you can't use textured stucco to repair a ceiling if half of it has fallen down. So the second choice of the do-it-yourselfer is ceiling tiles.

Figure 8-3 shows a ceiling tile job that I found in one of my houses. The owner fixed the ceiling but didn't stop the leak that caused the original damage. So, the new ceiling fell in too. When I bought the house there was a piece of cardboard concealing a hole in the corner of the room (A). The hole went all the way through to the bathroom above. A leaky tub drain had rotted out the bathroom subfloor and then the ceiling below (B).

Ceiling tile in the living areas of a home look cheap and out of place. They look just like what they are: a stopgap repair done by someone unwilling to spend the time and money to do the job right.

Another reason I don't like ceiling tiles is that they are impossible to clean. Over time they become yellowed and covered with airborne dust and grease. If you try to wash them, they dissolve. Painting the ceiling tiles makes them look even worse. The paint tends to peel off and the framework rusts through the paint.

Do-it-yourselfers will often cover damage with ceiling tile and leave the repairs undone. Any holes in the original plaster ceiling above the tiles will leak cold air even after tile is applied. Cold air from the uninsulated exterior walls or attic space will pour into the house. Drop-ceiling installation doesn't correct this problem, it just covers it up. In a cold climate, a few small air leaks will greatly inflate the monthly heating bill.

How do I deal with an acoustic ceiling in one of my houses? Simple. If it's any place but the basement, I usually remove it. I don't care if it was a beautiful installation job or if it's in perfect condition (although it rarely is). I'll take it out anyway. Acoustic ceiling tile does not belong in a home's living areas. It makes such a negative impression that it's *worth* taking out and replacing with drywall. I only leave ceiling tiles in the cheapest of property, where cost is such a constraint that I can't afford to do anything nonessential.

I'll admit that some homes have very professional, very attractive acoustical tile ceilings that harmonize with the room. But the ceiling has to look like something out of an Armstrong ceiling tile advertisement before I would want to keep it. You don't find those kind in fixer-uppers.

Ceiling tile isn't the worst type of ceiling. Sometimes I'm amazed by what people use to repair ceilings. I've been in houses with burlap covering the ceilings. Another home had a ceiling covered with hardboard paneling. These are third-rate repairs (not even as good as second-rate repairs), done by people who didn't know enough or care enough to use an appropriate repair material. I *always* tear ceilings like this out.

Decorated Ceilings

As I said, smooth white plaster ceilings are best. But I'll make an exception for ornamental plaster ceilings, the kind that were popular in quality homes built in the first quarter of the 20th century. I preserve the ornate plaster flowers or medallions that surround a light fixture or decorate the center of the ceiling. If they're damaged, I try to make repairs.

I like these decorations. They add a touch of elegance you rarely find, especially in new construction. It's just too expensive to reproduce this kind of work now. Buyers value these extra features in an older home. So if you have a nice ornamental ceiling, leave it. My preference for smooth, white ceilings doesn't keep me from salvaging architectural artwork.

The Walls

Damage to the interior walls is the most common problem you'll find in a fixer-upper. Some of the walls may look so terrible they're guaranteed to scare off other buyers. Again, damage like this can take thousands of dollars off your cost. The seller's loss is your gain — damaged walls are fairly cheap and easy to fix.

In an older home, the walls are probably plaster over wooden lath. Drywall wasn't popular until the early 1950s. If you have a house that was built before then, you may have plasterboard, plaster over wire mesh, or wooden lath. To add to the fun, you may have all of these surfaces, layer upon layer. You never know with a handyman special.

It doesn't really matter what the walls are made of, as long as they're solid and reasonably plumb. I've never had much problem with walls being too far out of plumb. I won't buy a house with walls that are obviously leaning. But I've had other problems with walls.

One of the first things you check when you're inspecting a house is the condition of the walls. Do this before you buy. Gently press against the walls to see if they have any give. Don't pound on them though, because if they're bad, big chunks might fall out. People get upset when you punch holes in their walls. Once the house belongs to you, feel free to punch as many holes in the walls as you like.

When deciding what wall repairs to make, begin by pounding on all the walls with the heel of your hand. If wall cover is going to collapse, it should happen before you make other repairs. Don't overlook a weak spot, and later have a prospective buyer fall through it when you're trying to close the sale. That won't make a very good impression.

Investigating the Damage

Don't repair damaged walls until you know what caused the damage. If it was an angry tenant who decided to put his foot through the wall on his way out, no problem. But if you fix something before the cause has been corrected, your repair is only temporary. Whatever caused the damage will cause it again.

If your house has plaster walls, you're fortunate. It's harder to make a hole in a plaster wall. Most older plaster walls have two layers of plaster over wood furring strips. Furring strips are spaced a half-inch apart. Wet plaster seeps through the spaces and hardens to form little fingers that hold the dry plaster firmly in place. These walls combine the strength of plaster and the strength of wood. That's why they're so desirable today. This is a good selling point. Only the most expensive luxury homes built today have lath and plaster walls.

Impact damage to plaster— I said it isn't easy to punch a hole in a plaster wall — but it *is* possible. One home I bought had a hole in a plaster wall made with a garbage disposal. Why would anyone throw a garbage disposal against a wall? I always wondered if it was frustration over a disposal that didn't work, or not being able to install it properly. Again, do-it-yourselfers often create more problems than they solve.

Impact damage is usually limited to a specific area. It doesn't spread like water damage does. An impact hole usually has a jagged, irregular shape, kind of like the glass in a broken window. It's safe to go ahead and repair these immediately. But keep in mind that an impact both knocks a chunk out of the wall *and* loosens plaster around the hole. Be sure to remove this loose plaster. Otherwise, the repair won't hold.

While you're patching impact holes, look for little craters in the plaster. These are generally caused by nails or screws driven into the wall to hold up pictures or shelves. When the fasteners come out, so does a little bit of the plaster. A little patching plaster will take care of these holes.

Impact damage to drywall— I rarely find more than one or two impact holes in houses with lath and plaster walls. Houses constructed with drywall are usually worse. It's easier to punch a hole in drywall. Carelessness when moving furniture can knock big holes in drywall. I've seen rooms that looked as though a war had been fought in them. There were huge holes in every wall. The house hadn't been vandalized; the tenants were just brutal.

If there's a small hole in your drywall, cut a small piece of scrap drywall and patch it in. This takes time, however. If you have more than one or two holes in a small area, it's easier to put up a new sheet of drywall.

Many people don't understand how to repair drywall. It's too bad, because making drywall repairs shouldn't be a mystery. Sure, drywalling is a skill, but it's not too difficult to learn. You can expect to mess up a few sheets in the beginning, but it's cheap. Give it a try. It just takes practice. The company that published this book offers a good manual on installing and repairing drywall. The address and phone number are on the order form at the back of this manual.

Massive wall damage will drive away most buyers. Even buyers willing to fix up a house may be driven away if they haven't worked with drywall. All they can think of is sheets of wood paneling. You wouldn't want to panel an entire house, would you? I've seen houses like that. They look like one big finished basement. One house I looked at even had paneling over the windows and doors. You couldn't find your way out. I almost panicked until I noticed that one sheet of paneling had a doorknob!

Once you get the hang of it, working with drywall is almost as easy as paneling — and it's less expensive. When you're finished, you have a clean, bright and attractive room. Once you master making drywall repairs, you'll never have to be afraid of damaged walls again. That's a big advantage.

Water Damage

Water damage is usually a much more serious problem than impact damage. It can show up anywhere below the point where the water entered. If water came in through a roof leak, you may find damage from the ceiling to the basement at several points in the wall.

While lath and plaster walls resist impact, they don't resist water damage very well at all. Typically, water damage produces an odd-looking bow in the wall. The water fills the plaster, making it soft. Eventually gravity pulls it away from the furring strips. With nothing to adhere to, it sags, and bows outward. If it bows out too far, the plaster will fall away, leaving a big hole in the wall.

When you see one of these bowed-out areas in a wall, check to see if it's hard or soft. Push it gently with your fingers. Is it solid, or is it mushy? If it's soft, that means it's still wet. There's probably an active leak somewhere above this point in the house. It's pointless to repair the wall until you've found and repaired the leak. Punch the bowed-out area. Your fist will go right through it; it has no strength. You might as well go ahead and tear out all the soft, loose plaster. It's not good for anything. Once it's out of the way you may be able to peek up into the wall and tell where the water is coming from.

If the bowed-out area is hard, that means that it was wet at one time but has dried out. Unfortunately, you have no way of knowing how long ago it hardened. It could have been years ago, or it could have been yesterday. If it hardened years ago, the leak that caused it has probably been corrected. On the other hand, the plaster may have hardened simply because it hasn't rained for a while or because nobody's flushed the toilet recently. You'll never know until you find the source of the moisture.

Finding mysterious leaks— The water source may be obvious or it may be almost impossible to locate, like in a house I now own. The problem was in the stairway wall between the first and second floors. There was a bow in the wall about 3 feet wide and 2 feet high. The plaster was hard and the area above and below it was solid. The ceiling above the wall was fine and there was no other water damage anywhere in the house. I couldn't imagine what had caused the damage.

I might never have figured it out, except that I noticed a glint of metal behind the furring strips when I removed the bad plaster. Metal? Sure enough, there was a sheet of galvanized steel inside the wall. It turned out to be a vent that went up the wall, through the attic and out the roof.

The vent was attached to an exhaust fan in the ceiling of the pantry. You don't often find exhaust fans in pantries. I checked with the former owners and found that this pantry had once been a bathroom. It had been such a tiny, inconvenient bathroom that they had changed it back into a pantry. But they left the fan.

Figure 8-4
Repairs in progress

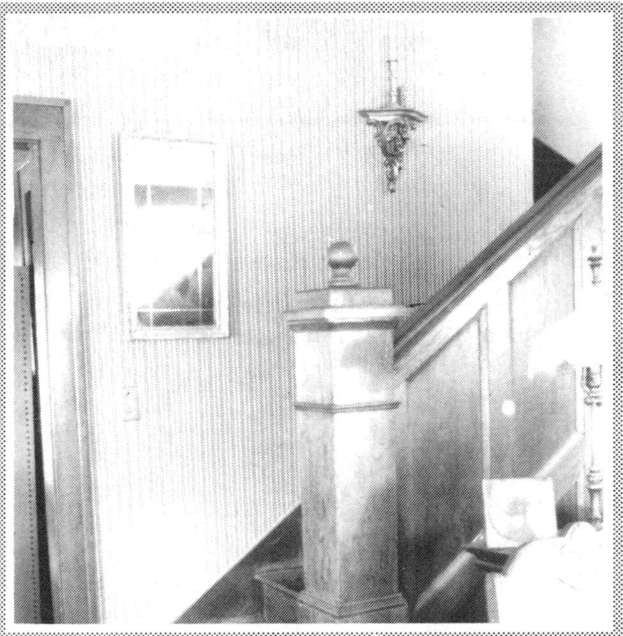

Figure 8-5
The completed wall

Whoever made the bathroom conversion hadn't installed the vent correctly. It wasn't sealed properly. Rainwater dripped down the vent tube, continuing 20 feet until it reached the point where the tube attached to the fan. There the water dribbled off the metal onto the plaster, creating the bowed-out spot in the wall. I went up onto the roof to check out the vent. The former owners had already sealed up the leak, and repaired the cause of the problem. Once the mystery was solved, I could go ahead and repair the plaster.

If you've ever tried to trace down a mystery leak, you know what a puzzle it can be. The leak isn't necessarily directly above or even close to the damaged area. Drops of water can drip and run along the undersides of rafters, eventually dropping off the end of a bent nail or other object. There are times when I would swear that water was defying the laws of gravity, flowing uphill. It's important that you find the source of the water and plug it up, or make sure that someone else has already done it. If you don't, your repair work may be wasted.

Repairing Damaged Plaster

There are several ways to repair damaged plaster. You can remove the old plaster and fill the hole with wet plaster. That's the right way. The February, 1987 issue of *Fine Homebuilding* magazine has some interesting information about working with wet plaster. You might want to read up on it. I find wet plaster hard to work with. So I usually take the easy way out, making repairs with drywall.

I used drywall to repair the water-damaged stair wall we just discussed. After I broke out the bad plaster, I found that 1/2-inch drywall was just a little too thick. When I laid it against the lath, it stuck out some. I didn't want to weaken the surrounding plaster by cutting out the lath. And besides, if I did that the drywall would have been too thin. Luckily, I had one of my favorite tools handy — a belt sander. I'm not afraid to take a belt sander to anything that displeases me. It usually makes short work of a task like this. Figure 8-4 shows the wall with the repairs in progress.

I took some panel adhesive and glued the piece of drywall into the hole. Then I sanded it flush and taped the seams. The sander did the job. Of course, the house was covered with a thick layer of plaster dust, but that's the price I had to pay. It was still a lot easier than using wet plaster. I covered the repaired wall with wallpaper. Figure 8-5 shows the finished job. You would never guess there had been a problem there.

Repairing cracks— A certain amount of cracking is normal in older homes. Vibrations from passing trucks or trains can shake some plaster loose over the years. Other cracks may be caused by the lath drying out and contracting. A little crack here or there is no big problem.

Extensively cracked plaster, however, is a danger signal. If you find several large cracks in the same room, that's what I term "extensive cracking." It's almost always caused by some kind of movement of the walls or ceiling. Plaster doesn't bend. It has no give. So tiny movements of the walls, which wouldn't be noticeable in a more flexible material, will cause large cracks in plaster. Cracking is the only way plaster can absorb stress. Figure 8-6 shows a large crack in a plaster wall.

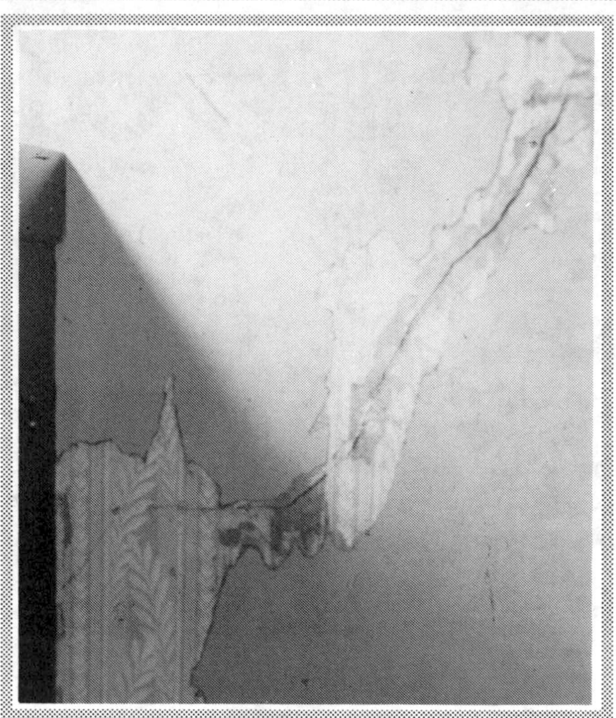

Figure 8-6
Lumpy wallpaper can conceal large cracks in plaster walls

Once you've determined that the area is stable and the cracks won't continue to grow, you can go ahead and repair them. But check the walls around the crack carefully before you begin. Push gently on them, using the same technique I described for checking bowed-out areas. Extensive cracking may have loosened the plaster from the lath. You don't want to take time to tape and repair the crack, only to have a big chunk of the plaster fall out after you're done. If a chunk is going to fall out, you want it to happen *before* you begin repairs.

It's a good idea to use drywall tape to repair any large cracks. It makes a strong repair that resists vibrations and air pressure changes which can loosen repairs that aren't reinforced. You apply the tape to the crack in much the same way you tape seams when installing drywall.

Lay down a bed of joint compound. Embed the tape in it, and cover the tape over with more compound. This will, of course, make a small lump. In order to keep this from showing, you need to smooth and taper the compound *very gradually* in all directions. It doesn't matter how large the crack is, you won't notice it as long as you've carefully smoothed and feathered the edges of the repair. Once the wall is painted with a flat (non-glossy) paint, it will almost be impossible to see. Remember, when you're working on a flat surface, anything with sharp edges (like a crack) will show. If there are no visible edges, like a very gradual lump, nothing will show.

If the cracking is extremely bad, there may not be much solid plaster left. In that case, you'll probably have to tear off all the plaster and replace it with drywall. It's a big job, but when you're done, you'll have an attractive, smooth wall that will impress buyers.

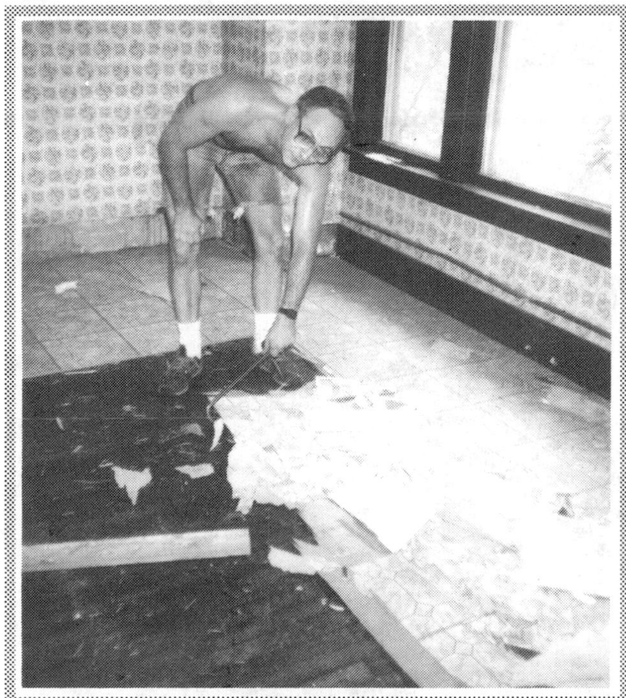

Figure 8-7

A beautiful oak floor was hidden under these tiles

A word about fasteners— When you're working with lath and plaster walls, be careful about the type of nails you use. Lath under plaster is often very springy. If you try to drive a nail larger than a brad into it, you may find that the nail springs right out of the wall and falls on the floor. Lath tends to flex with the blow, so the nail doesn't penetrate the surface. That's funny the first time it happens. But if the lath breaks loose from the plaster when you hit it again, a big chunk of plaster will probably fall out. Now you've got a whole new repair problem. That's not funny any more.

To prevent this, I use drywall screws for any fastening problems, whether I'm working with drywall or lath-and-plaster. These screws are designed to be installed with an electric screw gun or a variable-speed power drill with a Phillips-head bit. Driving screws this way is almost as fast as driving nails with a hammer. The screws won't damage plaster walls or any other delicate structures. And, they're easy to get out if you accidentally put them in the wrong place. Try drywall screws on your next repair job. Once you get used to them, you'll never want to use anything else.

The Floors

People who live in fixer-uppers are not very easy on their floors. You'll be lucky if you find one room in the house that has salvageable floor coverings. Since bad floors make a bad impression on buyers, you'll have to do some work on the floors.

Many years ago, most floors were wood, usually oak strips or parquet. Most new homes today have plywood flooring under carpet. Everyone seems to want wall-to-wall carpeting. There's no reason to spend money on oak floors if they're only going to be covered up by carpeting. Today, only luxury homes have real oak floors.

If you buy an older handyman special, you may discover an oak floor hiding under the dirty, ratty-looking carpet. There are few opportunities in this business where you can increase the value of your house without any cost on your part. This is one of them. Take advantage of it.

Discovering Oak

Always take the time to look under the floor covering. Check out the original flooring. I've salvaged some beautiful oak floors from some highly unlikely places. For instance, in one older home I bought, the former owners had covered the dining room floor with vinyl tile. It looked cheap and tacky, clashing terribly with the fine oak woodwork around the windows and doors. Given the overall condition of the house, I was fairly certain that the original floor would be ruined. Still, I decided to give it a try.

Figure 8-8

Oak floors and woodwork are attractive selling features in older homes

Fortunately, the tile had been installed by a craftsman. A layer of lauan underlayment was laid over the wood floor before tile was applied. I pried up the edge near the kitchen and peeked under with a flashlight. It looked pretty rough. I ripped off a big chunk, and what did I find? A beautiful oak floor in almost perfect condition! That's me in Figure 8-7, happily pulling up the old flooring. The rough area next to the kitchen cleaned up with a little light sanding. The rest of the floor needed nothing but polish. The polish even filled in the thousands of tiny nail-holes left behind when I pulled up the underlayment. When I showed the home to prospective buyers, I got a lot of compliments on the beautiful oak floor (Figure 8-8). And compliments weren't the only thing I got from that oak floor. Buyers *expect* to pay more for a house like that. And I like to give my buyers what they expect. It's just the way I am.

There are a couple of lessons to learn from this experience. First, always look under everything; you never know what you might find. Second, be very careful about making big assumptions from small samples. I thought the floor in this house was ruined when I peeked under the underlayment. I was wrong. I've been wrong in the other direction too, assuming a surface was good when it wasn't. You'll never know what you're dealing with for sure until you've uncovered the whole floor. Take the time to investigate it fully; it's worth it.

Damaged Oak Flooring

Of course, you won't always be lucky enough to find an oak floor in perfect condition. More often the flooring is in far less than perfect condition.

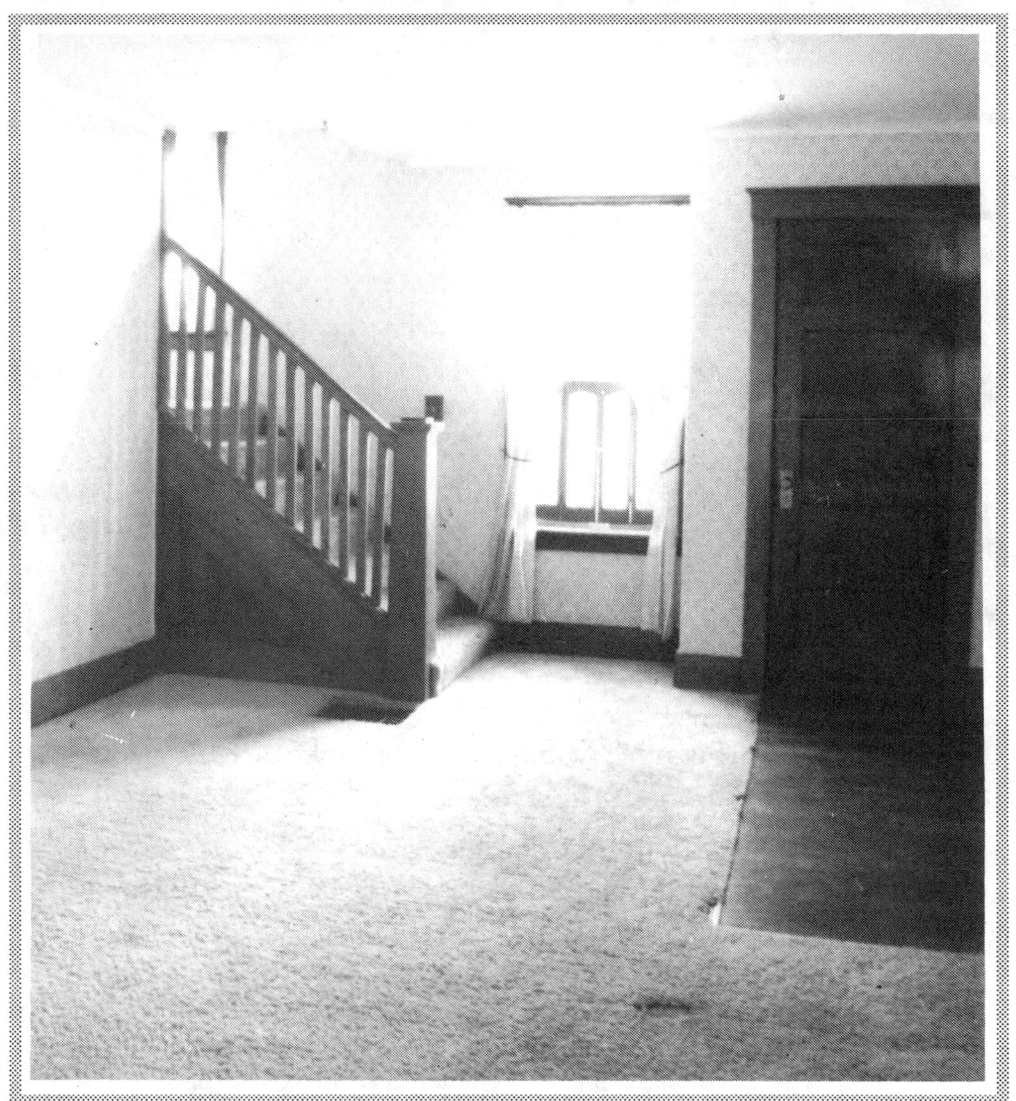

Figure 8-9

Worn carpeting in living room and on stairs

The house in Figure 8-9 had worn-out carpeting in the living room and on the stairs. I wasn't anxious to replace it, but I didn't think I had a choice. When I took the carpeting up, however, the oak flooring underneath was in surprisingly good condition. Only the stairs were badly worn. I thought about just carpeting the stairs, but it would have spoiled the effect if they didn't match the rest of the room. As much as I hated the job, I decided to refinish the stairs. Sanding and refinishing a floor is a big job, and one I really don't like to do. I think you'll agree it was worth the effort though, at least in this house. You can see in Figure 8-10 how beautifully the floors turned out. The house was far more attractive with the natural flooring than it could ever have been with carpet.

Patches— I've had a few really big disappointments working with oak flooring, too. Several times I've peeked under a corner of the carpeting and found perfect oak beneath. But when I uncovered it, there was a huge, ugly plywood patch in the middle of the floor. These

Figure 8-10

Sanding and refinishing natural oak is usually worth the effort

are usually the result of modifications to the heating system. You can work with small defects in the flooring, but a large patch in a prominent place is impossible to hide. If you have to rebuild the entire floor to correct a defect, it's seldom worth it.

You can sometimes make good repairs in small areas, especially in places that aren't too obvious. I'll consider patching a wood floor if the defect is less than about two square feet, and if I can get a good match with the wood. I always save scrap pieces of oak floorboards just for that purpose. Of course, you may have to refinish the entire floor to blend the patch in. But the effort usually pays off.

Surface damage— Here's another problem you're likely to have: a wood floor that's solid but has big stains. These are usually caused by pet accidents, leaky windows or radiators, spilled paint, or worn-off varnish. I've found that people who prefer carpeting rarely value what they cover up. They'll paint the walls without bothering to use a dropcloth and ruin perfectly beautiful floors. They don't care, they're just going to carpet over the flooring anyway.

Professional carpet installers are also careless about what happens to the floors they cover up. Unless someone specifically instructs them to, they won't bother trying to preserve the floors when they install carpet.

These kinds of problems can usually be repaired by sanding and refinishing the floor. But it's a big, tedious job. Sanding and refinishing is mostly labor. Materials don't cost much. You know the floor will look great when it's done — so just keep telling yourself it's worth the effort.

Most splotches will sand off easily. Standing water will warp and discolor the floor. That's harder to deal with. In most cases, however, a little extra sanding will take care of the problem. If all else fails, you can stain the floor a darker color. It's easier to spot problems on a light floor than a dark one. A dark stain will blend uneven shades together. Even if the discoloration is still a little noticeable, it will just look like the surface has been antiqued. After all, in an older home people expect an antique look.

Water damage— Carpet may be your only alternative if there's extensive water damage to the floor. Water left standing on a floor for a considerable length of time will cause cupping — the floorboards will curl up widthwise. This makes a very uneven surface.

How can you deal with this problem? If the cupping is moderate, you may be able to just carpet right over it. Lay down a thick carpet pad. If it's bad, however, you'll have to smooth out the cup by sanding down all the high spots. Use your trusty power sander. The results won't be a floor that looks good enough to leave bare, but you'll have a level surface suitable for laying carpet. If you end up with little gaps between the floor boards, they won't interfere much with the strength of the floor. Use a thick carpet pad though if cold air can leak in through the gaps. The carpet pad should help seal the cracks.

Another way to deal with water-damaged wood is to cover it with underlayment. If the warpage is extreme, quarter-inch underlayment may not be thick enough. It will bounce underfoot as it bridges over the little valleys. You may need to use half-inch underlayment. This can turn into a rather big, expensive job. I prefer sanding floors down. It's a lot of trouble, but the cost is less. Either solution will work. Choose the one that's best for you.

Carpeting

Your fixer-upper may be carpeted throughout when you buy it. But the carpeting will probably be an outdated style and color and in terrible condition. It may even be odd scraps of mismatched pieces patched together from room to room. Some of it may look decent at first, but beware. On a humid day it may smell terrible. I can usually tell from the carpet smell what pets the former occupants had, and sometimes how many. For some reason, people who live in these houses seem to have a lot of pets — and they are never housebroken.

Your first impulse will probably be to tear out all the old carpeting and replace it with brand new wall-to-wall carpeting in a current style. But don't do it, at least not right away. You're going to have to paint the walls and ceilings first. That dirty old carpet makes a great dropcloth. It's just the right size, and it's already in place. It will also protect the floor from any construction damage. New carpeting should be one of the very last things you install.

Job sequence is very important. It's always very tempting to rush in and clear out all the old junk. But don't get carried away. Toss out all the loose trash and garbage. But don't take out anything that may still have some use.

Pros and Cons of Carpeting

Installing new carpeting has several advantages, but it also has some disadvantages. Its biggest advantage is that it covers almost anything and requires minimal surface preparation. It's a simple and quick choice for floor covering. You can do the entire house in just a few hours. Another big advantage is that it's a unifying design element. Once you pick the color and style, you can carry it throughout the house and blend your decorating theme from room to room.

The most obvious strike against carpeting is its expense. Unless you can get a fabulous deal, it's going to cost you roughly a thousand dollars to carpet even a small house with low-quality carpeting. If you have a larger house, or you want better carpeting, well, the sky's the limit. Some people pay more for carpeting than I've paid for renovating an entire house.

It's easy to slip into thinking "Oh, it's only a thousand dollars. I'm going to make twenty or thirty thousand on this project, so I can afford it." That's not the point. Keep this in mind: the extra thousand dollars is *your* money, not your customer's. Every dollar you spend comes out of your pocket. Every dollar you save is yours to keep. If you take the easy way too many times, you'll have a beautiful home but little or no profit.

Many times in every project you'll be tempted to take the easy way out, to pay someone to solve a problem you don't want to handle. Before you do, consider this. Some things you'll *have* to hire done. They may be outside your area of expertise or require a license you don't have. So be very careful about hiring others to do what you can do yourself. Floor covering is an example. If you can refinish hardwood floors instead of putting down carpeting, you can pocket more of the profit. And, a nice hardwood floor is far more impressive than cheap carpeting.

What else is wrong with carpeting? It's too easy to ruin and too hard to repair. Of course, if you're certain that your house will sell quickly, this won't be a big problem. The carpeting should survive a few shoppers walking through.

What if your house doesn't sell quickly? If the market goes bad and you must rent your house out for a while, will your carpeting survive? You never know. You may have to replace it again before you can sell the house. Carpeting is the only part of a house that wears out regularly. Worse, replacing it can cost thousands of dollars. Think about it: what else could a tenant ruin that would cost you that kind of money?

You may have guessed that I'm not in favor of carpeting. It looks nice. And it's easy to put down. But the cost may outweigh the benefits. Of course if you buy a house built on a concrete slab, you probably won't have a choice. Carpeting may be your least expensive option. I only put in new carpeting when I have no better choice.

Choosing Carpet

If you do decide on carpeting, either because it suits your decorating scheme or because the floor is beyond repair, what kind should you choose? You have to consider color, texture, and style to determine what looks best.

Color— Trends in carpeting change almost as fast as clothing fashions. Carpeting that's outdated makes a house look tacky and unstylish, even if it's in good condition. For instance, if you buy a house that has orange shag carpeting, you'll have to take it out even if it's in reasonably good shape. Stay away from high fashion colors that will be out of style quickly. The more conservative the color, the longer its appeal.

Light-colored carpets are fairly neutral but they're not very practical. They show every little spot and stain. Unless you have some compelling reason to go with a light shade, don't. Stain-guard is supposed to protect carpeting from stains — but I've found that it guards against all types of dirt except the kind that gets on *my* carpet. And stain-guard doesn't help a bit when it comes to cigarette burns and other physical damage. Burns really stand out on light carpeting.

Dark solids are easier to care for than light colors, but they're still not ideal. Stains and burns are less apparent, but lint and other light-colored streaks are far more evident on darker shades. A medium to dark multi-colored carpet is your best bet for long wear. I prefer something in a varied pattern, like a gray tweed. It's not a uniform color, so dirt, stains, and burns tend to disappear into it. And, gray is a very neutral color.

Now, obviously, if you have a buyer lined up for your house, you can give them the option of choosing the color of carpeting they want. After all, once you sell, the carpeting is their problem, not yours. Just make sure the sale will go through before you put in pale blue carpeting! If there's any chance you'll be keeping the house for a while, *you* choose the color.

Texture— You also need to pick the texture of the carpet. You can get shag, plush, level-loop or Berber. Level-loop is a low, hard-textured carpeting. It comes in plain, or sculptured styles and is frequently used in offices and commercial establishments. It wears well. And in tweed-type patterns, it doesn't show dirt. But it isn't very homey. Also, because of its smooth texture, any cuts, burns or patches will show up. You can't cut out damaged sections and replace them using this type of carpet. The seams will show. The same applies to Berber.

My favorite texture of carpeting is plush. Plush is like a short shag, but it's much neater and smoother looking. It's made of narrow strands and isn't looped like shag. I prefer carpeting that has a pile deep enough to be soft and flexible, but short enough that it doesn't mat down. This is what I call plush.

There's a big advantage to carpet with this texture. If it gets torn or burned in spots, you can brush the plush pile over the defect and it won't show. Of course, this only works for a small defect, like a minor cigarette burn. Another advantage is that you can patch in pieces to replace damaged areas. This is difficult to do, however. It's hard to hide the patch completely unless you're a professional carpet installer. They can often do this type of repair flawlessly, as long as the patch is an exact match. Patching carpets is one of those last-resort techniques that you use if there are no other alternatives, short of recarpeting an entire room. But I like having a way to make emergency repairs at a fairly low cost.

Used Carpeting

When I have to lay carpet in one of my houses, my first choice is to put in good-quality used carpet. You can often find almost new carpet for next to nothing, sometimes even free. This overcomes the biggest drawback of carpeting — its high cost.

People spend thousands of dollars for new carpeting and decide to change it before it's hardly been walked on. Or maybe they buy a house or take over an office with new carpeting and it doesn't match their color scheme. Well, if they don't want it, I'll take it. I can always find a use for it. Sometimes you can have second-hand carpeting just for saving someone the cost of hauling it away. Watch for ads in the newspapers, sometimes under the giveaways.

Let your friends and associates know that you're interested in used carpeting. People in the building and decorating trades often know of large quantities of carpeting that someone is going to dispose of. An ideal source of used carpeting is commercial buildings. Commercial carpeting is usually high quality and wear-resistant. One advantage of commercial carpet is that it usually comes in large pieces. Even if it's worn in some spots, you can probably find big-enough pieces in excellent shape to cover each room in an average-sized home.

The carpet should look nice in the house or you shouldn't use it, even if it's free. It's false economy to ruin a beautifully remodeled house by putting in carpeting that doesn't do it justice. *Never use second-hand carpeting unless it's in like-new condition.* And never volunteer any information about the carpeting. There's no need to explain where the carpet came from.

Second-rate carpeting— I distinguish between what I call second-hand carpeting and second-rate carpeting. If some of your carpeting is usable, but not in like-new condition, it still may be useful. How about carpeting the attic? If your attic has a floor, adding carpeting will give you a nice, soft surface on which to store things. Stored objects won't get scratched, and the carpet adds insulation. People don't mind if carpet in the attic is a little worn (although it shouldn't be dirty or snagged).

Other areas can benefit from used carpeting as well. A small basement storage area or a garage workshop can be brightened up with carpeting, even if it's a little worn. And, it doesn't have to be installed perfectly; people aren't going to entertain there. Still, the area will be more cheerful and more inviting than before. Many women like to have the laundry area in the basement carpeted. It gives a warmer feeling and is easy on the legs. Every little bit helps.

Padding— Watch for good used carpet padding too. Many people think they have to replace the padding every time they replace the carpet. Often the padding is still like new. I've picked up mountains of perfectly good padding for free, and it even *smelled* new. You'll always be able to use padding. It doesn't have to be all in one piece or the same color. It can easily be patched together since it isn't going to show. All that matters is that all the padding in a room be roughly the same weight or thickness.

Other Floor Coverings

Carpeting isn't the only choice you have for floor covering. You can also install wood, ceramic tile, slate, sheet vinyl, or asphalt or vinyl tile. Each has advantages and appropriate uses in a fixer-upper.

Sheet vinyl and vinyl or asphalt tile— Vinyl or asphalt tile make very good floor covering when used in the right places. I use a lot of sheet vinyl and vinyl tile in kitchens, bathrooms and basements. I would never use it in a living room, dining room, or bedroom.

In the 1950s, bright-colored asphalt tiles in living rooms and bedrooms were stylish. Some of the houses I buy still have them. If they're covering up a good oak floor, I pull them up. Otherwise, you can usually lay carpet right over them. There's a slight danger here of moisture accumulating between the carpet and the tile, giving off an unpleasant, musty odor. Where I live, the climate is dry enough for this not to be a problem. But if you're in Florida, or Hawaii, or one of the more humid areas of the country, it's probably not a good idea.

I don't leave tile down in the main part of the house unless it's very cheap property — and only then if the flooring is in excellent condition. It would have to look *very* good before I'd want to keep it. We'll discuss these floor coverings more when we get to the rooms that are more suited for their use.

Wood— Many types of wood flooring materials are available. Some are squares, like tile squares, others are interlocking boards. Most are prefinished oak or teak and are ready to be glued in place just like vinyl tile.

These products look nice but are very expensive, about as much as the best ceramic tile. Because of the high cost, I don't use them very often. If you expect to make any money on a mid-priced house, you can't install floor coverings like these except in very small areas like the entry — to give prospective buyers the right first impression. Of course, if you can get a super deal on them, by all means go ahead. But if you have to pay regular price, you'll find it's cheaper to put in carpeting.

Ceramic tile and slate— You can install ceramic tile or slate in the entry or vestibule to add a touch of luxury to the house. It is also nice around the fireplace. Of course, these floor coverings, like wood, are expensive and not easy to install. As long as you install only a few square feet, however, the cost isn't prohibitive.

Does this seem a little crazy after I just told you to scavenge used carpeting for the living room? Why pinch pennies there and then spend extra money to add elegance to the entry? Are we trying to cut corners and get by cheap, or are we trying to do a luxury job? Actually, both. The object is to turn a fixer-upper into the nicest possible house, for the least possible money. You want to end up with a nice house and make money, so you only put in the luxury items you can afford. A few luxury touches here and there give an overall impression of more.

Here's my rule: Any time you can save money without cutting quality (at least, not cutting it very much), do it. Any time you can add luxury without spending too much, do it. If you do both of these diligently, you can produce a much nicer house for a much lower price than your competitors.

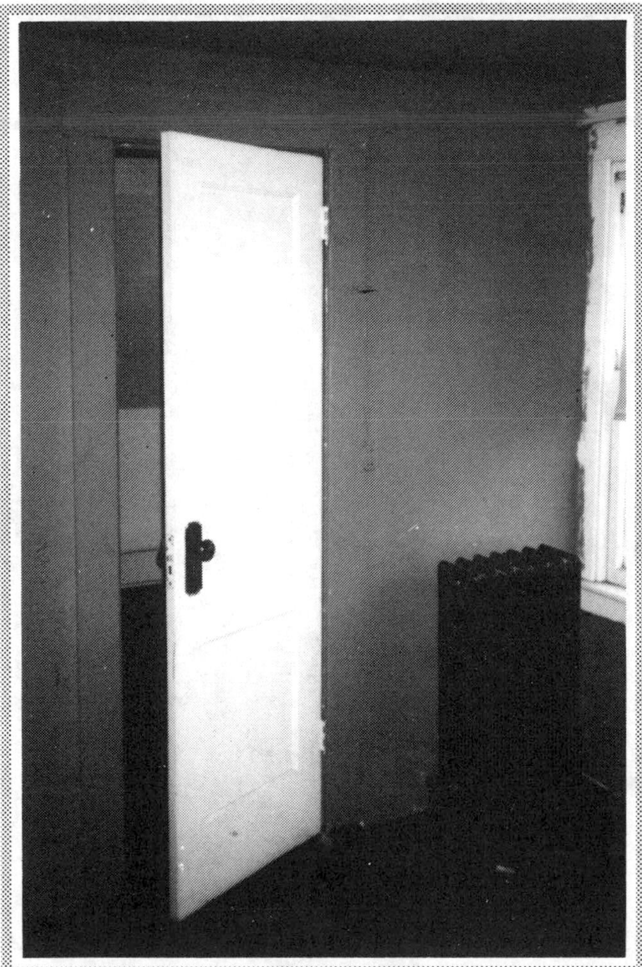

Figure 8-11
This claustrophobic room was painted royal blue — including the ceiling

Repairing the Bedrooms

Bedroom repairs are just about the same as living room or dining room repairs. The main difference is that bedrooms should have a simpler, more restful decor.

The decor in some of bedrooms I've restored has been pretty wild. Part of your repair task may be returning the room to a more conventional condition. The bedroom in Figure 8-11 just required a new paint job, although it took three coats of paint to cover over the bright royal blue walls and ceiling. The radiator was brilliant red and the doors and windows trimmed in white. Although it was patriotic, I got a headache from the colors. I couldn't imagine trying to sleep there.

Another odd decorating scheme I recently removed was the pecky cedar shingle wall covering shown in Figure 8-12. The natural wood finish had been painted over and several shingles had fallen off. The room looked pretty rough. I tore off the shingles, put up drywall and then wallpapered the room. It now looks like the bedroom it's supposed to be. These are fairly typical bedroom jobs. The only other significant problem I have with bedrooms is missing or mismatched doors.

Bedroom Doors

Bedrooms have more doors than other rooms. Every bedroom has at least one door and many have two or three. This is especially true in older homes where two bedrooms sometimes share a common bath or sunporch. You have doors for each of these exits as well as for small walk-in closets like the one in Figure 8-13. It's nice if all the bedroom doors match. Often, they don't. Trying to match doors is one of the biggest problems I deal with in bedroom repairs.

It's hard to match doors in an older home, especially if a door is stained instead of painted. Painted interior doors that don't match will look nearly the same when painted the same color. So, if you have mismatched doors that are already painted, you might as well apply a fresh coat of paint and leave them. But if a stained door doesn't match, it would be a shame to cover the natural wood tone. I try to find a door that comes close to matching. As long as the doors are similar in style and wood finish, a small difference won't be noticed.

Finding a door— As I mentioned earlier, I always save any usable old doors I come across. I can usually find a door in my collection that's nearly what I need. As long as they're the same general type, they'll pass. But I wouldn't mix modern doors and old-fashioned doors, or doors with totally different finishes.

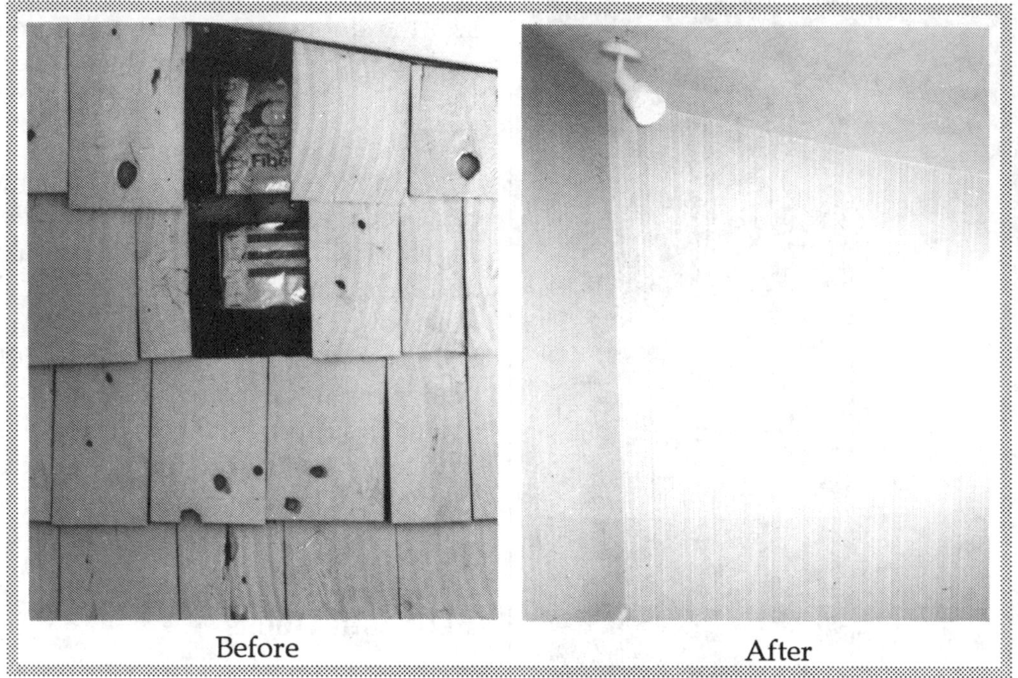

Before After

Figure 8-12

New drywall and wallpaper make a more pleasant atmosphere

Sometimes you can't find a door that comes close to matching the other bedroom doors. In that case, you may be able to steal a closet door from another room in the same house, as long as the doors are the same size. Most codes require that bedroom doors be at least 30 inches wide, but closet doors are often narrower. So if you can find a matching 30-inch closet door, you're in luck. You can move it to the bedroom doorway and you've solved most of the problem. Replace the closet door with something attractive, like a mirrored door. People will think it's an improvement, rather than an attempt to deal with an awkward situation.

If all else fails, you can probably buy a door that will come fairly close to matching the style of the other bedroom doors. Several manufacturers offer old-fashioned style doors. However, they are usually expensive. Buying one of these doors should be your last alternative. But do something. It's better to buy a new matching door than leave obviously mismatched doors in place.

Figure 8-13

Walk-in closet with wood finished door

Figure 8-14
Mirrored closet doors help make this bedroom look larger and better

Closet doors— Closet doors are often missing altogether. I prefer not to use doors that are a completely different style for closets. But this is just my preference. When you have to replace a closet door, one way to blend the new one in is to paint it to match the room. Of course, it won't match the other doors in the room, but it won't stand out either.

Replace bypass sliding doors with mirrored doors if you want to upgrade the bedroom. They add a nice touch and also make a small room appear much larger and brighter. The bedroom in Figure 8-14 is a good example of how mirrored doors improve a bedroom. This room seemed rather ordinary before, even with its built-ins. Now it *looks* like the master suite it is.

Before we go on to the kitchen and bathrooms, let's take a brief look at one of the features I'm always happy to find in a house — a fireplace.

The Fireplace

Fireplaces are a luxury in a low-cost home. Most of the homes I buy were built as low-budget housing. Few have a fireplace. But some have been upgraded over the years by the addition of a fireplace. Occasionally, one of the older houses I bought was actually built as a luxury home and had a lot of extra features, like fireplaces. I look for these extras when I'm buying for resale, though probably only about a quarter of the houses I've remodeled have had fireplaces.

A fireplace and a formal dining room are two items high on the list of special features that people look for in a house. Fireplaces are especially in demand in colder climates. They can add several thousand dollars to the value of a home. But there are a few people who don't care about either the value or pleasure you can get from a fireplace. They consider it a drafty nuisance. Some people even seal up the fireplace and panel over it. Take a look at your roof. Do you have more than one flue pipe coming out of it? Or more than one chimney? If so, what does the second one connect to? Maybe there's a fireplace hidden away under the paneling or wallboard. Don't be too surprised.

Fireplace Maintenance

Fireplaces need a little maintenance, and people who live in handyman specials never maintain a fireplace. Luckily, they don't use them very much, either. They just stow their trash in them.

The fireplace will probably need to be cleaned. The flue becomes coated with soot and creosote. A little bit is deposited with every fire. The more it's used, the more build-up there is. If it isn't removed, the deposits can catch on fire and a chimney fire can easily burn the house down. If the house goes up in smoke the day after you've sold it, you'll probably get some of the heat. It's best to clean out the fireplace and chimney as part of your fixing up.

I bought and use a set of fireplace-cleaning tools. It's a messy job, but doesn't take very long. Cleaning the fireplace yourself gives you the chance to check it over carefully.

You'll also need to clean the ash dump. This is the area under the floor where ash can be dropped. Most fireplaces have an ash drop so you don't have to carry the ashes out through the living room. I always find them full — of ashes and other trash. I've even found ash drops with thirty-year old beer bottles and cigarette packs. It's hard to believe that no one had cleaned out the dump for 30 years! But the proof was there.

Masonry Repair— You'll probably find more loose bricks and crumbling mortar on a chimney than on any other masonry in the house. I suspect that repeated heating and cooling causes the mortar to deteriorate. This is one of the things you'll discover while you're cleaning. Check the masonry while you're cleaning it. Expect to do a little mortar repair here and there.

Another place to check for loose bricks is at the top of the chimney. The last few bricks on the top tend to come loose, probably from weather exposure. Look the chimney over while you're up checking the roof for leaks. If the chimney needs repair, do it while you're there. Don't wait until bricks fall on someone's head.

Leakage— Look at the area around the chimney for signs of water leakage. You may find it on the ceiling near the chimney, on the walls, or even in the basement. It's amazing how far dripping water can travel before it falls off and causes damage.

Chimneys usually leak because the flashing is either deteriorated or missing. Flashing should cover the joint where the chimney meets the roof. Do-it-yourselfers often don't understand the need for flashing and don't bother with it when doing roof work. Cut-rate roofers know better, but they don't care. I've seen brand-new roofing jobs where the deteriorated flashing was ignored. I had one house where the space between the roof and the chimney was so big you could clearly see light all around the chimney from inside the attic. Obviously, in a rainstorm, gallons of water would have poured in through the opening.

Installing flashing is a lot of trouble. Nobody likes to do it, including me. But flashing isn't optional. If your flashing isn't in good condition, make some repairs before the next heavy rain.

Paint— Sometimes you'll find fireplace masonry that's been painted. It's too bad, because masonry looks better unpainted. Once painted, it's hard to undo. There isn't any practical way to get the original brick finish back. You can wire-brush the paint off, but then the brick will have that slightly odd, orange color you see on restored brick buildings. Personally, I don't like this color on fireplaces. Restoring brick isn't worth the effort.

My preference, once the brick has been painted, is to simply repaint it white. It looks much nicer than orange, and there's a valid architectural precedent for this. French chateau-style brick homes are often painted white. If you paint the fireplace white, it'll look like you were following the French-chateau style, not like you were trying to cover up someone else's mess.

One time I painted over previously unpainted masonry. I had to. The fireplace was badly damaged and a lot of repairs were needed. A coat of white paint covered it all up. The result wasn't as good as the original brick finish, but it certainly looked better than the patches.

Mantels

When an owner panels over a fireplace opening, the mantel usually gets tossed out. If you remove the paneling, you have a fireplace again, but a major part is missing. Don't give up. Look around in a few antique stores, used furniture stores, flea markets, or junk shops. I've seen many perfectly good antique mantels offered at reasonable prices. You might even find one for just a few dollars at a garage sale.

If you can't find a used mantel, buy a new one. There are quite a few manufacturers who make them. One I like is *Morgan Products*. They have a very attractive brochure, with many styles to choose from. You can write for a brochure at:

Morgan Products, Ltd.
Oshkosh, WI 54903
(800) 435-7464

I'm sure they'd be happy to refer you to the nearest dealer. Some companies make mantels to order, but they're very expensive. Don't buy a new mantel until you've given up on finding an inexpensive used one. Even if it costs you several hundred dollars to restore your fireplace, do it. Even in a cheap house, restoring an attractive fireplace adds more to the resale price than it will cost.

That's about all you're likely to have to repair in the living room, dining room and bedrooms. Now let's move on to the *big* jobs — the kitchen, bathrooms and basement.

CHAPTER NINE

The Kitchen, Bathroom and Basement

The Kitchen

Kitchens are the most heavily-used rooms in most homes. For many families, the kitchen is the center, common meeting place. That's why your house should have an attractive and functional kitchen.

Another reason is that if any room in the house has an influence on whether or not your house sells for a good price, it's the kitchen.

At least half the appeal of any kitchen lies in the decorating, which I'll cover in later chapters. The balance of its appeal is based on how functional it is — how well it's laid out for daily use. When you decide on what work has to be done in a kitchen, consider improvements in the layout as well as the usual repairs.

What Will You Find?

Kitchens in the houses you buy will usually be in bad shape. That's probably why I end up devoting the most time and money to the kitchen and baths. These are rooms that your future buyer will really care about. Doing a good job on the kitchen and bath can make a tremendous difference in the appeal and value of your house. They're worth the work.

Unlike the living room and bedrooms, the kitchen isn't just a box. It's a work area. You have to make sure it's equipped for the job of storing and preparing food. If it isn't laid out adequately or the appliances don't work, you'll have to make it right.

The Walls and Ceiling

The kitchen ceiling, like other ceilings, should be smooth and white. The only difference is that you should paint it with a water-resistant gloss enamel. Otherwise steam from cooking may make the paint peel.

Use a semi-gloss enamel on all the painted surfaces in the kitchen. An oil-base enamel is best. It's the most durable, and easiest to clean. Many kitchens don't have much wall visible; it's taken up by cabinets and appliances. You may not have to make any surface repairs. But if you do, simply use the same techniques you'd use for the other rooms. Patch the holes and cracks to make a nice, smooth surface for painting.

Wallpaper— Wallpaper is decorative, but it's also a great way to cover up small flaws. Brighten up your kitchen with wallpaper. Small holes, bumps, cracks, and imperfect repairs will disappear. Paper won't cover large holes or lumps, but it does cover repairs that aren't quite perfect — and would be obvious defects under paint. Any little defect shows up on a painted wall.

Use washable vinyl wallpaper for the kitchen, and remember to use a moisture-resistant adhesive. Otherwise, steam from cooking will make the wallpaper peel off. Good-quality wallpaper is expensive, but there's usually so little wall surface to cover in the kitchen that you can afford to splurge here. You'll probably only need a couple of rolls.

My wife always buys wallpaper when she finds a good bargain. A while ago she bought some beautiful, top-quality wallpaper, marked down from $30 a roll to $1.99. That paper is going to save me some cash later and add quality to some job I do in the coming months.

The Kitchen Cabinets

The kitchen cabinets are probably the first things your prospective buyers will notice when they enter the kitchen. You need plenty of cabinets and they need to look nice. Generally, handyman specials have too few cabinets and those that are there are in poor condition.

Buying a complete new set of top-quality cabinets could easily cost several thousand dollars. Kitchen cabinets are expensive. One of the advantages I have over many other renovators, including remodeling contractors, is my determination to keep my costs down. I can make a profit on a house that others pass by. According to their estimates, there's no money to be made on it. One of the easiest places to get carried away with costs is in the purchase of kitchen cabinets.

When you shop around you'll see items like the "European style" 32mm cabinets which you'll find very appealing. You'll think, "Hey, this is a great deal. They look terrific and cost less because you have to assemble them . . . and they're not even that difficult to work with!" It's easy to get caught up in good deals like these. But they're not inexpensive enough or a good enough deal to suit *my* budget constraints. The only time I would buy something like these is if I was redoing a very expensive home. I'd have to have a high profit margin in order to afford this extravagance.

You may think I sound silly and miserly, but you wouldn't believe how costs mount up! On my last project, I scavenged, scrounged, re-used, and repaired anything I possibly could, and I *still* spent over $20,000 on materials alone! If I hadn't been absolutely strict about cost control, I could have easily spent five times that much — and kissed my profit goodbye. I wouldn't be long in this business working like *that*!

There's no trick to building a gorgeous kitchen. Give me $20,000 or $30,000 and I'll build you a kitchen your friends will drool over. The challenge is to make your kitchen look like a magazine ad, without spending the kind of money that designers use to create that look. And you can — but you have to work at it. Buying a whole new set of beautifully-finished cabinets is

Figure 9-1
Inexpensive oak cabinets

Figure 9-2
New glass cupboard doors complete the unit

the easy route. The working man's route is to make your cabinets look like a new matched set and spending just a few hundred dollars to do it.

How can you provide good cabinets without destroying your budget?

First of all, I never buy top-quality cabinets. Most of the cost of these is in the finish. I usually buy the least expensive wood cabinets that I can find, provided they're decent-looking and sturdy. If they're cheap and flimsy, they never look good, even when they're new. My first choice is plywood cabinets. They're usually both sturdy and inexpensive. You can install an entire set in a kitchen for only a few hundred dollars. Buying them unfinished saves money, too.

Occasionally I use inexpensive oak cabinets like the ones in Figure 9-1. These I reserve for small spaces or where I need to blend with existing cabinets. I don't usually put in a whole new set; even inexpensive oak is expensive when you're dealing with more than one or two cabinets.

Sometimes I'll rebuild a cabinet rather than replace it. The cabinet in Figure 9-2 was in good condition, but the doors were missing. I built new glass cupboard doors and restored the unit to the style of the rest of the kitchen. It was easier to do than you might think. I used stock 1 x 4s for the frame, fastened at the corners with flat corner irons. A thin strip of wood beading made an edge for the glass to rest against. I set the glass in the way you would for a window, and filled the gaps with wood putty. Once the doors were painted, the wood putty blended right in. The whole job took about two hours. Even a beginner can do jobs like this — you don't have to be a master carpenter. Sometimes a simple repair can revitalize the whole kitchen. Evaluate what you have and try to work with it.

Figure 9-3
Remove obsolete tin cabinets like these

Can these cabinets be saved?— You'll almost always have to do some work on the kitchen cabinets, but that doesn't always mean replacing them. Real wood cabinets may just need a face lift. But tear out cabinets made of cheap metal, plastic, Masonite, or crumbling particleboard. Trying to make repairs will be a waste of your time and money. Figure 9-3 shows a typical metal cabinet and sink. I don't hesitate to replace units like this.

Figure 9-4
Old cabinets make good work benches

You can do a great job refinishing kitchen cabinets, but you need good basic material to work with. A sturdy wood cabinet, even if it's damaged or has pieces missing, will turn out beautifully. But if the base material isn't any good, you're wasting your time. It's better to clear them all out and start from scratch. You don't necessarily have to throw the cabinets in the trash. Cabinets that aren't good enough for the kitchen might be very handy in the garage or basement. People appreciate extra storage space in those places, and no one expects top-quality cabinets in the garage. As long as the cabinets aren't falling apart, you can find some useful purpose for them.

The old cabinet in Figure 9-4 became a basement work bench. I covered the sink top with a piece of sturdy plywood that I had on hand. The

Figure 9-5

A new oak cabinet added a lot to this kitchen

result was a perfectly good work area. The kitchen got the new inexpensive oak cabinet unit shown in Figure 9-5.

If the cabinets are just tired-looking or out-of-date, a good paint finish will update them. If you add some nice-looking new hardware, you'll be amazed how attractive your kitchen will become. Select paint and hardware carefully and the result can look like a completely new kitchen.

I've had some kitchens where refinishing the cabinet doors was all that was needed to turn an unpleasant, unattractive kitchen into a cheerful, stylish one.

Finishing cabinets— I prefer to buy unfinished plywood cabinets and apply the finish myself. Most homes have stained cabinets. That isn't practical with plywood. The laminated edge of the plywood shows through stain and varnish. So I usually paint the cabinets. It's surprising how nice inexpensive cabinets can look with a good paint finish. I've seen painted kitchen cabinets in very expensive luxury homes. Don't think that all kitchen cabinets have to be stained. Decorators paint cabinetry to harmonize with a decorating scheme. If you select a decorating scheme that harmonizes with painted cabinets, your buyers will be suitably impressed. They'll admire your kitchen, and never think that your object was to save money.

The important part of this decorating idea is the quality of the finish. You *have* to have a good paint finish. You can't just slop some paint on the cabinets. That's never the right approach. Do quality work. You need a smooth, flawless surface. If the surface of the cabinet is dented or scratched, repair the damage before you paint. Drips and dust in the paint won't do; the finish must be furniture-quality.

If you don't know how to apply a furniture-quality paint finish, that's another handy skill you should learn. It's rather a lot of work, but you'll use it again and again. You'll find step-by-step instructions on achieving a perfect paint finish in *Paint Contractor's Manual*, published by Craftsman Book Company. There's an order form for it at the back of this book.

Figure 9-6
White paint and new knobs transformed these cabinets — and the kitchen

I use only oil-base paint for cabinets. It's far superior. Some builders may be surprised to hear this. You've probably been impressed by all the advertising for latex paints that promise superior results. And, of course, with latex paint you can clean brushes with soap and water.

I've found that the new improved paints, like so many other things in our modern world, aren't really better, just *cheaper*. Latex paint is a lot cheaper than oil-based paint. It's also easier to apply. However, for most uses, it's utterly inferior. It doesn't adhere well, it doesn't wear well, and it doesn't protect surfaces well. Sure, it's easier to clean your brushes. But the object of the job isn't to have clean brushes, it's to have a good, durable finish. I'd much rather have a good finish, even if I have to throw the brushes away!

Oil-base paint will adhere to almost anything. I've even had good results using it over surfaces that you're not supposed to paint, like plastic. If I need to paint anything other than a plain, flat-paint interior wall, I use oil-base paint.

You can't always find oil-base paint at discount stores. You may have to go to a regular paint-and-wallpaper store and pay full price for it. That's a major drawback, in my opinion. I'm very cost-conscious. But if I'm willing to pay extra for something, you can believe it must be worth it.

Cabinet hardware— Your choice of hardware is very important to the overall effect of the kitchen cabinets. It's the visual focal point of the cabinet. This is especially true of painted cabinets. The painted surface is smooth and uniform. Your eye is drawn to any object that stands out, in this case, the handle, knob, or pull. Many of the cabinets I buy don't require handles. They have a lip on the underside that you can use to open them. I put handles on them anyway just to dress them up.

Good hardware makes a plain cabinet look expensive. It also diverts attention from any small defects that may make someone suspect that the cabinets are cheap. I spare no expense on kitchen cabinet hardware. I will sometimes spend several dollars per knob. That's a lot of money when you consider how many knobs are needed and how much cheap hardware is available. But a beautiful knob adds so much to the kitchen that the extra expense is worth it. Even the most expensive hardware will only add up to about a hundred dollars for the entire kitchen. The extra expense adds a lot more value to the kitchen, which pays off in the selling price.

The kitchen in Figure 9-6 had dark brown cabinets against black wallboard wainscoting. I painted the cabinets white and added pink knobs to match the pink tile on the countertop. I also put up pink and white wallpaper and painted the woodwork in the kitchen with the same semi-gloss white as the cabinets. The transformation was startling. The dark, dingy kitchen turned into a bright, stylish and very attractive room. The cost: $200.

How many cabinets do you need?— Most kitchens don't have enough storage space. I've never heard anyone say, "I don't like this kitchen. It has too much cupboard space!" On the other

Figure 9-7

Add cabinets to increase kitchen utility

hand, too little cupboard space is a serious drawback; one your prospective buyer will notice immediately. They may decide not to buy your house because of it.

Provide as much cabinet space as you can reasonably fit into your kitchen. Large areas of blank wall are nice in other rooms, but in a kitchen, that's wasted space. The kitchen wall area shown in Figure 9-7 was empty. The hookups for the stove and refrigerator were there, but no counter space and no storage area. I added the overhead storage and the center divider. Not only did these cabinets provide much-needed storage, but they gave the impression of built-in appliances and a "modernized" kitchen.

Suppose the kitchen cabinets in your house are sturdy and in reasonably good condition, but there aren't enough of them. You'd like to add more, but you can't find new cabinets that match the old ones. Unmatched cabinets just won't do. Should you tear out the perfectly-good cabinets and replace them, or settle for less cabinet space so everything will match?

I've had this problem a number of times. A couple of years ago I bought a house that needed substantial remodeling. The kitchen cabinets were custom-made and in good condition, but they were ugly. Replacing them would have been difficult and expensive, since the standard sizes didn't fit in the same space. Most of the cabinets were walnut-colored Formica in a simple, modern style. However, one floor unit was an Early American style, in a light wood. The kitchen needed at least one more large cabinet to provide adequate storage.

Figure 9-8
Paint and hardware blend mismatched cabinets into one style

I found that I couldn't match either of the styles that were already there. If I bought another cabinet for extra storage, I'd have three different styles of cabinets in the same kitchen. With all the other work I had to do, I simply couldn't see replacing all the cabinets just to make them match. My solution was to paint.

I painted the walnut Formica cabinets white. Paint Formica? Sure! I sanded the surface lightly to give it tooth, and used a quality oil-based paint. A latex paint would never have adhered to this surface. The paint would have beaded up. Oil-based paint, however, worked fine. The Early American cabinet took a little more work. Since all the styling was on the doors, I decided to replace them. I made a plain, plywood pull-out door that matched the modern style of the other cabinets. I'm not a finish carpenter, but even I can cut a couple of rectangles out of plywood and add hinges. I painted the door white and attached new, matching hardware. Figure 9-8 shows the painted cabinets with their new hardware.

What about the new cabinet? It didn't match, so I painted it white like the rest. I found a cabinet style that was nearly the same as the existing cabinets. It blended right in once it was painted and fitted with the same brass hardware. I ended up with a kitchen full of new-looking, matching cabinets, at minimal cost. All I had to buy was one cabinet, a gallon of paint and new hardware. I've done this several times, and always with good results.

Countertops

Because of all the wear and tear they're subjected to, kitchen countertops are rarely in good condition in the homes I buy. And they're usually too small to meet the needs of most families. I always try to put in additional countertop space if I can. Most people have more countertop appliances than they have countertop for. Even with half of them stored away, the remaining counter space isn't enough for normal food preparation. So add more if you can.

The problem, of course, with adding counter space is the same as adding cabinets. You have to match the existing tops. The best way to blend everything together is to redo them all the same. How you handle this depends on the type of countertop you're working with.

Luxury materials— You aren't likely to be dealing with some of the more exotic materials that are now available for kitchen countertops. For example, the shelter magazines today usually feature synthetic materials, like DuPont Corian. It's very expensive to buy and install, and it can be easily damaged. The advantage of this material over something like laminated plastic is that it can be repaired. Burns and chips can be sanded out and smoothed over.

Some European styled kitchens are using stainless steel countertops. Stainless steel is hard to damage, but very expensive. I've also heard of builders using oak. This must be for a kitchen that is strictly ornamental! It certainly isn't very practical for everyday family life. Like any wood surface, nicks and scratches can be sanded out. And a bar top or resin finish can help preserve the wood. But I never use materials like these and don't recommend them for anything but luxury homes.

Ceramic tile— I like ceramic tile countertops in kitchens. The look says "quality." But I don't use tile very often because it's hard to install and it's expensive. But if you're going to add a small countertop to a kitchen that's already tiled, you'd better stick to the same material. As long as you don't need a large quantity, it won't cost too much. Matching colors can be a real problem, though. If you have old tile and you can't match it, the only choice may be to replace all the tops with something less expensive.

If you want to add tile for accent, small quantities may be available at small prices. Odd lots of tile are often drastically marked down — sometimes for as little as $1.00 per square foot. Of course, installing tile is still a lot of trouble. But at least the tile cost will be small.

Formica— One of the most common materials for countertops is Formica-covered particleboard. It comes with a built-in splashback and is available by the foot in a variety of colors. It's easy to clean and water-resistant. The only major drawback to Formica is that it's easily damaged with a cigarette or an ordinary knife. You can't use any type of laminated plastic as a cutting board. And it will burn or scorch if hot pots are laid on it. But it looks nice when it's properly installed, and the price is right. So I generally use Formica in my kitchens.

I also replace the existing countertops with Formica when I add a new Formica top. This keeps the kitchen together visually. And if the countertops match perfectly, prospective buyers may not notice a minor mismatch in the cabinets.

Sometimes I don't replace all the tops, even if they don't match. A kitchen I worked on recently had two countertops. One was in poor condition, but the other was perfect. The bad countertop had to go, but I hated to tear out the good one. I had some especially nice ceramic tile in my garage, and it occurred to me that this tile would look good in that kitchen. I covered the damaged countertop with the ceramic tile and left the other one alone. The tile provided an interesting contrast to the other design elements of the kitchen and yet blended well with the existing top. The combination worked. It was less trouble than replacing all the countertops and it was considerably less expensive.

Repairing damaged countertops— Sometimes you can salvage a damaged countertop by setting ceramic tile into the damaged area. I insert a ceramic tile accent in the damaged area of the Formica. This works best when the countertop is in good condition but has one damaged spot. The damaged area will most likely be where food is cut up or next to the range where hot pots seem to get placed. What would be more natural than to insert a small tile surface there?

Tile, or even a nice wood cutting block, is just what's needed for those areas.

With a router, cut out an area the size of the insert. Set the tile into the Formica flush with the surface. It will look like it was designed to be there.

Use only the nicest tiles for this type of job. Since you're only installing a small area, like one square foot, the price of the tile isn't a problem. If you browse around tile stores, you'll find some beautiful tiles. You can install solid colors to carry out a color scheme, or use ornamental designs which make their own statement. Your buyers will be impressed by your effective design rather than wondering what the tiles might be covering up. I once inserted a 12-inch square marble tile into a damaged counter and added a small touch of luxury for only $7.99.

The Kitchen Floor

Have a look at the kitchen floor joists from below if you can. The framing is more likely to be damaged here than anywhere else in the house — except possibly the bathroom. Long-term plumbing leaks can cause local rot damage. It's best to fix it now, before the floor falls completely.

Kitchen floors may also be damaged or weakened during remodeling. If the remodelers moved plumbing lines, cabinets, doors or a stairway, the framing may have been cut or altered. It's best to do this investigation before you buy. Solving structural problems can be expensive and seldom add much to the resale value of the home.

Even if it's structurally sound, the kitchen floor on a fixer-upper will probably need work. It's rare when you don't have to replace the floor covering. I have to replace the kitchen floor cover in nearly all of my homes. One exception I remember was a fixer that had a beautiful quarry-tile floor in perfect condition. But the rest of the kitchen had to be totally redone!

Oak floors in the kitchen— Even in the kitchen, it's worth your while to peek under the floor covering to see what you can find. There might be oak or some other good-quality surface that's been buried for years. Before we were married, my wife bought a house with an ugly linoleum floor in the kitchen. She considered tiling right over it, but it had such deep gouges that she had to pull it up. The linoleum was laid over wood underlayment. Under that was more ugly linoleum. And then another layer of underlayment. She dug through three inches of junk before she hit pay dirt — oak flooring. She sanded and varnished the oak and wound up with a beautiful floor for only a few dollars.

Unfortunately, even if you find oak, you may find that linoleum was glued right to the oak. This will ruin any oak finish. As a rule, it's not practical to try to restore the oak after this has happened. It's just too much work. Occasionally, though, very old glue will have turned to powder. Then the linoleum will come right up. It's always worth taking a look. With a good, heavy coat of varnish, oak makes a beautiful kitchen floor.

Chances are, though, you won't be salvaging too many oak floors in the kitchen. Even if you find oak, it's more likely to be unsalvageable in the kitchen than in any other room of the house. And, though oak flooring is very nice, I'd never go to the expense of installing oak if it wasn't already there.

Carpeting— During the 1970s, carpeting in the kitchen was quite popular. The fad didn't last long, but then, neither did the carpet. Kitchen carpeting gets dirty very quickly, and about the only thing you can do is replace it. Even though kitchen carpeting is cheap, if you have to replace it often enough, it can become expensive. If you buy a house with carpeting in the kitchen, replace it with a better grade of flooring. Everyone knows that kitchen carpeting is cheap, so it makes your house seem cheap. That's not the impression you're trying to create.

To be honest, I tried installing kitchen carpeting in one of my first houses. I had some carpet on hand that had been given to me. It seemed like such a cheap and easy way to deal with the kitchen floor, I couldn't resist. I thought it looked pretty nice when I was done, but the reaction I got from the people who saw it was universally bad.

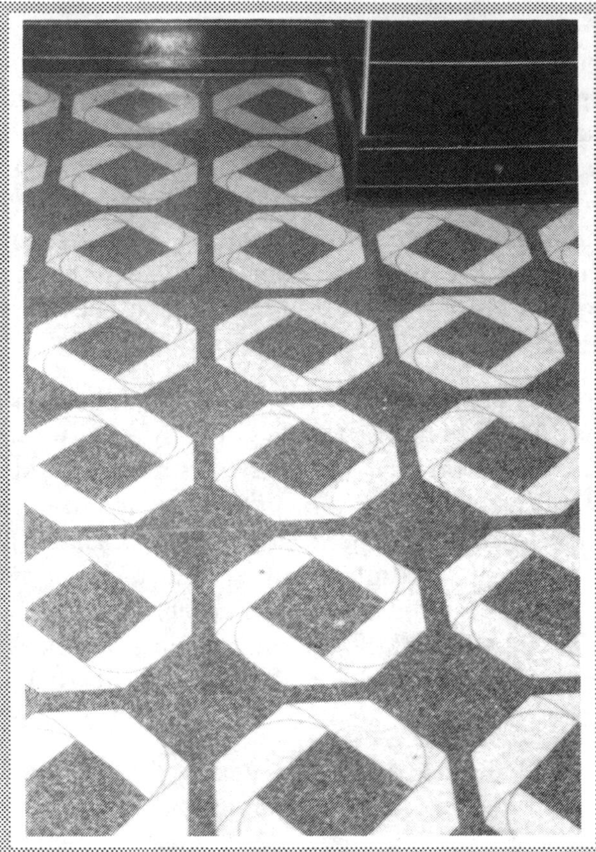

Figure 9-9
Choose good-quality vinyl flooring

Everyone said some variation of the following: "Kitchen carpet? I hate carpeting in the kitchen! How can you keep it clean? It never looks fresh! Why don't you put some nice floor tile down instead?" After a while, I got the message. I took up the carpeting and put in some cheerful-looking vinyl tile. The house sold right away. That was all the convincing I needed.

Vinyl tile— Most of the nicer floor tiles on the market today are made of some type of vinyl. Asphalt tiles are also available, but they don't look quite as good. I only use asphalt tiles in basements and utility rooms.

The kitchen floor isn't a good place to economize. It gets heavy wear and your buyers are going to spend more time checking out the kitchen than any other room. The kitchen floor should look nice. Don't try to save a couple of dollars by buying cheap tile. Buy good-quality, brand-name floor coverings. If you can save money by purchasing it on sale or in a factory closeout, fine. But don't compromise on quality. It doesn't have to be the very best money can buy, but it has to be at least average quality and a good brand. Don't bother with cheap or second-rate flooring. In the long run, it will cost you more than better quality goods.

You can get vinyl flooring in 12-inch squares or room-size sheets. There are advantages to using sheet vinyl. It makes a smooth, even surface. If the kitchen walls aren't parallel, use a pattern without lines or squares. That makes out-of-square walls less obvious.

Since sheet vinyl doesn't have seams, water can't seep in. This is important if you're installing the floor covering in a very wet area. Here's another advantage to sheet flooring. Sheets don't have to be glued tightly all over the surface. You can install them over a poor surface that might not hold glue well. Just make sure that the edges are secure. With vinyl tile, you have to be sure that each individual tile is glued firmly in place.

On the negative side, sheet flooring is harder to install. And you probably won't find as many choices in color and style in sheet vinyl. That limits my creativity a little. For example, I like sheet vinyl with a pattern in my color scheme. That makes it easier to carry a theme throughout the kitchen.

Figure 9-9 shows a vinyl tile floor I installed in a kitchen. It's a two tone, gray on gray. It looked very sharp against the black wallboard, and added nicely to the room's Art Deco scheme.

Surface preparation: I've found that you can skip some of the surface preparation the floor tile companies suggest. They recommend installing fresh underlayment every time you put down a layer of tile. But I've had good results installing new tile right over old tile, as long as the old tile is clean, solidly attached and has a smooth surface pattern. Getting the tile surface clean is sometimes half the job. I've worked on some floors where the layer of grease and dirt was so thick that it would almost have been easier to put down underlayment than clean the floor.

Remember, glue doesn't stick to grease. The floor must be clean.

I've only found underlayment to be necessary when the old floor coverings were crumbling or coming off, and the surface under that wasn't much better. There's no point spending all day trying to dig down to a better surface. There may not be one. It's easier to just put some fresh underlayment over the top. But installing underlayment is also a lot of work, so don't make that choice until you've eliminated your other options.

Self-stick vs. regular tile: I've had some problems with self-stick tile. Over a very smooth, clean surface, they usually have enough glue to stick. But if your surface isn't perfect, which is often the case, there may not be enough glue on each tile to get a good hold. I don't use them if the surface where I'm applying the tile has any problems. You can compensate for surface problems by adding more adhesive when you're using regular tiles. Of course, you can do the same with self-stick tiles, but you then eliminate the advantage you paid extra for. You might as well buy regular tile and apply your own glue.

Ceramic tile— Ceramic tile is beautiful. I'd love to use it in all my kitchens, but it's too expensive for a large area. People don't expect to see ceramic tile kitchen floors in moderately-priced homes. If you should happen to stumble across a great bargain on nice ceramic tile, then it might be worth considering. But only if your house will be selling at a premium price. Then you can justify that extra expense. In a medium-priced home, your buyers won't be able or willing to pay extra for ceramic tile.

Ceramic tile is much more difficult to work with than resilient flooring. You can't cut ceramic tile with scissors or a knife like you can cut vinyl tile. Ever try to cut a piece of ceramic tile into a complex shape? It's enough to make you tear your hair out. Just when you think you've got it exactly right, it breaks into a million pieces. After a few experiences like this, you may seriously consider going into some other line of work.

There's one more drawback. Ceramic tile must be installed on an absolutely stable surface, with no bounce or give. If the surface moves even a little bit, the grout will break loose and the tiles will pop out. A floor that's suitable for vinyl may need a lot of reinforcing before you can install ceramic tile. If your house has a basement, you may be able to reinforce the kitchen floor from underneath. But I rarely find that all the extra trouble and expense is worthwhile. If I can't put in tile easily, I just don't do it.

Other floor coverings— I've seen kitchens in magazines with wood planks, teak parquet, marble, and other luxurious flooring materials. These materials are very expensive. But I wouldn't use them in a kitchen even if I could get them for free. They just aren't practical. They damage too easily: marble chips and wood floors are vulnerable to water damage. Of course, if there's already an oak floor in the kitchen, I'd keep it. A heavy coat of varnish will help keep it reasonably waterproof. But as I said earlier, I wouldn't want oak flooring in the kitchen if it wasn't there already.

The Bathroom

Most older houses have one main bathroom near the bedrooms and a second convenience bathroom on the main floor or sometimes in the basement. The second bathroom is often just a half-bath, or a lavatory. Focus your attention on the main bathroom. Prospective buyers will scrutinize it closely. If it isn't up to their expectations, they may pass your house by.

Bathrooms, like kitchens, are very heavily-used rooms. And like kitchens, they must be convenient and able to stand a lot of use. What you find in most older homes is damaged, worn out bathrooms.

The Bathroom Walls

At one time, ceramic tile was the standard wall cover in bathrooms. Bathrooms had tile wainscoting, tile counters, tile floors and tile shower surrounds. If you're lucky, you may find an older house with some of this tile still intact. Ceramic tile is a very durable material.

But even if all the tile is there and still in good condition, the bathroom will look outdated. Styles change in bathroom design. Fixture styles change too. When one or two fixtures are replaced, the tile may look out of place. Tile that used to be in harmony with the design begins to clash with new additions.

Suppose you have a ceramic tile bathroom that looks outdated and awkward. What should you do? I recommend that you leave all the tile that's still in good condition. Instead of changing tile, change some of the other design elements. For example, change the wall color to blend with the tile. It's easier to paint and wallpaper than to tear out tile and replace it.

Alternatives to ceramic tile?— Suppose the tile really has to go. Should you replace old ceramic tile with new ceramic tile or should you install something else in its place? It's probably easier and cheaper to put in some other kind of wall covering. Imitation ceramic tile board products are available, but I don't recommend them. Most of them not only *are* cheap — they *look* cheap. Instead, I recommend using more tile. People value ceramic tile. They expect it in the primary bathroom. That isn't a good place to cut expenses.

Real ceramic tile will give your house a solid, quality look. Buy and install good-quality tile. Remember, the biggest cost of ceramic tile isn't usually the tile, but the labor to install it. It's a big job. And it's just as much work to install cheap, poor-quality tile as it is to install the good stuff. So don't waste your money and all that work on cheap materials.

You don't have to use tile everywhere. People expect the tub area and the floor to be tiled. It's nice if the walls are tiled too. But with most decorating schemes, it isn't really necessary. I've seen houses where every inch of the bathroom was tiled, including the ceiling. It looked very nice, but I couldn't justify the expense. If it's done already, keep it. If not, use paint or wallpaper on the bathroom walls. My rule is this: always use good-quality ceramic tile, but only tile as much as is expected. Tile is too expensive and too much work to get carried away with.

Salvaging damaged tile— Since I consider ceramic tile to be an absolute necessity in a primary bath, I go to great lengths to save the existing tile. Creative repair techniques have helped me save tile that most remodelers would have torn out. Since I've never seen these ideas mentioned elsewhere, I'll share some them with you.

Finding a match: You'll often find bathrooms with nearly all the tile in good shape except for a few missing pieces. You're stuck with an ugly-looking hole. How do you deal with this?

Well, you'll never be able to buy tile to match. Even when you buy brand new tiles, different lot numbers of the same tile, from the same manufacturer, in the same store, at the same time, won't match. There's no chance of finding tile that will match tile sold many years ago. But don't give up, you can still make the repair. It simply requires more creativity.

While you can't match existing tile from a new source, there is a source of matching tile — the bathroom itself. Take tile from one area and use it to repair another. Aren't you just trading one problem for another? Yes, but hopefully you can trade a big problem for a little problem.

You can often take tiles from hard-to-see corners or from behind the toilet. I've taken tile from an inconspicuous corner, made a repair with that tile, and then filled the corner with the best match I could find. Since the scavenged tile was part of the original tile work, the repair matched perfectly. The replacement tiles in the corner didn't match exactly, but no one noticed because the corner wasn't well lighted.

If you do this kind of repair, don't mix old and new tiles on the same surface. Replace all the tiles in one area. Only mix new and old tiles if you can do it in an area that's hard to see, like behind a corner toilet or under an enclosed sink.

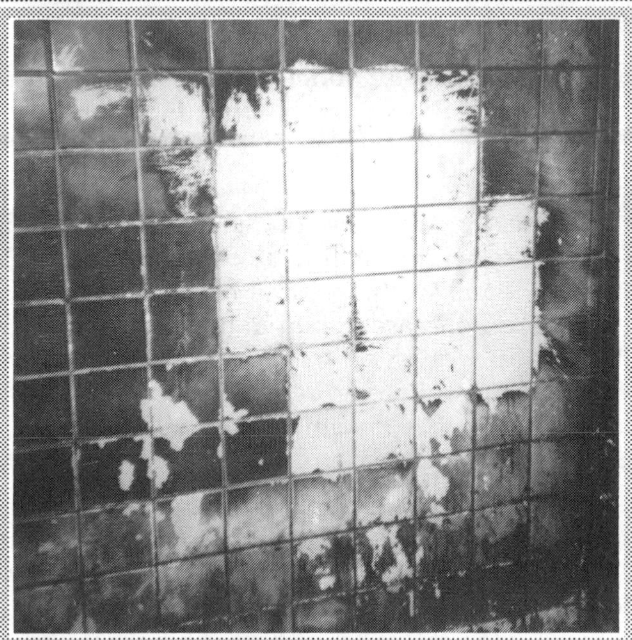

Figure 9-10

Epoxy paint peeling off of ceramic tile

Uncovering hidden tile: Do-it-yourselfers seldom try to repair ceramic tile, even if it's only slightly damaged. They just cover the tiles with some other material, like imitation-tile hardboard. If you find imitation-tile hardboard in a handyman special, take a peek under the hardboard. You may find salvageable tile. Of course, the former owners may have driven nails through the ceramic tiles and smashed them when installing the hardboard. Then the tile won't be salvageable, but you may find enough good pieces to repair the sink top or floor.

Occasionally you may find hidden tile in perfect condition. Someone may have covered it simply because they didn't like the color. Then you're in luck. You'll be able to salvage an expensive tile job at no cost. It always pays to peek under any removable surface. You never know what you'll find. Ceramic tile, like oak flooring, is worth preserving.

Adding accent tile: What if your bathroom is just a plain square, with no hidden areas you can borrow tiles from? You still have another option. Try changing the tile design. You could take out a row of tiles all the way around the edge of the room, and replace it with a row of contrasting tiles. It's quite an attractive technique if it's done well. You can then use the tiles you removed to repair damaged or missing tiles elsewhere.

Use contrasting accent tiles to make an attractive pattern on the wall. You may even devise an accent pattern that covers most of the broken or missing tiles. That way, you won't have to move many of the existing tiles.

Your tile dealer probably has brochures that suggest ways to use accent tiles. I've even seen a video that describes how to use accent tiles effectively. Accent tiles can be quite expensive. But if you're only using a few of them, it's certainly cheaper than replacing all the tile in the bathroom.

What not to do: Once, one of my neighbors had his bathroom tile painted with epoxy paint. He paid about $1,000 dollars to have this done. It looked very nice. So I bought some epoxy paint and painted the bathroom of one of my houses (this was one of my first renovation projects). The paint cost about $50. I was pretty pleased with myself. That was one twentieth of what my neighbors had spent!

If I had sold the house right away, that would have been the end of the story, at least as far as my awareness was concerned. But there was a serious recession at the time, and houses weren't moving. So I rented the house out instead of selling. After a few weeks, my tenants called to tell me that the bathroom was disintegrating. It was! The epoxy paint was peeling off. It was an awful-looking mess (Figure 9-10). I was glad I hadn't sold the house. My name would have been mud.

Had I applied the paint wrong? I checked with my neighbors to see how their epoxy-paint job was holding up. Theirs was peeling, too. It looked just as bad as mine — and they were upset! I'd say about twenty times as upset as I was. I had to scrub all the epoxy paint off the tile. It hadn't bonded properly to the tile surface. That at least made scrubbing it off somewhat easier. But it was still a big job.

Once I'd cleaned off the paint, however, I had to do something with the bathroom. I had painted the bathroom tiles because there were some pieces missing and I couldn't find any

Figure 9-11
Replace outdated and inconvenient sinks

matching replacements. So I had filled in the spaces with odd tiles I found around the house and painted everything to match. Now I was back where I started.

As part of my bathroom remodeling, I had installed a vanity to replace the original sink. It occurred to me that the wall behind the vanity had tile. Well, nobody was going to miss that tile. It didn't even show. I carefully removed the tiles I needed and used them to replace the ones that didn't match. It looked like new. Too bad I hadn't done that in the first place!

Moisture Damage

There's a lot of moisture in bathrooms. Think of the steam that rises when you take a hot shower. Where does it go? Most of it escapes out the window, door or through a vent. But a lot is left to soak into walls, ceiling and floor. Very few construction materials can tolerate constant moisture without showing the effects.

The most common problem created by excess moisture is peeling paint or drooping wallpaper. If you see this type of damage in any other room of the house, suspect a leak, probably from the roof. In the bathroom, however, it may be caused by simple condensation. Another common result of excess moisture is mold and mildew. I've seen bathrooms that were covered with it.

Luckily, this type of moisture damage is easy to fix. Mildew will wash off. Scrape off peeling paint and wallpaper and replace it. I always use a good oil-based paint in the bathroom. Oil-base paint won't peel from condensation. When you put up wallpaper in a bathroom, be sure to use vinyl with a moisture-proof adhesive. Self-stick paper won't do.

If you have moisture or condensation problems, consider installing a bathroom exhaust fan. It will help keep the bathroom dry and fresh-smelling. Building codes require them in bathrooms without windows. If your bathroom has a window but you still have excessive moisture, a fan will solve the problem. The fan must be vented to the outside, not into the attic. If you vent it to the attic, you'll simply transfer your moisture problem there.

Bathroom Plumbing and Fixtures

Most likely, some of the plumbing in your bathroom will need repair. Again, don't try to economize in the bathroom. If you must replace fixtures, use good-quality, brand-name fixtures and materials. Often you can update or improve the looks of existing fixtures by simply replacing faucets and handles.

Sinks— Your bathroom should have a nice sink. Nearly every sink in a home is used several times a day. Prospective buyers will certainly notice how the sink looks. If it's ugly, stained or worn, they won't like it.

Bathroom sinks aren't terribly expensive. It's better to replace a worn or chipped sink than try to repair it. But don't throw the old sink away if it's still in reasonably good condition. It may not be good enough for an upstairs bathroom, but it may be perfect for a basement lavatory. People are less particular about fixtures in the basement.

I usually replace old sinks like the one in Figure 9-11 with a new bathroom vanity. They come in all styles, sizes, and colors. A bathroom

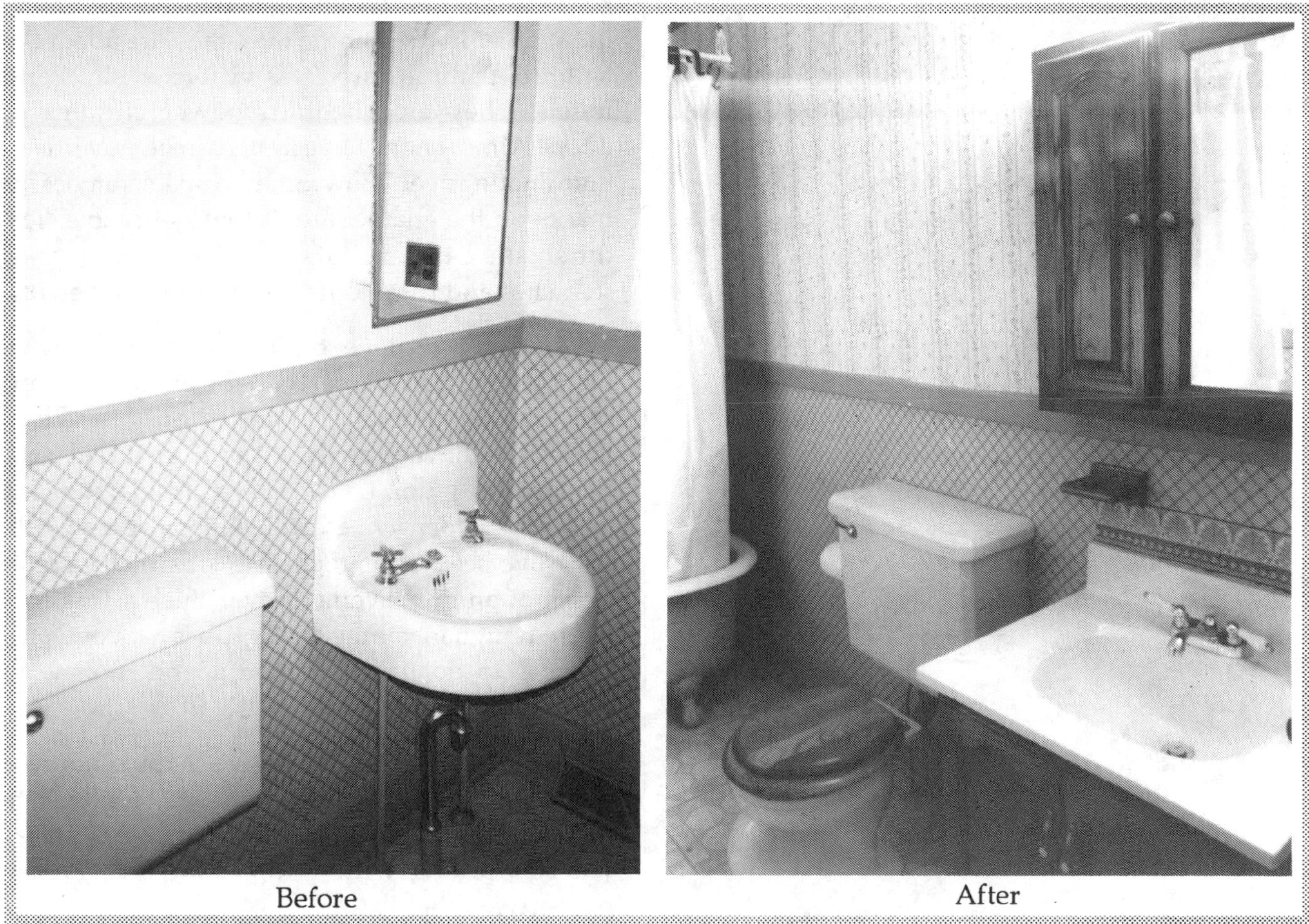
Before After

Figure 9-12
Replacing old fixtures can improve an unattractive bathroom

sink without a vanity is very inconvenient. It may be the only storage space you have room for in a small bathroom. And bathrooms, like kitchens, never seem to have enough storage space.

The price range for vanities is very broad, from less than $100 to well over $1,000. But you don't have to spend $1,000 to get an attractive, well-made vanity. I usually pay about $100. Your buyers expect a nice bathroom sink and an attractive vanity. But they won't pay $1,000 extra for a super-deluxe model. Figure 9-12 shows a bathroom in one of my homes before and after I remodeled it. The extra convenience and good looks of the finished bath came at a small price — just a vanity and matching mirror cabinet.

Faucets catch the eye, so make sure your faucets are attractive. Even if you decide to save the existing sink, consider replacing the faucet. If the sink is almost good enough to keep, a nice new faucet may make the difference.

Toilets— Toilets never wear out. The mechanical parts inside them do, but the china fixture itself will last forever, unless it's damaged by impact. You rarely have to replace a whole toilet.

Make sure the toilet is clean and works properly. If it doesn't work, replace the worn parts, but be careful. It isn't easy to break a toilet, but it can be done. You can crack the china if you overtighten the bolts.

Figure 9-13
Shelf makes tub fit odd-sized opening

If you have to replace the toilet, a plain, white fixture is best. Don't waste money on fancy toilets in decorator colors. Your buyers won't be impressed. You'll get better results spending money on something else.

One thing I *always* replace is the toilet seat. If it blends with the decor, I install oak toilet seats, like the one shown in Figure 9-12. This minor extravagance ($20) adds a nice touch. The toilet seat is highly visible. Spend a few extra dollars and buy a nice seat. It will go a long way towards giving your buyers a positive attitude about your house. People are attracted by small details like this, so I add them wherever possible.

Bathtubs— Most people prefer showers to baths. Buyers are usually more concerned about the shower in their home than they are about the bathtub. Bathtubs aren't as visible as sinks and toilets. They hide behind shower curtains or doors. Almost none have lights directly overhead illuminating every flaw. Small chips, scratches, or marks on the enamel aren't that noticeable. The tub should be clean, however. Removable marks, scratches and rust stains should be scrubbed off.

I don't replace bathtubs unless they're obviously in bad shape. If all the enamel is worn off, or if big chunks are cracked out of the tub, then you'll have to replace it or have it reglazed. Personally, I don't bother with reglazing. It's almost as expensive as an inexpensive new tub. And I've seen poor reglazing jobs that weren't much of an improvement over the existing tub. Even though installing a new tub is a lot of work, I prefer to do it rather than spend money on something less reliable.

If you do need to replace a tub, choose a plain, inexpensive white tub. Again, don't waste money on fancy tubs in decorator colors unless you're working with a top-of-the-line, luxury property.

A few years ago, I bought a house with a dreadful bathroom. Someone had decided to build a little wall around the sides of an old-fashioned tub with iron feet. They built the enclosure out of Melamine panels. Unfortunately, the enclosure leaked, water collected in the wall, and rot destroyed the bathroom floor. The old tub was beyond repair and had to be replaced. The problem was that after removing the tub and surround, I had an odd-sized opening to deal with. It was about 4 inches too long and 8 inches too deep for a standard, 5-foot tub.

I solved the problem with an idea I spotted in a magazine. I used a standard size tub and built a ceramic-tiled shelf along the side. It was just the right size for a soap dish or a rubber ducky. See Figure 9-13. Shelves like this are popular in luxury homes. So instead of looking like an awkward solution to an odd problem, my tile

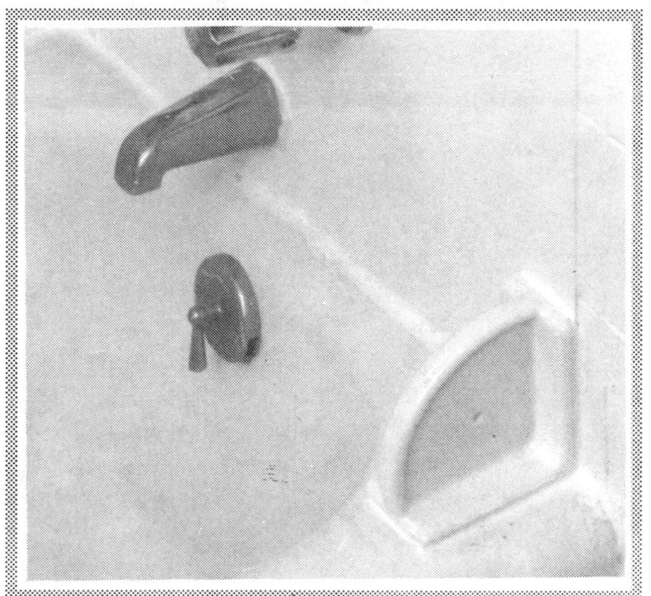

Figure 9-14
A ceramic corner keeps water in the tub

enclosure looked like a distinctive addition. You'll find good ideas like this in magazines published for home owners and builders.

Because most people like showers, I recommend installing one over the tub if it doesn't have one already. Shower installation may be a lot of work, but the cost of materials is small. You should be able to get more money for the house if you add a shower to a bathroom that doesn't already have one.

Another worthwhile addition is a ceramic tub corner like the one shown in Figure 9-14. Some bathtubs tend to dribble water out of the corner, especially when someone is showering. Eventually this will cause a great deal of damage to the floor and walls. This simple little improvement can save hundreds of dollars in future repairs.

If your tub has a shower, but the hardware is in poor condition, try to repair it. Don't replace it. I'll replace washers, re-grind valve seats, polish chrome, and do whatever else I can do to avoid replacing tub or shower hardware. Why? Because I often find that there isn't proper access to the tub plumbing. I don't want to tear up a wall just to replace a faucet. That's many times more work than replacing the faucet, and I don't need extra work. Anyway, I hate plumbing. I avoid doing any more than absolutely necessary.

If the hardware doesn't look as good as you'd like, add a new shower curtain or install shower doors instead. Your buyers may be impressed by the nice new curtain or doors and not mind the imperfect tub hardware.

The Bathroom Floor

Ceramic tile is the ideal flooring for the primary bathroom. Unless you're dealing in inexpensive properties, people expect ceramic tile in the main bathroom. Many older homes already have a ceramic tile floor in the bathroom. Preserve it if you can.

What if you find a primary bathroom with beautiful resilient floor covering? So far, I've never run into a bathroom like this. Resilient floor coverings don't last more than 5 or 10 years. I've seen 60-year-old ceramic tile floors in perfect condition. If you have to work on the floor at all, you may as well install something your buyers will really like. It's a waste of time to replace an inferior floor with something other than ceramic tile.

Water damage— Bathroom floors are the most likely to suffer water damage. A lot of water spills from the bathroom sink and even more from the tub or shower. If the floor surface isn't waterproof, the water will soak through and rot out the flooring. Plumbing leaks left unrepaired cause extensive floor damage, and will eventually damage the walls and ceiling below.

Remember the big hole in the dining room ceiling I had to repair? If you recall, the damage was caused by a leaky bathtub that hadn't been repaired right. Figure 9-15A shows the tub and the floor above that dining room. Loose tiles, mildew and peeling paint were the only signs in the bathroom of a very serious water problem. I

Figure 9-15A
Water leaks can be worse than they look

Figure 9-15B
Examination of the area revealed extensive rot damage

found the floor, part of the wall and a section of the ceiling below completely rotted away. See Figure 9-15B.

First I had to fix the tub. Then I reinforced the subfloor from below and replaced the floor. I also had to repair the ceilings in two rooms below, the walls in those rooms, plus the wall in the bathroom. The last step was salvaging the tile. When I pulled up the flooring, I was very careful to save every tile. When I finished the structural repairs, I reinstalled the original tile to preserve the bathroom decor. See Figure 9-15C. I was very happy with the results. Figure 9-16 shows my renovated "1930s style" bathroom.

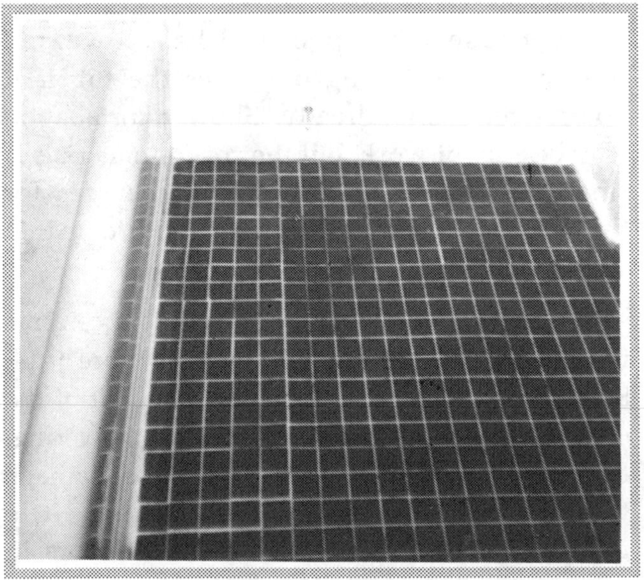

Figure 9-15C
The same area repaired

If you have a job with similar damage, remember to strengthen the floor from underneath. If your bathroom is on the first floor above a basement, you're in luck. If there's no basement, you'll have to work in the crawl space — and you know how I feel about that. Think about it before you buy! If your bathroom is on the second floor, make your repairs as I did. Remove the ceiling below the damage. Replace the ceiling joists from the lower floor. If the problem is severe, the ceiling will probably be sagging into the room below. No problem. That just makes it easier to strip off the ceiling cover.

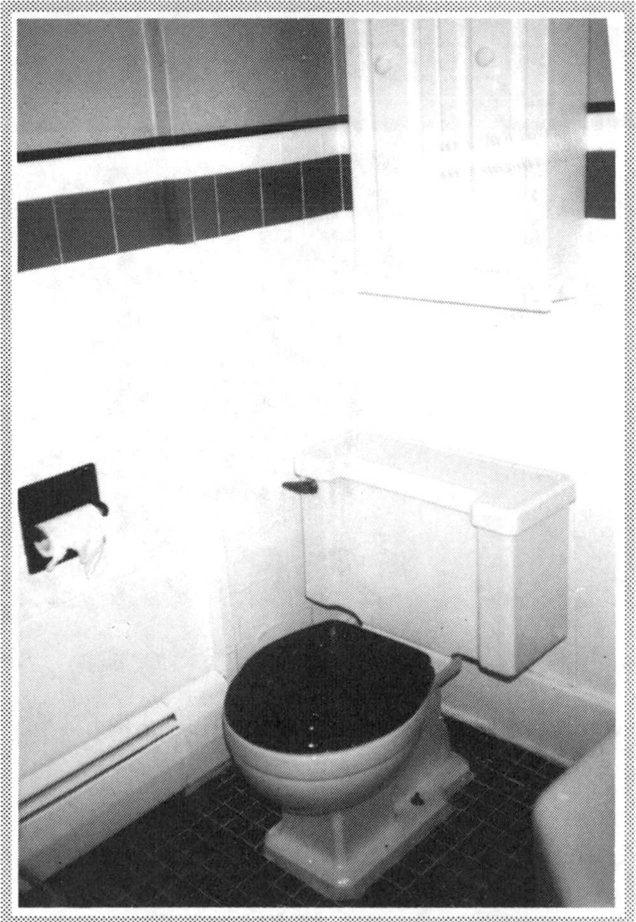

Figure 9-16
Renovated "1930s style" bathroom

The Second Bathroom

Many of the materials I reject for the primary bathroom work quite well in the second bathroom. People are much less demanding about that bathroom. In an older home, you're fortunate to have a second bathroom at all. Often it's just a half-bath downstairs used for convenience.

Since the second bathroom doesn't get the same amount of use as the primary bath, you don't have to worry so much about durability of materials. Melamine panels and vinyl flooring are fine. These materials don't wear as well as tile, but that's only a minor inconvenience in the second bathroom.

I almost always use sheet vinyl in second bathrooms. Vinyl tile has small seams where spilled water can get under the surface, eventually loosening the adhesive that holds the tile in place. You don't have to worry too much about this in a half-bath. But bathrooms with a tub or shower should have a watertight floor cover.

The Basement

Homeowners don't care if the basement isn't up to the standard of the rest of the house. Little nicks, scratches and dents that you would fix upstairs won't matter here. Most people use their basements as a storage, laundry, and workshop area. They want it clean, bright and functional. They don't expect more, but they do expect that much, and so do lenders.

Unfortunately, the bank didn't consider the basement in Figure 9-17 to be a functional room when I bought the house. I had to make repairs before they would approve a loan based on the whole house, including the basement. As you can see in the photographs, I did quite a bit of work to make this an acceptable basement. I added a wall to create a separate utility room, drywalled the unfinished areas and painted. It was a great improvement.

If the basement is in reasonable shape, I usually just add lights, repair broken fixtures, and paint. If I can make it look like the basement in Figure 9-18, I'm quite satisfied, and so are my buyers. Most of the work in basements is usually just cleanup. People leave all kinds of junk behind.

Occasionally I find something valuable, like the antique stove among all the clutter in Figure

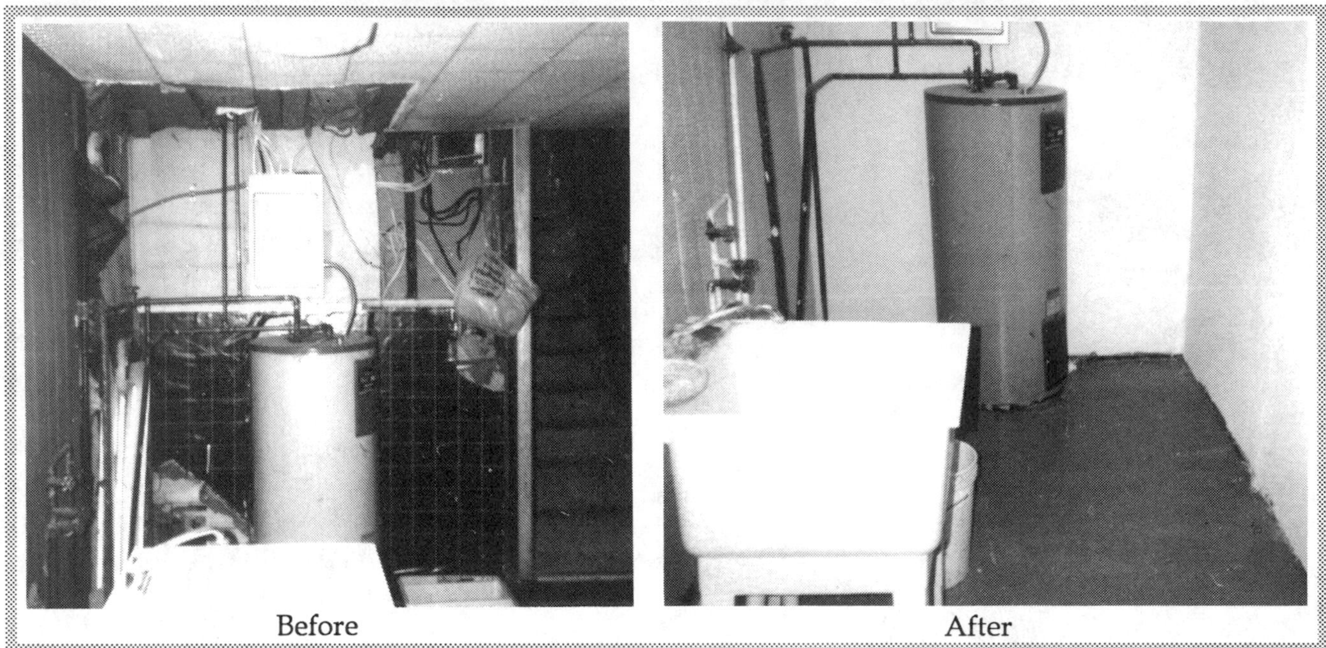

Before | After

Figure 9-17

Drywall and paint made a tremendous improvement to this basement utility room

9-19. This basement was actually in pretty good shape. After all the leftovers had been cleared out and it had been painted, it turned out to be a nice storage and work area (Figure 9-20). And, as a bonus, I got a very good price for the stove from an antique dealer.

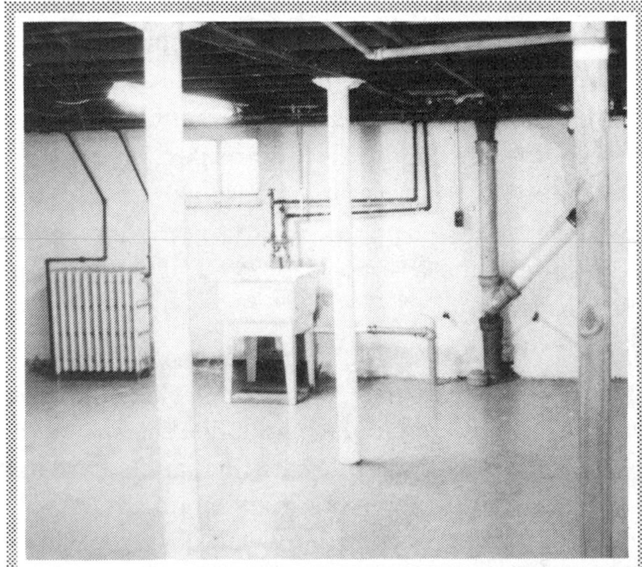

Figure 9-18

Basements should be neat, clean and bright

Finished Basements

As I mentioned earlier, finishing off a basement isn't really a worthwhile investment. It can cost more in money, time and effort than it's

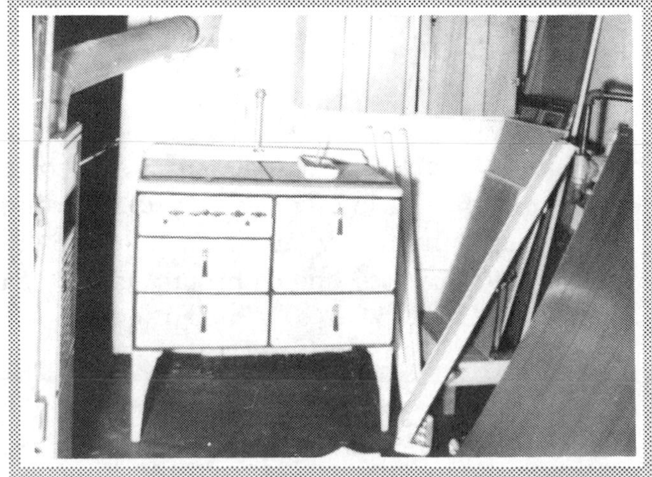

Figure 9-19

Antique stove left among the junk

Figure 9-20
A nice storage area is an asset

worth. Converting basements won't raise the value of the house in proportion to your expenditures. Some people like finished basements. Others don't care. Since you don't know who'll be buying your house, don't invest money and effort in something that your buyer may not even want. Put your resources into something you know everyone will like, such as the kitchen or bathroom.

However, if you buy a home that already has a finished basement and if it's in fair condition, you might as well repair it. Since most of the work has already been done, repairs shouldn't be too costly. If you end up with a cheerful and presentable room for a small investment of time and money, it's worth taking a chance.

I've bought houses with basement renovations that were in very poor condition, so bad that they weren't salvageable. If that's the case, remove the damaged finish materials and turn the room back into a plain basement. A basement room that has to be completely rebuilt isn't worth the effort.

Summing Up Repairs

Repairing a handyman special is a big job. I usually work with one or two helpers. That speeds the work along and is especially important if I have more than one project under way at a time.

I've found it helpful to make job lists, both for myself and my help. A list of what to do and the order to do it saves time and questions. It also helps me organize the tasks in my own mind. Figure 9-21 is typical of the job lists I keep for myself.

I leave lists like the one in Figure 9-22 for my helpers. The lists generally make up about one week's work. My helpers check the list every day. As long as I have all the necessary materials on hand, work should keep going whether I'm there or not. I've had the same assistants working with me for some time, so I can trust them to work with little supervision. Having a small team of workers you can depend on makes the job go much more smoothly. Develop a list of skilled craftsmen you

JOBS ON ROBINDALE

Job	Equipment needed
LIVING ROOM:	
Paint	
Wallpaper	— wallpaper, glue, brushes, sizing
Polish floor	— floor polish
KITCHEN:	
Paint ceiling white	— Walby's white, 2 gal.
Put up new light fixture	— light fixture
Repair wall	— joint compound, tape, spreaders/scrapers,
Paint	
Wallpaper	— kitchen wallpaper
DINING ROOM:	
Paint ceiling	— ceiling white, rollers, pans, brushes, paint thinner
Paint walls	
FRONT BEDROOM:	
Paint walls	— Winter white latex
BACK BEDROOM:	
Fix wall	
Paint wall	
BATHROOM:	
Paint ceiling white	— Walby's white
Repair wall	
Clean/repair tile	— scrubbers, steel wool, cleansers
Fix leak in sink	
UTILITY ROOM:	
Replace bad tiles	— find/bring tiles
Replace laundry tub	
EXTERIOR:	
Prune bushes	— hedge trimmer
Repair garage door	— hanger iron

Figure 9-21

Job lists help organize work

JOBS FOR NEIL & STEVE

PORCH:

Paint everything with Walby's white.

KITCHEN:

Paint cabinets with Walby's white. Be careful not to get paint on the floor.

UPSTAIRS:

Paint knotty-pine room with ceiling white latex.

Finish taping seams in other room, patch holes, and paint with texture paint.

UTILITY ROOM:

Paint walls with Walby's white.

Drywall the new wall (after the frame is up).

Prime and paint drywall. Prime with one coat of latex, then paint with Walby's white to match the other walls.

Paint ceiling tiles with ceiling white latex.

STAIRWAY:

Paint ceiling tiles with ceiling white latex.

BLUE BEDROOM:

Paint ceiling with Walby's white.

Thursday morning is trash pickup, so be sure to take the trash out of the garage and put it out front on Wednesday.

Figure 9-22

Job list for helpers

can depend on and then try to keep them in plenty of work.

If you've completed all the repairs we've discussed in the last few chapters, your house will be fully functional — a decent place to live. You might even be able to sell it now. But if you want to get the best price, you have more work to do.

In the next chapter I'll explain how to make your house even more desirable. To get top dollar, you have to provide more than a warm, dry place to live. You have to build in aesthetic values that appeal to the senses. You have to supply style and eye appeal. Offer what people want, not just what they need. Fortunately, it's not hard. And, most important, you can do it at a modest cost.

CHAPTER TEN

Improvements That Pay Off

Most of what I've talked about so far concerns functional repairs and replacements rather than improvements. To this point I've explained how to make an older, neglected home more like a new home. Making functional repairs isn't my favorite task. Most of these repairs involve a lot more labor than I like to do, and they're usually more necessary than profitable. But neglect these repairs and your house won't sell for any more than you paid for it. That's why I put so much emphasis on repair work.

I hope I haven't left you with the impression that real improvements aren't important. They are. Sometimes it pays to make the home even better than it was when new. That's the subject of this and the following chapter. In the next chapter I'll talk about decorative improvements, adding treatments, textures and colors to make a home more attractive.

The topic for this chapter could be called "adding livability." Most of what I'm going to discuss here concerns correcting design problems — eliminating mistakes that tend to reduce the value of a home. Of course, you can't solve every design problem. In fact, I usually leave well enough alone. But many times a few dollars and a few hours invested can yield a major increase in the selling price. That's an opportunity you shouldn't pass up. I'll suggest how to recognize mistakes in home design and visualize how these mistakes can become your opportunities.

Decisions on improving livability tend to be complicated. You want to improve marketability, but at the lowest possible cost. Some of the projects I'll explore in this chapter can be very expensive, both in terms of time *and* money. That's risky. You have to know what's *worth* doing and what's not. Otherwise these improvements are time and money wasted.

Let's begin with improvements that will make the available living space in the house more convenient for your future buyers. These improvements range from correcting traffic flow through the house to enclosing rooms and adding closet space.

Making Better Use of Space

Some homes are laid out in peculiar and inconvenient ways that make very little sense. For example: a house with wide hallways and tiny rooms. This is a good example of poor livability. People will be cramped and uncomfortable in the tiny rooms while all that space in the hallway goes to waste.

Houses with problems that involve a great deal of reconstruction, such as incorporating hallway space into rooms, require more work than I usually want to do. The best way to deal with houses like these is not to buy them. Moving one wall may be worthwhile. Moving *all* the walls is a waste of your time and money. It's almost easier to add onto the house. You may find a house like this at a very tempting price, but unless there's something really special about it, I recommend passing it up.

Many home improvement manuals are quick to tout the advantages of making modifications for the sake of improving livability. They'll have you moving doors and windows, and shuffling walls around like a deck of cards. That's fine if you're going to live in the house and you're making all these changes for yourself. You know what you like and what you're willing to pay for. But when you're remodeling a house to sell for profit, the modifications must be more than just desirable, they must be necessities. Never do anything expensive and difficult unless you're *sure* that it's going to improve the resale value. If you're in doubt, *leave it alone*. Confine yourself to modifications that *anyone* will like. Otherwise you'll limit the appeal of your house, and waste your time and money.

Simple Modifications with General Appeal

What kinds of modifications appeal to most home buyers? Those that improve the usefulness of the house. For instance, I recently purchased a house with a very odd layout. It was a good-sized house, with four bedrooms and two baths, but it was awkward to get around in. Originally the house had two bedrooms and one bathroom. Later someone added a large utility room at the end of the main hall. Then, two more bedrooms and a full bath were added onto the utility room. It was a confusing arrangement. The only access to the new bedrooms was through the utility room. Since you don't usually expect to find additional living area off a utility room, the bedrooms were "lost."

My first impulse was not to buy the house, but my wife thought it deserved some more consideration. After a second look, I realized that the problem was traffic flow. Figure 10-1 illustrates the point. You can see how the hallway directed traffic into a dead end in the utility room.

I solved the problem by adding a partition and simply extending the main hallway through the utility room. This carried traffic past the utility room and on into the bedrooms. The utility room was large, so taking a section away to make a hallway wasn't a problem. It was then separated off to one side of the hall behind its own door. This is a much more reasonable placement for a utility room. Figure 10-2 shows the hallway under construction and the finished job.

This modification made sense for a couple of reasons. First, it solved an awkward design problem. And second, it required little more than adding a partition. It wasn't difficult or expensive

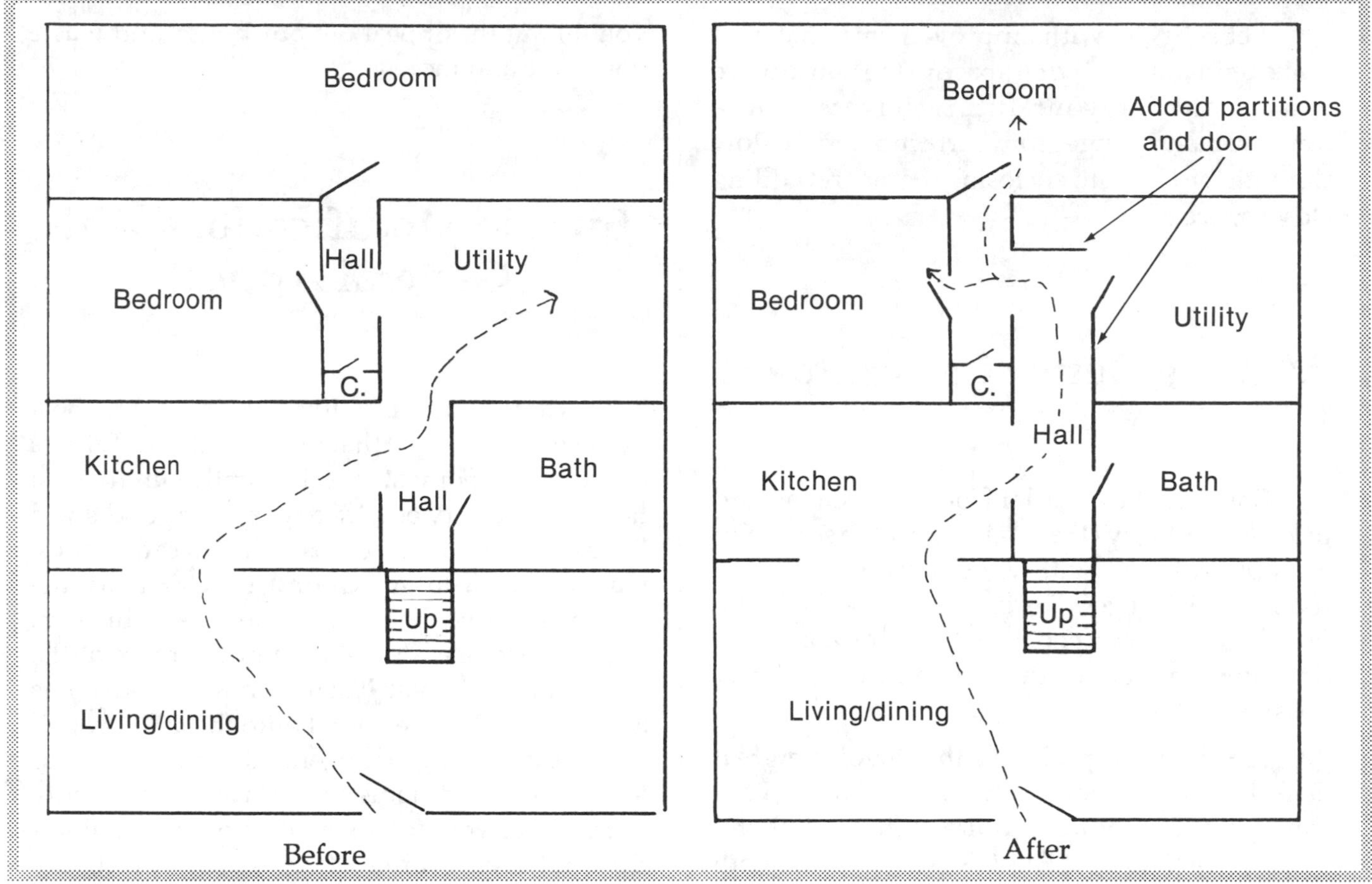

Figure 10-1

The bedrooms were lost, so I had to improve the traffic flow

because it didn't involve any structural changes. It was a good bargain for the money.

Understand this very clearly: I didn't buy the house until *after* I had figured out how to solve the problem. I can't overemphasize this point. Some problems just can't be solved. If you can't think of an easy and workable solution, don't buy the house.

Misplaced French doors— Another home I bought was a California Craftsman-style bungalow. The real estate listing advertised two bedrooms on the main floor and the added feature of French doors. It neglected to mention that the French doors led from the living room into the master bedroom (which had probably been a den or study when the house was built). The former owners had found this layout inconvenient, which isn't surprising. To solve their problem, they had added another doorway leading from the bedroom into the hall.

The problem with the French doors, aside from reducing the privacy of the master bedroom, was that they interfered with the placement of furniture in both the living room and bedroom. The solution seemed obvious — remove the French doors. Since there was already another door into the hall, they no longer served any purpose.

They were pretty, but they just didn't belong there. I removed the doors, filled in the space with drywall, and finished it with wallpaper. Figure 10-3 shows the bedroom wall, before and after the

Figure 10-2

Partitioning off the utility room redirected the traffic flow

modifications. There was very little cost involved, but a great improvement to the usefulness of the room. Of course, I saved the doors for later use.

Unenclosed Bedrooms

Bedrooms should always be private. Only very small children will tolerate a room that's open to any passerby. Yet, for some reason, quite a few houses have been built with small unenclosed rooms that end up being used as bedrooms. I suppose the builders thought that enclosing a small room would make it claustrophobic. This may be the case, but not enclosing them made them unsuitable as bedrooms.

It's usually worthwhile to enclose any space that could possibly be used as a bedroom. If you can enclose an awkward space and advertise your house as having three bedrooms instead of two, or four bedrooms instead of three, you increase its value and marketability. Figure 10-4A shows a small unenclosed room I found in one of my houses. Like many of these rooms, this one was open to the stairwell. All it needed to make it a nice bedroom was to have the half wall finished and a partition and a door added off the hall (Figure 10-4B).

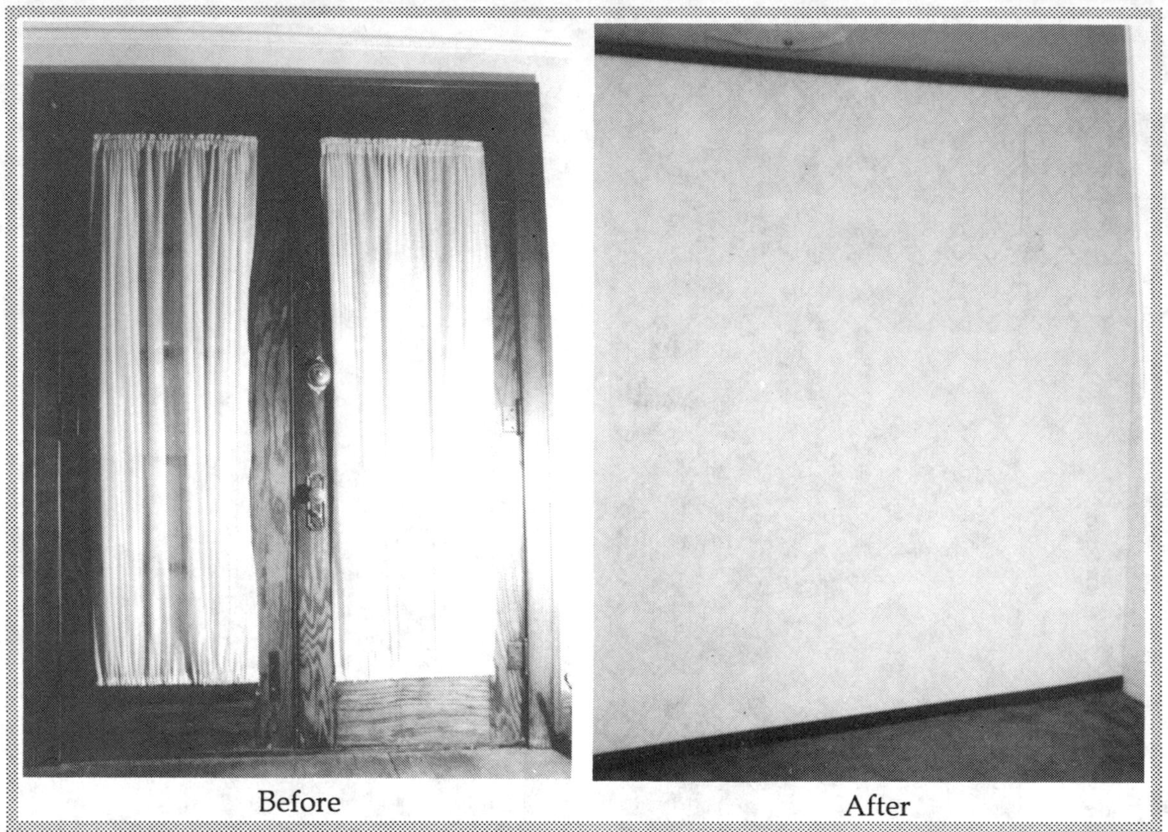

Before After

Figure 10-3

These French doors aren't suitable in a bedroom

What if your house already has four bedrooms? Should you go for five? Not many people need a five-bedroom house, but I still recommend enclosing any extra space. It can be used as a library, hobby room, guest room, or walk-in storage or linen closet. Or, you can incorporate the space into another bedroom as a giant walk-in closet. There are a lot of uses for an enclosed room, but open space is usually wasted space.

Closets

Extra closet space in hallways and bathrooms is always useful, but it doesn't make up for the lack of a closet in a bedroom. Closets are mandatory in main bedrooms. They're simple enough to build — just a box with a door on it. The problem is usually lack of space. Fixer-uppers tend to be small, and often the bedrooms are barely big enough to fulfill their function. If you take a piece out for a closet, the room may be just too small.

Every bedroom ought to have a closet, but I've discovered that you can usually get away with no closet in the smallest, least important bedroom. This room will probably be used as a child's room or sewing room. If there's space for a closet, add one. But if making a closet would make the room unusable, don't. Keep this in mind when you're enclosing space to make extra rooms.

When I enclosed the room shown in Figure 10-4, I had a carpenter add a half-height closet over the stairwell. A full-height closet would have extended too far down into the stairway headroom, creating a potential hazard. But a

Figure 10-4A
This unenclosed space is almost useless

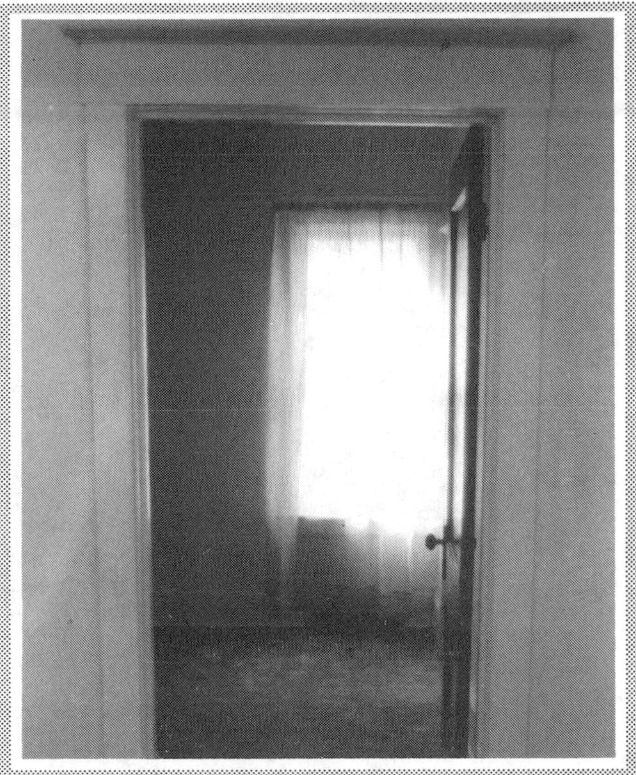

Figure 10-4B
Adding a wall makes a small bedroom

half-height closet left plenty of clearance. It wasn't quite as useful as a full-sized closet may have been, but it was certainly better than no closet at all.

Use a little creativity and you'll find space that might make a good closet. Borrow from an adjoining room or use wasted or underused space. A strange little area that doesn't seem to have any function might be fine for a small closet. Even a tiny closet is better than no closet at all. Figure 10-5A shows one end of a room that I turned into an extra bedroom. The roof slanted down at an extreme angle on one side, creating an area of wasted space. I turned this awkward space into a closet (Figure 10-5B). Not only was it a useful addition to the bedroom, but it visually balanced the room and made it more appealing.

Sometimes you can use attic space for an upstairs bedroom closet. I found a door leading from the bedroom in Figure 10-6 to an unfinished attic storage area. It was dark and dirty, and not very useful as it was. I drywalled it, painted it, added a light, and turned the space into a nice walk-in closet.

Hall closets— Hall closets and linen storage are less important than bedroom closets. You can usually find some place to put your linens. If you have available space in your hallway, by all means turn it into a closet. It never hurts to add closets. However, I wouldn't use bedroom space to create a linen closet.

Bathroom closets— Bathrooms are another convenient place for a closet. I often find a lot of excess space in older bathrooms once they've been modified for modern fixtures. The new fixtures take up less room than the old ones, leaving odd-shaped, unused space. I like to add closets or linen storage in the leftover spaces, especially if the house doesn't have a hall closet.

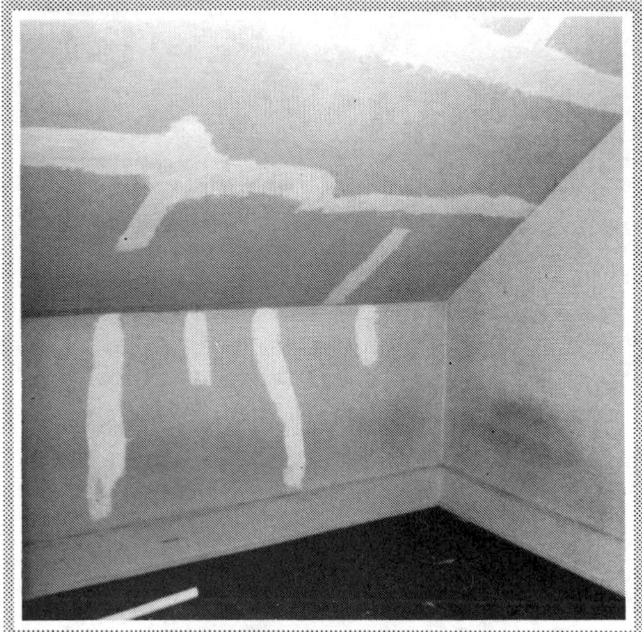

Figure 10-5A
The slope of the ceiling made this area useless

Figure 10-5B
Wasted space is now a closet

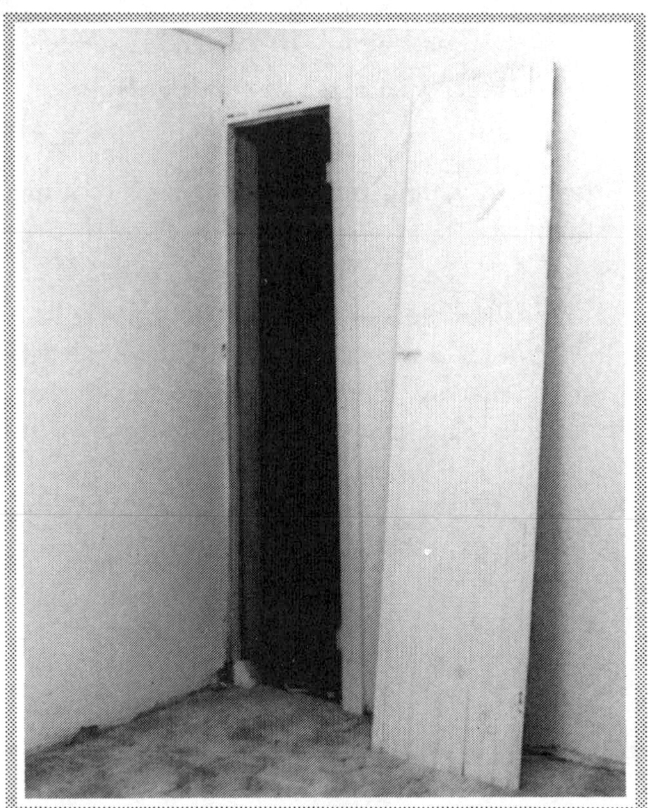

Figure 10-6
Attic storage is now a small walk-in closet

Unenclosed Bathrooms

Once in a while you'll run across a house with an unenclosed bathroom, like a toilet sitting in the corner of a basement. People may use this in an emergency, but they're never happy with the lack of privacy.

You could solve the immediate problem by adding a couple of walls. But if you go to that much trouble, you might as well put in a sink with a mirror as well. Then, instead of an unattractive fixture sitting forlornly in a corner, you have a half-bath. It doesn't have to be elaborate. As long as it's clean, bright, and cheerful, people will be very happy to have it. These simple modifications will only cost a couple of hundred dollars, but will add thousands to the value of your house. The series of pictures in Figure 10-7 shows a toilet fixture (A) in one of my basements that became part of a converted bathroom (B). Figure 10-7C shows the completed job. I even added a shower to this one, further increasing the value of the house.

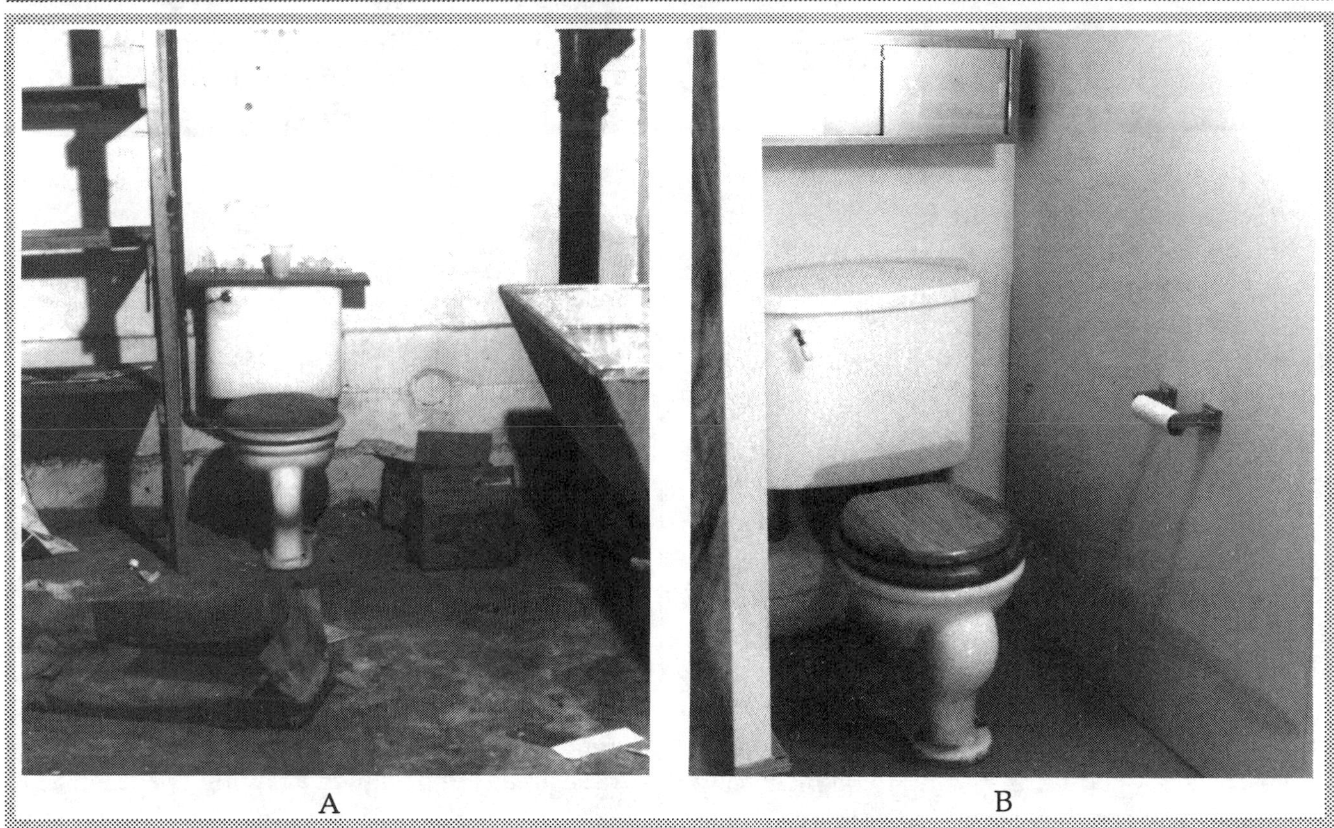
A B

Figure 10-7
I built a bathroom around this ugly basement toilet

Figure 10-7C
The new bathroom is neat, clean, and decent

When to Do Major Additions

You know by now that I try to avoid doing any major construction work on a house. It costs too much, it takes too long, and it's harder for me to make a profit. Once in a while, however, I come across a house that's worth the extra effort. It has to be a house that lacks *just one* important feature. By adding that feature, I can increase the selling price far more than the feature costs.

The most obvious example of this is a house that needs another room. Every house needs a kitchen, a bathroom, a couple of bedrooms, and a living room. Houses do not necessarily need formal dining rooms, dens, family rooms, or more than three bedrooms. If a house lacks one of the mandatory rooms, it's going to be practically useless. If you can think of an inexpensive way to add this missing room, you'll buy the house as distressed merchandise and sell it as quality goods. If a house has the basic rooms but could use a third bedroom or a second bath, consider doing it. These are very worthwhile and profitable additions.

People generally won't buy anything with fewer than two bedrooms. Three bedrooms are best. When you add a third bedroom, you increase the marketability of your house. Instead of a house which is too small for most buyers, you'll have an average-sized house, suitable for the majority of families. How many bedrooms is enough? That depends on the neighborhood. But remember, the biggest benefit in terms of price will come from bringing a house up to three bedrooms. Beyond that, extra bedrooms are desirable, but maybe not worth the extra money.

Adding an optional room, like a formal dining room, will also raise the value of your house, but not as much. However, if there's no other place to eat in the house, then a dining room may be a necessary addition. You can evaluate any house and decide if it's adequate for comfortable living. If it isn't, it may have the potential for a simple addition and a big profit.

Converting Space

When you select property, look for space in the house that can be converted into additional living area. This is the most cost-effective way to add rooms. Most of the work is already done for you. A little finish work may be all that's needed to turn unused space into a valuable bedroom. Porches, attics and attached garages are good candidates for converting into living space. However, while converting one of these areas will cost you less than adding a new room, it will also create some extra problems. After all, none of these areas are designed as living space.

Interior Walls

The most obvious thing these areas lack is finished interior walls. You'll have to finish them with plaster or drywall. In the case of an open porch, you'll have to add the exterior walls as well as the interior ones. But this is one disadvantage that's also an advantage. The open walls will make it a lot easier for you to run electric lines and heating ducts.

If lack of interior walls is your only problem, you're in good shape. Installing drywall (and adding insulation where it's needed) is quick, easy, and cheap. If that's all that stands between you and a finished room, then go ahead and finish it, regardless of whether the room is absolutely needed or not. The converted room will add much more to the value of the house than the simple finishing job will cost you.

Electricity

Most of the spaces you can use for converting won't have adequate wiring. Some will have no wiring at all. This is also cheap and easy to fix, especially if the drywall isn't in yet. For a bedroom, you don't need to add a lot of wiring. Some codes will let you get by with two wall outlets and a ceiling fixture.

If headroom is limited, don't install a standard ceiling light fixture. It will make the ceiling seem even lower. Worse, your buyers may hit their heads on it. Instead, install either recessed lighting that's flush with the ceiling, or a wall-mounted light fixture. Recessed lighting gives the room a modern look, and the fixtures are inexpensive. They're just slightly more than the little bent-glass fixtures that most builders put in bedrooms.

In a room with an old-fashioned look, use wall-mounted fixtures. Spend a little extra and buy something that's particularly attractive. That way, people will focus on the fixture and not the low ceiling.

Heat

Supplying heat is the biggest problem in a converted living area. Everyone knows someone who has a cold bedroom or den. They added space, but there's not enough heat circulating through the house to make the new room comfortable. You need to show prospective buyers that you have all the heat they'll need. If you show the house on a cold day, be sure to crank up the heat so your lookers will know that your new room is nice and warm.

Plumbed heat— How you'll bring heat to this new living area depends on what type of central heating the house has. If you have a system that uses plumbing, like steam or hot water, you can probably add an extra loop to the system to supply heat to your new room. If your room is near a main line, you're in luck. Otherwise, you may have to run a lot of pipe to get heat to the room.

This approach may not cost a great deal in materials, but it's a tricky, difficult job. Steam pipes, particularly, have to be installed at a precise angle. Otherwise, they'll make a lot of bubbling and banging noises, and won't heat well. I wouldn't attempt to do this job myself. It requires a master plumber — one especially qualified for this type of work. Finding someone like that may be difficult.

Forced-air heat— If you have a forced-air furnace, you'll have to run ductwork to the new room. This can be a real problem if there's no suitable ductwork running nearby. You may have to cut holes in several interior walls to get the ductwork to the new room. This can take all the profit out of your project. And a long duct run may deliver too little heat to be of any practical value. You'll have to install a booster fan somewhere along the way to help the air make it to your new room. Worse, the furnace may not have enough capacity to heat the extra space.

In a forced-air system, the warm air always takes the path of least resistance. If your room is at the end of a long run of ductwork, about 90 percent of the airflow will be gone by the time it gets to the end. You'll have to block off some airflow to the first rooms or install a booster fan for the last room on the line. Hot air systems, like plumbing systems, are balanced. Any time you modify one, you'll have to rebalance it. Otherwise, you'll wind up with hot spots and cold spots — and the most likely cold spot will be the new room.

Furnace capacity— Most furnaces are oversized for the house they're installed in. That ensures that there's enough heat, even on the coldest day. Thirty years ago it was common to oversize furnaces by 50 percent. Now many builders are lowering that percentage, since an oversized furnace wastes energy. But most are still oversized.

If the new room isn't very large, is well insulated and doesn't have large windows, the existing furnace will probably be able to supply enough extra heat. But if you're planning to convert a large garage to living space, you may be adding several hundred more square feet. If your original house was only 800 square feet and you add a converted 20 by 20 foot garage, you've increased the square footage by one-half. There's no way that the existing furnace is going to be able to heat all this space. You'll have to supply another heat source or replace the furnace. Consider this problem carefully before you begin a project of this type.

Other heat sources— If there's no practical way to bring heat from the main system, or if it doesn't have the capacity you need, you'll have to include a new heater in the conversion plans. The most common added heat sources are auxiliary gas heaters. Smaller units stand on the floor while the larger ones are mounted in the wall. Both types will require a gas supply, thermostat, fan, and flue.

These heaters have a few drawbacks. If you have a large room, the heated end of the room is usually too hot while the opposite end is cold. And, for some people, they're too noisy. They make whooshing sounds when they come on, and creak and clack after they go off. They're also difficult to install. You have to plumb in a gas line and build a flue. Once installed, they take up wall space and interfere with furniture placement. Nothing can be put close to them that might be damaged by the heat.

Auxiliary gas heaters are a dead giveaway that you have an added-on room. Most people expect that rooms with these heaters will be uncomfortable. Of course, an uncomfortable room is better than no room at all; but a room with proper heat is better.

Well, if that's the case, what good alternatives are there? Unfortunately, there aren't any. All the alternatives are bad, for one reason or another. But the best of the bad alternatives is electric heat. It's cheap and easy to install. You just wire it in, almost like a light fixture. The room has its own thermostat. The heat is distributed evenly and quietly and the small baseboard heaters are unobtrusive. The problem with electric heat is that it's very expensive to operate. However if you're only heating one small bedroom, the additional expense won't break anybody's budget.

If you're converting a large area like a two-car garage, insulate the new room as well as possible. If you do a good job of insulating, the energy cost for even an area this large should be moderate.

Fireplaces

A fireplace is both a heat source and a major improvement to a house. If your house doesn't have one, is it worth the expense to add one? This is a fairly expensive modification. Even if you put in the least expensive type available (a prefabricated zero-clearance unit and prefab flue pipe), and do all the work yourself, it's still going to cost you at least $1,000. You'll have to consider this carefully.

The Value of a Fireplace

A recent study by *Remodeling Contractor* magazine estimated that adding a fireplace increases the value of a home an average of $4,600. If you could be sure of that, adding a prefab fireplace would be a nice guaranteed profit. But you've got to remember their study came up with an *average* figure. Maybe on one house it raised the value by $9,200, and on another it raised it by zero. Where will your house fit in?

Consider the price range of your house. If you're working on a house that will sell in the lower price ranges, there's no way that adding a fireplace will add $4,600 to its price. In fact, there probably isn't any single item that will add that much to the value of your house. The reason is obvious. People who buy in the low price ranges can't afford extras, no matter how nice they are. If you raise your price, you risk pricing all your prospective buyers out of the market.

On the other hand, if you're working on an expensive property, a fireplace will probably add more than $4,600 to the value. People who plan to pay a lot of money for a house expect amenities like fireplaces. If they don't find them, they'll be disappointed. Not only will a fireplace add to the value of the house, but *not* having a fireplace will actually take away from its value. So if you're working on high-end property, the expense is justified.

What about middle-range property? As usual, this is where the decision-making can be difficult. Adding a fireplace here will definitely add to the value of your house. How much? Will it be $4,600 or $5,000 or just $2,000? In practice, it depends on where you locate the fireplace and how much it adds to the decor of the home.

Locating the Fireplace

Think about where a fireplace will fit in your house. With the mantel, hearth, and other trim, a fireplace takes up a lot of space, sometimes a whole wall. Can you afford to give up that much space in the living room? What about furniture placement? Will adding a fireplace make your living area too small to use? If so, then there's no advantage to adding a fireplace at all.

How about putting a fireplace in the den or in a garage conversion? That would help solve the heating problem and add value to your house. Many new homes have a fireplace only in the family room because that's where the family spends most of their time.

A fireplace is most valuable if it's in a convenient location. The best spot would be a large, featureless wall. It should be centrally located, so people can sit around it and enjoy the fire. It should also be visible from as much of the room as possible, and face towards an open space so the heat will be directed into the house.

Prospective buyers always imagine how they will arrange their furniture, and how they'll use the space. "Let's see, we'll put the couch here, and the TV will go there. Then we'll be able to sit in front of the fire and watch TV too." If they can't figure out how to fit their furniture, or if they won't be able to use the space adequately, they won't buy your house. And if the fireplace is in a position that makes it difficult to enjoy, people will figure it out, and they won't be happy. And unhappy people don't buy.

Installation Considerations

Installing a fireplace in a one-story house isn't a major problem. You can box in the fireplace, flue and all, all the way up to the ceiling. It will look more like a real masonry fireplace if you do that. Then just continue the flue through the attic space and out the roof.

Installation is harder in a two-story house. Where do you run the flue? Unfortunately, you can't run it through the middle of somebody's bedroom. Where will it go instead? In a closet? You can offset the flue pipe a little to work around the upstairs rooms. But there's a limit. You can't zigzag the flue pipe all over the house. That would create too much resistance in the flue, causing smoke to back up into the living room. So, think about the flue when you're thinking fireplace location.

Decor

Fireplaces will fit into almost all decorating schemes. There are traditional fireplaces for traditional houses, and modern fireplaces for modern houses. The more a fireplace complements your design, the more it adds to the value of your house. If you can coordinate the fireplace with the rest of your interior, it will add a great deal to your house. It won't add much if it just looks tacked on. Add trim and design elements that draw attention to your fireplace and emphasize its beauty. If it doesn't stand out, your effort, and your money, will be wasted.

Attic Conversions

Consider these points before beginning an attic conversion. First, how much work is required to make the conversion? Do you have adequate headroom, a usable staircase, access to

Figure 10-8
Low headroom made this conversion difficult

heat, and a foundation that can support a second or third story addition? If so, your choice is easy. Go ahead and convert the space. But if any of these items are lacking, your decision is more difficult. If they're all lacking, you should be making some other kind of improvement.

Structural Support

Check out your house's structural support system. An attic addition will add a lot of weight to the house. If the attic was framed with the idea in mind that it would be converted into living space some day, you may not need to do much. But for most attics, the floor joists will need strengthening to hold the weight you'll be adding. Exactly how much strengthening depends on how strong the existing joists are, and how much weight you're adding. Keep in mind that people and furniture add weight as well.

Remember too, that the weight added will have to be supported by the foundation. If your house has any foundation problems or other serious structural weakness, better find out now. Adding a few extra tons to the top of the house will make any of these defects a whole lot worse. This is something you'll need to investigate very carefully. If you're in doubt, call in a structural engineer to examine the house and advise you.

Headroom

How much headroom is actually available in your attic? Looks can be deceiving. At least 50 percent of the ceiling of any room must be 7-1/2 feet or higher, according to most building codes. If your attic doesn't meet these specifications, you may have some major problems. The attic shown in Figure 10-8 looks like it could easily be used for several rooms, but the low headroom made it difficult to convert. I had to add a dormer to get

Figure 10-9

Narrow attic stairway will have to be replaced

enough headroom to meet code requirements. And, you can only get by that easily if the ridge board of your roof is 7-1/2 feet or higher. Fortunately, this one was.

If your ridge board is low, you may have to change the whole roof design to get enough headroom. You can extend the roof upwards or take the roof off and extend the walls. Either way, you're cutting through the roof. You have to decide then whether the space you'll gain by expanding upwards will be worth the cost. This answer will depend a great deal on the shape of the house, its roof line, and whether you add on to the front or the back.

When you make an extension to the roof in front of the house, be sure it complements the style of the house. Adding to the rear of a home is usually less of a problem. Style isn't so important back there. Remember, few things spoil the look of a house more than an unsightly or awkward addition. Making a bad choice about design can eliminate any advantage you hope to gain from adding more space.

When you're opening up a house to the weather, you'll need to get the new roof and walls up quickly. Be sure you can get some additional workers to help you. That will boost your costs, but it's important to get the work done very promptly when the roof or walls are opened up.

Staircases

To convert an attic to living space, you have to provide an adequate staircase. Your house may have an unfinished attic with a stairway that's suitable for use with an unfinished attic. But the same staircase may be inadequate for use a finished room. For example, if the stairway is like the one in Figure 10-9, you'll have to replace it. A narrow stairway is fine for an attic, but not for the only access to a second story living area.

Adding a staircase is a lot of work, but that isn't the only problem. A stairway takes up living space. Most building codes require a main staircase to be at least 2 feet 8 inches wide with a rise of no more than 8-1/4 inches per stair. Figure those proportions and you'll see how much of the main floor is required. Is there room for the stairway? You may find that building the new stairway will take space from an existing bedroom. Losing the usefulness of one bedroom to gain another doesn't make sense.

Before you buy a house, consider carefully where you might find room for a new staircase. Don't begin thinking about this problem after you've bought the house. In many cases there's simply no good place to put a staircase.

Weigh the Benefits

Converting an attic can almost double the square footage of your house. If you have a house that's too small for most people, doubling the living area will greatly increase the home's value. But if the conversion takes up almost as much space as it provides (for the staircase, for instance), you're not making any progress.

Does the house need this extra space? If it's a small two-bedroom house, adding bedroom space will increase the number of potential buyers for your house. But if the house is already fairly large, you may not gain much by this conversion. Remember, most people want three-bedroom houses. They'll pay a little extra for four, or even five bedrooms, but they won't pay a lot more. Weigh the benefits of converting an attic against the effort and costs before you make any decisions.

Converting a Porch

Converting a porch, especially an upstairs porch, is one of my favorite projects. It can be a great way to add an extra bedroom to a smaller home. Porch conversions have several advantages over attic conversions. First, a porch doesn't need a staircase. That saves a lot of space as well as work. Second, you don't need to strengthen the floor, since it's already strong enough to support people and furniture. And finally, porches almost always have adequate headroom.

Problems with Porches

Porches do have other problems, though. Lack of heat is one. They usually need insulation and drywall. And there's one problem unique to porches: they often have sloped floors. They were designed to be fully or partially open to the weather, so the floor is often angled to allow the rain to run off. This just won't do for a bedroom. You'll have to level it. Otherwise, some people will feel off balance in the room.

I use *sleepers* to level this kind of floor. They're 2 x 4s cut in a long taper to reverse the angle of the floor. Space the sleepers about 2 feet in each direction. Then lay a new plywood floor over the sleepers. This is a lot of work, but it's still the easiest way to deal with the problem.

You'll have to enclose the porch, but that's a lot less work than building a room from scratch. It's also easier than adding a dormer to the attic because you don't need to cut into the roof. And, you have more scheduling flexibility since it isn't vital that you get the work done before it rains.

If your porch is enclosed, the interior walls will probably be made of paneling, shingles, or pine siding. If it looks good and is made with quality materials, you may be able to just leave it. These materials aren't common in a bedroom, but as long as it's attractive, people will accept it. If it isn't attractive, then replace it with drywall.

Check your porch carefully for wood rot damage caused by exposure to the elements. Make any repairs needed before you begin with your conversion. This may seem to be a lot of work, especially if the rot is extensive. But you'd have to replace anything that had rotted even if you didn't convert the porch. You can't leave a rotted-out porch. It isn't safe.

Some porch conversions are easy and convenient, but others are difficult because of their awkward locations. Some porches don't make good bedroom conversions, but you can usually convert the space into some type of living area.

Front Porches

Probably the most obvious porch on a house is the front entrance porch. These can be anything from a small stoop to a large glassed-in room. The front porch area doesn't easily convert to living

Figure 10-10
Sandstone porch doesn't match this Colonial-style house

space. A bedroom here would be ridiculous. Your best bet is to create a vestibule or add onto the living room with this area. People expect to see a living room in the front of a house. Adding another room in front of the living room will probably make your house less attractive, not more.

If you have a tiny living room and no den or family room in your house, consider expanding the living room into the porch space. This is a big job, and the new area must blend with the style of the existing living room. If you can't match it, you'll have to gut the whole area, both old and new, and redo everything.

I have, on rare occasions, seen front porches converted into very nice semiformal sunrooms. Restaurants sometimes arrange their entries like this. However, this looks good only on an informal or a modern house. It would never do to add a sunroom onto the front of a Colonial home. Consider carefully before attempting unusual modifications like this. Done correctly, on an appropriate house, they can be very attractive. Done incorrectly, they can be a total disaster.

Remember that both the interior and exterior of your conversion must match the existing house. Don't let your conversion stick out like a sore thumb.

The front of your house is very important. Don't spoil it with an ugly addition like the one in Figure 10-10. The sandstone brick detracts from the original Colonial look, and the third-floor Tudor-style oriel window adds further confusion to the home's exterior treatment.

Occasionally you'll run across a house that has a porch conversion that you'll want to remove. Figure 10-11 shows a front porch bedroom conversion that was virtually useless. It wasn't suited to be a bedroom because it wasn't

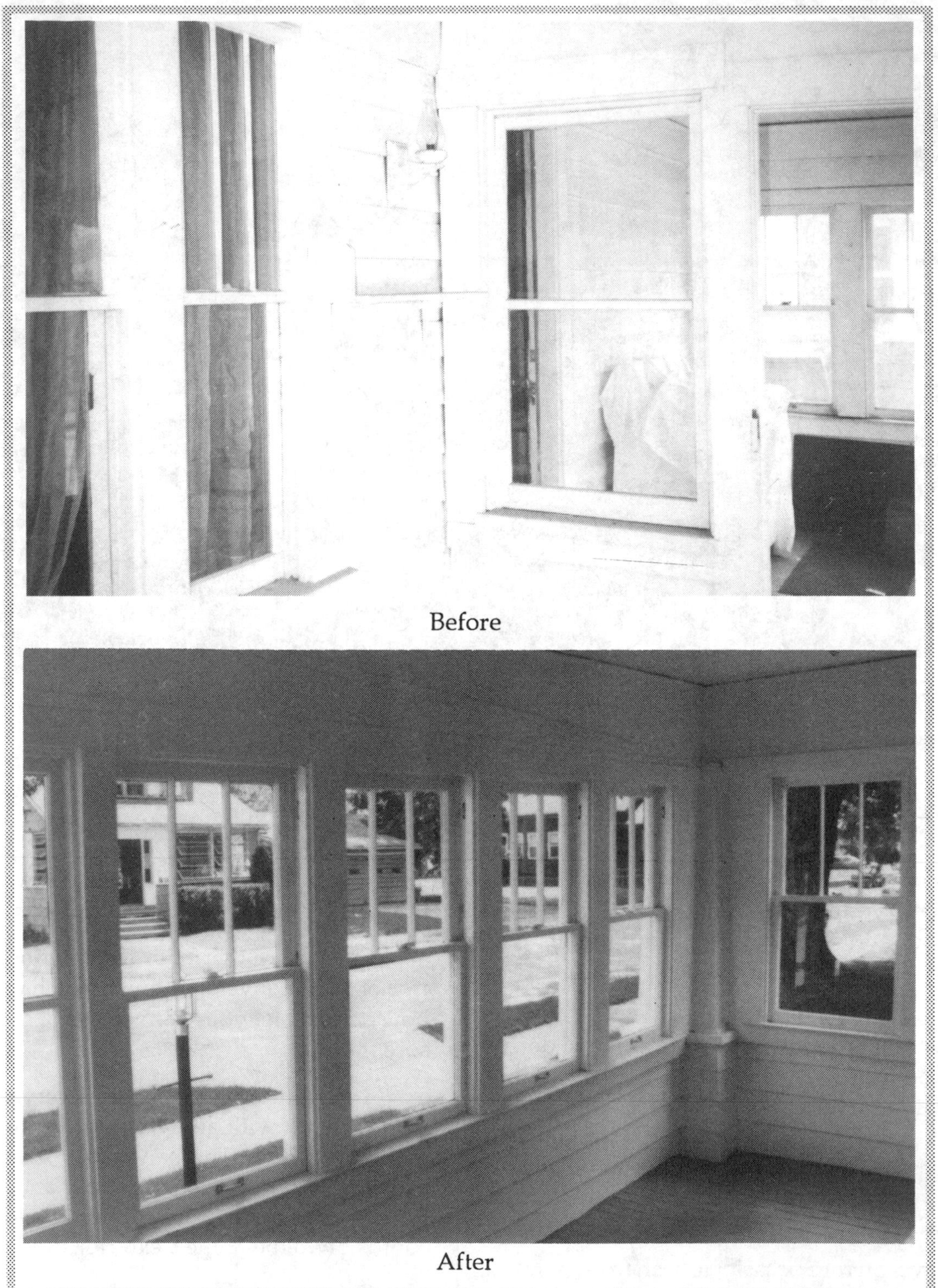

Before

After

Figure 10-11
Some converted rooms need to be removed

private, so it ended up being used as a storage area. I took out the partition and returned it to the original look.

Converting a front porch to living area isn't going to be worth the trouble unless there's a real need for more living space. Generally, you're better off using space other than the front porch for conversions.

Rear Porches

A main floor rear porch has far more potential than a front porch. You can use the space several ways. And you don't have to worry so much about blending the addition to the rest of the house. The appearance of the back of your house is much less important than the front.

Kitchens— A rear porch is prime space for expanding the kitchen. This is a huge job, and one I hesitate to take on unless it's absolutely necessary. Unfortunately you'll find that on some handyman specials it may *be* absolutely necessary. The kitchens may be hopelessly inadequate. Expanding onto a porch may provide the space needed for a really nice kitchen. You may even be able to retain a lot of the porch-like features, such as the large windows, unless they're too drafty. Big windows make a kitchen bright and cheerful.

Dining rooms and dens— Rear porches can also be easily converted into a dining room, den or family room. But these rooms aren't absolutely necessary in a house. In fact, they aren't worth much more to you than a porch. Adding a dining room, den or family room will raise the value of the house only slightly (unless there's no other eating area).

If you're considering converting a porch to a den or dining room, ask yourself this question before starting: How easily can I make this conversion? If you have an enclosed, heated porch, very little work may be necessary for the conversion. In that case, it's probably worthwhile, even though the value of the house will be increased only slightly.

Also consider how much your house needs the extra space. If the house is tiny, every additional inch of living space is precious. It will pay to convert any space you can. But if your house is already reasonably large, the space gained by adding these rooms won't pay for your effort.

Bedrooms— Converting a main floor porch to a bedroom can be a real problem if you aren't careful. You may wind up trading a perfectly good, enjoyable porch for a peculiar, undesirable bedroom. This will do nothing for the value of your house.

People are particular about their privacy and about their bedrooms. A bedroom won't fit in just anywhere. Inappropriately-placed bedrooms (like the one in Figure 10-11) are the sort of thing you end up taking out, not adding. You don't want to have a bedroom opening onto a kitchen, living room or dining room. When you convert space off these rooms, seal off the opening to the main living areas. Add a new entrance from some other part of the house, ideally a hallway.

Sometimes porches are attached to an existing first-floor bedroom. If you convert this porch, you'll have a "pass-through" bedroom. A room like this usually can't be considered a bedroom — at least not for mortgage purposes. What you really have is an extension of the existing bedroom, making it a two-room bedroom suite. If you desperately need space, a pass-through bedroom may be the best you can do, but it's far from ideal. Of course, if the existing bedroom is very small, this may work out just fine. Or you may just want to extend the existing room onto the porch and make it one large bedroom.

The best porch to convert is one that opens onto a hall. If there are already bedrooms on the first floor, adding another will be less noticeable. You may be able to blend the new bedroom in with the others. Ideally, no one will even realize that it's an add-on. This is the perfect project if your house needs another bedroom.

Upstairs Porches

Many older homes have sun porches on the second floor. Depending on the placement, this may be a great candidate for conversion. Unfortunately, many porches like this don't have a separate entrance. If not, stop and think. Is there any way to give the porch its own entrance? Could you add a door somewhere else? Could you add a hallway leading to the new room without doing too much damage to the existing bedroom? If not, the conversion may not be worth the effort. You'd end up creating a "pass-through" bedroom.

If the porch has its own entrance, but it's on the front of the house, then there are a few other things to consider: Can you enclose the porch and blend it with the existing exterior? If it doesn't match, can you give it a pleasing complementary design? Many houses were designed with contrasting elements that blend together when combined, like brick on the first floor and aluminum or wood siding on the second floor.

The best location for an upstairs porch conversion is in the rear, with a separate entrance off the hall. I'm always happy to find a two-bedroom house with a large, enclosed porch like this. I can easily convert it to a three-bedroom house. This moves the house up to an entirely different price range. That's the kind of situation I look for: a big profit without too much work. Finding a house like this is like finding money.

Converting a Garage

Attached garages are the only garages worth converting to living space. A bedroom 20 feet away and separate from the main house isn't an attractive addition for most buyers.

Garage Problems

Many of the problems you'll have when converting garages are like the problems you'll have in finishing porches. For instance, you'll probably have a sloping floor. Like porches, some garages have floors laid at an angle to carry water away. Fortunately, some are level, and others are almost level. If the pitch is just a few degrees off level, you might be able to ignore it. Probably no one will notice it. However, if your garage floor has a noticeable pitch, you'll need to level it somehow. If the garage is small, the easiest way to do this is with sleepers, as I described for porches.

For a large garage, however, a pourable floor-leveling mix might be a better remedy. There are a few different solutions you can use. The cheapest, though not necessarily the easiest, is ordinary concrete with a bonding additive. You simply clean the old concrete and pour the new concrete mix over the old. Finish it as you would any concrete job. You can also buy special floor-leveling powders that you mix up, pour, and smooth by hand. I've used the concrete and bonding agent in small areas and it works quite well. Don't worry if it comes out a bit rough. Put down a thick carpet pad and a nice carpet, and no one will realize it isn't perfect. If it comes out *really* rough, however, you may have to smooth it out with a plywood underlayment. This is extra work, so you don't want to do it if you don't have to.

Probably the easiest solution to floor leveling is to have Gyp-Crete or Forta-Fill installed by one of their franchise subcontractors. This is easiest because you don't do a thing. Someone else does it. However, you have to pay for it, and it isn't cheap. These are commercial gypsum concrete products that are pumped on as a liquid and then smoothed to a level surface. You can't do it yourself. I would probably only resort to using one of these products if I had a very large job. If you want information on a Gyp-Crete franchise in your area, contact:

Gyp-Crete Corporation
920 Hamel Rd.
Hamel, MN 55340
(612) 478-6072

The entrance— The location of the entrance is as much a problem when converting a garage as it is when converting a porch. Attached garages tend to open into kitchens or dining areas. If you plan to convert the garage to a dining room or den, this is acceptable. But it won't do for a bedroom. Try to find a better access point into the new bedroom and seal off the existing door.

If the house desperately needs another bedroom, the conversion may be worthwhile even if it has to open into the kitchen. Adding that bedroom will probably increase the value of your house anyway, even with the poor design. But everyone will immediately recognize the room as an add-on, with all the disadvantages that add-ons tend to have, like poor heating.

One way to get around the problem is to finish the room as a den rather than a bedroom. Since it's reasonable for a den to be connected to the kitchen, this placement won't seem odd. If your buyers like your house but need another bedroom, they're likely to look at the den and say, "You know, I bet we could use this room for an extra bedroom." If you had told those buyers that the conversion was a bedroom, they would never have been happy with it.

If you need the extra bedroom as a selling point, advertise it as a "Two- or three-bedroom home." People who wouldn't consider a two-bedroom house will be curious enough to ask about it. You can tell them "It's a two-bedroom house, but you could use the den as a bedroom if you wanted to." Most people will accept this explanation.

Windows and Doors

Unlike porches, which often have many windows, a garage may not have any windows at all. If the garage has no windows, you'll need to add some. Otherwise it will feel like a basement.

You want your new room to look as much like the rest of the house as possible. Add the same type of window as you have in the other living areas of the house, especially if the new windows will show from the street. If there's a nice view, be sure to emphasize it.

The garage service door, if any, may not be appropriate for your new room. Bedrooms don't usually have exterior doors, although dens may. Taking a door out is a simple task. And, you can easily replace the door with a window since there's already a framed opening. Of course, the new window must harmonize with the rest of your design. Don't install any window that's going to be awkwardly placed or unattractive.

Your next problem is what to do with the large garage door. I've seen some conversions where the garage door was simply nailed shut and left in place. Don't do that. Obviously the new room was once a garage. People may suspect that anyway, even if you do an excellent conversion, but there's no sense advertising the fact. A garage conversion shouldn't be any more obvious than it has to be.

It's best to remove the garage door and frame and finish the opening to match the rest of the house, both interior and exterior. The opening is a good place to add some nice, large windows, since the roof load is already headered off. Finish the interior of the garage door opening with the same material you're using for the rest of the room.

Finishing the Exterior

The exterior finishing may be a problem. You may not be able to get the same siding or finish materials that were used on the rest of the exterior walls. It may be a color or style that's no longer available. Then what?

This is a major problem only if your filled-in garage door opening will be visible from the street. If it isn't, you can probably get by with matching the materials as closely as possible. You should do a good job though, even if it isn't a critical design issue.

If it's visible from the street, and it can't be finished to match, then your best choice may be an interesting contrast material. The material must match the style of the house and complement the existing siding. Have a look at some books of home plans or magazines such as *Better Homes and Gardens*. You'll find a number of examples where contrasting materials are used to accent the original design plan.

Here's a trick that will help blend the new wall with the existing walls. Add some of the same elements to the rest of the house. If you use brick trim on your new room, add some brick trim somewhere else on the front of the house. This will give the house a unified look instead of an "added-on" look. Once again, the important concept is that your modification should look like part of the original design, not an afterthought.

Carports

It's possible to convert a carport into another room. Of course, this is harder than converting a garage. Carport space isn't closed in and may not even have a foundation. Many carports, in fact, are little more than a roof projecting over a driveway. And that roof may not be suitable for use over a finished room. A carport like this is essentially worthless for a conversion. All you have really is a space where a room could be added.

If you have to lay a foundation and frame the walls and roof, you might as well leave the carport and put the addition in a more convenient location. It might look better in the back of the house, where it won't be so obvious. What about your driveway and parking space? If you put a room where the carport was, you'll have to come up with some alternative parking or have no off-street parking at all. I only recommend using the carport if you absolutely *must* add a room and there's nowhere else to put it. But consider it carefully.

Here's a final suggestion for garages that doesn't involve a conversion. If the garage isn't attached but is very close to the house, you might consider building a breezeway to connect the garage to the house. This is one of those extra touches that costs just a little but offers a lot of convenience to your buyers. It doesn't do the selling price any harm either. People like attached garages. It lets them bring in their groceries on a rainy day without getting wet. Breezeways can also help give an older home a face-lift — a more modern look that's both attractive and useful.

That's all for major additions and modifications to increase "livability." We've discussed how to get maximum usable space for minimum cost, and evaluated which modifications are worthwhile and which are not. In the next chapter I'll talk about another type of modification — not one that increases livability or space, but one that simply makes your house more beautiful.

CHAPTER ELEVEN

Decorating the Exterior

I consider decorating one of the most important topics in this book. A perfectly functional house in reasonably good repair but with little eye appeal will sell for the standard price. The same home painted, decorated and color coordinated will sell for a premium price. Even a home with some serious repair problems will bring a good price if it's well-decorated. Most important, painting and decorating are much cheaper, faster and easier than making major repairs. From your standpoint, the best house to buy is one that needs decorating and a few simple improvements, not a major remodeling.

When should you begin to think about decorating? Right at the beginning, when you first see the home, not after you've bought it. Look for easy, inexpensive, but worthwhile improvements that greatly increase its value. Some properties can't be improved easily. If you look at a house and can't think of a simple way to improve it, you'd better buy another one.

Usually, my wife and I look over a property together before we buy. We both have a lifelong interest in architecture and design, and we trust each other's judgment. We've been working together and studying design and construction together. What one of us misses the other will probably see. A shortage of ideas is never our problem. It's usually just the opposite; we have more ideas than we have places to put them. As we walk through a house, we're weighing possibilities: "Well, let's see, what do you think would look good here? How can we fix this? What would you do with that?"

I have a backlog of good ideas that I haven't found a place to use yet. Sooner or later I'll get to use them, but by then, I'll have a dozen more. I hope you have dozens of good ideas that you've

Figure 11-1

Traditional home with modern porch deck

been trying to use. If you read books and magazines on decorating and design, you'll probably know what you'd like to do to almost every property you see.

Design and decorating are easy for me. Probably they will be for you after you've been doing them a while. But if they're not easy for you yet, this chapter and the next may be just what you need. In the next two chapters I'll explain how I resolve design and decorating problems that are common in older homes. Of course, what you do to any house should be in harmony with the style of the house. So that should be our starting point: architectural styles.

Why Worry About Architectural Style?

I prefer buying homes with a definite style, or something close to one. If a house is a hodgepodge of uncoordinated styles, it's hard to bring order out of the chaos.

Let's assume you've selected a house, made repairs and a few necessary improvements. Now you want to decorate it. Where do you begin?

First you need to decide what type of house you're dealing with. What style is the house? Is it large or small; formal or informal? The size and style of the house will determine the appropriate decor.

Formal houses are designed to be stately, elegant, and dignified. A Colonial style home is a good example of formal architecture. In keeping with a design like this, you could add shutters to the windows and carriage lamps around the front door. These are elegant features for an elegant house.

What shouldn't you do? Don't add informal decorations such as wagon wheels or rustic fencing to a formal house like a Colonial. They don't match the feeling, the style or the time period of the house. Informal accents belong on an informal house, such as a ranch style.

I'm not saying that you should never mix styles. Professional decorators do it purposely to create certain special effects. Once in a while it looks very nice — *if* it's done with a specific design in mind. But don't put wagon wheels in front of a Colonial house just because you like wagon wheels. They'll look out of place. *Always* look at the whole house.

An example— My neighborhood has several examples of homes with mixed styles. One home is clearly a traditional Early American design. Some years ago, it needed a new porch. Instead of rebuilding the original porch, or replacing it with a similar one, the owners decided to add a modern wood deck (shown in Figure 11-1). I'm sure they thought they were updating their old house. And, they were probably pleased with the result. But to me, it looks awkward. I cringe every time I drive by. The deck is informal, the house is formal. The deck is modern-style, the house is traditional. The deck is new, the house is old. Nothing matches. The deck simply looks out of place.

The problem is that the owners focused on the job, not on the house. The deck itself is fine. It just doesn't belong on this house, at least not in the front. For the same money, the owners could have built a porch more in keeping with the style and formality of the house.

Get the maximum benefit for each dollar spent. Improvements in harmony with the style of the house look better and bring a better return on money spent. Improvements that don't match don't add anything. The wood deck porch on the Early American house is better than no porch at all, but the deck's value is lost. It detracts from the look of the house instead of adding to it.

What if you don't know what style your house is? This can be a real problem, especially when you're dealing with a house that's been "improved" over the years. Many people aren't familiar with some of the older architectural styles. Some styles, like Colonials, are fairly easy to recognize. But many others are not. Let's look at a few.

Architectural Styles

The builder usually selected the original plan, but that plan may not have been based on any particular architectural style. This is especially true in the case of owner-builders (persons building homes for their own use). They don't always care about specific design types. Even if they do, they don't always get the details right. Style sometimes gets away from them.

Sometimes the construction budget forces compromises. The builder may have started with a beautiful design, but a tight budget may have forced him to leave out some of the best parts. Other homes were built with a great deal of care and attention to detail and style. But years later, after a few modifications, it may be hard to see what the original design idea was. Layers of unmatched additions can alter the style beyond recognition. Still, with some knowledge of architecture, you can find unifying factors that help establish an overall style for your house.

Learning About Architecture

Anyone who works with houses already has at least an informal knowledge of architecture. You've heard terms like Colonial, Tudor and Ranch and could probably identify each of these styles from a picture. A Colonial is usually a formal, two-story house. A Ranch is usually single story and modern. You'll make better decorating decisions if you understand what each of these styles includes.

If you're in the business of buying, repairing and selling homes, you should have a copy of *Field Guide to American Houses* by Virginia and Lee McAlester, published by Knopf. This book has hundreds of pictures of houses of every common American style, along with detailed descriptions and maps of where the various types of houses are commonly found. It's invaluable for anyone interested in architecture.

Use the *Field Guide to American Houses* or a similar reference book to find the style of your house. If you can't find your house, you may at least find something close among the common styles. Knowing what your house looked like when it was new, even though it may have been heavily modified, will help you decide how to beautify it now.

Most of the houses in use in the United States today were built during the 20th century. They fall into a few basic architectural categories. Let's go through them.

Victorian

This was the predominant style of the last century, but quite a few were built after 1900. This style includes a lot of substantially different variations, but it's still easily recognized by the unusual lines and detailed handicraft. Victorian houses tend to include a combination of different shapes with many projecting wings. The inner layout, as well as the exterior design, is very different from how our homes are designed today. Victorian houses frequently had many tiny rooms, each with a particular purpose. Most modern homes have larger rooms and more open space.

Renovating Victorian houses is a specialized subject. Because of their odd layout, it's hard to modify them for convenient living. Also, Victorian homes have lots of decorative woodwork that has to be carefully maintained. The home in Figure 11-2 is rather plain for a Victorian. However, it does show the gingerbread woodwork common to this style. Notice the varied design of the shingles, the sunburst at the peak of the roof and the sculptured wood detail.

Renovating Victorian houses is usually a labor of love, not a way to make a living. As historical properties, they can sometimes command high prices, but they can also absorb tremendous amounts of time, money and labor. I recommend leaving these projects for the experts.

Figure 11-2
A small gingerbread Victorian

Figure 11-3
A beautiful example of the Craftsman style

Craftsman

The Craftsman style originated in California just after the turn of the century. It was an extremely popular architectural style through and including the 1920s. Block after block of Craftsman houses were built in many cities. These houses are characterized by low-pitched roofs with wide eaves, porches that often go the full width of the house, and details like corner braces under the eaves and large pillars on the porch. Figure 11-3 is a beautiful example of a Craftsman home. A smaller, less expensive version of the design (Figure 11-4) was more typical.

Figure 11-4
A small Craftsman home

Figure 11-5

A Prairie house in the style of Frank Lloyd Wright

I find it surprising that this common style isn't appreciated today. Even people who make their living in real estate don't recognize this style. They just call them *bungalows*. When in doubt, they call just about any small old house a bungalow. That's why the term bungalow doesn't mean much anymore.

You may have dismissed the style in the past as "just an old house." These houses didn't just happen. They were very nicely designed, and the Craftsman house was impressive in its time. With all the modifications and alterations that these homes may have undergone in the last 70 or 80 years, you may not be able to appreciate its underlying style. But if you can restore the original style, your buyers may be favorably impressed. This, of course, is one of your options in any remodeling and redecorating job — not just to decorate, but to restore the house to its original style.

Prairie

This style originated with Frank Lloyd Wright's Prairie house. The best examples of this style look a lot like Frank Lloyd Wright's work. They are wide, massive houses with big roofs, big porches, and lots of leaded glass. Figure 11-5 is a nice example of this type of house. As you can see, a well-built Prairie-style house can be a really beautiful home.

Unfortunately, as the years went on, builders took more and more liberties with Wright's design, making it cheaper and easier to build. Eventually most of the fine, distinctive detailing was left out. Both the Prairie and the Craftsman style were simplified until it was hard to tell the two styles apart. Look at the house in Figure 11-6. Which it, Craftsman or Prairie?

Figure 11-6
A small Prairie style home

While Craftsman and Prairie styles may seem obscure and unappealing to you now, they usually included fine features that are hard to find in homes built today. There was a great deal of beautiful oak woodwork, built-in cabinetry, and leaded glass. I make a point of mentioning this, because a large number of these houses turn up as handyman specials. I've owned more houses of these types than all other styles put together. You can find them throughout the country, so you're certain to come across a few if you stay in this business very long. Take the time to study these styles and you're sure to develop an appreciation for them.

Tudor

Most people refer to this style as Old English. The best examples of this style are large, formal homes. Note Figure 11-7. But Tudor style has been used in many smaller homes as well. During the 1930s the small Tudor was particularly popular. It's still a common style today, especially in up-scale neighborhoods.

Colonial

This style was very popular in the 1940s and 1950s and is still being used today. The best examples of Colonial styling are the stately,

Figure 11-7
An example of the Tudor style

Figure 11-8

A beautiful Colonial home

two-story brick homes like the one in Figure 11-8. More frequently, you'll run into the less expensive version of this style. Colonials are commonly two-story, rectangular homes with attic dormer windows, shutters and front columns supporting the roof structure. It is a modernized version of the English Georgian style.

Many poor imitations of this style were built, particularly in the years immediately following World War II. These imitations include bits and pieces of the Colonial style. Virginia and Lee McAlester refer to these houses as "Minimal Traditionals"—a few traditional features are tacked on to a home that has very little style. Often these houses don't have a clear, consistent style throughout. It's up to you to establish one.

Modern Ranch

Huge numbers of Ranch-style homes were built in the 1950s and 1960s. They're still being built today. Many variations of this style are used in different areas of the U.S. They originated in the southwest and were based on the Spanish-Mexican rancho style. A Ranch house is typically a one-story home with a low-pitched roof and an open floor plan. You'll find that real estate agents will often refer to any one-story house as a ranch, regardless of the style or when it was built. My favorite ranch style homes are the spacious, rambling brick houses with all the modern amenities. Figure 11-9 shows an inexpensive ranch-style house.

Assessing the Style

If you're unsure which style category your house falls into, look carefully at the different styles and see which one it comes closest to. If it just doesn't seem to fit any style, there are a few more clues that may help you place it.

Age— One of the best ways to zero in on the style of the house is by its age. Certain styles were more popular in certain times. For instance, Craftsman and Prairie styles were very popular in the early part of the century, but declined in the 1930s. None were built after 1940. Ranches were built only after WWII, and were most popular after 1950. Colonials were most popular after 1940, although they may have been built any time.

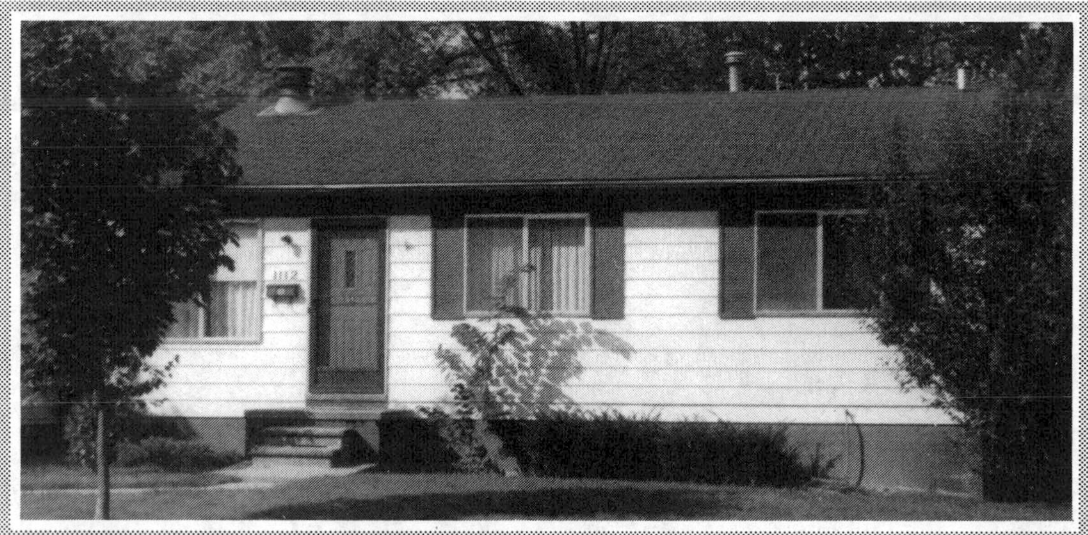

Figure 11-9
A small modern ranch house

Size— Another clue to the style of your house is the size. For example, very few *large* Craftsman style houses were built. Most of them are small (1000 to 1500 square feet), cottage-style houses. The larger homes built in the early part of the century were more likely to be Prairie style. Genuine Colonials are supposed to be fairly large houses. If you have a small house in that style, you probably have a Minimal Traditional house.

Trying to figure out the original size of a house that has had many alterations is like solving a detective story. Look for faint lines on walls where there might have been doors or windows. Look for changes in the style of trim, molding and other woodwork. Follow the old molding to the point where it switches to new molding. That's where the new addition to the home begins. Once you've found the perimeter of the original house, it may make it easier to identify the style.

Use the Stylistic Elements

You may be thinking at this point: "This is all well and good, but what practical use is it? Who cares what the original style was, anyway?"

You should care if you want to take pride in what you're doing. If you want to make good money at this *profession,* you have to work at it like it's a profession. You have to know how to decorate as well as renovate your house. If you can identify what you have, you'll know what you have to build on. You may decide not to restore the original style. In some cases, the original design may have too many drawbacks. It may not be suitable for modern living. But knowing what you have will help you get the most out of your house with the least effort.

Identifying the basic style helps you make decisions about fixtures, landscaping and decorating. There are thousands of choices in hardware, fixtures, fittings, trim and accessories. You have to decide which to select when making modifications or repairs. If the front door needs replacing on your Prairie-style house, you don't want to put a modern door on it. You may not be that interested in Prairie style, but at least put on something that blends with the basic style of the house.

Keep the style consistent throughout the interior and exterior of the house. If you're dealing with a genuine Colonial, stay with that style. Any modifications you make should follow the Colonial style. Otherwise they'll be out of place. If you

Figure 11-10A
This house had no particular style

Figure 11-10B
Now it's a Victorian

have a Minimal Traditional house, you'll have more leeway. This type of house already combines Colonial and modern features. You have plenty of options. Either add more traditional features or add more modern features. The point is this: be consistent and professional in what you choose to do. Don't add wagon wheels, carriage lamps, *and* a front porch deck to the same house.

Selecting a Style

Let's look at a few typical jobs and see how you might want to handle the style and decorating.

A home with no style— Figure 11-10A is a house I bought a couple of years ago. Essentially, this house didn't have any style at all. It was owner-built for basic shelter around 1920. An architect or a historian maybe could come up with some name to describe the style of this house, but I couldn't. It didn't make any clear statement. It started out as a two-story box. Someone added a porch and then shutters to dress it up. These looked OK , but they still didn't establish any particular style. The shutters are old fashioned, perhaps Colonial style; and the porch is rustic, with a sort of western type railing.

I had to decide what to do. Leaving it as it was wouldn't hurt, but it wouldn't raise the value of the house very much either. To make it more attractive to buyers, I needed to assign a style to it and decorate around that theme.

I had to pick a style that was consistent with the basic lines of the house. A plain front-gabled house like this one could have fit into a couple of different styles. It could have been Colonial, but then the porch wouldn't have matched. I didn't want to replace the porch just to create a style — that's too much work. It could have been a rustic farmhouse, but that style was a lot more popular in the 1970s than it is now. I didn't want my house to appear dated.

I decided on Victorian. While the house is not really old enough to be a real Victorian, I knew I could easily create a simple style that would be consistent with the Victorian look. The major reason I chose this style was, first and foremost, economy. All I needed to do was add some Victorian gingerbread to get the effect I wanted.

I bought some decorative woodwork from Vintage Wood Works and added it to the porch posts. Then I closed in the bottom of the porch with inexpensive lattice. For about $350 and one day's work, I had my Victorian house. I finished up with a fresh coat of gray/blue paint, white trim, and some colorful flowering plants.

As you can see in Figure 11-10B, the result is a striking improvement. The Victorian gingerbread immediately catches people's eyes. The house has character and a clearly definable style. Mine is the only Victorian house on the block; probably the only one in the entire suburb. It makes a statement. People may not know exactly what the style is, or the history behind it, but they understand that it's special. A house like this is a work of art. People respond to it just as they would to a Norman Rockwell painting.

Another reason I chose the Victorian style is because Victorian is currently quite popular. There's a revival of interest not only in Victorian homes, but furniture, knickknacks, and all kinds of other products. Walking through the shopping malls today, you'll spot more and more Victorian-type furnishings: lamps, mirrors and other decorating accessories. Fifteen years ago the rustic, farmhouse look was popular. If I had remodeled this house in the early 1970s, I would have chosen the rustic look, using lots of barn wood, milk cans, maybe even wagon wheels. I generally choose the look that's most popular at the time.

My preference for Victorian homes may have also influenced my choice. Remember, I'm my own boss, so I can do it my way. That's what's great about this business. You can do the things that please *you* (as long as your taste is marketable).

If you're interested in adding Victorian wood work to a house, you might want to send for a Vintage Wood Works catalog:

Vintage Wood Works
513 S. Adams #1140
Fredericksburg, TX 78624
(512) 997-9513

There are also a few chain stores, such as Builder's Square, that carry gingerbread wood work. It costs about the same wherever you buy it. It's an expensive addition, and the only way to cut the cost on something like this is to make it yourself. All you need is a jig saw and a lot of time and patience. I would only make it myself if I was doing it for my own home and I wanted something very special.

A Colonial or what?— Look at Figure 11-11. It's another house without a clear style. The design was probably influenced by the Craftsman style, but it wasn't really of that design. Once again, I had to assign a style to work with. This one was a problem.

I immediately ruled out Victorian because of the porch. Actually, the enclosed porch didn't match any established style. But again, I didn't want to remove it. This porch was functional and pleasant, warm in winter and cool in summer. People like that.

Because no particular style fits this house very well, I let the interior help me make up my mind. Inside, the house was very formal, with elegant rooms and a formal dining room. So I picked a formal style for the outside: Colonial. I painted it Early American colors, and added carriage lamps for a Colonial touch. It still doesn't look like a classic colonial, but at least it has some style now.

Your House as a Work of Art

All of this becomes a lot easier if you have some artistic talent. Look at your house as if it's a piece of artwork. That's how architects and designers look at their work — as a highly-developed art form.

Figure 11-11

Assign a style and decorate around it

Make your house a work of art—the kind of art that has wide popular appeal, like Norman Rockwell rather than Pablo Picasso. If your house looks like an all-American family home right out of a Norman Rockwell painting, it'll sell in minutes. Avant-garde houses that look as if Picasso had designed them don't sell well in middle-class neighborhoods. Pick it up and move it to Beverly Hills and you've got a winner. But if you can't do that, you better design homes that most working families can like and appreciate.

What if you don't have an artistic nature? What if all of this discussion of style and art sounds like utter nonsense to you? Well believe me, it isn't. You need some artistic advice. Do you know someone with an artistic nature you can call on for help? How about your spouse? How about your friends? Ask for people's opinions. Most people love to tell you what you should do with your time and money, as long as you don't ask them to contribute any. I've often had people get very enthusiastic about advising me on what they thought I should do with a house.

That's exactly what you want. You need to know what people will like in your house. Ask your friends and family. Ask the neighbors, too. As I said earlier, the neighbors will probably have similar tastes to the people who buy your home. Once you've heard enough comments, you can form a consensus of opinion. You'll get a sense of what most people like in a home. It may not be the same as what *you* like in a home, but then, you're not the one you hope to sell it to.

Getting Ideas

A general understanding of architectural design and style will help. So will friends and associates. But you may need to consult some other sources as well.

If you run short on ideas, where can you go? Where do you find out about current trends, new materials that are available, and how you can use them? Here are some suggestions.

Look at Magazines

Shelter and home design magazines are the best source for the latest ideas in decorating and remodeling. Decorating trends change constantly. Since you want your house to have the greatest appeal possible, try decorating it in a stylish fashion that's consistent with the design of your house. You want your house to look updated, remodeled, and current. Follow the latest trends if you can apply them gracefully. There are always new ideas available for every decorating style. This will give your house an advantage over others on the market that haven't been redecorated as recently as yours. You need every advantage you can get.

Better Homes and Gardens— One of the best sources for decorating ideas is *Better Homes and Gardens*. It's popular, the ideas are new and interesting, and they have wide audience appeal. No potential buyer will be offended by decorating ideas from *Better Homes and Gardens*.

It's a good idea to subscribe to a few home decorating magazines like *BH&G*. As a remodeler, you'll want to know what's new and exciting in the home decor field. Read the articles on remodeling and home design. Consider the ideas offered. Ask yourself, would any of these ideas work with one of my properties? Would they be practical? Would they be affordable? Would they be effective?

Better Homes and Gardens can provide you with many creative ideas. Most of the homes shown aren't million dollar estates. Instead, they show how to make a plain, average-looking house into a showcase. They show all the interesting things that can be done with a basic house. That helps stretch your imagination. If you look through some back issues (don't go too far back, though, the styles will be outdated), you may find a story on a house very much like one you're working on. Be careful not to get too carried away with their ideas, however. The magazine's publishers are in the business of selling magazines, not homes. Their ideas may be great, but they're not necessarily cost-effective.

For example, the May, 1987 issue had an article on a small, ordinary bungalow which was completely remodeled. The finished job is fabulous. But I calculated the cost of all the modifications they made. The total cost was at least $154,000. In my area, the whole house wouldn't be worth that much. And that didn't include the cost of the land and original building! It was a great job, one that anyone could appreciate, but it was still a small bungalow. There's a limit to how much money people will pay for a house like that.

You may not be able to use all the ideas in decorating magazines. But you should be able to use *some* ideas. Remember, *Better Homes and Gardens* is a showcase for new products offered by building material manufacturers. These are usually top-quality goods. You can probably find some similar, but less expensive products to substitute. For instance, *BH&G* may show kitchens with expensive European styled cabinets. I buy cheaper, unfinished cabinets and paint them to look like the ones in *BH&G*. Essentially, I do what women's clothing manufacturers do. When I see a new idea, I copy it using less expensive materials. The effect is almost the same, but the cost is much less.

Try to copy the *look* of the house, not the substance. For example, avoid major structural modifications. Look instead for highly visible features you can duplicate for a reasonable cost. Consider adding trim, decorator items, lights, stylish paint colors and possibly special windows and doors. Avoid moving walls, roofs, porches, or anything else big.

You can also copy landscaping — within limits. *BH&G* garden layouts often include elaborate decks, gazebos, and brick walkways. All these are very nice, but they're also very expensive. You can almost get the same effect by planting the same kinds of flowers and adding the same kinds of garden decorations. Certainly, the effect won't be as nice without all the decking, but it will be stylish, coordinated, and attractive.

I find it doesn't pay to get too carried away with landscaping. I generally add some flowers, planters, maybe a little garden seat or a small walkway. That's about it. I try to limit the cost of landscaping to a couple hundred dollars and a day's work. That's usually all you need to brighten up a yard. Beyond that, you simply won't get a good return on your investment. Many people just want a garden that's neat and tidy. An elaborate garden requires more maintenance, too much for most buyers. If you do too much landscaping, people who aren't gardeners will reject it.

Fine Homebuilding— Another magazine that has interesting design ideas is *Fine Homebuilding*. It's written for the custom builder and includes details on how to do the job, not just pictures of the finished work. *Fine Homebuilding* assumes that you'll do the work yourself and shows what's really involved in the project. That can keep you from starting on work that requires specialized skills or equipment you may not have. There are other magazines on the market that cover this subject, but *Fine Homebuilding* is my favorite.

I even find the advertising in *Fine Homebuilding* valuable. The magazine is full of ads from building suppliers, offering new products and free brochures for things that you might like to investigate further. It's a good idea to keep a file of brochures on hand for products you may consider using. That way, when you have the opportunity to use it, you'll be able to order it quickly. This is especially handy when you're dealing with hard-to-locate items, such as repair parts for antique fixtures.

The only problem I have with *Fine Homebuilding* is that it's aimed primarily at builders of expensive properties. A lot of the ideas are simply too expensive to use when remodeling mid-range houses. They also like to explore some really different and unusual ideas. I don't find it practical to get involved in projects that are more avant-garde than those found in *Better Homes and Gardens* — that magazine is my final authority. But I subscribe to both magazines, and I'd advise you to do the same. You can never have too much information.

Other magazines— Many building and decorating magazines are published. Several specialize on subjects like energy efficiency or solar heat. If you live where solar heat systems are popular, this subject may be of special interest to you.

I've discovered that most of my customers don't know much about energy efficiency, and don't care. I've tried to explain it to people, but most just can't be bothered hearing about it. Since that's the case, I just put in minimal energy improvements. I always insulate and vent attics, I sometimes insulate walls (if they're easily accessible), and I install good storm windows. That's about it. Nobody seems to care about anything more. And if they don't care enough to be willing to pay a little more, I don't care either.

I try to avoid exotic decorating ideas. *Architectural Digest* features some pretty unusual homes. This magazine may be a very effective showcase for interior designers, but you should stick to the basics for your fixer.

Architectural Digest features expensive decorating ideas that are appropriate only for the high end of the market. Ideas that look good in a multi-million-dollar mansion won't fit in your $120,000 bungalow. That kind of decorating is too extreme for the average home buyer.

Other Sources of Ideas

Model homes— Model homes at housing tracts are a very good source of decorating ideas. Since these homes are brand new, they usually have all the latest decorating schemes. The developers can well afford to hire some pretty expensive interior decorators. Sometimes some of their ideas seem to show up in houses I've remodeled. Must be coincidence. These homes also feature ideas that are likely to appeal to a broad selection of buyers. These models usually have products and features that are popular in your area. This is important, because preferences vary from region to region. Many ideas that work well in the northeast won't work in Florida, for example. Climate and taste are different.

I like to look at houses that are about twice as expensive as the ones I'm working on. I can't afford to copy the major features, but I look for details and colors that I can use to update the look of my house. Some of the prospective buyers that are looking at my houses will already have seen these same models. They'll be impressed by my use of similar decor.

There's a common pattern I've found among buyers. They usually start out looking at expensive homes. It doesn't take them long to discover that they can't afford the model home they like. If your house has some of the same features at a price they can afford, you'll have a quick sale.

Don't bother looking at homes selling for five or ten times more than what yours will sell for. Even if you like the ideas in these houses, you probably won't be able to afford to copy them. Buyers in your market may have looked at homes selling in the $200,000 range. But they won't even bother looking at million dollar mansions. So if your buyers aren't looking at these very expensive homes, why should you be interested in trying to copy them?

Restaurants— You can also get some good ideas from better restaurants. Many restaurants are remodeled every few years, so they remain up-to-date, cheerful, and inviting. They usually decorate in a style that's compatible with the type of customers they expect to attract. If you find a comfortable and inviting atmosphere in a particular restaurant, think about what they've done to make you feel that way. Use these ideas in your decorating.

Neighbors— One of your best sources of ideas is right around you — your neighbors. If anyone in the neighborhood has recently remodeled, use their house as a model for yours, assuming they've done a nice job. Let them pay the huge architectural and decorator fees. They probably won't mind if you copy them. After all, isn't imitation the sincerest form of flattery? And, any improvement you make to your house is also an improvement to the neighborhood.

You'll be surprised at the excellent ideas you'll find simply by driving up and down the streets in your neighborhood. Good decorating ideas from houses similar to yours will transfer very easily to your house. Just be careful not to copy ideas that are fading in popularity. Don't add something to your house that everyone else is tearing out of their house. Watch current trends.

Ideally, all the sources of ideas that I've mentioned should agree. That is, the magazines will show the same decorating ideas that you find in the model homes, which will be the same as the restaurants, which will be the same decorating ideas your neighbors are using. If there isn't any agreement, rely on the magazines as your primary authority. Their suggestions are probably the most current.

Specific Decorating Considerations

We've been considering decorating style in general for the whole house. Now let's look at a few specific areas that need special attention. We'll start at the top and work down.

The Roof

If you're planning to reshingle the roof, think about the style and color of the replacement roofing. You don't necessarily have to replace it with exactly the same shingles. What are your alternatives?

Luxury roofing— Luxury roofing materials include tile, slate, wood shingles, and copper. Any of these materials make a good roof. But all are more expensive than asphalt shingles. Unless you're working on an upscale property, you won't be able to make any money if you use these materials. Of course, if you happen to buy a house that already has luxury roofing, by all means save it. Tile, slate, and copper never wear out. If the roof structure underneath is damaged, you can remove the roofing, rebuild the roof and replace the roofing. That's a lot of work. But considering the value of the roof once you're done, it will almost certainly be worth it.

Patterned shingles— Fiberglass shingles with printed textures or patterns printed on them are a good alternative to luxury roofing. Brand names include Celotex Dimension III and Georgia-Pacific Summit. These shingles cost about 50 percent more than ordinary shingles, but they look 100 percent better. The patterns printed on them imitate slate or wood. Of course, they don't really look that much like the materials they imitate, especially up close. But no one sees them up close. From a distance they don't look bad at all. Some of these patterned or textured shingles are attractive and are worth considering.

Before installing these shingles, ask yourself this question: Will these shingles harmonize with the style of your house? Many old-fashioned styles, like Colonials or Victorians, look nice with wood shingles and imitation wood shingles. The only *original* roofs you'll see on Victorian homes today are made of long-lasting materials such as tile or slate, but many did have wood shingle roofs. The original roofs on these houses rotted away years ago.

Wood shingle roofing was considered standard back in the 1920s when most Craftsman and Prairie houses were built. Oak floors were standard back then, too. Unfortunately, unlike oak floors, wood shingle roofs don't last as long as the house. I can't afford to replace them with real wood shingles, but I can afford to replace them with imitation wood shingles. From the ground, hardly anyone can tell the difference.

Sometimes these more expensive patterned shingles aren't worth the cost. Better quality shingles add value to a house — but not that much. And sometimes very little of the roof is visible from the street. The type of shingles may not make any difference. A good example is my counterfeit Victorian house shown back in Figure 11-10. I had considered putting an imitation wood shingle roof on this house. It needed a new roof anyway. However, I discovered that the roof is almost invisible from the ground. The only place you can see the roof is from a small spot in the middle of the neighbor's lawn. Why bother with the extra expense of patterned shingles if nobody will be able to see them? I decided to use the plain shingles instead.

The Paint

I dealt extensively with the subject of siding in the section on repairs, since replacing the siding is more of a repair than a decorating option. However, I didn't go into much detail on color and style at that time.

Color— Color has a tremendous effect on a house. Light colors make a house look larger, and dark colors make a house look more solid. Think carefully about color before you select any siding.

Many handyman specials are small. Nothing ever seems to be quite big enough. So I do everything possible to make things seem bigger. I usually paint houses light, bright colors to make them look as large as possible.

I also use warm tones to make them look more cheerful. I'll use a color like light yellow rather than light grey (a cool tone) on a small house. Cool tones tend to give a house an air of dignity and elegance. That's wasted on a small house. A house needs to be big to be dignified. There's a limit to how dignified and elegant a small house can be. So it's better to try to make it look friendly and inviting instead. Warm colors do that. A small house is never going to be terribly impressive, but it can, and should, be friendly.

Look again at Figure 11-10. Notice that the trim is a light color and the house is darker. I did that because this particular house had mineral composition siding designed to look like cedar shingles. The siding was in good condition and perfectly functional. But it wasn't very pretty. I preferred not to call attention to it. So I painted it a dark gray-blue. Dark colors tend to make materials fade into the background visually.

There was another reason for painting the siding a dark color. I wanted the Victorian trim to be highly visible. The white gingerbread really jumps out against a darker background. This helps distract people from the siding. They see the highly-visible trim, and don't notice the dark-colored siding in the background. Many people have commented on this house; *everyone* mentions the Victorian gingerbread but *no one* mentions the siding. That's exactly the effect I wanted.

Dark siding was perfect for this house. Even though it was small inside, it appeared quite large from the outside. The dark siding seemed to reinforce its solid appearance. It never fails to amaze me that you can't judge the size of a house from the street. Big houses sometimes look small, and small houses sometimes look big. When it comes to color, the actual size of the house doesn't really matter. What's important is the visual effect of the exterior. If it looks big, you can use decorating suitable for a big house, even if the house is small on the inside.

Here's one disadvantage to dark colors. They absorb more heat than lighter colors. Heat can be hard on wood siding. It expands and contracts as it heats and cools. But that's not a problem with mineral siding. It's tough stuff and won't be harmed by excess heat.

There's another interesting point I'd like to make about the paint on my Victorian house: It's one of the few times I used exterior latex paint instead of oil-base paint. Latex is terrible for wood, but fine for masonry, mineral siding, metal, and other non-porous materials. And, since latex paint is half the price of oil-base paint, I saved a few dollars and still got a good paint job.

Style— Style is another important consideration when choosing colors. If you don't match the color to the style of the house, it will create a jarring effect, like any other mismatched modification. A Colonial house should be painted Colonial colors, like white, blue, or green. If you look at decorating books and magazines, almost all Colonial houses are painted in some variation of these colors. You want your house to look like a picture out of a magazine. You don't want people to look at it and say, "What's that supposed to be?"

When you decide to change the color of your house, be sure you pick a shade that's in style. Check the latest issue of *Better Homes and Gardens* for the most popular shades of the day. This will give your house an advantage over others, which may not have been redecorated as recently. Buyers always prefer the more stylish house.

Don't get carried away with color, though. While you want to use colors that are currently in style, you don't want to go overboard. A neighbor of mine painted his house in a combination of pink and mauve. These colors are currently used by a lot of expensive restaurants. I thought it looked nice. Not everyone agreed. Many people who came to look at my house (which was yellow and white) had something uncomplimentary to say about the pink and mauve house down the street. "Yuck!" was the most common reaction. It's usually best to go with subtle tones. You don't want your color combinations to have that effect on people. A bad choice of colors can drive away buyers who might otherwise be interested.

Grays and pale blues are fashionable now. My neighborhood has suddenly filled up with light grey houses with white trim, and just a little touch of bright red as an accent. A number of commercial buildings have appeared using this color combination as well. These are perfectly decent colors to use on a house. They're pleasant and inoffensive. *Better Homes and Gardens* uses them all the time. Depending on the size and style of your house, light grey may not be the best color for your house, but you can be sure that it won't be the worst choice, either.

The dark browns and barn reds that were popular in the early 1970s are out-dated now. These colors went well with the rustic, back-to-nature look that was popular at the time. If you buy a house painted in these colors, it probably needs a new coat of paint. Paint it even if it doesn't. Imagine it in another color, for instance grey, blue, or yellow. Wouldn't it look a lot better? Today, elegance is in.

I don't want to seem too dogmatic about colors. Styles change. The colors that are in favor now will be out in a few years. That's why it's so important to stay in touch with trends. What colors are featured in magazines this year? What are they using in model homes, and restaurants? Paint is fairly cheap, and a current paint job will make a strong, positive first impression. Any time you can make a positive impression for little cost, do it!

Styles of Siding

Unlike paint, siding is expensive. All colors of paint cost about the same, but all styles of siding don't. Therefore, cost will be important when selecting siding.

Luxury sidings— Many types of expensive and attractive siding are available these days. I like cedar shingles and fine wood clapboard or shiplap. These look very nice on new homes. However, I've never found them to be worth the money when remodeling. The only siding that my customers are willing to pay extra for is brick. As I mentioned in the chapter on exterior repairs, you may want to add brick siding to your house if you're selling to customers that are willing and able to pay for it. I wouldn't bother with any other expensive siding.

Vinyl or aluminum siding— If you're planning to install one of these siding types, dark colors may not be available because dark colors absorb too much heat and fade quickly. So most vinyl and aluminum manufacturers offer only lighter shades.

Choose the color of your siding as you would the color of paint. Pick a stylish but inoffensive color. Grey, yellow, or pale blue are good choices. Avoid pink — some people react badly to pink. White is acceptable, but dull. There are already too many white houses in most suburbs. Yours will have more visual impact if it's another color.

You can't paint vinyl siding, but you can paint aluminum if you use paints designed for that purpose. If your siding is perfectly usable, but ugly, a fresh coat of paint will freshen it up. Avoid the expense of replacing siding if you possibly can.

Wood— Lately people have begun stripping and restoring old wood siding rather than repainting or covering it over with new siding. Once they have all the old paint off, they stain the wood. Stained wood siding is featured in many expensive new luxury homes now. You can give your old "handyman-special" a new luxury look by imitating their exterior decor. I've seen a number of houses done this way, and they looked very nice.

In all honesty, I've never tried this technique myself. I'll try stained siding when I find a property that's right for it. Obviously, stripping all the old paint off a house is going to be a lot of work. But if it's an old house and the paint is peeling, you'd have to strip it off anyway before you could repaint. It may not be that much more work to strip off the last few bits of paint and get completely down to the wood. It won't cost any more in materials than painting. It may even cost less, since good exterior stain is cheaper than quality oil-base paint. Your extra cost will be your labor. Is it worth it? That depends on the neighborhood. If you're in an up-scale neighborhood where buyers will appreciate this look, then do it. In a lower price bracket, don't bother.

The Porch

The porch on your house is an important element of the exterior design. The quality and style of a porch can either add or detract from the look and value of a house.

Figure 11-12A
Craftsman house with 1960s porch trim

Figure 11-12B
White paint subdues ornamental trim

Porches are often altered a great deal over the years. They're exposed to the weather and may be poorly maintained. Sooner or later, they need work. Because it isn't part of the living area, people don't worry very much about maintaining their porches. Usually they do whatever is least expensive, using mismatched materials or styles for repairs. Sometimes they replace the porch with a new one that doesn't suit the rest of the house. Or, they may simply remove the porch altogether, leaving a house that was designed for a porch without any porch at all. *You* have to make something good out of these bad situations.

Matching the style— Look at the house in Figure 11-12A. It's obvious to me that most or all of the porch has been replaced. From the style of the work, I would guess that it was done in the early 1960s. The stairs, pillars, railing, and deck of the porch are 1960s style. They don't match the rest of the house, which is 1920s Craftsman style.

The best way to deal with a mismatched porch is the way I dealt with the pseudo-Colonial house we discussed earlier (Figure 11-11). That is, try to pull the house together visually using trim and color. Avoid doing any major building or demolition if possible. Remember that trim and color are major elements of design. It's often these easily-alterable elements that establish the look of the style. The basic shapes are important, but if they're close to the design you want, use color rather than rebuilding to get the effect you want. Rebuild only when there's no reasonable alternative.

Compare the *before* and *after* (Figure 11-12A and 11-12B) pictures of this house to see the difference trim color makes. I didn't make any structural style changes. Instead, I painted the wrought iron white to match the house. This subdued its "60s" ornamental style. The Craftsman style is still not obvious, but it's closer to its intended look. I could have spent a lot of money rebuilding the porch or making other major changes, but it wouldn't have added anything to the value of the house.

Closed-in Porches

A screened or glassed-in porch can be a real design dilemma. Usually the screens or windows were added years after the house was built and don't match the rest of the house. It's common to find modern aluminum windows in the porch of a very old-fashioned house.

The real problem with an enclosed porch is that it's both ugly and a valuable addition to the house. If you tear out the windows, the house will look better, but the porch won't be as useful.

Figure 11-13
Porch enclosure conflicts with original style

Which is more important? Your choice will depend on how bad the porch looks and how useful it may be to your potential buyers.

How does it look?— Was the original porch totally disfigured by enclosing it with mismatched windows? Or was it an ugly porch to begin with? If the porch was beautiful, it's a shame to allow the enclosure to ruin it. If the porch was nothing special, you won't gain much by changing it — just leave the ugly windows in place. Or, can you improve its looks by making some simple change in the window enclosure?

How about the quality of the materials used for the enclosure? Are they top quality windows, or just plain cheap glass with deteriorating screens? I leave porch windows in place if they're good quality and in good condition. However, I won't go to any trouble to repair those that are poor quality.

I had a house a few years ago with a screened-in front porch that needed repairs. I removed several screens to repair them. The porch looked so much better without the screens that I just left it that way. I guess other people must have thought it looked better too. I sold the house for a good profit with very little other work.

How useful is it?— Decide how useful the porch will be to your buyers. Again, let the neighborhood guide you. Young families in low-cost housing use their porches. They're less particular about the style of their house. I would leave the enclosure in place as long as it's good quality and in good condition. However, don't leave a poor quality job, even if it's in good shape. *Nobody* will like it.

Buyers of more expensive housing are more particular about the style of their house. They won't buy an ugly home, no matter how useful the porch might be. The extra porch space has little value because they tend to lead more private lives. In a more expensive neighborhood, your best bet is to remove the enclosure.

An example— I had a problem deciding what to do with the house in Figure 11-13. Ugly, modern aluminum storms and screens had been put on this 1920s Prairie-style house. My first impulse was to remove them, but the underlying porch wasn't particularly attractive either. The enclosure was a quality job, and it was still in good condition. My dilemma involved the neighborhood. It was changing for the better — gradually becoming an upper-middle-class area.

My decision to rent the house rather than sell it made up my mind for me. Renters are more concerned with living space than looks. I did the best I could to improve the looks of the addition by painting the aluminum white. At least then it matched the trim and took on more of a Colonial look. I also added carriage lamps. These small improvements helped to distract attention from the unattractiveness of the porch.

I decided to rent this property because home values were increasing at least 10 percent a year. As I mentioned in the section on property selection, this is just the kind of area you want to look for. The longer you hold on to a property like this, the more it will be worth.

I'm going to wait a few years until the area peaks in price, then I'll remove the windows, upgrade the porch and sell the house for a generous profit. The eventual buyers of this property will probably be very style-conscious. I'll make this house look as nice as possible, probably by restoring the original style. Buyers in upper price ranges appreciate these details and will pay top dollar for a really nice property. In the meantime, I'm making a profit by renting the house. I can afford to wait.

When you have a marginal porch like the one in the example, think about ways to work around the porch. Add decorator items to draw attention away from the windows: exterior lights, trim, paint, nice house numbers, a new mailbox or even landscaping can help. A well-maintained garden can do a lot to make a practical, but unattractive porch appear more desirable. Figure 11-14 shows examples of simple decorative additions which can improve the exterior appearance of your house.

Adding a Porch

Adding a porch can sometimes be a major design improvement. Most people appreciate a well-designed, attractive porch. It's nice to have one, even if all you use it for is to stay dry while fumbling for keys on a rainy day.

Many cheaper homes were built with plain, ugly fronts. A new porch can dress up a house like this. Of course, you need to match the porch to the style of the house. If the house has no particular style, you can create one with your addition. Remember to be consistent with the whole exterior of the home. Building a porch is a major job, and I never take on any major job lightly. But adding a new porch may actually be the cheapest way to beautify an undistinguished, unattractive house.

Other porch repairs— Sometimes you'll have to build or rebuild a porch on the rear of a house. An attractive back porch is also an asset. Often, you have little choice in whether or not to make improvements. A deteriorated porch will have to be fixed. And while you're at it, you may as well make it better. Figure 11-15A shows the rear view of one of my more recent jobs. Obviously, this porch had to be rebuilt. But this was an especially nice property. The new porch had to be nice too. Figure 11-15B shows the completed porch rebuilt in the home's original style. Notice I also added a small block patio as a convenience to fill in the area between the porch and garage. This kind of simple decorating adds thousands of dollars to the value of your house and costs relatively little. Figure 11-16 shows my impression of the return you can expect from improvements you make to a porch.

The Front Door

We discussed the importance of the front door in the section on repairs. An attractive front door says "Welcome." It sets the style of the home. I've seen a lot of modern doors with light finishes on old-fashioned houses. Usually these doors date back to the 1960s. At that time, anything old-fashioned was unstylish. I'm sure the owners thought that adding a modern front door improved the looks of the house. Today these doors look ugly and out of character.

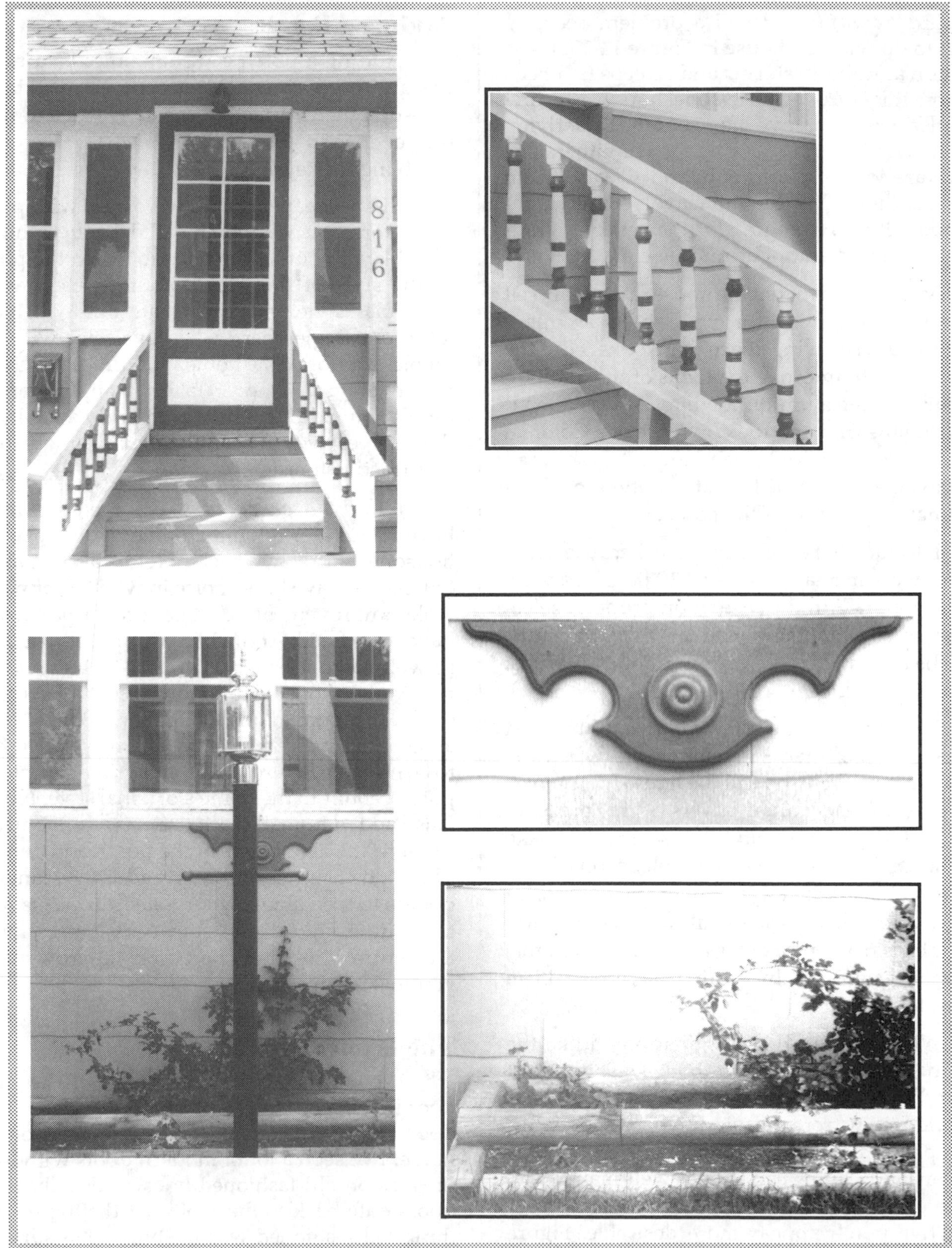

Figure 11-14
Examples of simple decorative additions for the exterior of the house

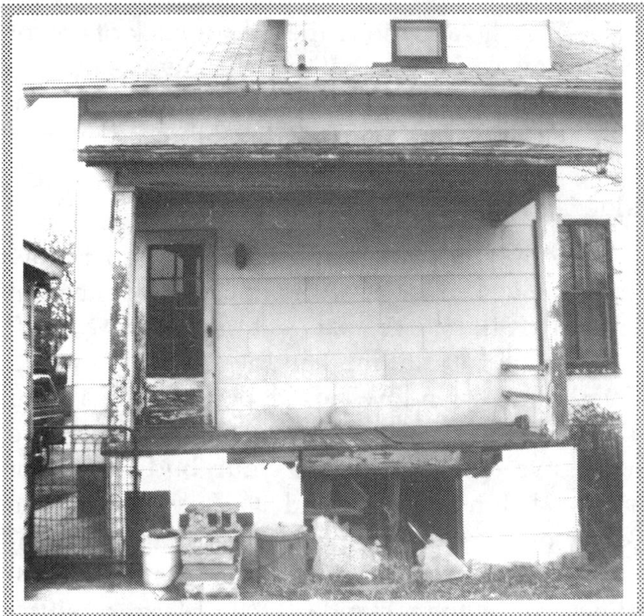

Figure 11-15A
This deteriorated porch needed to be rebuilt

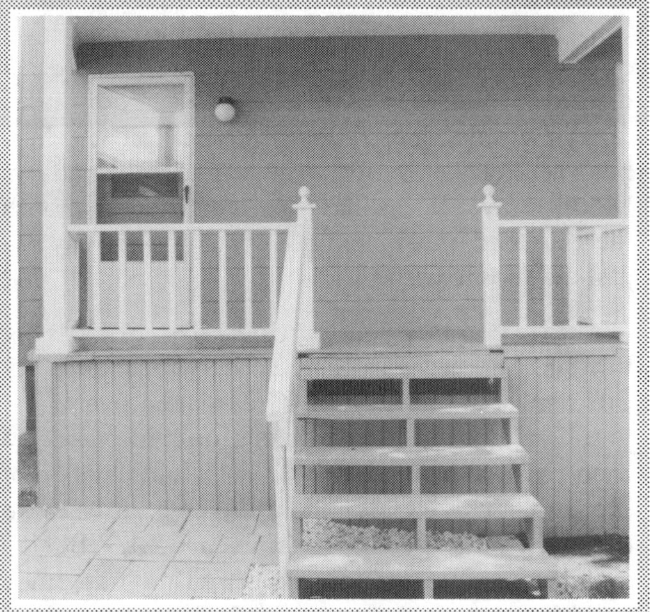

Figure 11-15B
The finished porch, reconstructed in the original style

Before buying a new door, I always try painting the old door with a good, oil-base paint. Most people don't think of painting this type of door. But a clear finish on a door doesn't keep you from painting it. In many cases, a coat of paint will make an ugly door perfectly acceptable.

Storm doors— Is there a storm door on the front of this house, or are you planning to put one on? In cold climates, storm doors may be useful on all the exterior doors, including the front. This is especially true in moderate-income neighborhoods. If you're dealing in luxury homes, it's more fashionable to leave the storm door off the front entrance so everyone can see the entry door.

A storm door obscures the view of your front door. If you have a beautiful front door, it won't show as much. If you have an ugly front door, it won't show as much either — this can be to your advantage. If you have an unattractive door, leave that door and consider installing a storm door. See how it looks with the storm door in place. Then decide if you have to replace the entry door.

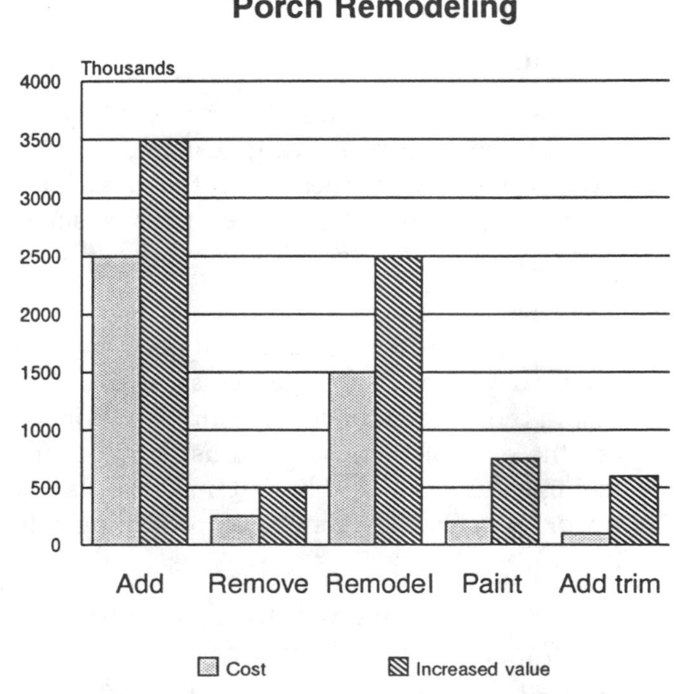

Figure 11-16
Cost vs. value of porch remodeling for a mid-priced house

Trim— One option most people don't think of is adding trim to the front door. The biggest difference between a plain modern door and a fancy Colonial door is the trim. The Colonial door has rectangular molding arranged in a pattern. Modern style doors have no trim, just a smooth face. Instead of replacing the plain door, why not just add some trim?

You can buy prefabricated trim at most big lumber or hardware stores. It comes in many different shapes and sizes. Create whatever effect you like. Cut the trim to size, glue it in place and then paint it. Your door will look just like one of those expensive Colonials. It takes a while to do the work, since this is precision carpentry. But it's still less trouble and less expense than hanging a new door.

If none of these remedies work, then replace the door. An ugly front door can cut thousands of dollars off your selling price. You want to create a good first impression for your buyers. One of the first things they'll see is the front door.

Windows

Some remodeling books blithely toss around the idea of moving installed windows from one wall to another — like they were pieces of furniture. Don't be misled. I never suggest moving windows. It's a big job and rarely worthwhile.

There are some houses that need *more* windows. If you have a big expanse of blank wall facing the street, add some windows. Windows are the eyes of a house. A house without front facing windows looks blind. It makes visitors feel uncomfortable, like they're approaching a fortress.

When adding windows, consider how placement will affect the appearance of the house. Look at the better houses on any street. Notice that they all have an attractive layout of front windows. This is true of any attractive house, regardless of size or price. This pleasing layout is one of the things that makes the house appealing.

Then go around to the side or back of any of these houses. Notice that the windows seem to be placed with less care and in no particular pattern. The windows are placed where they're needed inside the room. How they appear from the outside is much less important.

Sometimes you may want to add a window to improve the looks of the house. If so, keep in mind that the major cost isn't the window itself. It's the labor. Installing windows is a lot of work. Even cheap windows are expensive when you consider the labor cost. Buying more expensive windows can really push your budget out of shape. I don't recommend it. Very few people know or care anything about the quality of windows. Name brand windows can cost up to five times more than standard "builder's quality" windows. They won't raise the value of the house anywhere near what they cost.

You don't need expensive windows to get an expensive look. Most of your buyers won't pay extra for better quality alone. But they will pay extra for good looks. That's not right, I know, but it's the truth. Buyers prefer flash to substance. They buy the sizzle, not the steak. At least, mine do. I can't change it. Neither can you. So learn to live with it.

What do people like? They're impressed with bay windows and leaded-glass windows. They're highly visible. They also cost more than plain windows. But they're no more expensive to install. You'll get a good return on your investment there. People pay extra for bay windows and leaded glass windows because they are getting something special. Of course, you shouldn't install any window in a house if the design is out of character with the house style.

Alternatives to adding windows— What if the house has windows in the front but they're too small? That's common in older homes. Sometimes it's easier to improve than replace. Maybe you should just enlarge the windows.

If you have a large expanse of wall with small windows, make the windows *look* bigger by adding simple decor items: shutters, window boxes or decorative trim over or around the windows. These make the existing windows look bigger than they really are and make the front of the house look more appealing.

Instead of people saying, "Gee, that's an awfully small window for that big wall," they'll say, "Oh, look at those shutters, and that nice flowerbox! Isn't that pretty!" The window is still small, and the rest of the wall is still big, but it isn't as noticeable as it was.

Put on a pleasing face— The front of your house makes the first impression — either good or bad. If you're adding shutters or other window trim, just put them on the front. Continue your decorative window treatments around the side or back only if the house is on a corner lot and these areas are highly visible from the street. Even then, they don't need to be quite as detailed. For instance, if you have shutters and window boxes on the front, put only shutters on the side. Or, if you have ornate trim on the front, a simple molding in the same color will do for the sides.

The sides and back should be clean, neat, a pleasing color, and in good repair. They don't need the same decorative treatment as the front of the house.

Garages

Include the garage in your design scheme if it's at the front of the building or is easily seen from the street. Make sure the paint and trim match the rest of the house. Again, it should be clean, neat and sturdy, even if you can't see it from the front of the house.

Landscaping and Yard Decor

There are a million ways to landscape a home. A look down any block will confirm this. For some families the yard is a playground for their children, for others a pen for their dog, and for others it's an outdoor retreat with beautiful gardens and walks. Some want all lawn or ground cover, others prefer a deck, patio, or even a pool for entertaining.

There are as many choices in landscaping as there are yards to landscape. Your problem is that you can't anticipate what your buyers want, need or can afford. A deck is wasted on someone who wants to plant a garden and grow vegetables. It covers up valuable growing space. Gardens are wasted on people who only want an exercise area for their dogs. Don't try to second guess your buyers. Let them decide how they want to use the property. If your house already has a nice patio, some buyers might consider it a plus. But don't spend a lot of money putting one in. No matter what you do, there's a chance that your buyers won't like it. Put your money into something with a guaranteed return, like the kitchen.

I'll spend time and money on landscaping only if I have a *problem yard* that will discourage buyers. The problem could be an ugly view, a drainage problem like ones we discussed earlier, or maybe a yard so small that it appears useless. How should you deal with problems like these?

Fencing

Fencing, when used correctly, is a strong, positive design element in your exterior decor. It serves to define the yard and set limits. Used incorrectly, however, it can have a negative effect.

Many subdivision developers use fencing to create a sense of identity and exclusivity. They surround their subdivisions with brick walls, a gatehouse, and a sign with the name of the development written on it. The subdivision becomes a private community, cut off from the rest of the world. Other developers ban fences altogether. You may have seen subdivisions like this, where no house has a fence. The idea is to create an open, flowing area, like a park or commons. New owners have to agree that they won't erect any fences on their property.

As you can see, there are several viewpoints on fencing. Your buyers will have their own ideas on fencing, too. Some people love them, some hate them. So I don't put up fences unless I have a reason to.

Figure 11-17A
This yard lacks privacy

Figure 11-17B
New fence blocks off unpleasant view

Privacy fences— One obvious reason for installing a fence is to screen off an ugly view. A simple 6-foot pine privacy fence will cover up just about anything. Figure 11-17A shows the side-yard of one of my houses. It faces the rear of a warehouse where trucks pull in and out of the driveway. The fence in Figure 11-17B completely blocks off this unpleasant view. These fences

Figure 11-18
Small patio is an easy and inexpensive addition

Figure 11-19
Small back yard can have charm

aren't expensive or difficult to put up and they can solve a lot of problems. I use privacy fences regularly.

Another good use for this type of fence is to insure privacy. This is particularly true in a "problem yard." Sometimes a neighbor's house is very close or oriented so it seems your yard is more part of the neighbor's property than yours. People feel uncomfortable in a yard like that. It makes them feel like trespassers on their own property. When you fence the yard, you remove it from the neighbor's view, and the neighbor's house from your view. You define your property, making it more comfortable to use.

Defining space— Outlining the perimeters of a small yard can give it character. Perhaps the neighbor's larger yard seems to overpower yours, or *all* the other homes around you have large expanses of property and yours seems small by comparison. Add a fence and the yard becomes an entirely different sort of space.

Well-defined space is very important in high density housing such as condominium complexes. Many condos come with a tiny yard, maybe as little as ten feet by ten feet. Builders usually surround these yards with a wall and put in a little deck, planter, fountain, or some other features. The yard becomes a cloistered garden, a private piece of the outdoors.

Use some of these same ideas when dealing with a very small yard. Often people will look at a small yard and say, "What could I possibly do with a yard like that?" You'll have to show them. Put in a small patio like the one in Figure 11-18. Add some seats or planters. Create a little decorative walkway or a cozy corner with a birdbath, like the one in Figure 11-19. These aren't expensive items. Then install some decorative exterior lights.

When people look at the yard they'll think, "Oh, how nice! I can sit outside on the patio and enjoy the quiet; and I can plant some colorful flowers in the planters. It's not too much to keep up, in fact it's just right. The lights are pretty; this would be a nice area for a party." You've provided the inspiration which replaces the idea that the buyer is getting shorted on land area. For more ideas on fences, order a copy of *Fences & Retaining Walls* from this publisher. This book describes most of the fences you're likely to encounter, and tells you step-by-step how to build them.

Don't even consider putting in the fancy landscaping that condo developers use: brick walls, spas and decks. You can create the same feeling at a fraction of the cost. Instead of a brick wall, use pine fencing. For a small yard, this will only cost a couple hundred dollars. You can make

Figure 11-20A
Deteriorated fence is an eyesore

Figure 11-20B
Removing the fence is a big improvement

a small patio out of patio blocks, and planters and borders out of landscape timbers or scrap 2 x 4s. The whole project should cost less than $500 and take only about two days' work.

As I said before, don't overemphasize the landscaping. If your house has a nice yard, or even an ordinary yard, leave it. Plant grass seed if the lawn is dead and add some colorful flowering plants to the front garden. Adding something fancy won't increase the value enough to make it worthwhile. Do just enough so the yard doesn't detract from the value of your house.

When to remove fences— Sometimes it helps as much to remove a fence as to build one. This is particularly true if the fence is ugly or deteriorated. Figure 11-20A proves the point. I

Figure 11-21
A classic handyman special

tore the fence down with the intention of rebuilding a new one along the property line. But as you can see in Figure 11-20B, the trees now define the property line and the yard looks far more attractive without a fence. Simply removing the fence added to the value of the property in this case.

Remove any fence that obscures a nice view. It's also a good idea to take down any fence that either interferes with use of the yard or defines space in a way that makes the property seem less valuable.

A few years ago I bought a house from a man who had several dogs. The dogs were kept in the back yard and away from the garage, driveway and side yard by a large chain-link fence. This fence made it look like the property ended at the driveway. The driveway, garage and side-yard seemed to belong to the neighbor's property.

You don't want to create confusion in the minds of potential buyers. If the chain-link fence fooled me, I knew it would confuse my potential buyers as well. Most people wouldn't stick around long enough to find out where the property line really was. They would drive away thinking, "That's a nice house. Too bad it doesn't have a driveway or a garage."

I think that chain link fence helped me buy the house at a big discount. Other people probably assumed that the house sat on a small lot. In this case the defect was easy to repair. I simply took down the fence. Instantly the yard seemed twice as large. The actual property boundaries became obvious. That made the home appealing and easier to sell.

Figure 11-22
The finished project

Decorating Completes the Package

Your goal in exterior decorating is to create a coordinated and organized look for your whole house. It's important that everything appears to belong, as though it were planned, not like it just happened. The front of the house is the key. Your house needs to have *curb appeal*. If people don't like what they see from their car, they won't bother getting out for a closer look. The sides and back of your house are much less important. Potential buyers won't see these until after they've gone through the interior. By that time, their overall impression of the house, good or bad, will already be formed.

Once people form an impression of your house, it's very hard to change it. That's why decorating is so important. You can turn a house like the one in Figure 11-21 into showplace. Figure 11-22 is the same house a few months and more than a few dollars later. I was very pleased with the results of this particular job — and so was the rest of the neighborhood.

Now that we've completed our survey of the exterior, let's step through that beautifully-renovated front door and take another look at the interior.

CHAPTER TWELVE

Decorating the Interior

Interior decorating is an important part of your project. Remember that what you're creating is somebody's home. People can be very emotional about their homes. They should be. For most buyers, a new home is both their dream and their biggest expense. People want a place that's friendly, cheerful, warm, inviting, and most of all, comfortable. Your goal is to create a house that people can love living in. You don't need to love it yourself; you're not going to live there. But someone has to like it enough to take out a 30-year loan to buy it. That takes both rational and emotional commitment. Rational commitment comes from the number of bedrooms, the plumbing and heating system, and the type of things you see described in the multiple listing service. Emotional commitment comes mostly from the interior decor you create.

I like all my houses. If I'm getting ready to sell one that I don't like, I keep working on it until I do like it. When it's likable, liveable and lovable, I know it's ready to sell.

When people are out house shopping, they may not know why they like a particular house. They just know that it gives them a good feeling — and that feeling sells houses! If a house makes prospective buyers feel good, they'll want it — and probably buy it if they can possibly afford it. If they don't like it, they won't buy it at any price. It's as simple as that.

That's the secret of success in this business. Buy houses that no one wants and turn them into houses that people can love.

Choosing Your Interior Decor

Your interior color scheme is the basis of all of your other decorating decisions. Once you've decided on that, you can work out the details in each room. The major decorative items — floor covering, tile, window treatments, paint, wallpaper and lighting — should harmonize with the overall look of the house. So our first step will be to make the most basic decorating decisions; then we'll go through the house room by room, looking at the details.

Your first question probably is, "What color should I paint it?" That's a good question, and worth some serious thought.

The Importance of Color

Color has a psychological effect on people. It's important to understand how to use colors so they can work *for* you, not against you. When you look at homes, you'll discover that many people don't understand how critical color is to the sales appeal of a home. They decorate the inside and outside of their houses at random without any apparent plan. The wrong colors or combinations of colors can actually lower the value of a house by thousands of dollars.

Commercial establishments, such as stores and restaurants, hire decorators to create pleasant, inviting interiors for their businesses. They want people to come in, relax, and spend money. Study the colors used in the stores where you shop and the restaurants where you eat. Why were these colors chosen? What were the decorators trying to do? Were they successful? You can develop good judgment on use of color just by observing what experts have done.

Dark vs. Light

Dark colors are close, intimate, and luxurious. Many expensive restaurants use dark colors, rich woods and subdued lighting to create an elegant atmosphere. The larger the room, the darker the shade you need to make the room seem cozy and intimate. Decorators use colors the same way in homes. Many luxury homes are very large. Designers often choose dark shades of wood and subdued wallpaper to create a solid, refined and elegant atmosphere in a large luxury home. I'm sure you've seen examples of this in architectural design magazines.

Large rooms painted in light colors seem too open, more like a public place or hotel lobby than a home. Use light colors in small rooms, where you *need* a feeling of spaciousness. It's hard to make a small home appear elegant, so try for a friendly, inviting decor instead. Light, warm colors will make a moderate-sized home seen cozy and cheerful. Dark colors will make the same home seem drab and claustrophobic. Dark colors close space in; light colors enlarge space and push the walls back.

Notice that fast-food restaurants always use bright cheery colors in their decor. They want to appear fresh, open and friendly so they'll attract as many people in as possible. They make money on quantity, not quality. They want to pack as many people in as small a space as possible without making them feel crowded. They manage this through their choice of colors.

Poor color choices will cost you— A while ago, I bought a house that was a perfect example of the wrong decorating approach. The former owners had tried to decorate a small, three-bedroom house in a very trendy, stylish way. Unfortunately, they didn't understand the use of color and scale. They painted the walls dark brown, installed Art Deco light fixtures and then brought in massive wood furniture. The furniture took up so much space that you could barely get in the door, and the dark walls made the small rooms look like caves. But that's all that was wrong with the house.

I bought this house for $18,500 under market value, simply because of bad decorating. This is a perfect example of how powerful a coat of paint can be. Once the furniture was out and the house was repainted, it was a very likable home. Best of all, it was in a neighborhood where property values were increasing. This is another house I'm sitting on for future gain. Buying under market makes it a perfect rental property. Rent provides enough income to cover expenses while the home appreciates in value.

Light vs. White

When I suggest using light colors, that doesn't necessarily mean white. Many people paint everything white, inside and out. Can't go wrong with white, right? Wrong! White isn't the worst color you can use for rooms, but it's far from the best. If you think it's too much trouble to pick out colors, and just paint everything white, your prospective buyer will pick up your "why bother?" attitude. People are sensitive to this. Your lack of interest in decorating may create a lack of interest in buying.

It's easy to preserve a neutral look without using stark white. I often use off-white shades like antique white, Navajo white or light beige. Light pastels are also worth considering. I prefer *warm* colors, like light shades of yellow, tan, or peach. These colors appear friendly and actually make dark or cold rooms seem warmer. Cool colors, like blue or green, are good for rooms that tend to be too bright or hot. Use them in rooms with a western exposure that get the hot afternoon sun in summer.

Unifying with Color

Our mind tends to group together things that are the same color. People perceive boundaries between rooms that are different colors. So if you have a small home with an "L" shaped living and dining area, paint it all the same color. This makes the house seem more spacious.

Create separate spaces with color by painting different areas different colors. However, make sure the colors blend well with each other, and don't change colors in the middle of a wall. Find a natural breaking point between the rooms to make the color change. Individual rooms can be painted different colors, but they should be in complementary shades. Never have startling distinctions between rooms, like red to blue, or even gray to yellow. People find this kind of visual disruption disturbing.

Coordinating Colors

Coordinate your colors to show off the other elements of the room. For instance, if you have natural woodwork, choose colors that go well with wood tones. Not only will the walls look better, but it will help draw attention to the woodwork. Highlight the positive features in a house. Nice woodwork is rare these days. If you have it, use it to best advantage.

Match the wall color to the carpeting if carpeting is already down. If you're lucky, the carpeting will be a neutral color, like gray or beige. Most colors go well with colors like these. Just keep your color groups together, cool colors with cool colors, and warm colors with warm colors. For instance, pale blues and grays go well with gray carpeting, and Navajo white, peach or beige look nice with beige or brown tones.

If the carpeting is a strong color, it's even more important to coordinate the wall colors. If nothing looks good with the carpet, you can always paint the walls white. I didn't say that you should *never* paint a room white. There are certain times when no other color will work with features that are already there. White is fine in moderate amounts. But don't use white just because nothing else comes to mind. Use white for a reason. And never paint all the rooms white.

You put a lot of time, money and effort into fixing up a house, so don't neglect the interior decor. I've seen many competent remodeling jobs lose their impact because they didn't follow through on the decorating. Take the time to decorate your house carefully. Pick out attractive colors, ones that people will respond to. Many times people have said to me, "You put a lot of tender loving care into this house! It really shows!" Actually, it was the potential profit I had in mind when I brought all that tender loving care into action, but I didn't see any need to tell them that.

Ceiling Treatments

Decorating magazines and model homes often feature special ceiling treatments. Among these are wood ceiling planks. They look just like the wood planks used for expensive flooring, except they're usually finished in lighter shades, like whitewashed pine or oak.

Figure 12-1

Tin walls and ceiling found in an old house

These ceilings look very nice in decorator houses, particularly Colonial, country and southwest-style homes. The better Early American homes often had ceilings covered with planks, so this treatment goes well with period houses. Are they really useful for your average decorating plans? Probably not. Unless you're doing a particular style or authentic reproductions in high-end housing, you won't want to invest that much money in the ceiling.

Another ceiling treatment I'm seeing again is ceiling tin. You may have seen pressed tin ceilings in restored Victorian stores, restaurants or bars. They usually have a raised pattern and are painted. Today, they're reproduced in genuine tin, or in plastic patterns that look like the tin.

I'm very fond of tin ceilings (you may have gathered by now that I like Victorian styles). Unfortunately, I can't justify their cost in my houses. If I find them in a house, like the one shown in Figure 12-1, I try to preserve the ceiling. It's a unique feature, worth a little extra effort.

Occasionally the extra cost of exotic ceiling treatments may be a good investment. For example, some material may fit so well and add so much that it raises the value well beyond the cost.

High-Fashion Ceiling Treatments

High-fashion decorating magazines occasionally show ceilings painted in brilliant, stylish colors. Some are wallpapered. Others have painted murals. That's great for magazines, but I wouldn't recommend it for one of your renovating jobs.

Ceilings like this belong in grand, million-dollar houses. The same ceiling wouldn't look good on a small scale. It loses all impact. My advice is to stick to a plain white ceiling.

Wallpaper

My wife loves wallpaper. I think she'd wallpaper every room in every house if I let her. Certainly, wallpaper can add a great deal of personality and charm to a house. But don't overdo a good thing. Buyers have their own ideas about how much personality, and *whose* personality, their home should reflect.

Wallpaper is also fairly expensive, unless you take the time to shop for bargains. Sometimes you can find wallpaper that won't cost more than paint for the same area. However, wallpaper requires a lot more labor to install than paint. It has to be hung right. A careless job of papering is no improvement at all.

Know What You're Doing

Hanging wallpaper requires skilled labor. You can't just hire a kid off the street and expect a decent job. It's not terribly difficult to learn, but you have to take the time to do it, or train an employee to do it.

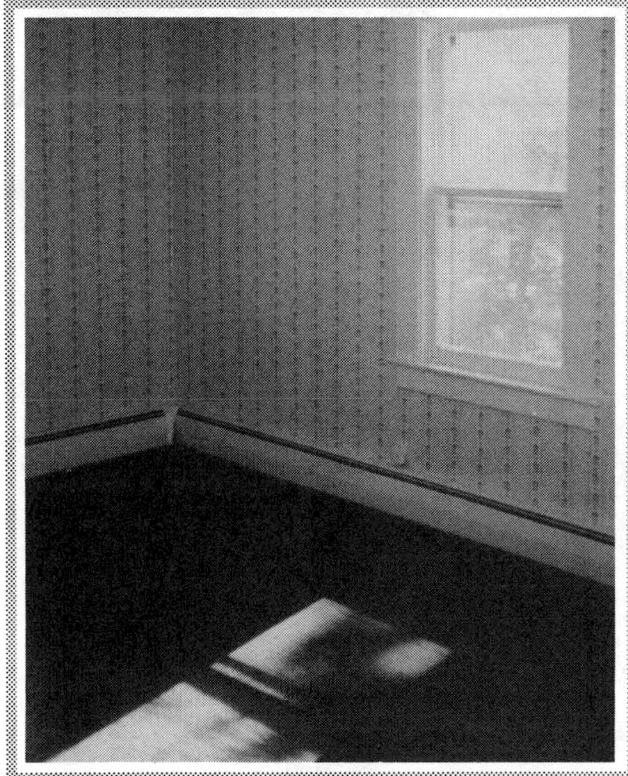

Figure 12-2
Wallpaper complements the oak flooring

When you hang wallpaper, the pattern has to match. It's a lot easier to hang wallpaper with a simple, repeating pattern, such as lines or dots, than one with large pictures that have to be matched carefully. I've seen countless wallpaper jobs where the pattern wasn't matched properly.

I bought a house where the wallpaper had been slapped on so carelessly that the corners had all been bridged over, creating a rounded room! If you leaned a hand on one of those rounded corners, you'd poke a hole right through the paper. If you're going to go to the expense of putting up wallpaper, do it right.

Advantages of Wallpaper

Wallpaper has quite a few practical advantages. Its best use is for covering minor wall damage. Hairline cracks and small nail holes disappear under it. You may find it easier to wallpaper than to spend the time filling and sanding a whole wall full of tiny cracks and pits. However, wallpaper won't cover large holes or hold badly cracked, unstable plaster together. You have to apply wallpaper on a fairly smooth and solid surface. Otherwise the results are unpredictable.

It's often easier to repaper a wall that was previously wallpapered than to strip and clean the wall for painting. Even if you can remove all the old wallpaper (which is sometimes very difficult), the wall will be covered with glue residue. Any paint you apply over this will peel off. Removing this residue may be even harder than removing the wallpaper itself. I generally don't bother. I just hang new wallpaper.

You don't necessarily need to remove old wallpaper before hanging the new. If the old paper is on tight, you can wallpaper right over it. If it isn't, it may peel off, taking your new paper with it. I've never found it necessary to steam off old wallpaper. If steam's needed to get it off, don't bother. It's on tight enough to hold one more layer.

Design Aspects

A nicely-papered wall gives the impression that the house has been carefully decorated. Most people think of wallpaper as an expensive "upgrade." After all, you don't see wallpaper in low-budget tract housing.

Choose wallpaper that matches the overall style of the house. That is, a formal house needs formal, traditional wallpaper. An informal or modern house should have informal or modern wallpaper. Now and then you can mix styles to create a special effect, but not unless you're sure you know what you're doing. When in doubt, keep the styles matching.

Wallpaper accents the existing features of a house. Natural woodwork looks particularly nice when set off against wallpaper. Keep this in mind when you're choosing the wallpaper for a room. The bedroom in Figure 12-2 has a beautiful wood floor. The wallpaper picks up the wood tone in

Figure 12-3

Wallpaper really brightened up this kitchen

the pattern while brightening up the room with an overall light, warm color.

You don't have to wallpaper an entire room. You can paper just one wall as an accent. That creates a nice effect and is perfect where one wall has defects that paper will cover. A 6- or 8-inch wallpaper border around the top of the walls in a room is another nice touch. You can put a border around an entire room for less than $20. Try a border in small kitchens and baths where too much wallpaper would be overpowering. You can also use a border instead of molding or trim if you want to paper only half the wall.

Do's and Don'ts

Follow the same principles when selecting wallpaper that you use when selecting paint. Don't use a dark print in a small room. Choose a light colored print with a small pattern. Never use a large pattern in a small room. The large print will make the room seem even smaller.

Wallpaper, like paint, can either unify or separate adjacent areas. Wallpaper adjoining areas with the same pattern to make it look like one large area instead of two small ones. If you paper one area and paint the other, it separates them visually. Don't use contrasting wallpapers in adjoining rooms. You don't want to look through the living room and see something that doesn't match in the dining room and something even worse in the kitchen beyond. Coordinate your papers and colors for a unified look throughout the living areas of a house.

Here's one very important "do:" Select wallpaper that's inoffensive. If you happen to be fond of wallpaper with giant pink roses, paper your own home with it. Don't put it on houses you plan to sell. Simple patterns are best. You want results that will tend to please everybody. For example, see how the wallpaper and airy curtains brighten up the rather ordinary kitchen in Figure 12-3. Attractive paper turns plain into charming. That's the kind of results you want from simple decorating.

Figure 12-4

Pine molding stained to match oak floor and woodwork

Decorative Trim

Decorative trim can give a home a special appeal. Trim is expensive and takes time to install. But sometimes the time and trouble are good investments.

The cost of trim varies a great deal. You can buy beautifully-detailed, solid oak crown moldings at many home improvement or building supply stores. This molding is terribly expensive. I'd love to use it, but it would wipe out my decorating budget.

Plastic trim comes in many different styles and costs a lot less. The most common example is the polystyrene ceiling medallions used around ceiling fans. You can find those for just a few dollars. They're also good for covering holes in a ceiling where someone tried to install a light fixture or ceiling fan. The medallions conceal the damage and save replastering or patching. Most ceiling fans must be installed by amateurs, because stores sell a lot of these medallions.

Between expensive oak trim and cheap plastic trim there's my old standby, pine. While pine moldings aren't very expensive, you can still run up a big bill buying large quantities in elaborate styles. It *can* be worth the cost however. Look at Figure 12-4. Although the floor, stairs and window moldings are oak, I used pine for the moldings around the floor. I stained it to match, and none of the dozens of people who looked at this room noticed that the trim wasn't exactly the

Figure 12-5
Crown moldings save time and add elegance to the room

same. They only commented on how beautiful all the wood looked.

I like to add trim to my homes. But I don't add a lot — just in the places where it's really needed — where I can increase value by more than the trim costs.

Trim as a Cover-Up

One of the best uses of decorative trim is to cover damaged areas. I've already mentioned how you can do that with ceiling medallions. I also use crown molding to cover the ceiling seam between a freshly drywalled ceiling and the plaster walls. Drywalling a ceiling goes a lot faster if you don't have to make a perfect joint where the ceiling and wall meet.

I used crown molding in the formal dining room in Figure 12-5. It covered the drywall joint *and* accentuated the elegant molding around the windows and door. True, molding does cost a lot more than a roll of drywall tape, but in this case it was worth the extra expense. It was a particularly nice house. The extra cost increased the value of the home while reducing the labor and effort required.

What about using trim in a room that's already in perfect condition? Is it worth the extra cost to add it? Maybe not. Add trim where it serves two purposes: adding style *and* saving time and labor. Think carefully before adding trim just as a design element.

When to Use Trim in Decorating

Consider adding trim to a room that lacks any pleasing features or that has imperfections in the wall or floor that can't be easily repaired. Trim adds interest to a boring room, and distracts your attention from the problems of an imperfect room. Adding trim will pull a decorating scheme together, particularly if the house has no definite style. A little trim or wallpaper can make the house appear "decorated."

Figure 12-6

Ornamental fire screen

Be careful when adding trim in a small room. You want to create an open, spacious atmosphere. Accenting the borders of a small room with trim or decoration will only make the walls seem closer. Instead, emphasize the windows and keep the colors light and bright. In a small room you want the walls and ceiling to visually disappear. The less you notice about them, the better.

Other Interesting Accent Options

A stroll through an antique store can give you some good ideas. For example, cast iron ornaments, like eagles or crests, add a decorative accent over a fireplace. Ornamental wood balls and turnings can also add interest.

One of my houses had an artificial fireplace across one end of the living room. It really didn't do much for the room, so I decided to brighten it up. I put a grate and some logs in it to give it some authenticity, but it still lacked any real charm. My wife found the interesting fire screen and brass fireplace tools you see in Figure 12-6. The fire screen was strictly ornamental. It would have been useless with a real fireplace. I suppose that's why we got it for such a good price. It served our purpose perfectly.

Figure 12-7

Stained-glass window adds to the appeal of this room

Another good example is a stained-glass window I found in an antique store. I had been looking for something to brighten a rather uninteresting dining room I was working on. I came across the inexpensive shield-shaped window shown in Figure 12-7. I didn't have a shield-shaped space for it, but I did have an idea. I bought the window and attached it to a sheet of window glass. The combined unit fit perfectly in one of my dining room window sashes. I spray-painted the clear glass a color that harmonized with the stained glass, and installed the new window in the dining room. It turned out to be a beautiful and elegant addition to the room.

Windows and Window Treatments

Windows can make a big difference in any room. How much money should you invest on windows? That depends on the house. If you can add a major decorative touch for less than a

Figure 12-8
Wood mini-blinds came with the house

hundred dollars, as I did with the stained-glass window, do it. Should you add expensive window treatments, such as custom drapes or mini-blinds? There's a simple answer to that question: *No.*

Window treatments need to match the furniture more than they need to match the house. Buyers don't really expect you to provide purely decorative items like these. If the former owner left custom drapes or blinds behind, you may as well profit from your good fortune. But don't go out and buy them. I was very lucky with the house in Figure 12-8. It's an attractive Craftsman home with plenty of beautiful wood-trimmed windows in the living room. The windows had wood mini-blinds already installed. You won't find many badly-deteriorated homes with good window blinds.

I don't recommend buying expensive window coverings, but I don't recommend leaving the front windows of a house bare either. Bare windows look cold, unfriendly, and uninviting. They also make the house look vacant from the outside, and that invites vandalism.

What's the solution? I buy inexpensive white or neutral-colored sheer curtains like the ones in Figure 12-9. All you need is something simple to cover the windows and give the house a lived-in look. You don't need to put them on every window, just the living room windows and other windows that face the street. Your buyers may just toss them out, but in the meantime they've served a purpose.

Lighting

I consider lighting to be one of the most important design elements available to the remodeler. You can impress buyers very easily by controlling lighting effects. When you're showing the house, take care to light up things you want people to notice. Leave undesirable

Figure 12-9
Put up sheer curtains

features in the dark. Of course, most undesirable features will still be fully visible in the daytime. But you can call attention to what you want buyers to notice by lighting it well, especially if it's even a little cloudy outside.

Most houses don't have any lighting fixtures in the living room. I bring a small table with a lamp into the living room when I show houses to prospective buyers. Use a nice table lamp, not a naked bulb. It should provide normal light, like you'd have if you lived there.

Look for Bargains

Most rooms have at least one lighting fixture. Modernizing that fixture can change the whole effect of a room. But don't think good light fixtures have to be expensive. You can easily spend hundreds of dollars on one fixture. Don't do it. I often buy really beautiful light fixtures for no more than $25. They add a lot to the value of the house without costing me a fortune. It's difficult to say how much each lighting fixture is worth when you sell a house. I'd guess that every deluxe fixture adds from $100 to $300 to the value of your house — that's not bad for a $25 investment!

Light fixtures are often the featured sale items in home improvement stores. Both national chain stores and local specialty stores run sales on beautiful light fixtures. Why? Because they're perfect for do-it-yourselfers. They're easy to install and tend to build store traffic. So they're offered cheap and advertised heavily.

I'm always on the lookout for nice lights at a good price. If I find something I like, I'll buy a dozen of them. I may not have exactly the place for them at the moment, but I'll find a spot soon enough.

Here's a helpful hint: Look for light kits for ceiling fans. For some reason, these are much cheaper than the equivalent fixture in ready-to-install form. To use them as regular fixtures, you just need to add a mounting plate. The plates screw on easily, and cost about $2. Is this worth the trouble? I think so. I can buy a light kit for $15 that, when completed, is almost exactly the same as a fixture that costs $75. For five minutes work I save almost $60.

I've also found you can save a great deal of money on "look alike" light fixtures. Many popular, expensive styles of lights have been copied by other manufacturers and are offered at a fraction of the cost of the original. Like copies of designer clothes, these aren't the same quality as the originals, but the difference hardly matters. The originals may last a hundred years, but most of us won't be around to care. Since fixtures are frequently changed to suit style changes, the less expensive models with the shorter life expectancy are perfectly adequate. I've never had any problem with them.

Another thing to look for is the cheapest version of any particular style that you find yourself using a great deal. I like recessed ceiling fixtures, the kind that use interior reflector floods

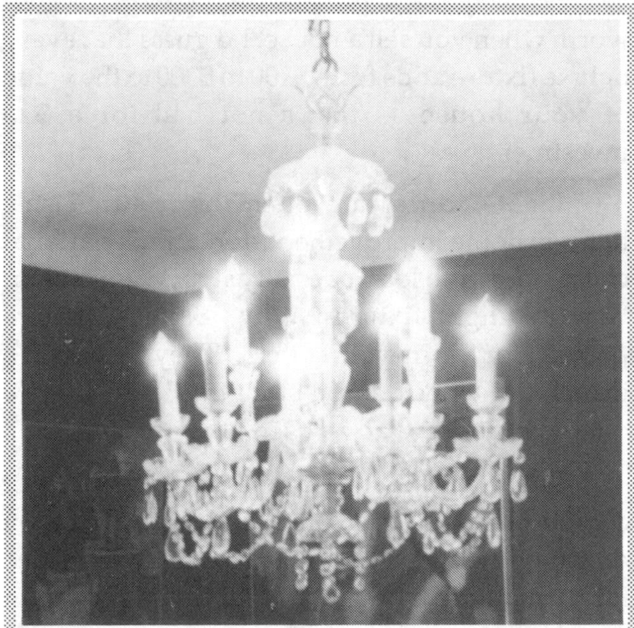

Figure 12-10
Crystal chandelier left in "fixer upper"

to create spotlight effects. Many builders use them in expensive homes to create luxurious lighting effects. They're particularly nice when you use dimmers. Again, when I can find a closeout sale on this type of fixture, or a brand that's being discontinued, I pick up all I can. I use them in a variety of places in the home: kitchens, baths, dressing areas, master bedrooms, even in the living rooms of some of my more modern houses. I buy in quantity when I see a special deal available.

Styles

Choose light fixtures that match both the decor and the style of the house. Be sure the right fixture goes in the right place. For instance a crystal chandelier, like the one in Figure 12-10, would be out of place anywhere except in the formal dining room of a formal house. (This chandelier, by the way, was left in one of the houses I bought. It's worth well over $1,000, and was quite a bonus.) Ceiling fans, on the other hand, belong in the informal atmosphere of a den or breakfast area, unless the house itself is very informal. Then you could put them in the living/dining areas as well.

Use fixtures like the ones in Figure 12-11 to accentuate a modern or very informal decor. Each is different and adds its own style to the house. The lovely antique fixture in Figure 12-12 was in an old house I bought. It was much too nice for the house it was in, so I moved it to a house where it would be appreciated. The right fixture in the right place provides the finishing touch to a beautiful old-fashioned decor.

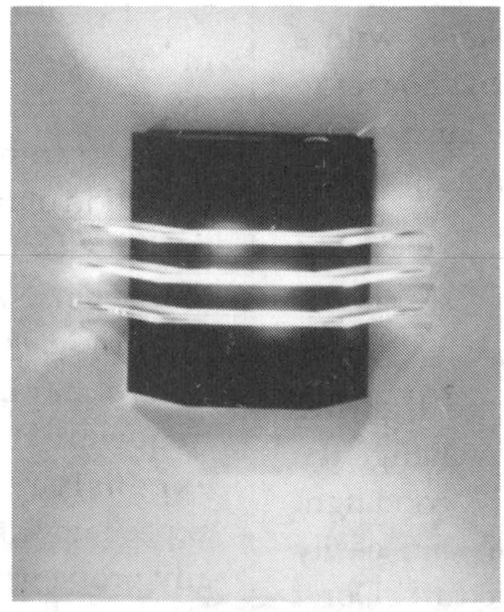

Figure 12-11
Modern light fixtures

Figure 12-12
This antique fixture provides the finishing touch

Track lights— Track lighting is a nice option for a modern home. It used to be rather expensive, but now several manufacturers have come out with inexpensive models. If this style of lighting is appropriate for your house and convenient for you to install, it has many advantages. Not only does it provide good lighting and look nice, it's great for spotlighting special features. And, unlike recessed ceiling lights, you can easily redirect track lights. Your buyers will be able to highlight any area of the room after they have their furnishings set up.

Recessed ceiling lights— Some types of fixtures can be used almost anywhere, with almost any style. A few modern styles fit into this category. A good example is recessed ceiling lights. You can't actually see these fixtures, so they don't interfere with your decor. While these fixtures are generally used for modern decorating schemes, they aren't really out of place with any style.

Lamp prices vary tremendously. You can pay $50 or $60 each for a deluxe model — and you may need six or eight of them. But I've seen modern recessed lights on sale for $7.96 each, and they look almost exactly like the more expensive models. I used several to create a luxurious-looking lighting effect for about $50. Of course, the fixtures I bought weren't quite as nice as the $60 ones, but you'd have to look closely at them to tell the difference. That's pretty hard to do with recessed lighting. When they're turned on, they're too bright to look at. When they're turned off, they're too dark to see.

The problem with recessed ceiling fixtures is that they're difficult to install. Because of that, I only use them in houses where I need to replace the ceiling. If I had to fish cable through an existing ceiling and try to hook up the lights, it would never be worth the trouble. But if the ceiling has to come down anyway, it's no problem to install some interesting lighting.

Placement is very important when you install recessed ceiling lighting. They light only the area below the fixture. So you need quite a few to adequately light a large area. Their best use is to highlight special features in your house, like the fireplace. You can also use them to show off windows or especially nice woodwork. Unlike track lights, the light from most recessed ceiling fixtures can't be redirected from one point to another (unless you buy the very expensive fixtures with directable eye lenses). Therefore, choose the location carefully. Be sure you're lighting areas people will want to see.

When you install the wiring, consider connecting several switches for each bank of lights. That lets you turn some on while others are off, instead of having them all on or all off at the same time. Using dimmers as well will create a lighting effect similar to the most expensive homes. With economical light fixtures, material cost for a bank of recessed lights on individual dimmers will cost only about $100.

Dining Room Lighting

Lighting requirements are different for each room in the house, but there are certain locations where a particular type of lighting is expected. People like to have adequate lighting for dining, for instance. So most homes have a light fixture centered over the area where the dining table is most likely to be. If your house has a dining room, then have a nice fixture centered there. Otherwise, the fixture should be in the kitchen or a dining area that's part of a living/dining-room combination.

This is probably the most important light fixture in the house. To many people, the dining table is the center of family life. A nice light fixture makes the dining area the center of attention — and a good selling point. It makes people think about pleasant evenings around the dinner table in their new home. That's a good first step in making the sale.

I usually try to put up the nicest dining room fixture I can find for around $50. This isn't very much for a dining room light, but it's triple what I pay for most of the other fixtures I install. If you shop carefully, you can get some beautiful light fixtures for that price. Last year I found a 52-inch ceiling fan and an elaborate light kit for $50. It was perfect for the "plain Jane" dining room I was working on. I also bought a nice-sized crystal chandelier at a closeout sale for $50.

Occasionally I'll buy an antique light fixture at a flea market or antique store. But be careful here. Old light fixtures almost always have to be completely rewired. That's a lot of work. Also, a nice antique fixture is going to be quite expensive, and it may not be appreciated by the people who buy the house. Many people would rather have a new, modern fixture. Buy genuine antiques only for very special properties.

Dining room light fixtures may or may not come with the houses you buy. I've looked at quite a few houses where the listing specified that the dining room light was not included. These, and occasionally ceiling fans, are about the only installed items that people take with them when they leave.

With this in mind, choose your dining room fixture carefully. Remember, your buyer may take down what you put up and install Grandma's chandelier instead. That's why you don't want to spend *too* much on it. However, anything you put up should be appealing and well suited to the decor of the house. An ugly lighting fixture will undermine your best sales efforts and detract from your house. You're better off with no dining room fixture than an unattractive one.

The Entry

Few "fixers" have formal entrance halls. If yours does, don't neglect it. Most entry areas are small. But they're important because they introduce a prospective buyer to your house. Remember, *first impressions count most.*

An elaborate light fixture will make a very positive first impression here. Also consider wall treatments and even a luxury floor covering, like slate or ceramic tile. This space isn't very big, so expensive materials won't add up to much money. Luxury materials in the entry make a good impression that lasts as buyers look through the rest of the house. Once the idea is formed, it's usually there to stay. The entry offers an opportunity to get a lot of benefit from a small amount of work. Don't pass it up.

The Living Room and Dining Room

The living room and dining room are usually together, or even in the same area. Their decorating needs have to be coordinated. Actually, you can never decorate a room as though it were separate from the rest of the house. All the rooms need to be coordinated to some extent, but the living room and dining room are especially important.

Coordinating the decor doesn't mean that they have to match in every detail. But they must blend from one to the other and be the same style. You could wallpaper the dining room and paint the living room, for instance. But it would be a poor idea to wallpaper them both using unrelated patterns. In the same vein, you shouldn't switch styles between these rooms. Don't have a modern living room and a traditional dining room. These two rooms should always be the same style.

As I mentioned earlier, the light fixture is probably the most important decision you'll be making for the dining room. The living room however, generally sets the tone for the rest of the house. All the elements that we have discussed are important here. Your choice of colors, wall coverings, floor coverings and style will carry through the rest of the house. Pick a color theme and style that fits the house and will be easy to decorate around.

Emphasizing a Special Feature

If your house has a special feature, show it off. Wood and trim can be accented with color and wallpaper. But what about other features, like a fireplace, built-in cabinet or buffet? These are valuable features in any house. So you want them to appear as attractive as possible.

One way to make the fireplace stand out is with color. For example, natural brick stands out against a lighter wall background. If the brick has been painted over, repaint it white. Then wallpaper the wall around it in a darker textured print. The fireplace will seem to stand out better against the wall. Nobody could miss that! Use the same technique when dealing with built in woodwork, like china cabinets. Set dark wood off against a contrasting background.

Another possibility is to use trim or molding to accent the fireplace or other feature. Your eye will naturally follow molding around the room. If you frame the fireplace area with molding as well, the molding will attract attention to the fireplace.

Lighting is another way to draw attention to a particular feature. You can use recessed lighting, as we mentioned earlier, to highlight an area. Wall-mounted light fixtures on either side of the fireplace will set it off in a traditional style. Or you can add interior lights to a china or curio cabinet. Of course, these suggestions are only practical if you can conveniently run wiring for these lights. In a modern-style house, track lights directed towards the fireplace or other special feature are usually a better (and easier) choice.

Pick up accent items that draw attention to the fireplace or cabinets. Include a unique fireplace tool set or screen as I mentioned earlier, or perhaps add brass pulls or hinges to the cabinets. You don't have to pay a fortune for things like these. Many times I find them in the houses I buy — all I have to do is clean them up.

A Living Room Renovating Project

The living room in Figure 12-13 incorporates many of the points we've just discussed. This beautiful older home had about the worst living room decorating I'd ever seen. Unfortunately, the black and white photograph doesn't do justice to the sheer awfulness of the room. The walls and fireplace were mustard yellow. Above the mantel was dark wood-grained contact paper — the kind you use on shelving, and all the beautiful oak

Figure 12-13

The wood is starting to emerge from under the heavy brown paint

woodwork was painted brown. In this picture, we've begun to strip the paint off the wood and remove the contact paper.

I don't bother stripping woodwork that's been painted unless I'm working on an exceptionally nice house. This one was. The cabinets, windows, mantel, molding and even the bannister on the stairs leading to the second floor were beautiful oak. The paint came off the wood fairly easy with a heat gun. You can see some of the refinished woodwork in Figure 12-14. Unfortunately, there was no practical way to uncover the brick in the fireplace. So, I painted the fireplace white and put up a nice textured wallpaper on the walls and above the mantel.

The light fixture in Figure 12-15 is an antique style designed to hold a candelabra bulb. It had been painted brown, and someone had taken the bulb out and burned candles in it! Cleaning the wax and paint off was a tedious job, but as you

Figure 12-14

Some of the fine oak woodwork we uncovered

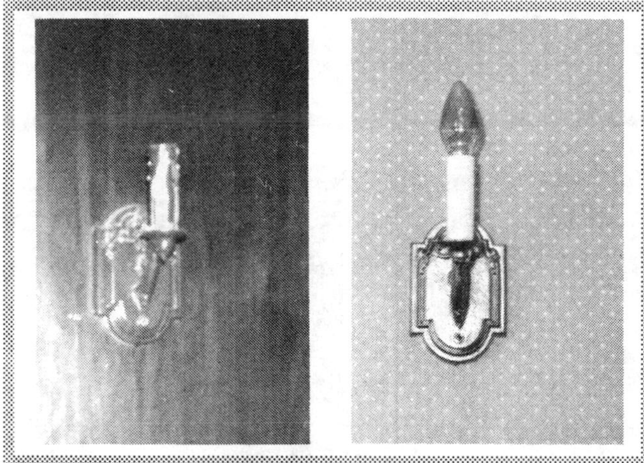

Figure 12-15
Restoring old fixtures

can see the effort was worth it. The refinished fixtures glow against the new wallpaper, and set off the mantel above the fireplace.

I also replaced a very ugly ceiling light with an antique fixture that matched the style of the room. That fixture creates a nice nighttime lighting accent. The many windows with their matching wood trim add daytime light and unity to the style of the room. Figure 12-16 shows the renovated room. Notice the brass hinges on the cabinets. They were already there. Like the candelabra, it just took some work to uncover their beauty. New carpeting finished up the job.

Looking at the *after* pictures, I'm sure you'll agree that the results were well worth the extra effort we put into this project. Our buyers did. They happily paid a premium price for all the beautiful details.

In most homes, a hallway connects the bedrooms and the living area. On your way through, stop and consider what you can do to *improve* the hallway.

Figure 12-16
The new room in all its glory

Decorating the Halls

Most hallways are painted white — and that's all. With a little TLC, the hall can be an attractive addition to a house. An interior hallway is the artery that carries people from one room to another. You want it to be as pleasant as possible.

Never use dark colors in a hallway; they close it in. People will feel uncomfortable, like they're entering a tunnel or cave. Children seem to be especially sensitive to dark halls. A child who's uncomfortable in an area will let their parents and everyone else know it. Chances are, your prospects will be right out the door with their child — and they won't be back. That's no way to sell a house!

Make the hallway a positive feature. Some hallways seem very long and dark, even during the day. A bright, attractive light fixture can solve this problem. Instead of a dark tunnel, your hallway becomes an attractive space, almost like a room itself. A nice light fixture attracts people. They'll come into the hallway to get a better look at it and then just naturally go on to see the other rooms. Make sure you *always* have the hall light on when you're showing your house.

You can also make the hall more attractive by continuing your decorating scheme into the hallway. For instance, if the hallway is connected to the living room, paint it the same color and add similar trim. This creates a feeling of continuity. People will flow easily from room to room and hallway to additional rooms if they don't perceive a barrier. An abrupt change of style or color creates a visual barrier to passage. Use your decorating skills to create a comfortable environment where people want to come in and stay awhile.

The Bedrooms

Many of my comments about decorating the living and dining rooms apply to the bedrooms as well. However, there are a couple of differences that I want to discuss.

Choosing Colors

I like to pick out a separate color for each bedroom. These should always be inoffensive; pale pastels, such as pale blue, or perhaps pale peach. You can use various colors, depending on what seems to be in style at the moment. Just stick to light, inoffensive colors that won't make the room seem smaller or irritate prospective buyers.

I've found that people really respond to the colors in a bedroom. When they look at your house, you'll hear them saying, "I want the blue room!" or "Let's put the baby in the yellow room!" What would they say if all the rooms were white? They wouldn't be able to relate to the rooms as well. People are much more likely to buy a house that they can relate to.

Carpeting

While it's possible to use different carpeting in each bedroom, I wouldn't recommend it. If you have hardwood floors throughout the house and you're only carpeting the bedrooms, let each bedroom have its own personality. The wood will be the unifying factor. But if you're planning to have the house carpeted throughout, do the bedrooms in the same color. If you buy neutral carpeting, this should be no problem. Just remember that the wall colors in each room must harmonize with the carpeting.

Suppose you've decided to use a particular non-neutral color of carpeting throughout the house. What if this color isn't going to match the walls? Then you're going to have to change the walls. It's a good idea to consider this before you paint, not after. It saves a lot of wasted effort.

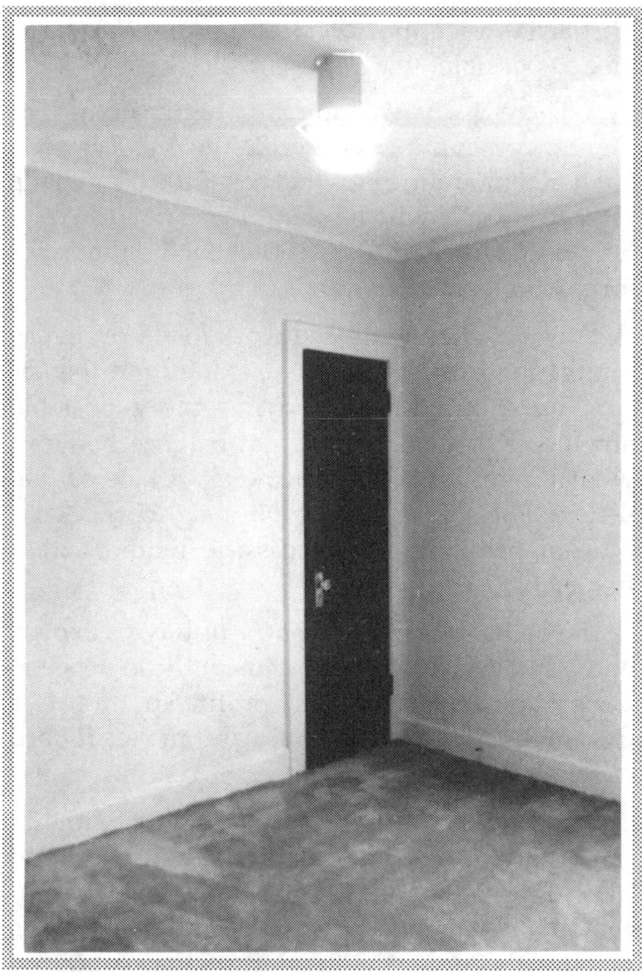

Figure 12-17

New paint, carpeting, and lighting improved this bedroom

Lighting

People don't really expect an elaborate bedroom lighting fixture. Most builders just put in cheap, bent-glass fixtures — even in expensive houses. Buyers have come to expect them. In the past, I used to replace them with better fixtures. Then I found out that no one even noticed the difference. So in spite of my prejudice against cheap fixtures, I don't replace them anymore unless they're broken. But if I do have to replace one, I always get something a little nicer than the plain, bent-glass type.

The only time I use an elaborate bedroom light fixture is in a "problem bedroom." This is a bedroom that's too small, has a peculiar shape, no closet, or some other problem that's difficult to fix or cover up. A bedroom is just a plain box. There isn't much you can do to hide an undesirable feature except maybe install a nice light fixture. I use my most elaborate, elegant, dramatic light fixtures in my worst bedrooms.

Figure 12-17 shows a typical finished bedroom in one of my remodels. It has new paint and carpeting and an attractive light fixture that echoes the Art Deco style of the rest of the house. The room is simple, but inviting. No one mentioned how small the bedroom was when they looked at the house, but there were many positive comments on the light fixture. That's about all you can hope for.

Dens

A den can be an important addition to a house. It's valuable for people who like to entertain, since it can accommodate the overflow of people from the living area. It's an extra bedroom for overnight guests and a place for the kids to play while adults are using the living room. Even people who don't have any particular use for a den are never disappointed to have one. Let's face it, everybody can find a use for an extra room.

One important benefit of a den is that it's easily converted into a bedroom. Some dens may be a bit inconvenient to be used permanently as a bedroom, but they're better than nothing. When I decorate, I leave the den somewhat ambiguous. That is, I don't put any features in it that clearly say "This is a bedroom," or "This is a den." If it's plain, the buyers can decide how they want to use it. If they need another bedroom, it's there for them.

Obviously, this strategy won't work if the room is located in a position that isn't appropriate for a bedroom, like right off the kitchen. When a den is adjoining the kitchen, I usually decorate it to harmonize with the kitchen. However, a plain decor lends itself to converting to a hobby room, sewing room, family room or whatever your buyers prefer. You want the room to be attractive to as many buyers as possible.

Dens are generally informal rooms. If you want to dress them up, you can add special features, such as a ceiling fan. If your den is adjacent to the rear yard, another interesting addition might be a patio door leading to the outside. You can buy patio doors in many different styles to go with your decor. Putting in an exterior door is fairly expensive however, and they're a big job to install.

A den is also be a good place to install a fireplace, especially if there isn't room for one in the living room. It's easy to imagine how you can transform a plain, uninteresting room with the addition of a lovely fireplace, patio doors, a ceiling fan, and miscellaneous trim and decor items. Then just imagine how your budget will be transformed by the cost of all of these items!

That takes some of the fun out of it, I'm afraid. However, you have to consider the cost of everything you add to a project. You can always go ahead with the inexpensive items, like the ceiling fan and trim. They won't hurt your budget much, but the expensive items need to be considered carefully. If someone overlooks your $35 ceiling fan, it's sad, but it's no tragedy. However, if they overlook your $2,000 fireplace, you've just wasted a lot of money. Ration your expensive improvements carefully.

As usual, there's an exception to this rule: expensive property. People who buy expensive houses expect lots of extras, and that's not at all unreasonable. For the kind of money they're paying, they ought to get everything you can afford to provide.

Now, let's go on to an extremely important part of the house: the kitchen.

The Kitchen

I generally spend more time, care, and money on the kitchen than on any other part of a house. In fact, I often spend more on the kitchen than on all the rest of the house combined. The kitchen is very important; it absolutely *must* be as nice as possible.

There really isn't any limit to the amount of money you could spend on a kitchen. I've seen kitchen remodeling jobs that cost $100,000. That's great for people who have lots of money and own homes that need a $100,000 kitchen. But that's not for my buyers.

The kitchen will need work in almost every renovation project you have. Don't omit the basics, but don't try to provide every possible amenity either. Find the right balance between what's required and what merely a nice convenience. For example, in some neighborhoods a built-in dishwasher is a necessity. In others, it's a luxury.

You have to know what your buyers expect, and you have to remodel to meet those expectations if you expect to make a profit. Anything less lowers the value of the house and makes it hard to sell.

One way to approach this problem is to find out what the other houses in the neighborhood have, especially the ones that have been sold or remodeled recently. You may find that everyone is perfectly content with no more than a built-in range, double sink, formica countertop and garbage disposal. In that case, the essentials are enough. But if you find homes with new cabinets, dishwashers and ceramic tile countertops, your next step should be obvious.

If you decide on the more elaborate additions, are you planning to sell the house for enough money to make them worthwhile? Will you be able to appeal to buyers who are looking for a neighborhood in upward transition? If that's the trend, climb on board the bandwagon. Go for the higher market.

All New or Semi-New?

The simplest thing to do with any old kitchen would be to tear it all out and replace it with a beautiful, stylish, all-new kitchen. But that's usually not an option if you're remodeling for profit. Sometimes, however, you may not have a choice. You may run into a kitchen or two that's almost a total loss. In that case, a new kitchen may be all that stands between you and a substantial profit.

Before ordering all new materials, evaluate the existing kitchen. What can you salvage? Most kitchens have plenty that's still good: the cabinets, the countertops, maybe even the sink. If that's the case, decorating skill is needed to blend the old with the new.

Usually at least some of the cabinets are salvageable. They'll need refinishing and repair, and you'll almost always need to add more (and match the old with the new). That's one reason why I usually buy unfinished cabinets. After finishing, any differences will hardly show.

Countertops, walls and floors should get special attention. Countertops get heavy use and usually need to be replaced. Even if the kitchen has been recently painted, you'll probably need to paint or wallpaper again. Chances are, the former owners' decorating taste was determined by what was cheap and available when they decided to paint. You can usually count on replacing the floor coverings as well.

What you usually end up with is a combination of the new with the best of the old. Careful decorating can harmonize the two. When you're done, it should look like it was planned that way. You'll get the benefit of an all-new, matching kitchen, at a fraction of the cost.

Personal Choices

Decorating a kitchen is very different from decorating any other room of the house. In other rooms, you simply provide the framework for the new owners. They personalize rooms by adding furniture, drapes, and decorations that create a finished look.

The kitchen is different; furnishings are built-in: cabinets, countertops, sink, and appliances. The kitchen and the bathroom are the only rooms where *you* do the final decorating. This is a big responsibility. You have to make choices for people you've never even met, and they, not you, have to live with your choices. To make matters worse, there's a great deal of money riding on your decisions.

Years ago, kitchens and baths were easier. They had far fewer built-in cabinets. Most storage was provided by movable pieces of furniture, such as cupboards, and shelving units. If you ever come across an old house that's in original condition, you'll notice that it has a very large kitchen with nothing in it except a sink, and that too may be part of a portable unit.

This "kitchen furniture" look seems to be coming back. Some custom builders are installing kitchen cabinets that look like they're made out of several pieces of old furniture. This is perfect for scavengers like me. I can "one-up" these custom builders by creating a kitchen that *really is* made up of pieces of old furniture! And I can do it for a fraction of their cost, too.

Wall Treatments

There's very little exposed wall in most kitchens. One advantage to this is that you can afford any kind of wall treatment you like. Since there are so few square feet to cover, you can use good quality paint or decorative wallpaper for very little money.

Use wall treatments to coordinate the look of the kitchen. Wall color or texture that contrasts with the cabinets will make slightly unmatched cabinets look more similar. If your cabinets are plain white, create contrast by painting the walls a solid color or using a bright, patterned wallpaper. The cabinets will stand out against the background of the wall. People perceive things that are a similar color and texture as the same, and things that are different colors and textures as being separate. They will pick up the contrast between the wall and the cabinets and not notice the slight differences between the cabinets themselves.

Use color perception as part of your design. You don't have to paint all kitchen cabinets white. Other contrasts work as well. Dark wood against a lighter background is also a good contrast. The point is that you need to create consistency in decor. Do it with color.

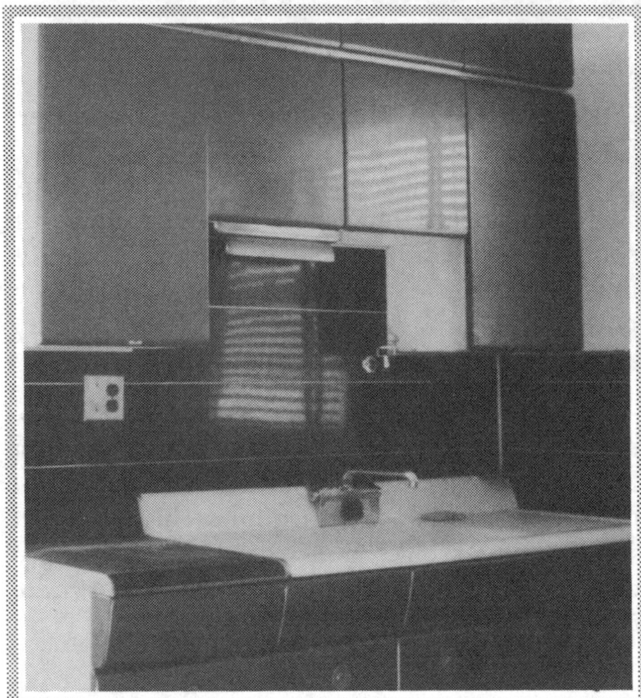

Figure 12-18

Dark brown cabinets and black wallboard

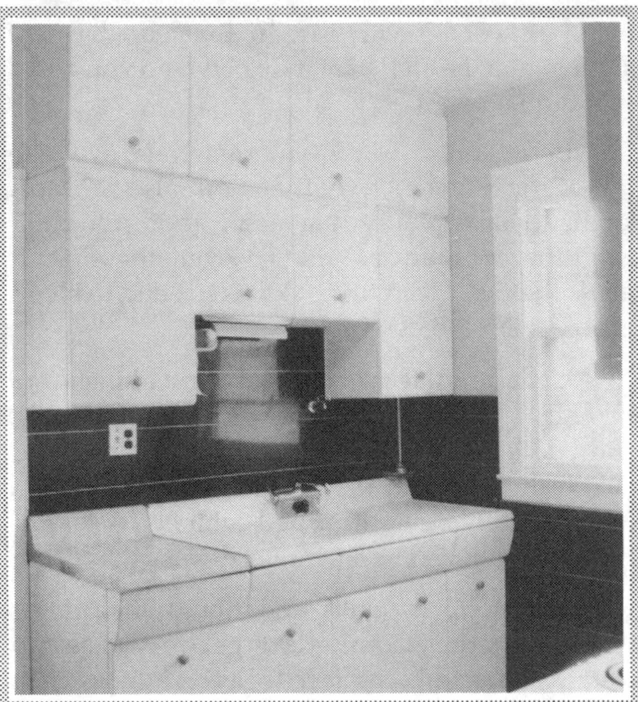

Figure 12-19

We painted the cabinets white, and added pink knobs to match the wallpaper

As styles change, trends in colors and textures change. But the basic principles of color remain. Light colors make a room look bigger; dark colors make it look smaller. And coordinating the visual elements in a room helps organize and blend new materials with old.

Cabinet Color and Trim

What makes one kitchen cabinet different from another? Essentially, it's only the color and trim. They're all just boxes of various sizes. Color and trim, therefore, are the keys to coordinating your cabinetry.

We've discussed painting mismatched cabinets in the section on repairs. So, once you select the color, you then have to match the trim. If one type of cabinet has some trim, and the other doesn't, either remove the trim from the cabinet that has it or add similar trim to the cabinet that lacks it. The trim doesn't need to be the same color, or even the same material. Once it's painted, it should blend nicely.

If you apply trim to the cabinets, try using it elsewhere in the kitchen. For instance, install matching crown moldings, or perhaps door or window moldings. This makes the cabinets seem to be integrated right into the walls. The cabinet trim leads the eye right into the wall trim, and away from things you would prefer not to have people notice, such as mismatched cabinets. Use trim wisely to give the appearance of an all-new, coordinated kitchen. Your buyers may never even realize that the cupboards don't match exactly.

One advantage to white cabinets is that they give the room a spacious feeling. This is true of all light, bright colors. I use white a lot because I'm constantly looking for ways to make everything appear bigger. Dark cabinets create the same closed-in effect as dark colored walls; it's best to use them only in large kitchens.

Figures 12-18 and 12-19 are before and after shots of a kitchen I recently finished. The kitchen was in good condition, but the combination of black wallboard and dark brown cabinets gave the room a dark, gloomy feeling. Since the rest of the house was decorated in an Art Deco theme, I decided to carry it on into the kitchen. I painted all the cabinets white and added pink knobs, replaced the dark tile countertop, and put up pink wallpaper. The combination of bright white, pink and black turned the small kitchen from dreary to cheery and brought raves from the people who came to see the house.

The Floor

The kitchen floor is important. If it's less than attractive, stylish, and in good repair, replace it. A new floor gives you another opportunity to coordinate your design scheme. The style and color you select should harmonize with the color and style of the walls and cabinets. If you want an old-fashioned theme, pick a floor covering with an old-fashioned pattern, like little Victorian flowers. This will give the room that "Grandma's kitchen" look which many people find very homey. If you're creating a modern kitchen, choose a modern pattern for your floor covering.

Lighting

Always provide good light for cooking and working in the kitchen, and be sure the fixtures match the style of the room. This restricts your choices a little. You can't put in a fixture that's simply decorative if it's the only light source. You need a fixture that gives plenty of light. You can add other lights as well, but the bright fixture needs to be there.

Most older kitchens have just one light fixture in the middle of the ceiling. If you want to move that fixture or add additional lighting, rewiring will be needed. However, I've found that a single bright decorative fixture in the center of the ceiling is usually all that's necessary.

Some kitchens may have a single fluorescent fixture in the middle of the ceiling. These were supposed to be an improvement when they were installed (probably in the 1950s), but they're very unattractive and cast an ugly, harsh light. Even though they're economical, I don't like them. They remind me of basement or workbench lighting. Never leave these in a kitchen! Replace them with something nice. If they're in good condition, you can use the fixture in a basement or garage where it belongs.

It's not hard to find attractive kitchen light fixtures at reasonable prices. You can buy a very nice fixture for $20 or $30. Installation takes about five minutes and will raise the value of your house by hundreds of dollars. This is the type of modification you should watch for. It's cheap, easy, and makes a big difference. That's maximum "bang for the buck."

Never make the mistake of thinking your kitchen light fixture is "good enough." If you can use that phrase to describe it, it isn't! Remember, the kitchen is a very important room. The light fixture should be nice enough to draw favorable comment. Don't cut corners here. If it isn't beautiful, replace it.

***Deluxe lighting*—** You'll see model homes with elaborate kitchen lighting such as recessed ceiling lights or track lights. They even add fluorescent fixtures to the undersides of cupboards to light up the countertop work areas. Some of these arrangements aren't expensive, but they are a lot of work to install. If you need to replace the ceiling anyway, consider track or recessed lighting. Rewiring the ceiling lights can be a big job, but it's a chance to get a million-dollar lighting effect for about $100.

Track or recessed lighting looks best in a fairly large, modern kitchen, although it will work with nearly any design. If the kitchen is small, however, the effort will be wasted. One of the big advantages of recessed or track lighting is its ability to highlight certain areas. In a small kitchen you can't separate the lights far enough apart to really spotlight one area. The light from one area spills over into another, spreading the light evenly throughout the room. That's virtually the same effect that you get with one central fixture. Don't bother with elaborate lighting unless you're going to get the full benefit of it.

The Unsalvageable Kitchen

What if the kitchen in your house is totally ruined, and nothing can be salvaged? This means you'll have to do more work and spend a *lot* more money, but it makes your decorating job considerably easier. You don't have to work around existing fixtures. You can just go to your favorite home-improvement store and pick out a complete, coordinated kitchen. Some dealers will even have photographs of the finished jobs so you know how the kitchen will look when you're done.

Depending on what's available, you may be able to do a luxury job without busting your budget. Home-improvement stores often feature very good sales on kitchen products. For instance, a short time ago one of my local stores featured oak-veneer cabinets at a price below the plain, birch cabinets I usually use. So one of my houses got a beautiful oak kitchen, and it didn't cost me any more than I had planned to spend.

Since the cabinets are the most visible — and the most expensive — part of your new kitchen, pick them out first. You want the nicest cabinets you can get, for the lowest possible price. This is where careful shopping pays off. A set of kitchen cabinets can easily cost $5,000. However, if you shop carefully, you should be able to outfit a medium-sized kitchen with nice-looking, sturdy, (although not deluxe) cabinets for under $1,000.

Since you've paid a lot of money for those new cabinets, help people appreciate them. Select other kitchen decor items that accent the cabinets. Pick colors and wall treatments that emphasize the cabinets. Check the cabinet manufacturer's catalogs. Do they suggest a complementary decor for their cabinets? They pay decorators a lot of money to pick out colors and designs that highlight their cabinetry. You can usually be pretty safe following their recommendations.

Look carefully at the floor coverings, light fixtures, window treatments and appliances in the catalogs too. You may not be able to find identical items at your favorite store, but you can probably find something similar. Just make sure the catalogs you're looking at aren't old and out-of-date. The cabinets may not have changed, but styles in color, wallpaper and trim may. You don't want to put in a new design scheme that's already dated.

Coordinating the Rooms

The kitchen should match the style of the rest of the house. It's less important for the kitchen and dining room to be coordinated than for the living room and dining room to be coordinated. But usually the kitchen and dining room should at least be complementary. If you have a really compelling reason, decorate the kitchen in a distinctly different design to make it more of a separate room.

A good example of this would be a modern kitchen in a traditional house. I'm not going to tear out a kitchen that's in good condition just because it doesn't match the style of the house. It isn't *that* important. But if the kitchen needed to be redone, I'd do it in traditional-style.

The Bathroom

I devoted a great deal of space to the bathroom in the section on repairs — and for good reason. It's probably the second most important room of the house. The first, of course, is the kitchen; and like the kitchen, the bathroom or bathrooms must be attractive. An ugly or outdated bathroom will take thousands of dollars off the value of your house.

The fixtures are to the bathroom what the cabinets are to the kitchen. Essentially, they're the "furniture" of the bathroom. They need to look nice and be in good working condition. Besides the fixtures, your decorating scheme has to be expressed through the walls and floor.

Working Around Ceramic Tile

Bathrooms usually have very limited wall space for decorating. If you have ceramic tile in the tub and shower area, its color and style may largely determine the rest of your decorating scheme. It's much cheaper and easier to try and decorate around the existing tile than to replace it and start from scratch.

Generally, if there's ceramic tile on the floor, it will match the ceramic tile on the walls. Usually all the tile is installed at the same time. If one was done later, hopefully it was designed to harmonize with the earlier job. I'll assume it was, and consider both the walls and the floor together.

I suppose it's possible that you may buy a house with bathroom walls and floor of ceramic tile that doesn't match. But I've never had that problem.

If you're lucky, all your bathroom tile will match and be in good condition. If you're really lucky, the tile will be stylish and attractive. This makes your decorating job very easy. Select coordinating wallpaper or paint, perhaps upgrade some of the fixtures, and presto, you're done. Unfortunately, it's hardly ever that easy.

Poor condition— I frequently find really ugly tile jobs or tile that's in such bad condition that it's hard to repair. Then, the decisions are easy. You demolish the tile and start fresh. This is like the unsalvageable kitchen. Pick out the tile you like. Take your inspiration from tile catalog pictures so you know ahead of time what the finished job will look like. You can even get color-coordinated wallpaper and fixtures, if you like. The only problem is the cost and the labor.

Good condition, but... — What if the tile is strange or an ugly color, but it's in perfect condition? That's more of a problem. I hate to tear out anything that's in good condition, but I don't like ugly tile, either. Decide if there's a way to work around it or improve it without tearing it out. First consider what's wrong with the tile.

In the early 1970s there was a fad for very strange tiles. They were often dark colors with peculiar patterns or designs. Some of them had a very odd texture as well. They were considered very creative. Today they just look weird. When I come across tile like this, it has to go.

Outdated color schemes— More often, the problem is the color, or the combination of colors. In the 1950s, the fad was mixing bright colored tiles together. You'll find colors like shocking pink and turquoise, or lime green and dark blue used together. Designers do the same thing today, but with much more muted pastel colors.

If the tile is in good condition but an ugly color, decorate in white or another neutral color like gray or beige. This reduces the amount of color in the room. If there isn't too much tile, you'll end up with a predominantly light-colored bathroom, with a splash of shocking pink, lime green, or whatever the old color is. This treatment will tone down the bathroom considerably.

It's OK to use bright colored tile as accents. You can include little bits of shocking pink or lime green in an otherwise pale earth-tone color scheme. Of course, in your bathroom the colors may be reversed. The bright colors may form the main part of the tile and the pale colors may make up the accent areas. Add some pale or earth-tone accents to neutralize the bright colors. It will look modern and up-to-date even though it isn't quite perfect.

Bright colors look garish when closely combined with strong contrasting colors. For example, black combined with shocking pink creates a strong contrast. Black trim makes pink look even more brilliant than shocking pink normally would. I would replace the contrasting accent trim with trim that blends with the predominant color. In a shocking pink and black bathroom, you might replace the black trim with white or even a pale pink that blends with the other tile. Reducing the contrast will tone down the pink. Use stylish colors as accents for an effect that will look like it's straight out of an American Olean Tile catalog.

By the way, if you don't have an American Olean Tile catalog, you should get one. They're full of good ideas, and they're free. Call *Ideas Line* for brochures at 1-800-548-4060. Or write:

American Olean Tile Co.
1000 Cannon Avenue
Lansdale, PA 19446

Collect and save all the free product catalogs you can get. Look through them for ideas when you're stumped. One advantage product catalogs have over decorating magazines is that you know immediately where to get what you're looking for.

Play up the style— Here's another option to consider when you've got good tile that happens to be out-of-date. Go with what you've got. If you've got a 1950s bathroom, cash in on the "Fabulous Fifties" theme. Maybe you can find a free-form mirror, or some '50s style light fixtures. People will be amused by your 50s-style bathroom. Few will understand that you're cutting corners by keeping outdated tile.

The biggest problem with this approach is that not everybody likes the 1950s style. It isn't as well accepted as other, more traditional styles. Young people tend to think it's great, but a lot of people who were adults in the 1950s won't be amused. So who do you think your buyers are likely to be? Young people, or the middle-age to older set? Is your house a move-up property, where everything needs to be perfect? Or is it an entry-level property, where anything that's decent and has a little style to it will be appreciated?

These questions come up over and over again when you make remodeling decisions. Keep your buyers in mind. Who's going to buy this house and how much are they going to be able to pay? That's your bottom line.

Working Around Older Styles

Occasionally you'll have a bathroom in an older home (1930s) that's still in good condition. These bathrooms are a real decorating challenge because 1930s style is popular again.

1930s Art Deco— A 1930s bathroom might be decorated in an Art Deco style that people are currently paying a lot of money to copy. Look at Figure 12-20. This Art Deco styled bathroom was in good shape, except for the shabby carpeting on the floor. Under the carpeting was deteriorated linoleum, but under that was a sturdy oak floor. The oak was an excellent base for new ceramic tile. Figure 12-21 shows the final result — a handsome, coordinated bathroom in keeping with the original style. I used expensive floor tile. Anything less wouldn't have been up to the standards of this particular house. But because the bathroom was so small, the cost of tile was very little.

Victorian— Occasionally I find an older bathroom done in the Victorian style that's also very popular now. The original wallpaper is gone, of course, but the tile and fixtures are sometimes in good condition, especially if the house belonged to an older couple.

I always feel it's a shame to tear out these nice old features, especially when people are now paying a lot of money to put them in. But there's a problem with retaining the fixture. The bathrooms in older homes weren't designed for modern conveniences. They usually have bathtubs with no shower. The sinks have separate hot and cold faucets. There's no vanity or storage area under the sink. Some of the fixtures may be in good condition, while others are damaged beyond repair. You can't mix old fixtures with new fixtures. It just doesn't look right. So, what do you do?

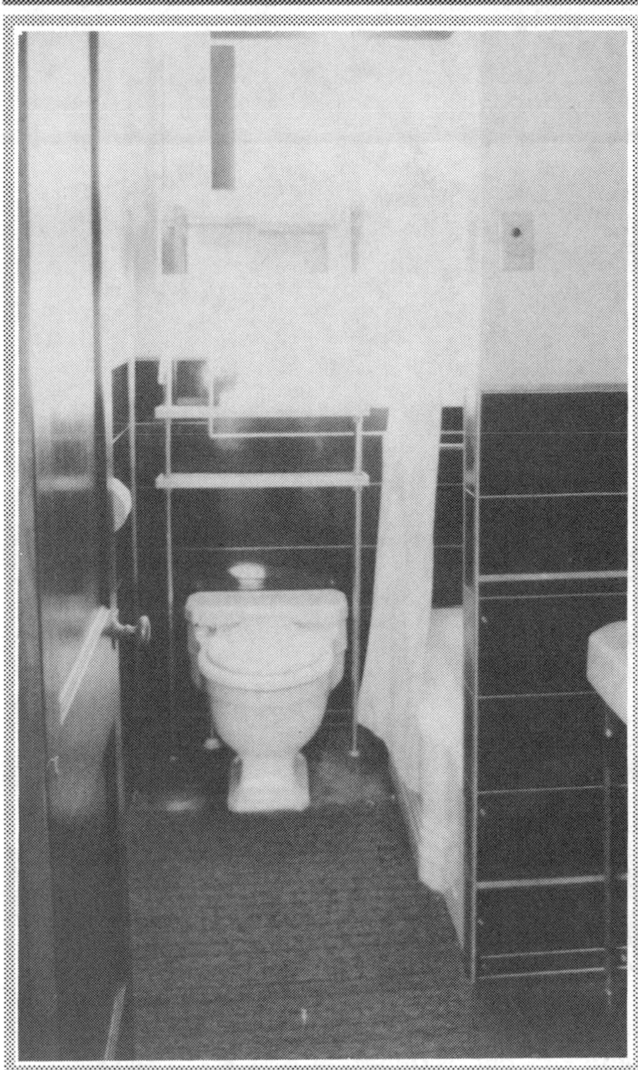

Figure 12-20
Art Deco bathroom needed new flooring

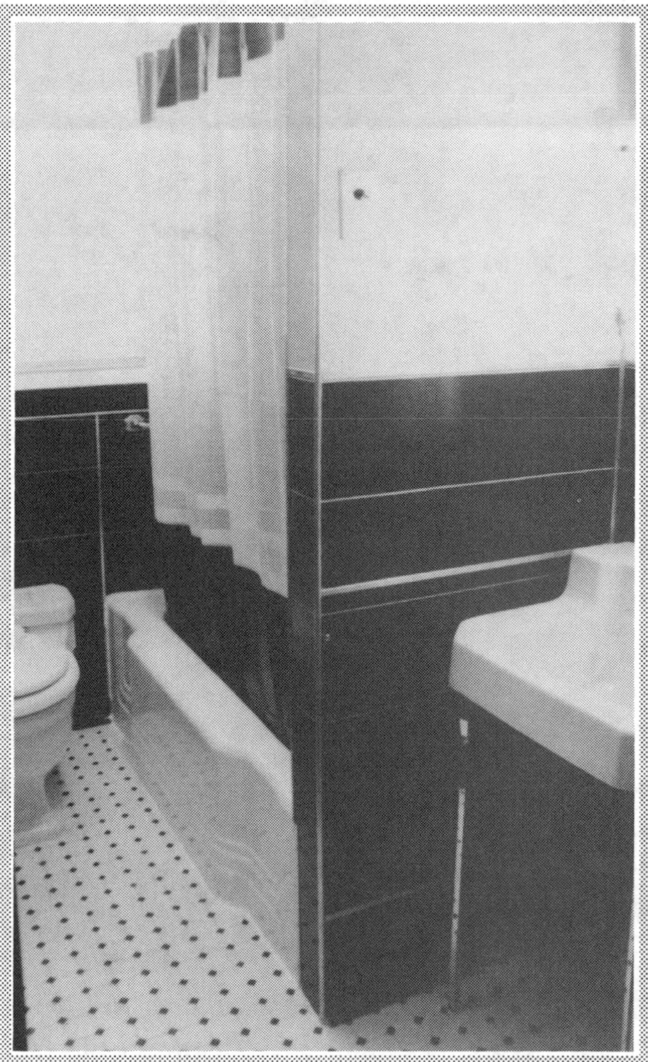

Figure 12-21
New tile floor accents style of bathroom

I try to save as many of the older features as possible and emphasize them in my decorating scheme. It should look like you wanted these features to stand out, not like you've got them and you're trying to hide them. The bathroom in Figure 12-22 has the original fixtures, including a claw-foot bathtub. I added old-fashioned style wallpaper and wainscoting, and oak trim and accents to match the oak flooring. This Victorian-style bathroom looks almost exactly as it would have in 1920 when it was new.

Solving Decorating Problems

How do you preserve the style of an old bathroom while adding the modern conveniences people want? That's sometimes my biggest challenge. One advantage to older bathrooms is that they tend to be fairly large (at least by today's tract-home standards). Most new homes have bathrooms that measure about 5 feet by 6 feet. Bathrooms in older homes are usually much larger. That gives you elbow room to work in and gives you options that aren't available in bathrooms built after the 1940s.

Figure 12-22
A genuine old-fashioned 1920s bathroom

One of the houses I bought had a large bathroom located on the main floor of the house. There was a beautiful claw-footed bathtub in it, but no shower. The bathroom was large, 10 by 12 feet, and was over a basement, so I had easy access to the plumbing. It was a very good property, and I was willing to spend some extra money to make it especially nice. I could have torn out all the fixtures and put in a new bathroom, but I didn't. I decided to keep the bathtub and add a separate shower enclosure.

That gave me an attractive, claw-footed tub for those who like to take baths, and a modern shower stall for people who prefer showers. My quaint, old-fashioned bathroom had a feature that only today's luxury homes have, a separate tub and shower. That gave my house appeal without destroying its uniqueness. Don't pass up an opportunity to make the most out of an opportunity like that — especially if it doesn't cost too much.

This solution won't always work, even if you have a large area to work with. If the bathroom is on the second floor, it's hard to add new plumbing, unless you're willing to tear up the ceiling of the room below. And if you're working on a tight budget, large scale modifications like that aren't practical. Essentially, you have two choices. You can remove the old tub and replace it with a modern tub-shower combination, or modify the old tub for a shower.

If you decide on replacing the tub, the finished effect will be attractive and modern, but it

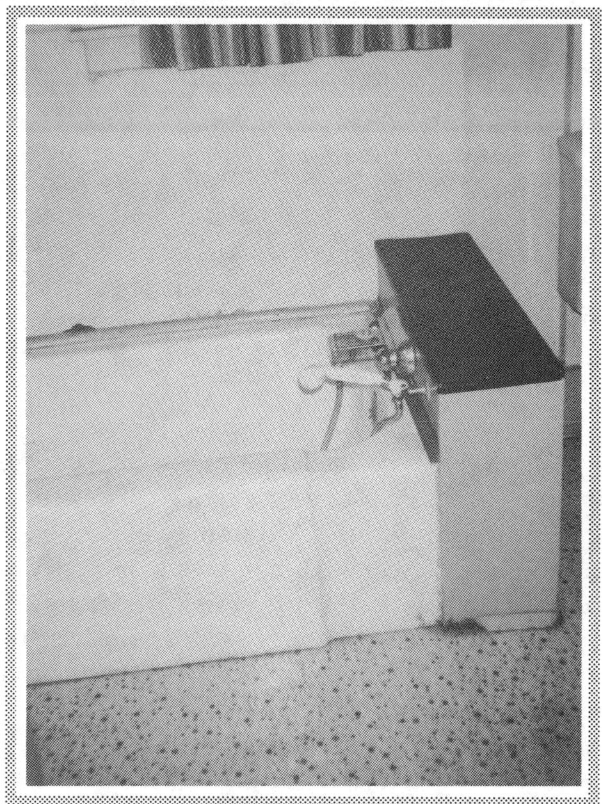

Figure 12-23

This bathroom is *not* "good enough"

Figure 12-24

New tiled bathroom is stylish

can also be a great deal of trouble and expense. Remember that tubs weren't always built in the standard 5-foot "tub pocket" that modern bathtubs are designed for. You may have to frame a wall around the tub. That adds a lot to your costs.

The less expensive choice would be to modify the footed tub for a shower. That's common where older homes and apartments are being updated. You can buy the parts you need at any well-stocked hardware store: a shower faucet with a diverter and a connector with pipe attached for a shower line. Then either buy or make a rectangular framework to suspend over the tub for the shower curtain. It takes several standard size shower curtains to make a complete enclosure.

What you do depends on how much you want to spend. If your bathroom is both attractive and functional as it is, spend as little money as possible just to test buyer reactions. If the house doesn't sell right away, spend the extra money. Replace the tub. But if you're lucky, the house will sell before that's necessary, saving you a lot of money and effort.

That raises the most difficult question in this business. How much time and trouble should you invest and where should that investment be made? You want to offer a product that's really attractive, not just good enough. Skimp on too much and people recognize it. They won't pay a good price for an inferior home. You can get by with a few items that are "just good enough" if the rest of the house is nice. But too much of that and you've got a house that's impossible to sell except to another speculator like yourself.

I could have said that the bathroom in Figure 12-23 was "good enough." The previous owners had been using it the way it was. A little paint and some new flooring was all that was really necessary. But I knew that improving it would make the house far more marketable. So I completely gutted the bathroom, leaving only the tub. I removed the half-wall at the head of the tub and put up a full wall with a built-in shower. The new wall created a complete tub and shower enclosure as well as a privacy alcove for the toilet. I chose gray with black trim for the new ceramic tile, and coordinated the flooring, wallpaper and trim to match. The result was the pleasant, stylish bathroom in Figure 12-24 — and that's more than "just good enough."

Matching Sinks to Styles

What about keeping old sinks, the kind with separate hot and cold water faucets? Should you bother to save something that's functionally outdated?

Believe it or not, replacement parts are still available for these old fittings and they seem to be coming back in style. A lot of decorating magazines are featuring items like these in their show pieces.

With this in mind, my decision usually depends on the style of the house and the quality and condition of the particular sink. If I find a beautiful, top-quality unit in good repair, I'll keep it. On the other hand, if it's a cheap utilitarian model with the glazing coming off, I'll replace it. You might even want to do a little repair work on a good quality sink that's slightly damaged. But don't bother on a cheaper sink.

If I'm going to use most of the bathroom fixtures but replace the sink, I try to find a sink that matches the other fixtures as closely as possible. I wouldn't keep the old style, with the inconvenient separate hot-and-cold water spouts, just because it fits in. I may use a completely different size and shape as long as it blends with the decor of the house.

For example, I had a house with an antique-style bathroom that was trimmed with lots of oak. The sink was an old, ugly cast-iron type with worn glazing. I replaced it with an old-fashioned oak vanity. It wasn't an authentic restoration. Vanity cabinets are a much more recent innovation. However, it *looked* right and the oak on the vanity matched the oak in the rest of the room. It was well suited to the style of the bathroom.

Another home I was working on had a 1930s-style bathroom with a worn sink that had to go. The sink was very plain. I replaced it with an attractive porcelain pedestal sink. Pedestal sinks were common in the 1930s and several manufacturers offer them today at reasonable prices. They aren't exactly the same design as was sold 50 years ago, but they're similar. Instead of separate hot and cold spouts, the new ones have mixer valves and one water spout. That's a big advantage.

If you're very particular about old fixtures, you can get authentic reproductions. They're too expensive for my projects, but may be worth the extra money if you're doing an historic restoration. I find similar, but unauthentic reproductions, to be perfectly adequate for my houses. They look as nice (sometimes even nicer) than the authentic reproductions and cost much less.

Decor Items

Spend a little extra money on bathroom trim and decor. A few dollars spent wisely will give buyers a more positive impression. Since most bathrooms are small, trim items stand out more. You get the maximum benefit from small items that might get lost in larger rooms.

Most home-improvement stores stock a large selection of bathroom trim and specialty items: towel bars, soap dishes, toilet seats, shower curtains, and decorative mirrors in a good assortment of colors, materials and styles. Include some of these items in your decorating scheme. The cost will be small. A new toilet seat and a colorful shower curtain will brighten up a bathroom for less than $30. It may even draw attention away from problems that are unpractical to solve.

Choose colors carefully. For a small room like a bathroom, light colors and small wallpaper prints are best. Use mirrors to make the room appear larger and give it depth.

Finished Basements

Good decorating will create extra value if you're lucky enough to have a house with an extra room like a finished basement or enclosed porch. Decorating an extra room isn't as important as decorating kitchens and baths. But you want to emphasize the positive features and get maximum value from the extra space.

Basements have a disadvantage. Most people think of them as cold, damp, and dark. Your buyers will discount the value of the basement if it's exactly that — cold, damp and dark. Fortunately, it's easy to make basements much more attractive.

Lighting

There isn't usually any natural light in the basement. Providing adequate light is probably the easiest and best thing you can do for most basements. The most common type of lighting in basement rec rooms is fluorescent fixtures, often recessed in the ceiling. I think that's a mistake. They cast a cold light which makes the basement seem even colder and more dreary than it really is. Save fluorescent lights for laundry and utility areas.

I prefer bright incandescent lights for a rooms where families relax and play. You'll be amazed at the difference they make. The basement will instantly become warmer and more inviting.

There's a good reason why most basements have fluorescent lighting. There's always a shortage of headroom in basements and fluorescent fixtures are easy to build into the ceiling finish. However, fluorescent lights aren't the only fixtures that can be recessed. Remember the recessed incandescent fixtures that I recommended earlier? They look gorgeous in a basement. And because basements usually have acoustical drop ceilings or no ceiling at all, they're easy to install. Install a dimmer switch to get the same kind of lighting effect as in a formal dining room.

If you don't like recessed incandescent fixtures, or if for some reason it isn't practical to install them, don't give up. Obviously, anything that hangs down too far is likely to be a hazard — the basement may not be the best place for a ceiling fan. But many other fixtures are available. If you can't find a ceiling fixture that fits, put in some attractive wall-mounted fixtures. Use enough fixtures to illuminate your finished basement with a bright, warm light.

Adding good light makes a big difference in a basement. If you're only going to make one change, it should be the lighting. You'll be amazed at the improvement!

Colors

Always use light, warm colors in a basement. This helps offset the cold, damp perception that people have about basements. Colors like yellow, peach, or beige create a sunny atmosphere that makes the basement more like other rooms with natural light from windows. Dark, cool colors, like blue or purple, will make your basement look like a cave. People may not even want to do their laundry in it, much less have a party there.

If a basement wall is covered with dark paneling, your choice of colors is more limited. If the paneling is already there and in good condition, you're probably going to be stuck with it. Work around it with better lighting and white ceiling panels. You could replace the paneling, but the extra work and expense aren't worth it. If the paneling is damaged, consider painting it a lighter color. True, painted paneling doesn't look very good. But it's better than badly damaged paneling.

I don't like using paneling in a basement. My goal in finishing a basement is to make it as much like an upstairs room as possible. My first choice in wall treatments is painted drywall. Not only does it look better than paneling, it's cheaper, too. If you drywall a basement, paint it a cheerful color, and install a bright, attractive light fixture.

That makes your basement as nice as any upstairs room. The last basement I did like that was converted to an extra bedroom by the buyers. I had advertised it only as a rec room.

Some people like the casual look of wood paneling. If you're going to use it in a basement, either because you like it or because you think it's easier to install than drywall, use a light wood tone such as oak.

Before installing any wall finish in a basement, insulate the walls. Insulation will keep the room warmer and help eliminate the dampness you find in so many basements. Styrofoam insulation is best for this purpose. If the concrete or block walls leak moisture, it won't soak through the Styrofoam.

Floor Treatments

Water damage is common in basement floors. Consider all the possible problems before deciding on the floor covering. The walls may leak, there may be laundry spills, condensation on humid days, and spilled soda pop. Ordinary carpeting in a basement may get wet, stay wet and eventually mold. Nobody likes a moldy house.

I usually install vinyl tile. Vinyl is flexible, waterproof and immune to water damage. Of course, all tile can come loose from the subfloor because adhesives aren't completely waterproof. But because they're flexible, they won't break when you glue them back down.

If you really want carpeting, use one of the indoor/outdoor types. They aren't as nice as regular carpeting, but some of the new styles are quite attractive. There are two advantages to indoor/outdoor carpet: it isn't harmed by water, and it's relatively cheap. In any case, don't spend too much on basement floor cover. It won't add much to the value of your house and many buyers don't want or need a finished basement. Keep the cost of floor cover down to a few hundred dollars, at most.

Dealing with poor surfaces— Sometimes you have to make decorating decisions for practical reasons that have nothing to do with your design scheme. The most common problem is bad floors. A number of houses I've bought had basement floors that were sound but extremely rough and uneven. There was nothing wrong with the concrete slab except the cement finishing job was very poor.

Unfortunately, you can't lay tile on an uneven floor. You can repair holes here and there and put tile down, but if the entire surface is hills and valleys, the tile will never go down right. Even if you could get the tiles to stick, the glossy surfaces will highlight all the defects. Anyone who sees it will notice the problem immediately.

If you plan to lay tile on a floor like that, level the surface with underlayment first. If the floor is very uneven, either install sleepers (wood spacers under the flooring) to fill in the valleys, or use underlayment heavy enough (3/4 inch plywood) to bridge the gaps. Another choice is to smooth the surface with a pourable floor-leveling mix.

These are time-consuming and expensive alternatives. You can easily spend a couple of hundred dollars on underlayment and then that much more for the tile. With choices like that, I usually just install carpeting. The hills and valleys will still be there, but they'll be hard to see.

Choosing colors— Treat basement floors, like the walls, in light, bright colors. You want the whole environment to be bright and cheerful. Carry the same colors you use on the walls down onto your floor; warm shades like yellow, beige and peach are best. If you're putting down carpeting however, these shades are a bad choice. Light carpeting gets dirty fast. Unless you're sure you'll sell the house right away, it may be more practical to use a medium gray or brown tweed carpet. These are durable colors. If you have to rent the house for a while, the carpet should survive your tenants' muddy feet.

Major Improvements

What about adding major improvements in the recreation room, such as a wet bar or built-in entertainment center? You can probably guess what I would recommend. These are nice features, but may or may not appeal to some buyers.

Figure 12-25

This basement rec room was cold, damp and dreary

Suppose you put in a wet bar and your prospective buyers don't drink? You've wasted your money. Buyers who want a wet bar will install one themselves.

I make one exception to that rule. If I happen to have something on hand that suits this particular job exactly, I'll usually install it on the chance that some buyer will fall in love with it. For example, I enjoy good stereo equipment. Every few years I improve my system, replacing the old with new state-of-the-art features. What I've removed is still good equipment and still works, but I don't need it any more. Twice I've added a built-in stereo system to a den or rec room I remodeled. To the buyers, that equipment seemed like a real luxury feature. The value added to the house was almost certainly more than what I could have sold the equipment for. And my installation labor was minimal. My old stereo created a very strong positive impression in the minds of the potential buyers. They don't expect features like a fine-quality stereo. It makes the house seem special and cared for, and creates pride of ownership.

I would do the same with a basement bar if I found one for sale at an unbeatable price. I saw a beautiful hardwood bar (with sink) selling for $50 at a garage sale. That's a bargain I couldn't pass up — and you shouldn't either. The most you could lose is the $50 and a few hours work. But you could add $1,000 to your selling price.

Improvements in expensive homes— Should you spend more to improve a finished basement in an upscale property? Absolutely not! In upscale property, the basement is used only for storage and laundry facilities. There's usually plenty of space upstairs. Basement space doesn't appeal to upscale buyers. They won't accept it.

I don't mean to imply that a finished basement is absolutely worthless in upscale property. It can be useful as a playroom or as hobby space. But it isn't considered prime living space and won't be used the same way a den or family room would on the ground floor. It's more likely to be used for storage space. Even nicely-finished storage space doesn't add much value to the house. In this kind of property, any work done in the basement will probably cost more than the value it adds to the house.

A Successful Basement Renovation

Figure 12-25 shows the basement in a house I bought a few years ago. This picture was taken *after* we cleaned out the junk. Not only was this recreation room poorly built, it was water

Figure 12-26
Remodeling in progress

damaged. I decided that the house was worth the extra expense it would take to turn this into an inviting, usable room. More living space was just what this small house needed.

We stripped all the old finish off the walls and ceiling, then framed in a new wall to divide the basement into a recreation room and a storage area (Figure 12-26). Then we drywalled and painted the ceiling and walls, installed indoor/outdoor carpeting, added new, very stylish lighting fixtures and finished off with a built-in stereo system! You can see the stereo and speakers on the right-hand wall in Figure 12-27. The

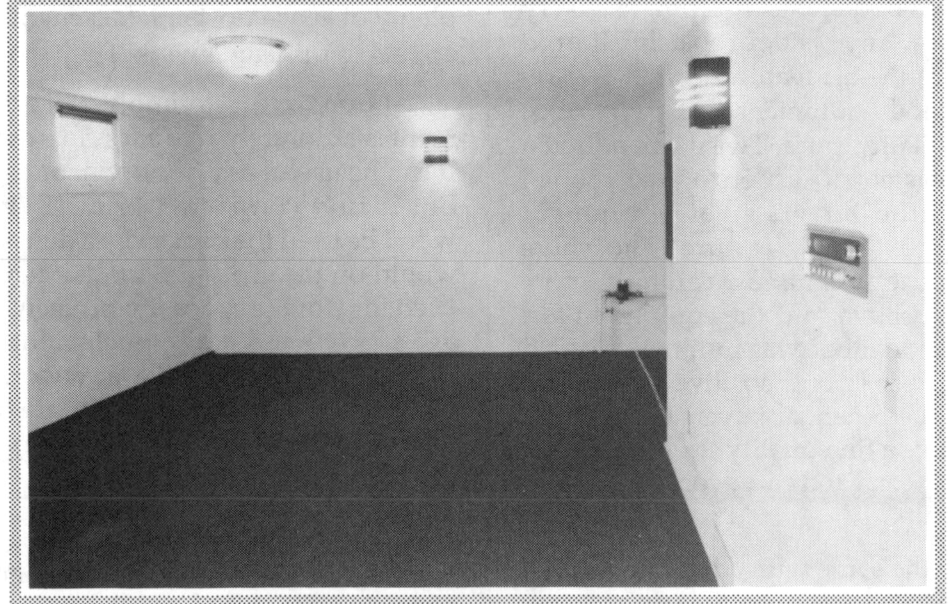

Figure 12-27
The completed room

entire project took about a week to complete and cost $800, mostly for the carpet. It added about $10,000 to the value of the house when I sold it.

Porches

It's hard to decorate enclosed porches. They're more exposed to the elements because windows and doors are often left open (or may not close entirely). Porches are exposed to extreme temperature ranges. Many decorating items that you could use elsewhere would be destroyed by weather in an enclosed porch. Still, a porch is extra living area and an attractive addition to a house. So it's worth decorating if you use "indoor-outdoor" items that can survive the elements.

To avoid confusion, I want to explain what I mean by *enclosed porch*. I'm referring to a porch that was originally open, but was later enclosed. I'm not referring to sunrooms, greenhouses, or Florida rooms that were added to the house. Those rooms aren't converted from something else. You don't often find these types of rooms in a handyman-special house. They're generally added to more expensive homes that don't often deteriorate into fixers.

Porch problems

In most of the homes I buy, the enclosed porch was used to store all the junk the owner couldn't bear to part with. When I buy the house, the junk usually comes with it. And until I haul the junk to a dump, it's hard to tell what needs to be done to the porch. Usually it's in pretty bad condition.

Most enclosed porches are a jumble of styles, colors, and finishes. One of the quickest and easiest ways to improve the porch is to give it a coat of paint. Remember to use exterior grade paints only. Interior latex will peel off if it gets too much moisture. Depending on the condition of the porch and the selling price you anticipate, a coat of paint may be all the decorating your porch needs.

Lights— Enclosed porches often have exterior light fixtures, since they used to be open porches. An interior-type fixture will make the porch seem more like part of the interior. Never leave a naked bulb dangling from a wire, or a "jelly-jar" fixture with the jelly jar missing. Replace missing or broken fixtures with an inexpensive but appropriate unit.

Floors— Porch floors are often gouged, dented, rotted, or splashed with paint. A fresh coat of floor paint in a nice color will improve the appearance. Avoid painting the floor gray. Porch and floor paint comes in many colors, yet for some reason many people automatically use gray. The color on the floor should harmonize with the rest of the porch. Certainly, if you have light gray walls, a gray floor is fine. However, if your walls are yellow or beige, a brown floor would look better than gray. A fairly neutral color is generally best for the floor.

Indoor/outdoor carpeting is a good choice on a porch. It covers floor damage very well and it's cheap. But don't install green carpet. Amateurs install green carpet on the porch. Gray, brown, or beige carpeting will look a lot better. New carpeting, plus a fresh coat of paint and an attractive light fixture will turn that former junk bin into an appealing semiformal sun room.

Costs

I don't recommend spending too much money on an enclosed porch. As with basements, there are some people who won't pay anything extra for an enclosed porch, no matter how nice it is. Since you don't know your buyers, it's best to keep your costs down. But always create a porch that's clean, in good repair, and has a fresh coat of paint. Never leave any part of the house dirty, unrepaired or unpainted.

If an enclosed porch requires major repairs, you may want to turn it back into an open porch, or remove it altogether. It just isn't worth making major repairs to an enclosed porch. If it's important to the exterior look of the house, then restyle it so it complements the exterior appearance of the house. A beautiful open porch will add a lot more to the value of your house than a peculiar-looking enclosed porch.

In medium- or low-priced property, people are usually happy to have a converted porch. They're glad for any extra usable space, but they won't necessarily be willing to pay more for it. A porch is, after all, second-rate space. If it comes free with the house, that's fine. Don't plan on making any money off decorating a porch conversion unless it's very well done.

Enclosed Front Porches

An enclosed front porch may be a disadvantage rather than an asset — especially if it doesn't complement the house exterior. You may want to demolish the porch and return the house to its original design. If you decide to keep the front porch, decorate it to harmonize with the home. Try to make it less like an afterthought and more like a real part of the home's interior.

The most important part of decorating this "room" is making it harmonize with the living room. It's the entry to the living area. If you have a formal living room, try to make the enclosed front porch appear more formal. Use a neutral color scheme and nice floor covering like carpet, wood or tile. If your living room is informal, make the porch informal as well. Cheerful colors and cute decorator touches are a good choice. Avoid mixing styles from the porch to the living room.

Reaching the End

Congratulations! Your "fixer-upper" is now completely fixed up. If you've followed my advice, you should get the results I get. At least a 10 to 25 percent profit margin after all expenses are considered — and sometimes a lot more! It's not uncommon for me to have a profit margin as high as 50 percent.

Before ending this section, let me make one important point. What I've suggested has worked very well for me. Everything in this book is based on my own experience in fixing up and selling dozens of homes. But there's no single formula that's bound to work for every renovator in every community and for all time. The rules I've recommended are designed to be flexible. Follow my suggestions until you develop your own judgment and your own set of rules. Then, when the reasons for those rules no longer apply, change them. That's what makes this business so much fun. New rules, new materials, new procedures and new opportunities are being created every day.

You may make good money but you won't have fun in this business unless you use a few of your own ideas. If you want to do something unconventional with a room, and you think it's really great, chances are other people will too. What's the good of being your own boss if you can't make your own decisions?

When your house has been repaired, remodeled, and decorated inside and out, you should be very proud of it — and yourself. Your finished house is a showcase of your skills. It's your calling card and should generate extra business if you do any custom home building or remodeling. Anyone who can create attractive, appealing housing on a small budget should have no trouble finding plenty of work in any community.

When the decorating is complete, your beautiful home is ready to greet willing buyers. If sold right, it should bring a good price and earn you a fair profit. In the next chapter, I'll explain how to get that good price.

CHAPTER THIRTEEN

Selling Your House

Now we come to the critical last step: finding a buyer for the finished product. If eager buyers are fighting over your house when you're ready to sell, congratulations! You're now a success. You've passed the course. You can skip the rest of this chapter and the next. You're a successful speculator in rehab properties.

If your house hasn't sold yet, no problem. Don't worry. Just keep reading. This chapter explains how to get top dollar for your house. The next chapter explains what to do if the market turns soft and you can't sell (temporarily, at least) at your intended price.

Critical though this step may be, if you've followed all my suggestions up to now, selling your house shouldn't be very hard. You're offering a beautifully-remodeled home, stylishly decorated, in a desirable area, that you can afford to sell for an attractive price. It's usually easy to find buyers for a home like that.

In some cases, you may not have to put much effort into selling at all. Buyers may actually come looking for you if the market is really hot. There may be more buyers than there are houses for sale. People might even ask you to sell before the work is done. That can happen if you've been dropping hints to neighbors, real estate agents, associates, or anyone who might know a willing buyer. They probably told friends or relatives who were looking for a house in that neighborhood.

Of course, you can't always count on selling a house by word of mouth. And even if people are begging for it, you may decide not to sell without testing the market. It's one thing for people to *want* to buy your house, and other for them *to be able* to buy at the fair market value (more on qualifying your prospects later). In any case, you'll like getting unsolicited offers for the house. That's a good position to be in.

You estimated the asking price way back when you started on the project. If you stayed within your estimated budget, the asking price shouldn't have changed. All during your renovation you should have a good answer ready when someone asks how much you want for it. "Gosh, I dunno," doesn't fall in the category of a good answer.

You'll usually have to put some effort into selling. So let's talk about where you begin.

Should You Sell It Yourself?

The first decision you'll have to make is whether you'll sell the house yourself or list it with an agent. Probably the most important factor in making this decision is your comfort level in real estate transactions. If this is your first home sale, you may want to let a professional handle the paperwork this time. Just pay *very* close attention to how everything is done. If you've bought and sold homes before, try making the sale on your own. Of course, many people, even those with a great deal of experience, prefer to leave the buying and selling to the professionals. As an experienced seller, I'd say there are several good arguments on both sides.

Pros and Cons of Using an Agent

Remember that I recommended *buying* through an agent. As a buyer, the advantages of working with an agent are overwhelming. For one thing, the seller pays the agent's commission. But the situation is a little different when you're selling. Why? Because this time *you* have to pay the agent's commission! As a buyer, you don't care how much commission the agent gets — it's not your money. Now that you're a seller, however, it's your money. So you need to weigh this decision carefully.

How much money are we talking about? A seller generally pays commissions of from 6 percent to 7 percent of the actual selling price of the house. If your property sells for $120,000, then you'll have to pay $7,200 to $8,400 in commissions. That's a pretty big chunk of your profits. You did a lot of work for that money. I hope you think twice about giving it away!

On the other hand, a good real estate agent earns that commission. They provide valuable services and take the burden of the sale off your shoulders. You can probably get a higher price for your house through an agent because your house gets more exposure to a wider pool of prospects.

Suppose you're asking for $125,000 but will take $115,000. What if the agent has an offer at $122,000. Have you really lost anything? At 6 percent, you'll pay $7,320 in commission and come out with $114,680 (less the selling costs you have to pay regardless of who sells the house). You'll be paying someone $320 off your bottom price to do all the paper work and handle all the headaches. That's a pretty good deal.

Of course, if the agent can only get you $115,000, and that's what you need for an acceptable profit, you'll be at a loss. I found myself in a situation once where I wouldn't have made any profit at all if I'd paid 6 or 7 percent commission on the sale. In that case, there's no choice. Handle the sale yourself. At least you'll learn how it's done.

Assessing the Market

In a hot housing market, an agent, even a top-flight agent, isn't really necessary. You may start getting offers on your property before it's ready to sell. An agent's most important service is finding a buyer for your home. If the market is hot, you can easily find your own buyers.

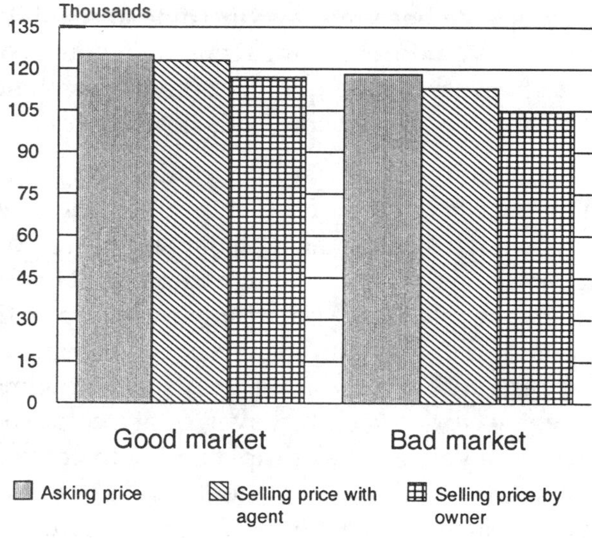

Figure 13-1

For sale by owner vs. real estate agency sales

In a seller's market, there are more buyers than there are houses available. That means buyers can't afford to dicker too long about any property. If they do, someone else will snap it up. After this happens a couple of times, buyers begin to panic. They'll jump at anything decent. In fact, they may even offer more than the asking price, to be absolutely sure they get the house they want.

Neighborhood quality is an important part of your sales strategy. Market conditions change from time to time in a good neighborhood, but *they're always bad in a bad neighborhood.*

Selling in a Bad Market

When you're caught in a slow market, an agent is a genuine necessity. There are lots more houses for sale than willing buyers. Then it's a buyer's market. They can afford to be very picky, take their time, and drive a hard bargain.

In a bad market, you still have some advantages. You bought low, and you have a nicely-remodeled house to offer. Your house should be one of the most appealing in its price range. But people won't buy what they don't see. So having your house in the multiple listing is vital. You need that exposure.

Also, by putting your house into the multiples, you're enlisting the aid of all the agents in your area. Agents get very hungry in a bad market. Sales are down and they're not making much money. They'll try desperately to sell anything. Offering another listing is a big plus for everyone.

It takes longer to make a deal in a bad market. Buyers are fussier. They take the time to examine every possible house before they decide, and they shop for price and terms as well. They may also experiment with lowball offers, just to see if a seller is desperate. Eventually, someone will buy your house. And they may even pay you a decent price for it. But not until they've considered everything else on the market.

Even in good times, it takes longer to sell a house yourself than it will by going through an agent. Since your pool of purchasers is smaller, it takes more time to find a qualified buyer. But the extra time isn't really a problem if you know the market is good and your house will sell. In a bad market, time becomes a real problem. Even with an agent, it can easily take six months to sell your house. Selling it yourself may take a year. That's a long time to be making payments on an empty house. It may be a lot better to pay an agent's commission and have it off your hands.

Figure 13-1 compares sales by owners and sales by agents in both good and bad markets. As you can see, an agent can usually get a higher price for your house. That doesn't mean, however, that *you* will end up with more money.

Consider Seasonal Variations

The housing market varies substantially throughout the year. But it's always better in the spring. The slowest market of the year tends to be in the dead of winter in cold climate areas, or in the heat of summer in hot climates. It's no fun to look at houses in bad weather. So unless people *have* to move, they'll wait until the weather improves.

It's important to understand seasonal variations. They can work for you or against you. Whenever possible, try to put your house up for sale in the spring. If you can't get your house on the market in time for spring, the next best time is early fall. If you miss the fall season, you've got a problem. Houses don't sell well during the holiday season. From Halloween through New Year's Day the market is usually slow. After New Year's Day, the market remains sluggish until it starts to look like spring. In my area that can be as early as February or as late as May. It all depends on the weather. As soon as the weather breaks, people start shopping.

Of course, seasonal changes aren't the only market variables. If the economy is great and the market is hot, it won't suddenly turn bad before Christmas. It just won't be quite so hot. You might still get a good price for your house, but not the great price you'd get in May. And if the market is terrible, it isn't going to suddenly become wonderful when spring rolls around. It just won't be quite as terrible.

What does this mean to you? Simply that you should include seasonal changes in your selling strategy. For instance, if you've had your home up for sale in the winter, don't accept a low offer for it in March. Spring is coming — lots of better offers are probably on the way. Hold out a little longer if you can.

On the other hand, if spring is over and your house hasn't sold, take a fair offer if one comes along. Time is running out. You may have priced your house too high in the first place, or there's something else wrong with it. If it hasn't sold during the best season of the year, odds are you won't be able to sell it later. So unless you want to take chances on a weaker market, do something to make your home more desirable. The easiest thing you can do is lower the price.

Changes in the season may affect your decision to work with an agent. If you're planning to sell in the spring, consider selling it yourself. If you have to sell in winter, an agent may be a big help.

Assess Your Time and Ability

Before deciding to make the sale yourself, consider whether you have the time and ability to do it. If you don't use an agent, then you have to do the work: find a qualified buyer, negotiate the deal and get it closed. That's not always easy.

Remember that selling requires not only knowledge, but also a certain type of personality. Do you have a salesman's personality? Are you prepared to be pleasant and good-natured to obnoxious people? Are you willing to put up with insults and fault-finding? When a persnickety shopper turns up his nose in disgust at some carpentry work *you* slaved over, or at a color *you* chose, will you see it as simply a ploy to get you to lower your price, as an agent would? Or will you be ready to throw him out the door? Are you willing to spend every weekend (and many evenings as well) answering stupid, pointless questions from people who are wasting your time?

You have to go through a lot of lookers before you find a buyer. And remember, "the customer's always right." You can't afford to be rude or impatient with someone who may buy your house, no matter how irritating they may be. If you're not prepared to deal with this sort of thing, you're better off paying a professional to do it. Otherwise, you'll just alienate potential customers and waste both time and money.

A good agent will take over your house so you can devote time to the next one. Your agent will handle all the details of the sale. All you have to do is follow their advice and sign the papers. The rest will be neatly taken care of.

What an Agent Can Do for You

Exactly what services should you expect an agent to provide in exchange for his or her commission?

Multiple listing service— First and foremost, they'll put your property into the multiple listing service. That gives you access to a large, sophisticated home-sales network. Once your house is multi-listed, every real estate agent in your area is working for you. They'll all be competing to find a buyer for your house.

Advertising and promotion— Good agents will also aggressively promote your house. They'll advertise your home in the classified ads and hold open houses on the weekends. These services can help your house sell fast, for the best possible price and terms. The wider your exposure, the better your sales opportunities.

Set sales price— An agent can help you settle on the best sales price for your house. Of course, you should have a good idea of the selling price before you even buy it. But an experienced agent can usually zero in on an exact figure. They watch sales on a daily basis and know what houses are listed for and what they actually sell for. They want you to get a good price for your house. After all, the higher the price, the higher their commission. But they'll be less biased and more realistic about what your house will actually sell for. They won't ask so much that the house sits on the market for months and months.

Provide information on comps— Your agent should review all comparable sales for the last few months and work up a list of "comps" for your neighborhood. "Comps" are houses that are comparable to yours. Comps should indicate the fair market price for your house. Appraisers also gather comps when evaluating homes for lenders. Remember, your house will probably be appraised for a loan, so it must be priced at a level that a lender will find acceptable too.

Of course, you compared and priced homes before buying the house you're now selling. But that was three to six months ago and a lot may have happened to the housing market in the meantime. Prices may have gone up or down. You need current information to make good decisions — and agents have it all at their fingertips. If you decide not to work with an agent, you still need this information. You'll just have to find another way to get it.

Expect a lot from your agent. After all, you're providing the best kind of property — a newly-remodeled, stylishly-decorated house in a desirable neighborhood. And, the house is vacant. That's easier than showing an occupied home where an agent has to work around the residents.

A good agent should be eager to list your house. It has the potential for a quick and easy sale. Time and effort spent should be rewarded quickly.

Follow through on paperwork— An agent should keep the paperwork moving smoothly and make sure everything is completed on time. A home sale can drag on for months if no one is pushing to make sure the paperwork is distributed, the loan gets processed, and escrow closes on schedule. Most of this paperwork concerns the buyer. Your part of the deal is pretty simple: either you get the money or you don't. Your agent should follow up on the buyer's part of the deal.

Good agents will keep track of everything. They don't just sit back and relax once the Offer to Purchase is accepted. They'll check with the buyers to be sure they've applied for the loan. They'll check with the lender to see how the application is doing. They'll make sure you've carried out any promises you've made as part of the deal. And if anything seems to be going wrong, they'll work hard to straighten it out promptly. You may not appreciate a good agent when things run smoothly, but you *will* when the deal hits a snag. Their efforts can be invaluable.

Watch Out for Bad Agents

Of course, not all real estate agents are created equal. There are good agents and bad agents. A good agent can be a tremendous help in selling your house. A bad agent will waste your time and money.

Incompetents— There are agents who are incompetent. In fact, you wonder how they ever passed the licensing exam. There are others who are lazy; some who are both lazy *and* incompetent. An agent who's incompetent can still be of some value to you. At least you'll get your house in the multiple listing service. Unfortunately, that's about all you'll get. If you're lucky, some other agent will see the listing and find a buyer for you. You'll have to do most of the negotiating and protect your own interests. Your agent will probably rely on the buyer's agent to do all the work.

Lazy agents— Lazy agents are eager to get your listing, but that's where their efforts stop. Once they list a house, they forget all about it. No open houses, no classified ads. They just sit back and wait for a buyer to walk in off the street or for some other agent to make the sale. Remember, no matter who sells the house, the listing agent gets a piece of the commission. A lazy agent will be satisfied with that. Since they don't do any work, the commission is practically free money. If the house sells, that's great. If it doesn't, who cares? There's no loss to him.

Agents like this won't help you gather information and can't help you set a price for the house. They aren't current on market trends and haven't studied the comps or listings. They have no idea what your house is worth. You'll know a lot more about your neighborhood and market than they do. They aren't anxious to handle paperwork associated with the sale. Since they hardly ever sell a house themselves, they don't know what to do. They would never dream of calling all the parties involved and checking on their progress. It may take many months to close a deal when you're working with an agent like this.

It's my impression that there are fewer incompetent agents around in a bad market. There's no easy money in a slow market — they have to earn it. But every time the real estate market starts warming up, a flood of new agents come into the business. Then you have to watch out.

Unscrupulous agents— Unfortunately, every profession has its share of dishonest or deceitful practitioners. The real estate business is no exception. Watch for agents who promote the sale aggressively, *but always for their benefit, not yours.*

One trick is to avoid putting your house in the multiple listing service. Of course they've signed a contract with you promising to do this, but they'll put it off. They don't want the competition. If they both list and sell the property, they get double the commission. That's a strong incentive for anyone to sell their own listings. But keeping your property out of the multiples deprives you of the exposure you bargained for. Instead of the thousands of home buyers who look through the multi-list, you'll be limited to the ones who see the "For Sale" sign or those who happen to come into the listing agent's office.

I've seen listing agreements that don't obligate the agent to put the property in the multiples for a month or so. But it's pointless to agree to an arrangement like this without some extra incentive from the agent.

Without the multiple listing service, few people will see your house. If your agent withholds the listing without your knowledge, you may begin to wonder if your house will ever sell. When someone finally makes an offer, the agent will pressure you to accept because it may be a long time before another offer comes in. They'll try to convince you that your house is undesirable. "It must be," they'll say. "Otherwise, you would have had other offers by now!" Of course, there probably *is* someone out there who would quickly buy your house for full price, if they only knew it was for sale.

Even if your house sells at a big discount, the agent's commission will be higher because it isn't split between buying and selling agents. You end up selling at a discount so the agent can make a few extra bucks. If you find out you've been tricked like this, complain to the state authority that regulates licensed real estate professionals. Both the agent and broker can lose their licences, even if the broker wasn't in on the deceit. Unfortunately, most sellers never find out they've been victimized.

Bad or unscrupulous agents will pressure you into accepting unwise terms. They may, for example, advise you to sell to unqualified, untrustworthy buyers on a land contract. Once the sale is closed, they get their commission. If the buyer never makes a payment, the agent doesn't care. That's your loss, not theirs. Does this seem farfetched? I thought so too — until it happened to me. Be on guard against this sort of thing.

Learn to Protect Yourself

How can you protect yourself against incompetent or dishonest agents? Take the time to find a good agent and stay with him or her. Review my suggestions in Chapter 3. Ask your agent these questions:

- Are you going to have an open house?
- Are you going to run ads in the paper?
- How much have houses like mine been selling for?

Remember, incompetent agents don't identify themselves. They try to act like they know what they're talking about. You have to distinguish between those that do and those that don't.

Make sure your agreement with the agent gives you the option of canceling after a reasonable time. You should be able to cancel the listing prior to receiving an offer without any obligation. Of course, you can't beat the agent out of a commission by canceling. If they bring you an acceptable buyer, you owe the commission. But if you've given an agent a 90-day listing and they haven't shown your property or performed up to your expectations in the first few weeks, you should be free to look for a better agent.

Ask to see your house in the multi-list book once it's been listed. Tell the agent that you want to check the information to be sure it's accurate. Be sure your property is really in the book. It's always a good idea to double-check the accuracy of a listing. Many agents automatically show you the listing so you can check if over — it's good business.

Don't let yourself to be pressured into anything. When you get an offer, ask the agent what real estate agency the buyers are working with. If it's the same agency that listed the property, be careful. Your agent will have an automatic bias towards the offer. Even if they aren't trying to put something over on you, they'll just naturally tend to favor their own office, possibly over your interests. Be aware of the conflict of interest.

Finally, once you've accepted an Offer to Purchase, *stay on top of the deal.* Don't let weeks go by without news. If your agent doesn't call to keep you posted, call them. If they're no help, call the buyer's agent. Maybe the buyer's agent can get things moving. After all, it's to everyone's advantage that the deal goes through quickly.

Develop a good relationship with a competent, experienced, trustworthy agent who's a proven self-starter. An agent like that will work hard to sell your property quickly, and at a good price. You'll have to pay for this service, but at least you know you're getting something for it.

For Sale by Owner

Selling your house without an agent takes a lot more work. You won't have the obvious advantage of using the multiple-listing service, but many of the other tools an agent uses are available to you. Begin by making people aware that your house is for sale. A sign in front of the property is a start. That isn't the most effective way to advertise — even in a hot market. But it does spread the word among the neighbors and help people find your house when they're looking for it. It has a definite value.

Use Classified Ads

Classified ads are most effective. If your area has a local paper, that's the place to run your ad.

It will be seen by people specifically interested in your neighborhood. You should also put an ad in the area's metropolitan newspaper. You can't get too much exposure. Most people who are shopping for real estate check the papers on Sunday. I find the most effective advertising is in the Sunday edition. But I also run ads in the local papers on Thursday through Saturday.

When in doubt, run your ad in every paper sold in your area, on every day of the week. The advertising bill may be high, but it's a fraction of the cost of an agent's commission. Remember, the point is to find a buyer for your house, and the sooner the better. It doesn't do you much good to save a few dollars on advertising costs if your house remains unsold.

Here's a typical newspaper ad for an open house. In this case, I'm describing the house you'll see a little later in the fact sheet, Figure 13-2.

> *Willow Glen. Near downtown. Beautiful 4 bdrm, 2 bath, lrg liv & din rms, bsmt, gar. Many extras. $124,900. OPEN HOUSE, Sun. June 11, 2-6. 423 E. Elm, S of 4th St, W of Main. 555-1234.*

Willow Glen: I always start with the name of the suburb or subdivision. Remember, people shop primarily by area. The name of the area is the most important piece of information in the entire ad, so put it first.

Near downtown: For this particular area, being near downtown is highly desirable. That's why it goes second.

Beautiful: Always start your description with some positive word like *beautiful, desirable,* or *lovely.* This puts the reader in a positive state of mind while reading your ad. Don't use an uninspiring work like *clean.* A public toilet might be clean, but would you want to live there?

4 bdrm . . . : This describes the basic size and shape of the house, the next most important information. You can use abbreviations to save space and money, as long as you use the same ones everyone else does. Readers usually understand them. But don't make up new abbreviations that will leave readers puzzled.

$124,900: If you don't include the price, you'll be wasting time with people who can't afford the house. Just put the price *after* the description, so the readers are enthusiastic about the property before you hit them with the price.

OPEN HOUSE: Don't abbreviate these important words, and put them in bold type if possible. And be sure to include the date and time.

423 E. Elm, S of . . . : Always include the address *and* directions! Otherwise, most of the calls you get will be from people who just want to know how to get there. Real estate agents may omit the directions because they want people to call. After all, they have other houses to sell as well. But you don't want to waste time repeating directions all day.

555-1234: You might want to leave off the phone number. We often do. What can you tell someone over the phone? All of the information is in the ad. They really have to see the house to appreciate it. If you don't want to be interrupted, omit the phone number. Interested buyers will drive by the house. Your number is on the For Sale sign.

Once your ad comes out, every real estate agent in town is likely to call. They read the ads too. They'll all come and tell you how hard it is to try and sell your house on your own, and how happy they'll be to help you when you finally give up and decide to list with an agency. They'll ask you if you're "cooperating with agents." That means, will you negotiate a commission with an agent if they bring you a buyer? You can usually get by with offering them a 3 percent commission (some will take less if they really have a buyer). Most likely, you'll never see any of them again. Real estate agents don't like to work with owners unless they're forced to by an interested buyer. They come around just hoping to get a listing. No matter what they say, yours is the last house in town they'll show until it's listed. You are, after all, undermining their profession.

Hold an Open House

The best way to show your house to the public is with an open house. Always mention the open house hours in your ad. It's a lot easier than making individual appointments with everyone who calls. Also, people are more relaxed coming to an open house. They don't feel like they're making any kind of commitment. Some people who are reluctant to make an appointment will show up at the open house. Some are no more than curious. But an open house gets a lot of exposure in a short time.

Try to get as many people as possible to come to the open house. That way, you only tie up one or two afternoons instead of the whole week. Also, the more people who show up at once, the more your buyers are likely to feel that they must respond quickly or lose out to competitive shoppers. Of course, some interested buyers can't come to the open house. By all means, make a special appointment to show the house.

Open houses are traditionally held on Sunday afternoons, between 2:00 and 5:00 p.m. Many families like to cruise around Sunday afternoons visiting open houses. Put Open House signs on the cross streets near your home to attract more buyers. Some people come by just for the entertainment value. They have no intention of buying. They just like to look — or to dream. So don't get too excited about how many people show up at your house.

Weather will have a great effect on the success of your open house. If it's pouring rain, people might not go out. On the other hand, if it's an absolutely gorgeous day, people may decide to go to the beach instead. Something in between, weather that's tolerable but not perfect, is best for open houses. Unfortunately, that's something you can't control.

When you hold an open house, have an information sheet available to give everyone who comes in. It saves repeating the same information to every prospect and lets buyers concentrate on the house itself. And most important, visitors have something to take home that reminds them of your house.

Figure 13-2 shows the kind of information sheet I use for my houses. Notice that it includes a nice, clear photo. I *always* include a photo. It helps people remember which house the sheet applies to. (They probably looked at several houses while they were out.) I also include a description of the house as well as the price, terms, and any outstanding features of the house or its location.

It takes time to find a buyer. Don't expect to sell the house the first afternoon. Keep running your ads, and keep holding open houses. Don't give up. Sooner or later, the right buyer will be there.

Prequalify Your Buyer

Let's suppose you have someone who wants to buy your property. The next issue is, of course, can they afford it? You'll get offers both from people who can and people who can't qualify for the loan required. Most offers will probably come from the "can't" category. These people know very little about qualifying for a loan and probably have never bought a house before. They don't realize that they have no chance of getting a loan. You have to weed out people like this before they waste weeks of your time.

One way to do this is with a table like Figure 13-3. It shows how much the buyer with a 10 or 20 percent down payment must earn to qualify for a $139,900 home. It gives the monthly payment, including taxes and insurance based on an adjustable interest rate beginning at 8.25 percent or fixed interest rate of 9.875 percent. The figures shown are for the maximum ratio of payments to income (36 percent) that lenders would allow for a buyer with perfect credit and no significant monthly payments. You might make up a table like Figure 13-3 (using the current interest rate) for each house you sell. You might have to adjust the ratios slightly to reflect the policies followed by lenders in your area.

WELCOME TO: 423 E. ELM

Take a moment to look around the neighborhood. This is one of the nicest areas of Willow Glen. You are only two blocks from downtown with all the new stores and restaurants, yet you have the quiet atmosphere of the country. And just down the street there are dozens of huge, beautiful mansions leading to one of the city's nicest parks.

Price: $124,900

- *3 or 4 bedrooms (large room behind the dining room could be used as either a bedroom or a family room)*
- *1900 sq. ft. of living area*
- *2 full baths*
- *Formal dining room*
- *Breakfast nook off kitchen*
- *New garbage disposal & dishwasher*
- *Gas gravity heat*
- *Electric hot water heater*
- *1-1/2 car garage with electricity*
- *Full basement*
- *New insulation in attic*

House is available immediately.

Cash or new conventional loan

Figure 13-2

Fact sheet for open house

Suggested Income for Loan

	Adjustable rate loan		Fixed rate loan	
	10% down	20% down	10% down	20% down
Sales price:	$139,900	$139,900	$139,900	$139,900
Down payment:	13,990	27,980	13,990	27,980
Loan amount:	125,910	111,920	125,910	111,920
Interest rate:	8.25%	8.25%	9.875%	9.875%
Interest rate caps:	2/5	2/5	N/A	N/A
Margin:	2.75%	2.75%	N/A	N/A
Index:	8.648%	8.648%	N/A	N/A
Principal and interest:	$945.92	$840.81	$1,093.34	$971.86
Tax:	145.73	145.73	145.73	145.73
Hazard insurance:	31.48	27.98	31.48	27.98
Homeowners association dues:	N/A	N/A	N/A	N/A
Other:	N/A	N/A	N/A	N/A
Total monthly payment:	$1,123.13	$1,014.52	$1,270.55	$1,145.57
Suggested income required to qualify:	**$3,119.80**	**$2,818.11**	**$3,529.30**	**$3,182.13**

Figure 13-3
Suggested income required to qualify for purchase

Someone could qualify for this house with lower earnings if they had a larger down payment. The lower the earnings, the larger their down payment would have be to keep payments in line with monthly income. Sometimes when people see these figures, it's easier for them to understand what's required. If their income is well below what's needed, they won't waste any more of your time.

I recommend that you ask potential buyers to fill out a financial statement. This should include employment information, current debts, and assets available to complete the purchase. The lender will need this information as well, but you should prequalify the buyers as soon as possible. Figure 13-4 is the prequalification questionnaire I use. It contains most of the information that lenders want to know, like the applicants' job stability and the source of funds for the down payment.

As the seller, it's your job to look over this questionnaire and decide whether you think the applicants can qualify for a mortgage. Most of the financial information in the questionnaire plugs

Prequalification Questionnaire

For (address): ______________________________

Cost of house ______________ Amount of down payment ______________

Source of funds ______________________________

Applicant #1

Name ______________ Home phone ______________ Work phone ______________

Date of birth ______________ Social Security # ______________ Driver's license #______________

Present address ______________________________

Present occupation ______________ Title or position ______________

Employer ______________ Phone ______________

How long with this employer? ______________

With previous employer? __________ Supervisor______________ Phone ______________

Current gross income per month (before deductions) $ ______________

Amount of alimony or child support you pay $ __________ or receive $______________

Other income ______________ Source ______________

If married, number of years __________ Number of dependent children ______________

Applicant #2 (Co-purchaser)

Name ______________ Home phone ______________ Work phone ______________

Date of birth ______________ Social Security # ______________ Driver's license #______________

Present address ______________________________

Present occupation ______________ Title or position ______________

Employer ______________ Phone ______________

How long with this employer? ______________

With previous employer? __________ Supervisor______________ Phone ______________

Current gross income per month (before deductions) $ ______________

Amount of alimony or child support you pay $ __________ or receive $______________

Other income ______________ Source ______________

If married, number of years __________ Number of dependent children ______________

Figure 13-4

Prequalification questionnaire

Assets

Available cash ____________ Personal property ____________

Stock & bonds ____________ Other assets ____________

Savings account:

Bank ____________ Branch ____________ Account # ____________

Checking account:

Bank ____________ Branch ____________ Account # ____________

Credit reference ____________ Amount owed ____________ Monthly payment ____________

Credit reference ____________ Amount owed ____________ Monthly payment ____________

Credit reference ____________ Amount owed ____________ Monthly payment ____________

Credit reference ____________ Amount owed ____________ Monthly payment ____________

Vehicle(s)

#1 Make ________ Year ________ Approx. value ________ Amt. owed ________

Monthly payment ____________ Lien holder ____________

#2 Make ________ Year ________ Approx. value ________ Amt. owed ________

Monthly payment ____________ Lien holder ____________

I declare that the statements above are true and correct, and I hereby authorize verification of references given and a credit check.

Date ____________ Signed ____________

Date ____________ Signed ____________

Figure 13-4 (cont'd)
Prequalification questionnaire

Worksheet

Monthly gross income	$3500	
Monthly installment payments	300	
Total available income	$3200	
Purchase price of home	$125,000	
Down payment	25,000	
Total amount financed	100,000	
Down payment percentage	20%	
Term of loan (years)	30	
Interest rate	10%	
Monthly payments (P & I)	$877.58	
Monthly taxes & insurance	$150	
Calculated PITI	$1027.58	
Ratio of PITI divided by income		29.36%
Ratio of (PITI + installment payments) divided by income		37.93%

Figure 13-5

Worksheet to qualify prospective buyers

into the worksheet in Figure 13-5. I've got a simple computer program that figures the monthly payment and ratios, but you can do it with a calculator and an amortization schedule.

If they meet all the criteria with room to spare, they're practically a sure thing — unless there's something they haven't told you. If they meet none of them, they're wasting your time. If they meet some but not all, then it's a judgment call. You could ask for a bigger down payment. Otherwise, you'll have to consider the circumstances. Do you have other offers that are more likely to go through? Personally, I'll often take a lower offer from a solid-gold applicant rather than a higher offer from a risky one. I'd rather not go through the whole process and come up with nothing.

In some states, mortgage brokers will pre-qualify buyers for you. They'll do this as a complementary service in hopes of getting your buyer's business. Since they don't want to lend to unqualified parties, they'll let you know right away if your buyers can qualify for the loan. Your buyers are under no obligation to go through the broker for their loan, and it doesn't cost them anything. All it takes is a phone call. Sometimes people feel more comfortable dealing with a "professional" financial person than with you, the seller. Many real estate agents use mortgage brokers to screen buyers as well.

If you screen buyers yourself, use the same criteria that banks use. Look for long-term, stable employment. Call the buyer's employer to verify the information they've given you. The employer may not tell you how much they earn, but they *will* tell you how long they've worked there. If they're currently renting, you should also call their landlord and find out if they are reliable tenants.

Ask your buyer how much money they have in savings. You'll have to rely on what they say. If they don't have any savings, they're not likely to get a loan. Lenders want buyers to come up with 10 to 20 percent of the purchase price or have that much equity in another house. They want to know *where* the down payment is coming from so they can verify that it exists.

Figure out what your buyer's monthly payments will be in relation to their monthly income. Banks prefer that monthly payments be no more than 25 percent of the buyer's monthly income.

If the buyers have a marginal income, there's still a chance that they can get the loan. Lenders will sometimes approve a loan with payments up to one-third of the buyers' income if the buyers don't have too many other long-term obligations.

Although some prospective buyers may be offended by your questions, don't compromise. As the seller, you're entitled to this information. Explain this as tactfully as possible. Tell them that these are not *your* criteria, but the bank's. By screening them in advance you're saving them a lot of time and money. The loan application fee is usually at least $250 and it's non-refundable. If they have no chance of qualifying, the sooner they know that the better for everyone. And, you can't be expected to tie up your house for unqualified buyers.

Prequalifying buyers is important, because if you accept an Offer to Purchase from someone, you'll be taking your house off the market. You can lose good potential buyers while you wait weeks, possibly months, for the lender to decline the loan. Then you have to start the selling process all over again. A delay like that can cost you thousands of dollars and may cause you to miss the best selling season.

Of course, even if you screen buyers very carefully, there's no way to be absolutely sure that the application will be accepted. After all, it's easy to lie about finances. They may fool you, but they won't fool the bank. And, even if they tell you the truth, they still may be rejected. Your buyers can be rejected for some odd reason that you would never think to ask about. There's no way to avoid this risk entirely.

The Offer to Purchase

If the buyers appear to be qualified, your next step is to sign an Offer to Purchase. Agents use a standard form for this. An Offer to Purchase is a binding contract that describes the property and specifies the purchase price and the terms of the agreement. When signed by both parties, it obligates them to perform — the buyer to come up with the purchase price in the time agreed upon, and the seller to sell.

The Offer to Purchase in Figure 13-6 is a standard agreement for purchase via a conventional new mortgage. But I don't recommend using a purchase agreement copied out of a book. Remember, it's a contract. And not all of the provisions in this sample agreement are necessarily valid in every state, since requirements vary. If there are any unusual circumstances about the sale of your house, they need to be noted in the Offer to Purchase. You may want to adapt my sample form to fit your situation. But have your lawyer go over it before you print up and use any copies.

You can include other specific items in your contract as well. Are the buyers going to apply for a new mortgage? If so, you can specify that they apply within a reasonable period like three or seven days. Most purchase agreements allow buyers 60 days to obtain a new loan. If they can't get one in 60 days, they probably never will.

Offer to Purchase Real Estate

1. The undersigned hereby offers and agrees to purchase the following land situated in the City of ______________________________, County of ______________________________, State of ____________________, more commonly known as ______________________________, together with all improvements and appurtenances, including all light fixtures, garbage disposal, dishwasher, curtains and blinds now on the premises.

2. The purchase price for the property shall be______________________________ ______________________________ Dollars, payable in cash or by certified check.

3. Seller agrees to deliver the usual Warranty Deed conveying a marketable title. This agreement is contingent upon the Purchaser being able to secure a Conventional Mortgage in the amount of $______________ and pay $______________ down plus mortgage costs, prepaid items, and adjustments in cash. Purchaser agrees to apply for such mortgage within __________ days from acceptance of this offer at his own expense. If a firm commitment for such mortgage cannot be obtained within __________ days of acceptance, at the Seller's option, this offer can be declared null and void and the deposit returned.

4. As evidence of good faith, Purchaser has deposited with the Seller the sum of ______________________________ Dollars in cash. The Seller shall not commingle Purchaser's deposit with Seller's own funds, but shall instead place it in a standard FDIC guaranteed passbook savings account in a bank of his own choosing. Seller shall not claim entitlement to Purchaser's deposit until the earlier of the closing contemplated hereunder or a default by Purchaser. If the terms of this contract are met, and if the purchase and sale contemplated hereunder are consummated, the deposit shall be applied to the purchase price at closing. If the Purchaser defaults on his obligation hereunder, the Seller has the right to retain the deposit, plus any interest accrued thereon, and demand specific performance of this Offer to Purchase, or, in the alternative, to terminate this agreement, and retain Purchaser's deposit as liquidated damages.

5. As evidence of title, Seller agrees to furnish Purchaser as soon as possible a Policy of Title Insurance in an amount not less than the purchase price, bearing a date later than the acceptance hereof and guaranteeing the title in the condition required for the performance of this offer.

Page 1 of 3

Figure 13-6

Offer to purchase real estate

6. If this offer is accepted by the Seller and the title can be conveyed in the condition required hereunder, the Purchaser agrees to complete the sale as soon as the mortgage application is approved and a closing date can be obtained from the lender.

7. If any unpermitted matters of title are disclosed by the title commitment, Seller shall, at their option, have a reasonable time to cure them. If Seller is unable to cure all unpermitted exceptions within a reasonable time, or elects not to do so, Buyer shall be returned the deposit made hereunder, in full termination of this agreement.

8. All taxes and assessments which have become a lien upon the land, whether recorded or not recorded, at the date of this agreement shall be paid by Seller. Current taxes, if any, shall be prorated and adjusted as of the date of closing in accordance with due date basis of the municipality or taxing unit in which the property is located. Interest, rents, and water bills shall be prorated and adjusted as of the date of closing.

9. The Purchaser shall have possession of the property on the day after closing.

10. The covenants herein shall bind and inure to the benefits of the executors, administrators, successors, and assigns of the respective parties.

11. Seller agrees to maintain premises in the same condition as existing at acceptance of this offer until possession is delivered to Purchaser.

12. This agreement supersedes any and all understandings and agreements and constitutes the entire agreement between the parties hereto. No oral representations or statements shall be considered a part hereof. Purchaser understands and acknowledges that he is purchasing a used home in "as is" condition and that the Seller makes no warranties as to the land and structure purchased or the condition thereof. Purchaser acknowledges that he has inspected the premises covered hereby and that he is satisfied with the condition thereof. Purchaser also acknowledges the receipt of a copy of this offer.

Page 2 of 3

Figure 13-6 (cont'd)

Offer to purchase real estate

By the execution of this instrument, the Purchaser acknowledges receipt of a copy of this agreement.

Purchasers: In the presence of:

_______________________ _______________________

____

Address: _______________________________________

____

ACCEPTANCE: The foregoing offer is accepted in accordance with the terms stated.

By the execution of this instrument, the Seller acknowledges receipt of a copy of the agreement.

Sellers: In the presence of:

_______________________ _______________________

____

Address: _______________________________________

____

Page 3 of 3

Figure 13-6 (cont'd)
Offer to purchase real estate

If you don't put a time limit in your contract, the buyer can keep you tied up for years.

Consult a lawyer. An Offer to Purchase is a contract. It's a good idea to have a lawyer look over any document of this type. You might even want your lawyer to draw up the Offer to Purchase for you. If you don't have a lawyer, you should get one. I don't advise trying to sell something as valuable as a piece of real estate without some kind of professional help. If you don't work with an agent, at least consult a lawyer.

If buyers want you to sign any documents that they or their lawyers have drafted, be sure to have *your* lawyer review the documents before signing. I've been asked to sign documents which outrageously favored the purchasers. If I had signed them, I'd have been stuck. I had my lawyer look at them, and only signed after he had replaced the unfair requests with more equitable terms.

Pushing the Deal Through

Be sure to keep in touch with your buyer after signing the Offer to Purchase. Don't assume that they're taking care of everything, just because you haven't heard to the contrary. Even if they have taken care of everything, call to reassure them that things are progressing on schedule. Don't let them hang in limbo wondering what they're supposed to do next. Keep them informed.

Make sure that they've applied for the loan. Find out the name of the lender. Then call the lender and ask how the application is going. If the lender is having a problem with the application, as often happens, call the seller back and see if you can help solve it. If you don't work to keep everything moving, the deal could fall through. Lenders don't nag applicants about completing the forms. They just set the application aside until it's completed. Until the buyer supplies all the information the lender needs, nothing's going to happen. The lender will just sit on the application, or worse, reject it. Keep after the buyer. That's what a good real estate agent would do.

Closing

Closing procedures vary from state to state. It may be handled by the buyer's lender, by a title company, by a lawyer, or by an independent escrow company. A lot of documents need to be presented and verified at the time of closing. You must present evidence of secure title, usually in the form of Title Insurance. Depending on where you live, you may need a structural soundness report or termite inspection. These verify that the property is free of dry rot, termites or other destructive organisms. The buyer needs to have homeowner's insurance, paid up a year in advance at the time of closing, and a title insurance policy for their lender. They must bring a certified check for their down payment (not a personal check), and have a loan approved for the balance due.

Certain documents are required for the transfer of title. If any of these documents are missing, everything stops. The closing can't be completed until all the documents are together. This is where your lawyer can be of tremendous help. He can review all of the requirements for real estate transfers in your state and make sure you've supplied all the necessary documents, stamps and fees. He can also review the buyer's document package to make sure that's complete as well. Some states require a lawyer to represent each party in this kind of transaction. It isn't a bad idea, even if it isn't required in your state. You may have to pay a couple hundred dollars for their services, but since you've saved thousands of dollars in real estate commissions, you can afford the benefit of a lawyer's counsel.

What If Your House Doesn't Sell?

Whether you decide to sell through an agent or on your own, it's always possible that the house won't sell. If you've followed my suggestions, the risk of that happening is much smaller. But there's no way to eliminate all uncertainty.

A sudden downturn in the real estate market could affect all home sales. This happens, for example, if a major employer in the area lays off a lot of employees. Or it could be the result of a nation-wide recession or soaring interest rates.

Recession

In a recession, real estate prices drop sharply. When the economy is down, some businesses close or are forced to lay off workers. People who are out of work can no longer afford their house payments and have to put their homes up for sale. This creates a surplus in the housing market. Some people have to sell quickly to avoid foreclosure, or raise cash to meet the demands of creditors. These sellers price their homes below market value to guarantee a quick sale. But buyers are scarce. In an uncertain economy, even those who haven't been laid off are too worried to make a major financial commitment. Buying a new house can wait. So houses sit on the market a long time, and when they do sell, it's at a low price.

This is a great situation for a buyer, but a disaster if you're a seller. How can you deal with this dilemma? Offering terms isn't going to do any good. Terms aren't the problem; the economy is the problem. Lowering the price will work, but you'll lose all your profit. You don't want to do that if you can possibly avoid it.

Strangely enough, I've heard of people who managed to sell their home in a weak market by *raising* the price. I know this sounds strange, but it has worked!

In a buyer's (weak) market, as I've said before, the pool of buyers is small. People look at houses in limited price ranges, such as $90,000 to $100,000, or $120,000 to $125,000. Since there are so few buyers, it's possible that all the buyers looking in your price range have seen your house and disqualified it, possibly for reasons other than price. Maybe they wanted something bigger, or they don't care for your decorating. In any case, this group of buyers is used up. You need to get another group of people to look at your house.

Certainly, one way to bring your house to the attention of another group of buyers is to lower the price. But why not try just the opposite, raising the price? Serious buyers generally don't bother looking at houses that are too expensive for them . . . and they'll also avoid houses that are priced too low. When they see a low price, they assume that the house isn't nice enough to be what they're looking for. Who wants to live in a $90,000 house when you can afford $120,000? Raising the price attracts a different group of buyers. Who knows, they may love your house — and you can now afford to deal, accepting an offer thousands of dollars below your new asking price and still getting more than your old asking price. Your buyers will think they got a great deal.

Unfortunately, of course, this doesn't always work. Some prospective buyers may look at your house and say "It's overpriced." However, it's worth a try, especially if your house isn't getting any offers at its present price. If this doesn't work, you can always lower the price. Then you can advertise a *huge price reduction.* That's bound to capture interest.

In a real recession, your best bet is to wait it out. Renting can be an ideal solution. During recessions, the demand for rentals increases. People have to live somewhere. The people who were forced to sell will be looking for a place to live. And those who put off buying will continue to rent as well. In times of economic uncertainty, people don't want to tie up their money or commit to new long-term obligations. People line up to rent houses that no one wanted to buy when they were for sale.

That's how I got started in the rental business. In the early 1980s, I found myself with a newly-remodeled house that wouldn't sell because of a local recession. I had always sold my remodeled houses without any problems before. But this house sat on the market for months with literally no offers. I knew that it would sit vacant for a year or more unless I slashed the price and took a loss. I decided to try renting it.

I was astounded at the response to my "for rent" ad. Everybody wanted to rent my house. In fact, the entire deal turned out to be much easier and more profitable than I had ever anticipated. It worked out so well, I continued to rent the house out after the market improved. Now I have several rental houses, in addition to those I remodel for resale.

High Interest Rates

Mortgage interest rates have been volatile over the last twenty years. I don't expect much change during the next twenty years. In 1978, I could get a fixed-rate, 30-year loan for not much more than 7 percent interest. Three years later people were paying 20 percent! Changes like that make loans risky, both for the lender and the borrower. Adjustable rate loans shift some of the risk from the lender to the borrower. For example, as this is being written, I can get an adjustable rate loan at 8 or 9 percent. But the rate will be adjusted up to the "cap" which is 14 percent. As the interest rate changes, the monthly payments are adjusted periodically — usually up. The loan is soon a burden if the borrower's income doesn't increase as quickly as the payments.

Rising interest rates can quickly price home buyers out of the market. High interest rates make monthly loan payments so big that buyers can't afford the homes they want. For example, a $125,000 house bought on a 20 percent down conventional loan at 8 percent interest, would have a principal-and-interest payment of $734. If we assume property taxes of $100 per month, the total monthly payment would be $834. A family with a monthly income of $2,600 could qualify for this loan.

But if interest rates went up to 20 percent, the same house, with the same terms, would require a monthly payment of $1,771! Monthly income would have to be over $5,500, or $66,000 a year. That's a big difference. Anyone who could afford to make that payment would be outraged at getting so little for their money. Most people would postpone buying until interest rates came down.

As a seller, you have three choices: offer terms, lower the asking price, or wait it out. Let's consider them all.

Terms— When interest rates skyrocketed in the early 1980s, land contracts and other private financing deals suddenly became very popular. Before this time, land contracts had been considered suitable only for people or property that didn't qualify for conventional financing. However, in the early '80s, land contracts were the only way many people could buy property. In my area, land contracts were being written at 11 percent interest, the maximum rate allowable for land contracts in Michigan. At 11 percent, the payments on a $50,000 mortgage were $589.29 a month. This was affordable; it was certainly a lot better than the $1071 the banks were getting for the same loan at 20 percent interest.

At that time it was possible to sell a house on land contract while you were still making payments on a mortgage. The seller paid you, and you paid the bank. If you were paying off a mortgage at 5 percent, you could keep the difference, so it was a good deal for both the buyer and the seller. Unfortunately, the Due on Sale clause which now goes into almost every fixed-rate mortgage, eliminated the advantage of selling on a land contract. Today, when you sell a house with an existing mortgage, the amount owed on that mortgage becomes due immediately.

You can still sell on a land contract, but you have to pay off the mortgage first. If you can do that, your house will have a big advantage over others on the market. You can offer good terms and sell the house quickly at a good price. Most other sellers won't be able to do that.

Lower the price— When interest rates skyrocket, most sellers have to cut the price to attract buyers. The higher the interest rate, the lower the price has to be to maintain the same monthly payment. For example, suppose a buyer with 20 percent down on your $125,000 house can afford the monthly payment ($751.27, not including taxes and insurance) at 8-1/4 percent interest. If interest rates go to 15 percent, you would have to reduce the selling price to $74,200 to maintain the same $750 monthly loan payment. Of course you can't do that, not if you'd planned on selling for $125,000.

Wait it out— Most sellers simply wait until the interest rates go back down. No one sells under these terms unless they're desperate. Unfortunately, there are usually enough desperate sellers to satisfy all available buyers.

If you're living in your newly-remodeled house, you can probably afford to just wait. After all, you're getting something for your monthly payments. You have to live somewhere, right? That's one reason why this business is so attractive. It's like owning a grocery store. If the food doesn't sell, you can always eat it. If your home doesn't sell, move your kids or in-laws in! That's one way to wait out the bad times.

If the house is vacant, rent it out. If you bought low, you can usually rent it for enough money to cover the payments, and maybe even make a small profit. Since you're taking in good money for the property, you can afford to wait for the economic cycle to take another turn.

Unloading a Lemon

Now we come to the worst case: You didn't buy wisely. You ignored some of my advice. You bought a bad piece of property. What do I mean by bad property? You should know by now. It's a property in a bad or declining neighborhood. As I've said over and over again, neighborhood is by far the most important consideration in selecting property. If you have a piece of property in a bad neighborhood, you've got a real problem.

Waiting this one out isn't going to work. Times are always hard for bad property. Waiting will just make it worse. The property probably isn't worth any more than you paid for it, regardless of the improvements you've made. So how can you bail out of this mess?

Offer Favorable Terms

First of all, forget about selling to a nice, middle-class family that can qualify for a loan. Middle-class people don't buy bad property. They can afford better. They don't need the problems that come with buying in a declining neighborhood.

Your buyers will be low-income people, and your house is probably a lot nicer than they expected to get. They'll be thrilled to get it — if they can qualify for the loan.

To low-income families, terms are more important than price. They probably won't be able to get a conventional mortgage. Even if their credit is good, they'll have trouble coming up with the down payment and the closing costs that most lenders require. Banks won't let you help with the down payment for your buyers. But you *can* pay some of the closing costs. You may have seen real estate listings with notes like: "Seller pays points," or "Seller to help with closing costs." If you're having real trouble finding a buyer for your house, this approach might be worth a try. In some cases, your buyer may be just a little short of the money necessary for closing. This extra help may be enough to make the sale.

The actual down payment itself must be paid entirely by the purchaser. And they have to prove it's their money. If your buyer doesn't have the cash for a down payment or has a credit rating that would frighten any lender, there are still some options. One is through government programs. Another is seller financing, such as a land contract.

Government Programs

The federal government has a number of programs specifically designed to help low-income people buy homes. You can find several books on the subject. Probably the best one is *How to Make Money in Real Estate with Government Loans and Programs*, by Albert Lowry. I covered government-backed loans in Chapter 5, so I'll just discuss a few additional points that are important to you as a seller.

FHA loans— The Federal Housing Administration (FHA) is responsible for maintaining these government programs. Your house must meet FHA standards before it will qualify for a government-backed loan. Chances are, once you've fixed it up, you'll be able to pass an FHA inspection. They're very particular about building standards however. They won't approve homes with cracked slabs, substandard plumbing or any other problems fundamental to the livability of the home.

Your buyers will have to meet FHA lending requirements: a stable work record and a favorable debt-to-income ratio. As we discussed earlier, government-backed loans often take longer to process than conventional mortgages. Suggest that your buyers use a lender who specializes in this type of loan. That saves time and prevents problems. A lender who isn't familiar with government-insured loans can delay closing for months.

VA loans— Buyers who have been in the military during certain periods may qualify for a VA loan. Most lenders handle VA loans without any problems, *as long as the buyers can provide documentation of service.* Lenders won't finance more than the VA-appraised value, even if the appraisal is less than your selling price.

FHA- and VA-backed loans require little or no money down. I'm not an expert on these programs. I don't want to be. They require extra paperwork, take longer, and the seller has to pay discount points and some closing costs. But if you're trying to unload a lemon, it's one way to get a decent price without taking a big risk.

By the way, you should know about the HUD Section 8 rent subsidy program for low-income tenants. Many landlords like this program, and for good reason. You get rent supplements directly from the federal government. Once qualified, you're guaranteed a tenant. If the government can't find you one, they have to pay anyway. They also insure you against tenant-caused damage. If a tenant wrecks your house, Uncle Sam will pay for it. Of course, like all government programs, there's a lot of red tape. But it's another way to get out of what might otherwise be a loss.

Land Contracts

If your buyers (or your property) can't qualify for any government programs, the only option may be seller financing. Use a land contract if you, or your buyer, can pay off the existing mortgage. If the loan balance is small enough, the buyer's down payment may cover it.

The more money your buyers can put down, the safer the sale is bound to be. However, selling on land contract is always risky. You should be able to get your asking price — but you have to rely on the buyers' ability to pay. If they aren't reliable, you'll have real trouble.

Protect yourself. Make the buyers fill out a detailed application. Check their references carefully. Your buyers probably have a checkered credit history. That's why you're selling on a land contract. Others may not qualify because they have no credit history, or they are self-employed and have income from unconventional sources.

Your best prospect may have no credit history at all. They may be hard-working, responsible people who don't use credit cards, don't borrow, and they pay their bills with cash. They have no credit history because they've never used credit. I have a number of tenants like this. They pay their rent in crisp $100 bills and I never have a problem.

The only problem is that there's nothing on this person's credit report. For all anyone knows, they could be criminals using a phony name. There's no way to tell. That's one of the risks.

If you can't sell under a land contract, then the only option may be renting the property. That may not be your preference, but it may not be a bad choice either. It's much easier to find renters than buyers for almost any property. So, if you can't sell your house, take heart. There's one more way to make money in this business. That's the subject of the last chapter.

CHAPTER FOURTEEN

Keeping Rental Property

Keep your options open. Sometimes renting a home is a good alternative. If you can't sell at your price, renting can cover holding costs until the market improves. It's an extra margin of safety. Heads, you win. Tails you get a chance to play again later.

The Advantages of Rental Property

It's always easier to rent property than sell it. And, of all the residential rentals available, single-family homes are the most desirable. They offer privacy and the convenience of a true home. That's not available in anything but the most expensive apartments.

Rental houses have almost always been in short supply. And new tax laws have reduced the availability of nice middle-income rental properties even more. People used to rent their houses for just enough money to break even. They weren't interested in making a profit; they wanted rentals for the tax write-offs. Under the new law this doesn't pay anymore. So, many people have sold off their properties and left the rental business. However, this doesn't really affect you very much. You're not in business to get write-offs. You want to make a profit on your rents. Any tax advantage is only an extra bonus.

You'll make money renting a remodeled house if you bought wisely and remodeled correctly. Once it's fixed up, it's worth a lot more. Houses rent on the basis of their livability, not how much they originally cost. If you own a nice house in a nice neighborhood, you can charge good rent for it. Because you bought low and your payments are low, you should have money left over after meeting expenses.

Here's an example. I bought a house a few years ago and took a loan for $64,500. My payments on the loan, including principal, interest, and taxes, come to $660 per month. Since this is a nice home in a good area, I can rent it for $835 per month. The $175 difference between my payments and the rent I take in is my return on the original down payment. Of course, I have to maintain the house, keep it occupied and collect the rent. I do most of this myself, so the cost is minimal.

Property Appreciation

While your property is paying for itself, more than likely it's appreciating in value. That's another reason I prefer to rent some of my properties. If I own a house in an area where property values are rising, I'll hold on to it. The house I just mentioned has been going up in value an average of 10 percent a year. A $125,000 house would gain more than $1,000 a month. I'll make a $12,500 profit on this one house every year for doing nothing! Add this to the $2,100 I clear on rent and you see why I'm happy to hold on to the property. Of course, I won't actually get the profit on the appreciation until I sell the property. But with figures like that, I can wait.

Tax Depreciation

Even though the value increases, I can deduct depreciation on my income tax return. That's the write-off mentioned a few paragraphs back. Even though the Tax Reform Act of 1986 requires depreciation of rental property over longer periods now, it's still a windfall for property owners like me. My well-chosen properties are appreciating, not depreciating. The depreciation allowance offsets most of the income I get from rentals each year. For example, if that $125,000 house has a cost basis (total costs minus land value) of $60,000, I'm allowed a depreciation of $2,000 per year. I can deduct that from the $2,100 I clear on the rent, so I only pay income tax on $100! Find a job anywhere with an advantage like that!

Spreading Out Your Income

If you've made a good profit from selling houses already this year, consider delaying any more sales (and profits) until next year. Averaging your income over the years tends to reduce your state and federal tax burden.

So another advantage of renting is that you can choose when to sell. Pick a year when you have less money coming in. The taxes will be due in the year when you actually get the money. Sometimes, if you sell late in the year, a long escrow period will carry profits over into the next year. The point is this: choosing when to sell reduces your tax burden and spreads income more evenly.

Under the Tax Reform Act of 1986, capital gains became ordinary income. That's too bad (and will probably change). A capital gain is a profit on an investment. It's not a wage in exchange for labor. Most of the money you make on a remodeled property is, in fact, a capital gain. The value of my properties increases more than the value of the work time and materials I invest. In the past, you paid less tax on capital gains than wages. If we're lucky, Congress will reinstate the tax break for capital gains. Many economists feel this would be good for business. I agree; I know it would be good for *my* business. That's one reason I'm renting instead of selling some of my properties: I'm waiting to see if the tax break is reinstated. If it is, I'll save a lot on taxes when I do sell.

Scheduling Extra Time into Projects

Consider renting while *you're doing the renovations.* I do this all the time, and my tenants don't mind. Of course, you have to complete all the interior work before renting the house, but the exterior can wait. Complete the interior first. Then, when weather permits, finish the exterior — while the home is occupied.

Tenants are far more concerned with the inside of a home than the outside. If they can see that the interior has been beautifully remodeled, they'll wait until spring for the exterior to be completed. Exterior work usually won't disturb tenants. You won't have to bother them, dirty their carpets, or disturb their personal possessions.

As a matter of fact, I've often found that the tenants, rather than being irritated by this ongoing work, often find it entertaining. They're amazed at all the effort I go to, and the work I do, to make their rental home nicer. Of course, it isn't just for their benefit. But it makes them feel like they're getting something extra for their rent money. I'll often see them watching me work and hear the comment: "Boy, I'm glad I don't have to do all that work!"

You couldn't make the same arrangement with a buyer: finish the exterior work during escrow or even after the sale closed. It would be nice if you could. Most of the time you sell property in "as is" condition. What you see is what you get. If the work isn't done, people assume it isn't going to be. Even if you promise to do it, your buyers wouldn't believe you. They would expect a discount for the work yet to be done.

As a landlord, you have a continuing relationship with tenants. The house is still your property, not theirs. They know that if you don't finish the work, you're the one that suffers the loss, not them. They can move and find a better place to live. It's in your best interest to finish work on the exterior, so they know you'll get it done.

The Income

Rental income is inflation-proof. If prices and wages start spiralling upwards, as they did in the 1970s, I'll just raise my rents proportionately. The value of my properties are protected from inflation, too. As the value of the dollar declines, the value of my real estate should go up.

Retirement Planning

Rental property makes a good retirement plan. Buy property now on a 30-year loan. These are probably your most productive years. Thirty years from now, when you're ready to retire, you'll own it free and clear with no expense other than maintenance and taxes. Income should be many times expenses. In the worst case, you'll always have a place to live!

Most of the people I know who are in their 60s and 70s haven't saved enough to retire completely. Very few people win the lottery. Rental property can insure a comfortable retirement in your old age. If you're 35 or younger, any loan you get will be paid off by the time you reach 65. If you're older than 35, or you want to retire sooner, you can get a 10 or 20 year loan or make extra payments on the principal for an early payoff. You'll have a nice income while you're young. Then, when the mortgage is paid off, your spendable income will explode!

If you don't want to bother with rentals when you retire, you can sell some or all of your property sooner. Since you own the property free and clear, you'll get to keep whatever you sell it for. If you have no other income, you'll have to pay less tax on the profits when you sell. You could get by nicely selling off houses, one at a time, every few years.

Protecting Your Investment

No doubt you've heard horror stories from landlords. I've seen some builders turn pale when I explain that I'm planning to rent out one of my houses. "*Don't do it!*" they cry. Then they proceed to tell me about all the terrible experiences that they or their friends had with rentals: the tenants never paid on time, tore the property to pieces, got physically abusive when pressed to pay rent, and so on. The stories can get pretty gruesome.

My experience is just the opposite. I've had extremely good results renting. Is is luck? I don't think so. I'm successful because I have a system that works. I'll explain.

Know the Business

Landlords that have serious problems don't take the time to do it right. There's a right way and a wrong way to rent property. If you don't do it right, you won't get good results.

If you plan to do any renting at all, take the time to educate yourself. By far the best book I've come across is *Landlording,* by Leigh Robinson, published by ExPress. If you only read one book on how to handle rental property, this is the one. It explains how to avoid all the problems landlords run into. If you follow Robinson's advice, you may never have a horror story of your own to tell.

Another good book on the subject is William Nickerson's classic, *How I Turned $1,000 into $1,000,000 in Real Estate.* This book is really a "must read" for anybody who invests in residential real estate. Nickerson's advice is to hold on to your property. He offers a great deal of valuable advice on renting the property you own.

Robert Allen advocates the rental system he uses in his book *Creating Wealth.* I agree with him on the need for a system, but I don't agree with some of his complaints. He says that he never had a tenant say "thank-you." That's too bad; maybe he didn't deserve one. I get thank-yous from my tenants all the time. I haven't had the problems he's had either. Could my system be better?

You can probably find these books at any bookstore. If they're not in stock, ask the store to order them for you.

My Advice

Here are the rental do's and don'ts that I consider most important.

Take the time to pick your tenants carefully— Don't rent to the first person who comes along. The best way to rent property is to hold an open house, much the same as if you were planning to sell the property. I make up a fact sheet to hand out to all the prospective tenants. It's similar to the one I use for selling a house. Figure 14-1 is an example. You don't need to have a photo of the house on this one, but you do need to clearly explain what your renter's responsibilities are. *Make sure there are no misunderstandings right from the start.*

Take applications from every interested person. Figure 14-2 is the application I use. When you've collected a stack of applications, go through them and pick out the people who you think will make the best tenants. I use this technique, and I've been very happy with the tenants I've selected.

Check references— It's extremely important to *check the references* of anyone you consider renting to. You don't need an elaborate procedure to do it. Just make the phone calls. I call the prospective tenant's employer to see if they really have a job. Then I call their current (and previous, if possible) landlord to make sure they pay their rent on time. Further checking might help, but these calls are absolutely necessary. The book *Landlording* goes into considerable detail on how to check the references of your prospective tenants.

I've had several interesting experiences when checking references. In one case, a very polite and well-dressed woman with two well-behaved children came to look at one of my properties. She filled out an application, showing that she had an income of $70,000 a year, including her job, child support and alimony. I was impressed. However, as she left, I noticed that she drove away in a beat-up rust-bucket. That made me wonder about her income. It seemed to me that someone with an income of $70,000 a year ought to drive a better car.

WELCOME TO: 311 Magnolia Ave

This lovely home has been recently redecorated, and includes many luxury features not usually found in rental homes.

TERMS

Rent	$835.00
Security deposit	$835.00
Total required to move in	$1,670.00

Lease: One-year lease is required.

Availability: The house is available today. We would like to have people move in as soon as possible, but no later than Nov. 1.

Utilities: You pay all utilities: electric, gas, phone and water.

Pets: We do allow pets, within limits. However, if you have pets we require one-and -a-half month's security deposit, or $1253.00.

Included: Stove and refrigerator, lawn mower, snow shovel.

Your responsibilities: You must mow the lawn, shovel the snow, and in general keep the grounds up to the standards of the neighborhood.

Repairs: We will take care of necessary repairs. We will either fix it ourselves, or pay for having it fixed. You will not have to pay for anything unless you break it.

DESCRIPTION

Central air

4 bedrooms, all with brand-new carpeting

2 baths

Formal dining room

Full basement

Large attic, with permanent stairs and lights

Extra storage area under back room. This house has a huge amount of storage

Gas forced-air heat, with automatic humidifier

Gas hot water

1-½ car garage with electricity

Beautiful park only one block away

INTERESTED? If you would like to rent this house, fill out an application. It is non-binding (you can change your mind). We will look over all the applications, check the references, and then select a tenant. We will notify the applicant we select as soon as possible, hopefully by tomorrow evening.

Figure 14-1

Fact sheet for rental open house

RENTAL APPLICATION for ____

All relevant spaces must be filled in for application to be considered. The most important items are your landlords and employers.

Personal

Name______________________ Home phone______________ Work phone______________

Date of birth______________ Social Security number______________________ Drivers License number______________

Present address ____

How long at this address______________ Rent $______________ Reason for moving______________________

Owner/manager______________________________ Phone______________

Previous address ____

How long at this address______________ Rent $______________ Reason for moving______________________

Owner/manager______________________________ Phone______________

Name, relationship, and age of every person to live with you:______________________

____

If you are accepted for this property, date you would be planning to move in______________

Do you have your own: Stove______________ Refrigerator______________ Lawnmower______________

Waterbed______________ Any pets?______ Describe______________________

Employment

Present occupation______________ Employer______________________ Phone______________

How long with this employer______________ Supervisor______________________ Phone______________

How long with previous employer______ Employer______________________ Phone______________

Current gross income per month (before deductions) #1 ______________ #2 ______________

Amount of alimony or child support you pay $______________ or receive $______________

Credit

Savings account:

Bank______________ Branch______________ Account #______________________

Checking account:

Bank______________ Branch______________ Account #______________________

Major credit card______________________ Account #______________________

Credit reference______________________ Acct. #____________Owed $________Payment $______

Credit reference______________________ Acct. #____________Owed $________Payment $______

Have you ever filed bankruptcy? _______ year______ Have you ever been evicted?______________

Vehicle(s)

#1 Make______________ Model ______________ Year ______________ Payment $______________

#2 Make______________ Model ______________ Year ______________ Payment $______________

Which newspaper did you see our ad in?______________________

I declare that the statements above are true and correct, and I hereby authorize verification of references given and a credit check.

Date______________ Signed______________________________

Date______________ Signed______________________________

Figure 14-2

Rental application

When I went over her application, I noticed that she had put her uncle down as her personal reference. No real harm in that. However, the same uncle was her employer. And her current landlord? You guessed it: her uncle. At this point I began to have serious reservations about this lady. I called her uncle to ask about her employment. When I questioned him about her salary, he said, "Oh yeah, she makes . . . uh . . . $40,000? Or was it $50,000? Hold on . . . oh yeah, it's $70,000. Right, she makes $70,000 a year!" Somehow, I didn't find this very convincing. I scratched her off my list.

In another case, a very pleasant older couple wanted to rent one of my houses. They told me they were quiet people, with no children or pets. They both had good jobs, and could easily pay the rent. Their favorite pastime was watching TV. They spent a lot of time looking around our house, trying to find the very best spot for their big-screen television.

Although these people seemed like ideal tenants, I was glad I called their current landlord to check on them. He told me that they were, in fact, very nice people. They just had one little problem: they didn't pay their rent on time. He had to make at least one and sometimes several trips to their home each month to pick up the rent check. They never sent it in the mail and never had it ready when he came by to collect. If he didn't collect in person, he never got paid. Maybe they were so involved in their favorite TV programs that they lost all track of time. It really saves time and money to check with former landlords!

You Have the Advantage

You can afford to be picky about the tenants you select. Rental homes in good neighborhoods are hard to come by. And often, the homes that are available are neglected. Frequently you'll find that rental property, even in good neighborhoods, is handled by rental agencies for absentee owners. Agencies, and even many owner/landlords, don't take care of property like they should. Some landlords and most agencies don't keep their properties in tip-top condition. Many of them begin to look like my handyman-specials *before* I fix them up. They're rented out in what I consider totally unacceptable condition. In fact, many of the fixer-uppers I buy are former rentals that no one would rent any longer.

My houses are always in good condition when I'm ready to rent them. They're newly remodeled and redecorated, often with new fixtures. This is rare in rental houses today. Very few quality houses are for rent. Those that are usually rent for far more or are in poor condition. I can afford to charge a moderate rent and still make money. That gives me an advantage over landlords with high loan payments. If I'd paid full market price for the house, of course, I'd be in the same position they're in. But I never do, so I can charge less rent and attract the best tenants.

Why don't I charge more if I could? Because then I wouldn't get as many applicants for my house. Very few people can afford rent of $1000 per month. At that price, I'd have fewer applicants to choose from. I'd have to be less selective. That's one way to get into serious problems. Bad tenants will agree to any monthly rent because they don't plan to pay it. I prefer to have reliable tenants paying just slightly less than the full market rental value. That's better than worrying about evictions.

I usually have several good applicants for every house I offer for rent. I've even been offered money to give someone first choice on one of my homes. But don't rent to the person who promises you the most. Instead, pick reliable tenants worthy of the trust you're placing in them.

My screening process reduces the number of problems I have with tenants. My tenants have to meet my qualifications and check out financially. The people I choose always pay their rent, don't destroy the property, and tend to stay a long time.

They know they've got a good deal: an attractive, well-maintained house at a reasonable price. People usually stay until they buy a home of their own or get transferred to another area.

Summing Up

That brings me to the end of my story. You have my entire recipe for buying, renovating, and selling homes for profit. You now know how to select a good property, what to repair and remodel, how to decorate, and how to sell or rent for a tidy profit.

I've tried to explain everything I know about this business. That's because knowledge is what you need most. Remember to always do your homework. Read over what I've written. Stay informed on trends in residential real estate, banking, finance, building, remodeling, and interior decorating.

Of course, getting advice and taking it are two different things. Let me suggest that nothing in this book does you any good if you don't try it. You'll never know if you've got a career in the spec rehab business unless you buy that first house.

When you finally take the plunge, you'll probably have a few surprises. That's normal. Every job is a little different. It's also why this business is so interesting. You never stop learning. At least I haven't.

But I've made a good living while I learned my profession. I've sold a lot of homes and plan to sell a lot more. And I have several that aren't going to be sold — at least not yet. The rent from these homes gives me a good monthly income, enough to cover my expenses, including house payment, utilities, and food for my family. If I can't work (or just don't want to), I have plenty of income to pay my bills. That's better security than most wage earners ever have. If I never remodel another house, I could live comfortably on my rental income. That's a nice feeling.

But it didn't happen overnight. In my case, it took 15 years. Will you do as well in your present job over the next 15 years? If not, consider trying what I suggest. I started with very little capital, some basic construction skills, a few tools and a willingness to learn and take chances. If you've got that, you're half way there already.

Of course, I had some help along the way. I'm grateful to my wife, Mary, who's been my business partner over the years. I couldn't have done it without her. I'm lucky to have a wife who shares my interest and enthusiasm for each project. We work together and share in the sense of accomplishment when the job's done. That's another benefit in this business. You get to work with the people you want to work with — whether it's your spouse, your brother, your sister, or your best friend.

Am I Just Lucky?

Could anyone have done as well by working as hard and following the same system? I think a lot of people working in construction trades could have done as well as I have. That's why I wrote this book. I feel there's room in this business for a lot more people like me. Some of the builders I talk with aren't so sure. They say it wouldn't work where they live because houses are cheaper in my area than in their communities. They insist my system won't work where home prices are high. I don't agree. Here's why.

I have a friend who does what I do, but on Long Island in New York State. Home prices there are much higher, more than double what homes sell for in most neighborhoods where I work. Still, my friend makes a good living year after year — usually well into six figures. His experience makes me suspect that potential profits in this business are proportional to prices. The higher the market goes, the greater the margin that's available. The only thing that's indispensable in this business is run-down houses — houses selling at below-market prices. If you've got those, you've got opportunities.

Spec Rehab Building

I've been called a *speculator*. A real builder, I'm told, makes his money developing raw land, pouring sidewalks and driveways, and laying sewer lines and foundations. He doesn't go around buying wrecks of homes at distress prices. They're partially right, I suppose.

I admit that I'm a speculator. And I make a speculator's profit — if I guess right and do my best work. What I'm doing isn't conventional building or remodeling. I buy something no one wants and turn it into something anyone can use. Most important, I provide a valuable service to my community. If I don't rehabilitate these homes, or if someone else doesn't, what's going to happen to them? They're going to sink deeper into decay — and pull the rest of the neighborhood down with them. The owners are never going to repair them. The government won't. No one will. That's a loss to all of us. And it brings me to my final point.

Good Reason Is on Our Side

Our cities aren't (and shouldn't be) disposable. Neighborhoods shouldn't decay into slums just because the homes are 40 or 50 years old. We can't abandon the residential hearts of our larger cities and continue covering the countryside with new housing tracts. What's desirable about living out on the fringe of a city and commuting 50 to 100 miles to work every day? It isn't practical and it isn't logical. But it's *very* wasteful.

Maybe more important, it's unpopular. There's a big movement to stop urban sprawl, unmanaged growth, and continued land development in many communities. City councils restrict it, voters protest it and every government agency tries to tax it. The result: there's going to be less and less land available for our nation's large merchant builders. Maybe they're becoming a dying breed, like dinosaurs that fattened until they exhausted the land that fed them.

The only raw material I need is an old house. I'm never going to run out. Best of all, my homes are in neighborhoods with streets, sidewalks, sewers and utilities already in and paid for. They're close to schools, shopping centers, airports, libraries and all the major government buildings. They're near the best paying jobs where people want to work. And no city council ever objects to what I'm doing. They're relieved that someone is finally eliminating the eyesores and improving the community. I'm a recycler, and I make a profit doing it.

Opportunities for You and Me

Unless I'm way off base, I detect a change coming in this country. Most of us consider a home old when it reaches 40 or 50. By world standards that's still young. In Europe and parts of Asia, many people are living quite comfortably in homes more than 100 years old. Europeans haven't turned the centers of their cities into sprawling slums. They remodel and renovate, replacing decay and neglect with charm and elegance. I think we in the U.S. are going to learn to do the same.

That's why I'm optimistic about the future of this business. I expect it to be one of the fastest growing industries during the next century. And it's a business custom-made for a builder-entrepreneur. City governments understand the need for urban renewal, but they can't afford to do on a large scale what many small business people like you and I can do on a small scale. There's an enormous opportunity for builders like us all over the country.

I hope this book helps you make the most of that opportunity. Good luck!

Buyer's Checklist

for inspecting and evaluating a possible home purchase

Property address:____

Exterior

Sidewalk: Cracks - large______ small ____________
Heaved __________ Holes - large ______ small _________________

Driveway: Cracks - large______ small ____________
Heaved ___________ Holes - large ______ small _________________

Service walk: Cracks - large ______ small ____________
Heaved ___________ Holes - large ______ small _________________

Front yard: Overgrown _______ Excess trash ______ Holes _________________
Lawn damaged/dead __________________ Graded wrong _________
Fence damaged/missing _______________

Back yard: Overgrown _______ Excess trash ______ Holes _________________
Lawn damaged/dead __________________ Graded wrong _________
Fence damaged/missing _______________

Roof: Sagging___________ Uneven ___________ Wavy _________________ Holes ____________
Patches ___________ Discolored________ No vents ______________

Shingles: Curled____________ Cracked ___________ Missing ______________ 3 layers __________

Soffits/fascia: Need paint ______ Loose _____________ Cracked/broken _______

Gutters/downspouts: Rusted/damaged _______________ Loose _________________ Missing __________

Chimney: Cracked/broken ___ Missing bricks ____ Crumbling mortar______

Windows: Broken panes______ Need paint _______

Storm/screens: Missing ________ Loose _____________ Rusted/rotted _________

Siding: Wood ____________ Brick_____________ Aluminum/vinyl ______ Block ____________
Asbestos ___________ Asphalt ___________ Stucco _________________ Other ____________
Needs paint _______ Rotted ___________ Damaged/dented ______ Pieces missing ____
Insect damage _____ Cracked ___________ Walls crooked _________
Missing mortar ____ Loose brick/blocks

Front porch/stoop: Wood ______ Masonry _________ Needs paint ___________
Sagging___________ Crooked___________ Excessive bounce_______ Holes in floor _____
Rot damage _______ Holes in ceiling ___ Style doesn't match house __________________

Porch stairs: Wood ____________ Masonry _________ Other _________________
Cracked __________ Rotted ___________ Broken_________________ Sagging __________
Excessive bounce __ Missing __________

Porch light: Missing___________ Broken ___________

Front door: Cracked/broken/dented ______________ Doesn't close right _____ Needs paint_______
Ugly/doesn't match house _____________ Damaged/missing storm door ______________

Back porch/stoop: Wood _______ Masonry _________ Needs paint___________
Sagging ___________ Crooked _________ Excessive bounce ______ Holes in floor _____
Holes in ceiling ____ Rot damage ______ Style doesn't match house _________________

Porch stairs: Wood _____________ Masonry _________ Other _________________ Missing __________
Excessive bounce ___ Sagging _________ Cracked/broken_______ Rotted ___________

Porch light: Missing ___________ Broken ___________

Back door: Cracked/broken/dented ______________ Needs paint___________
Ugly/doesn't match house _____________ Doesn't close right _____
Damaged/missing storm door ___________

Foundation: Full basement______ Slab _____________ Piers ________________ Crawl space ______
Cracked ___________ Heaved ___________ Crooked ______________
Holes _____________ Needs mortar ____ Missing/broken block/bricks _______________
Not visible ________

Crawl space: Workable space ___ Access available __ Unworkable space _____

Garage

Floor: Dirt_______________ Slab _____________ Excess trash ___________

Siding: Wood _____________ Brick ___________ Aluminum/vinyl ______ Block ___________
Asbestos __________ Asphalt __________ Stucco _______________ Other ___________
Needs paint _______ Damaged/dented_ Rotted _______________ Insect damage ____
Pieces missing _____ Cracked _________ Walls crooked _________
Missing mortar ____ Loose brick/blocks _______________________

Roof: Sagging ___________ Uneven __________ Wavy _______________
Holes _____________ Patches __________ Discolored ____________

Shingles: Curled _____________ Cracked _________ Missing _______________

Soffits/fascia: Cracked/broken __ Loose ___________ Need paint ___________

Gutters/downspouts: Rusted/damaged _____________ Loose _________________ Missing __________

Garage door: Overhead ________ Swinging ________ Roll-up________________
Material - Wood_____ Steel ___________ Other _________________
Rusted _____________ Rotted ____________ Crooked _______________ Doesn't close______
Needs paint _______ Dented ___________ Doesn't lock ___________

Service door: Cracked/broken __ Doesn't close _____ Doesn't lock ___________ No service door ___

Windows: Broken panes ______ Rotted ____________ Need paint ___________
Missing/broken hardware_____________ Won't open/close _____

Interior

Living room

Floor: Not level - slopes toward center ________ Toward exterior _______ Extreme __________
Excessive bounce ___ Needs carpet _____ Needs refinishing ______
Holes ____________ Gaps ___________ Water marks _________
Rot damage________ Buckled/warped _ Animal smells _________

Walls: Solid _____________ Loose __________ Wet ________________ Not plumb________
Cracks - large ______ small ___________ Holes - large __________ small_____________
Water marks - wet __ dry _____________ Wallpaper - peeling/loose/lumpy ___________
Paneling - damaged/ugly _____________

Windows: Broken panes ______ Rotted ___________ Need paint ___________
Missing/broken hardware_____________ Won't open/close _____

Electrical: Insufficient outlets __ Insufficient switches ____________________
Needs new light fixtures ______________

Fireplace: Cracked ___________ Missing/broken bricks __________________
Painted ___________ Mantle/trim damaged ____________________ Dirty_____________
Not wood-burning _ Clogged ________ Separated from wall ___

Coat closet: Door missing/damaged/doesn't close ____ Too small ____________

Dining room

Separate room _____ Dining area ______

Floor: Not level - slopes toward center ________ Toward exterior _______ Extreme __________
Excessive bounce ___ Needs carpet _____ Needs refinishing ______
Holes ____________ Gaps ___________ Water marks _________
Rot damage________ Buckled/warped _ Animal smells _________

Walls: Solid _____________ Loose __________ Wet ________________ Not plumb________
Cracks - large ______ small ___________ Holes - large __________ small_____________
Water marks - wet __ dry _____________ Wallpaper - peeling/loose/lumpy ___________
Paneling - damaged/ugly _____________

Windows: Broken panes ______ Rotted ___________ Need paint ___________
Missing/broken hardware_____________ Won't open/close _____

Electrical: Insufficient outlets __ Insufficient switches ____________________
Needs new light fixtures ______________

Family room/rec room

Family room ______ Rec room ______ In basement ______

Floor: Not level - slopes toward center ______ Toward exterior ______ Extreme ______
Excessive bounce ___ Needs carpet ____ Needs refinishing ______ Holes ______

Floor: Gaps ______ Water marks ____ Rot damage ______ Buckled/warped ___

Walls: Solid ______ Loose ______ Wet ______ Not plumb ______
Cracks - large ______ small ______ Holes - large ______ small ______
Water marks - wet ___ dry ______ Wallpaper - peeling/loose/lumpy ______
Paneling - damaged/ugly ______

Windows: Broken panes ______ Rotted ______ Need paint ______
Missing/broken hardware ______ Won't open/close ____

Electrical: Insufficient outlets ___ Insufficient switches ______
Needs new light fixtures ______

Kitchen

Floor: Not level - slopes toward center ______ Toward exterior ______ Extreme ______
Excessive bounce ___ Needs new tile ___ Holes ______ Gaps ______
Water marks ______ Rot damage ______ Buckled/warped ______
Badly decayed floorcovering ______

Walls: Solid ______ Loose ______ Wet ______ Not plumb ______
Cracks - large ______ small ______ Holes - large ______ small ______
Water marks - wet ___ dry ______ Wallpaper - peeling/loose/lumpy ______
Paneling - damaged/ugly ______

Windows: Broken panes ______ Rotted ______ Need paint ______
Missing/broken hardware ______ Won't open/close ____

Electrical: Insufficient outlets ___ Insufficient switches ______
Needs new light fixtures ______

Cabinets: Not enough cabinets ______ Doors missing/damaged ______
Cabinets ugly/unmatched ______

Countertops: Damaged/ugly/unmatched ______

Plumbing: No garbage disposal ______ Disposal broken ______

Sink: Damaged/ugly ____ Doesn't drain right
Faucet - damaged/ugly/doesn't work ___ Inadequate water flow ______
Plumbing leaks ____ Rot ______ Water damage ______

Main bath

Floor: Not level - slopes toward center ______ Toward exterior ______ Extreme ______
Excessive bounce ___ Needs new tile ___ Holes ______
Gaps ______ Water marks ____ Rot damage ______ Buckled/warped ___

Floor: Badly decayed floorcovering ___________

Walls: Solid _____________ Loose __________ Wet _________________ Not plumb ______
Cracks - large _____ small __________ Holes - large __________ small ___________
Water marks - wet __ dry ___________ Wallpaper - peeling/loose/lumpy __________
No closet/cabinet __ Doors missing/damaged ________________

Wallcovering/tile: Damaged/ugly/decayed ________

Windows: No windows _______ Broken panes ____ Rotted ______________
Need paint _______ Won't open/close_ Missing/broken hardware _______________

Electrical: Insufficient outlets__ Insufficient switches ________________
Needs new light fixtures _____________ Needs fan/vent _______

Plumbing: Sink damaged _____ Sink ugly _______ Doesn't drain right ____
Faucet damaged/ugly/doesn't work ____ Inadequate water flow __________________
Tub damaged _____ Tub ugly ________ Doesn't drain right ____ No shower ______
Shower doesn't work _______________ Missing/inadequate shower enclosure ______
Faucet damaged/ugly/doesn't work ____ Inadequate water flow __________________
Toilet - damaged/ugly/unmatching ____ Doesn't flush _________ Runs ___________

Second bath

No 2nd bath ______

Floor: Not level - slopes toward center ________ Toward exterior ______ Extreme __________
Excessive bounce ___ Needs new tile ___ Holes ______________ Gaps ___________
Water marks _______ Rot damage _____ Buckled/warped _____
Badly decayed floorcovering ___________

Walls: Solid _____________ Loose __________ Wet _________________ Not plumb ______
Cracks - large _____ small __________ Holes - large __________ small ___________
Water marks - wet __ dry ___________ Wallpaper - peeling/loose/lumpy __________
No closet/cabinet __ Doors missing/damaged ________________

Wallcovering/tile: Damaged/ugly/decayed ________

Windows: No windows _______ Broken panes ____ Rotted ______________
Need paint _______ Don't open/close _ Missing/broken hardware _______________

Electrical: Insufficient outlets__ Insufficient switches ________________
Needs new light fixtures _____________ Needs fan/vent _______

Plumbing: No sink __________ Damaged/ugly ___ Doesn't drain properly _______________
Faucet - damaged/ugly/doesn't work ___ Inadequate water flow __________________
No tub ___________ Tub/shower damaged/ugly ______________ Doesn't drain _____
No shower _______ Shower doesn't work _________________
Missing/inadequate shower enclosure ___________________
Faucet - damaged/ugly/doesn't work ___ Inadequate water flow __________________
Toilet - damaged/ugly/unmatching ____ Doesn't flush _________ Runs ___________

Hallway

Floor: Needs carpet/refinishing ________

Walls: Solid ________ Not plumb ________ Need paint ________

Cracks - large ________ small ________ Holes - large ________ small ________

Paneling - damaged/ugly ________ Wallpaper - peeling/loose/lumpy ________

Electrical: No light ________ Needs new fixture ________

Main stairs

Stairs: Too steep ________ Shaky ________ Broken treads ________

No handrail ________ No smoke alarm __ Needs carpet/refinishing ________

Bedroom 1

Floor: Not level - slopes toward center ________ Toward exterior ________ Extreme ________

Excessive bounce __ Needs carpet ________ Needs refinishing ________ Holes ________

Gaps ________ Water marks ________ Buckled/warped ________ Rot damage ________

Walls: Solid ________ Loose ________ Wet ________ Not plumb ________

Cracks - large ________ small ________ Holes - large ________ small ________

Water marks - wet __ dry ________ Wallpaper - peeling/loose/lumpy ________

Paneling - damaged/ugly ________

Closet: No closet ________ Too small ________ Door missing/damaged/doesn't close ________

Windows: Broken panes ________ Rotted ________ Need paint ________

Won't open/close __ Missing/broken hardware ________

Electrical: Insufficient outlets __ Insufficient switches ________

Needs new light fixtures ________

Bedroom 2

No 2nd bedroom __

Floor: Not level - slopes toward center ________ Toward exterior ________ Extreme ________

Excessive bounce __ Needs carpet ________ Needs refinishing ________ Holes ________

Gaps ________ Water marks ________ Buckled/warped ________ Rot damage ________

Walls: Solid ________ Loose ________ Wet ________ Not plumb ________

Cracks - large ________ small ________ Holes - large ________ small ________

Water marks - wet __ dry ________ Wallpaper - peeling/loose/lumpy ________

Paneling - damaged/ugly ________

Closet: No closet ________ Too small ________ Door missing/damaged/doesn't close ________

Windows: Broken panes ________ Rotted ________ Need paint ________

Don't open/close __ Missing/broken hardware ________

Electrical: Insufficient outlets __ Insufficient switches ________

Needs new light fixtures ________

Bedroom 3

No 3rd bedroom ___

Floor:	Not level - slopes toward center ________		Toward exterior _______	Extreme __________
	Excessive bounce __	Needs carpet _____	Needs refinishing ______	Holes ____________
	Gaps _____________	Water marks _____	Buckled/warped _______	Rot damage ______
Walls:	Solid _____________	Loose ___________	Wet ________________	Not plumb _______
Walls:	Cracks - large ______	small ___________	Holes - large __________	small ____________
	Water marks - wet _	dry _____________	Wallpaper - peeling/loose/lumpy __________	
	Paneling - damaged/ugly _____________			
Closet:	No closet _________	Too small _______	Door missing/damaged/doesn't close _______	
Windows:	Broken panes ______	Rotted __________	Need paint ___________	
	Won't open/close __	Missing/broken hardware _______________		
Electrical:	Insufficient outlets _	Insufficient switches ____________________		
	Needs new light fixtures ______________			

Bedroom 4

No 4th bedroom ___

Floor:	Not level - slopes toward center ________		Toward exterior _______	Extreme __________
	Excessive bounce __	Needs carpet _____	Needs refinishing ______	Holes ____________
	Gaps _____________	Water marks _____	Buckled/warped _______	Rot damage ______
Walls:	Solid _____________	Loose ___________	Wet ________________	Not plumb _______
	Cracks - large ______	small ___________	Holes - large __________	small ____________
	Water marks - wet _	dry _____________	Wallpaper - peeling/loose/lumpy __________	
	Paneling - damaged/ugly _____________			
Closet:	No closet _________	Too small _______	Door missing/damaged/doesn't close _______	
Windows:	Broken panes ______	Rotted __________	Need paint ___________	
	Won't open/close __	Missing/broken hardware _______________		
Electrical:	Insufficient outlets _	Insufficient switches ____________________		
	Needs new light fixtures ______________			

Attic/attic space

Inadequate insulation _______________	Inadequate vents _______
Rot/insect damage __________________	Evidence of roof leakage ________________
Damaged/inadequate rafters joists ______	

Basement

Stairs:	Too steep ________	Shaky __________	Rotted _________________	No handrail ______
Door:	No door __________	Door damaged/rotted ___________________		Doesn't close _____

Floor: Dirt floor ________ Concrete cracked/damaged ______________
Missing/broken posts ______________ Evidence of rodents ____

Walls: Poured concrete ____ Block __________ Brick ______________ Other __________
Holes - large ______ small __________ Light visible __________
Dirt/water leaking through __________
Cracks - large ______ small __________ Light visible __________
Dirt/water leaking through __________
Broken/missing bricks/blocks ________ Crumbling mortar _____

Dampness: Standing water _____ Water marks______ Unusually high humidity ______________

Smell rot/mold/fungus ____________

Ceiling: Low ceiling _______ Sagging beam ____ Cut/cracked joists _____
Water marks - wet __ dry __________ Rot/insect damage _____
Damaged/missing ceiling tiles ________

Electrical: Main service inadequate ____________ Not enough circuits ____
No dryer outlet_____ No washer outlet__ Insufficient basement lights ______________
Dangling/improperly installed wiring ___

Plumbing: Leaks __________ Rust __________ Improper size pipes ____ No cutoffs _______
Old/no washtub ___ Clogged drains ___ No sewer cleanouts ____

Water heater: Leaks __________ Doesn't work _____ Improperly vented _____
No cutoff ________ Improper/missing pressure release valve ____

Heating: No central heat _____ Furnace - damaged/doesn't work __________
Furnace very old ___

Furnace type: Gas forced air _____ Oil __________ Electric __________
Gas gravity _______ Gas-fired steam ___ Gas-fired hot water ____
Smell gas ________ Furnace dirty _____ Inadequate/damaged duct work__________
Leaky water/steam pipes ____________ Noisy/chattering pumps/relays/valves _____

Notes:

Index

A

B

C

S

T

U

V

W

Y

Z

Practical References for Builders

Renovating & Restyling Older Homes

Any builder can turn a run-down old house into a showcase of perfection — if the customer has unlimited funds to spend. Unfortunately, most customers are on a tight budget. They usually want more improvements than they can afford — and they expect you to deliver. This book shows how to add economical improvements that can increase the property value by two, five or even ten times the cost of the remodel. Sound impossible? Here you'll find the secrets of a builder who has been putting these techniques to work on Victorian and Craftsman-style houses for twenty years. You'll see what to repair, what to replace and what to leave, so you can remodel or restyle older homes for the least amount of money and the greatest increase in value. **416 pages, 8½ x 11, $33.50**

Construction Forms & Contracts

125 forms you can copy and use — or load into your computer (from the FREE disk enclosed). Then you can customize the forms to fit your company, fill them out, and print. Loads into *Word* for *Windows*™, *Lotus 1-2-3*, *WordPerfect*, *Works*, or *Excel* programs. You'll find forms covering accounting, estimating, fieldwork, contracts, and general office. Each form comes with complete instructions on when to use it and how to fill it out. These forms were designed, tested and used by contractors, and will help keep your business organized, profitable and out of legal, accounting and collection troubles. Includes a CD-ROM for *Windows*™ and Mac.
400 pages, 8½ x 11, $41.75

Rough Framing Carpentry

If you'd like to make good money working outdoors as a framer, this is the book for you. Here you'll find shortcuts to laying out studs; speed cutting blocks, trimmers and plates by eye; quickly building and blocking rake walls; installing ceiling backing, ceiling joists, and truss joists; cutting and assembling hip trusses and California fills; arches and drop ceilings — all with production line procedures that save you time and help you make more money. Over 100 on-the-job photos of how to do it right and what can go wrong. **304 pages, 8½ x 11, $26.50**

Basic Lumber Engineering for Builders

Beam and lumber requirements for many jobs aren't always clear, especially with changing building codes and lumber products. Most of the time you rely on your own "rules of thumb" when figuring spans or lumber engineering. This book can help you fill the gap between what you can find in the building code span tables and what you need to pay a certified engineer to do. With its large, clear illustrations and examples, this book shows you how to figure stresses for pre-engineered wood or wood structural members, how to calculate loads, and how to design your own girders, joists and beams. Included FREE with the book — an easy-to-use limited version of NorthBridge Software's *Wood Beam Sizing* program.
272 pages, 8½ x 11, $38.00

Finish Carpentry: Efficient Techniques for Custom Interiors

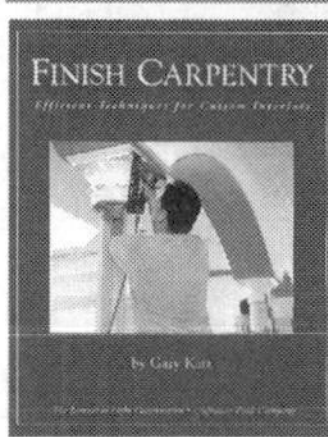

Professional finish carpentry demands expert skills, precise tools, and a solid understanding of how to do the work. This new book explains how to install moldings, paneled walls and ceilings, and just about every aspect of interior trim — including doors and windows. Covers built-in bookshelves, coffered ceilings, and skylight wells and soffits, including paneled ceilings with decorative beams.
288 pages, 8½ x 11, $34.95

How to Succeed With Your Own Construction Business

Everything you need to start your own construction business: setting up the paperwork, finding the work, advertising, using contracts, dealing with lenders, estimating, scheduling, finding and keeping good employees, keeping the books, and coping with success. If you're considering starting your own construction business, all the knowledge, tips, and blank forms you need are here. **336 pages, 8½ x 11, $28.50**

2002 *National Electrical Code*

This new electrical code incorporates some of the most sweeping improvements ever to make the code more functional and user-friendly. Here you'll find the essential foundation for electrical code requirements for the 21st century. Includes over 400 significant and widespread changes, this 2002 *NEC* contains all the latest electrical technologies, recently developed techniques, and enhanced safety standards for electrical work. This is the standard all electricians are required to know, even if it hasn't yet been adopted by their local or state jurisdictions.
720 pages, 8½ x 11, $59.50

Contractor's Guide to the Building Code Revised

This new edition was written in collaboration with the International Conference of Building Officials, writers of the code. It explains in plain English exactly what the latest edition of the *Uniform Building Code* requires. Based on the 1997 code, it explains the changes and what they mean for the builder. Also covers the *Uniform Mechanical Code* and the *Uniform Plumbing Code*. Shows how to design and construct residential and light commercial buildings that'll pass inspection the first time. Suggests how to work with an inspector to minimize construction costs, what common building shortcuts are likely to be cited, and where exceptions may be granted. **320 pages, 8½ x 11, $39.00**

CD Estimator

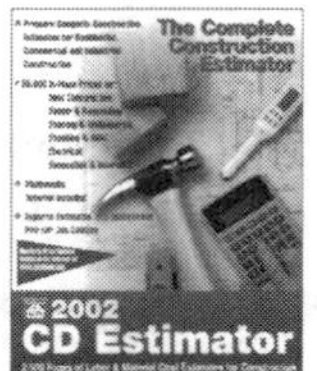

If your computer has *Windows*™ and a CD-ROM drive, CD Estimator puts at your fingertips 85,000 construction costs for new construction, remodeling, renovation & insurance repair, electrical, plumbing, HVAC and painting. Quarterly cost updates are available at no charge on the Internet. You'll also have the *National Estimator* program — a stand-alone estimating program for *Windows*™ that *Remodeling* magazine called a "computer wiz," and Job Cost Wizard, a program that lets you export your estimates to QuickBooks Pro for actual job costing. A 40-minute interactive video teaches you how to use this CD-ROM to estimate construction costs. And to top it off, to help you create professional-looking estimates, the disk includes over 40 construction estimating and bidding forms in a format that's perfect for nearly any *Windows*™ word processing or spreadsheet program. **CD Estimator is $68.50**

Plumber's Handbook Revised

This new edition shows what will and won't pass inspection in drainage, vent, and waste piping, septic tanks, water supply, graywater recycling systems, pools and spas, fire protection, and gas piping systems. All tables, standards, and specifications are completely up-to-date with recent plumbing code changes. Covers common layouts for residential work, how to size piping, select and hang fixtures, practical recommendations, and trade tips. It's the approved reference for the plumbing contractor's exam in many states. Includes an extensive set of multiple choice questions after each chapter, and in the back of the book, the answers and explanations. Also in the back of the book, a full sample plumber's exam.
352 pages, 8½ x 11, $32.00

Contractor's Guide to QuickBooks Pro 2002

This user-friendly manual walks you through QuickBooks Pro's detailed setup procedure and explains step-by-step how to create a first-rate accounting system. You'll learn in days, rather than weeks, how to use QuickBooks Pro to get your contracting business organized, with simple, fast accounting procedures. On the CD included with the book you'll find a QuickBooks Pro file preconfigured for a construction company (you drag it over onto your computer and plug in your own company's data). You'll also get a complete estimating program, including a database, and a job costing program that lets you export your estimates to QuickBooks Pro. It even includes many useful construction forms to use in your business.
328 pages, 8½ x 11, $46.50

Also available: **Contractor's Guide to QuickBooks Pro 2001, $45.25**
Contractor's Guide to QuickBooks Pro 2000, $44.50
Contractor's Guide to QuickBooks Pro 1999, $42.00

Contractor's Plain-English Legal Guide

For today's contractors, legal problems are like snakes in the swamp — you might not see them, but you know they're there. This book tells you where the snakes are hiding and directs you to the safe path. With the directions in this easy-to-read handbook you're less likely to need a $200-an-hour lawyer. Includes simple directions for starting your business, writing contracts that cover just about any eventuality, collecting what's owed you, filing liens, protecting yourself from unethical subcontractors, and more. For about the price of 15 minutes in a lawyer's office, you'll have a guide that will make many of those visits unnecessary.
272 pages, 8½ x 11, $49.50

National Repair & Remodeling Estimator

The complete pricing guide for dwelling reconstruction costs. Reliable, specific data you can apply on every repair and remodeling job. Up-to-date material costs and labor figures based on thousands of jobs across the country. Provides recommended crew sizes; average production rates; exact material, equipment, and labor costs; a total unit cost and a total price including overhead and profit. Separate listings for high- and low-volume builders, so prices shown are specific for any size business. Estimating tips specific to repair and remodeling work to make your bids complete, realistic, and profitable. Includes a CD-ROM with an electronic version of the book with *National Estimator*, a stand-alone *Windows*™ estimating program, plus an interactive multimedia video that shows how to use the disk to compile construction cost estimates.
296 pages, 8½ x 11, $48.50. Revised annually

Roof Framing

Shows how to frame any type of roof in common use today, even if you've never framed a roof before. Includes using a pocket calculator to figure any common, hip, valley, or jack rafter length in seconds. Over 400 illustrations cover every measurement and every cut on each type of roof: gable, hip, Dutch, Tudor, gambrel, shed, gazebo, and more.
480 pages, 5½ x 8½, $22.00

National Construction Estimator

Current building costs for residential, commercial, and industrial construction. Estimated prices for every common building material. Provides manhours, recommended crew, and gives the labor cost for installation. Includes a CD-ROM with an electronic version of the book with *National Estimator*, a stand-alone *Windows*™ estimating program, plus an interactive multimedia video that shows how to use the disk to compile construction cost estimates. **616 pages, 8½ x 11, $47.50. Revised annually**

Basic Engineering for Builders

If you've ever been stumped by an engineering problem on the job, yet wanted to avoid the expense of hiring a qualified engineer, you should have this book. Here you'll find engineering principles explained in non-technical language and practical methods for applying them on the job. With the help of this book you'll be able to understand engineering functions in the plans and how to meet the requirements, how to get permits issued without the help of an engineer, and anticipate requirements for concrete, steel, wood and masonry. See why you sometimes have to hire an engineer and what you can undertake yourself: surveying, concrete, lumber loads and stresses, steel, masonry, plumbing, and HVAC systems. This book is designed to help the builder save money by understanding engineering principles that you can incorporate into the jobs you bid. **400 pages, 8½ x 11, $36.50**

Basic Plumbing with Illustrations, Revised

This completely-revised edition brings this comprehensive manual fully up-to-date with all the latest plumbing codes. It is the journeyman's and apprentice's guide to installing plumbing, piping, and fixtures in residential and light commercial buildings: how to select the right materials, lay out the job and do professional-quality plumbing work, use essential tools and materials, make repairs, maintain plumbing systems, install fixtures, and add to existing systems. Includes extensive study questions at the end of each chapter, and a section with all the correct answers.
384 pages, 8½ x 11, $33.00

Craftsman Book Company
6058 Corte del Cedro
P.O. Box 6500
Carlsbad, CA 92018

☎ 24 hour order line
1-800-829-8123
Fax (760) 438-0398

Name

e-mail address (for order tracking and special offers)

Company

Address

City/State/Zip ❍ This is a residence

Total enclosed________________(In California add 7.25% tax)

We pay shipping when your check covers your order in full.

In A Hurry?

We accept phone orders charged to your

❍ Visa, ❍ MasterCard, ❍ Discover or ❍ American Express

Card# ________________

Exp. date________Initials________

Tax Deductible: Treasury regulations make these references tax deductible when used in your work. Save the canceled check or charge card statement as your receipt.

Order online http://www.craftsman-book.com
Free on the Internet! Download any of Craftsman's estimating costbooks for a 30-day free trial! http://costbook.com

10-Day Money Back Guarantee

❍ 36.50 Basic Engineering for Builders
❍ 38.00 Basic Lumber Engineering for Builders
❍ 33.00 Basic Plumbing with Illustrations
❍ 68.50 CD Estimator
❍ 41.75 Construction Forms & Contracts with a CD-ROM for Windows™ and Macintosh.
❍ 42.00 Contractor's Guide to QuickBooks Pro 1999
❍ 44.50 Contractor's Guide to QuickBooks Pro 2000
❍ 45.25 Contractor's Guide to QuickBooks Pro 2001
❍ 46.50 Contractor's Guide to QuickBooks Pro 2002
❍ 39.00 Contractor's Guide to the Building Code Revised
❍ 49.50 Contractor's Plain-English Legal Guide
❍ 34.95 Finish Carpentry: Efficient Techniques for Custom Interiors
❍ 28.50 How to Succeed w/Your Own Construction Business
❍ 47.50 National Construction Estimator with FREE *National Estimator* on a CD-ROM.
❍ 59.50 2002 *National Electrical Code*
❍ 48.50 National Repair & Remodeling Estimator with FREE *National Estimator* on a CD-ROM.
❍ 32.00 Plumber's Handbook Revised
❍ 33.50 Renovating & Restyling Older Homes
❍ 22.00 Roof Framing
❍ 26.50 Rough Framing Carpentry
❍ 22.75 Profits in Buying & Renovating Homes
❍ FREE Full Color Catalog

Prices subject to change without notice

Craftsman Book Company
6058 Corte del Cedro
P.O. Box 6500
Carlsbad, CA 92018

☎ 24 hour order line
1-800-829-8123
Fax (760) 438-0398

Name

e-mail address (for order tracking and special offers)

Company

Address

City/State/Zip ❍ This is a residence

Total enclosed______________________(In California add 7.25% tax)

We pay shipping when your check covers your order in full.

In A Hurry?

We accept phone orders charged to your
❍ Visa, ❍ MasterCard, ❍ Discover or ❍ American Express

Card# ______________________

Exp. date______________Initials ______________

Tax Deductible: Treasury regulations make these references tax deductible when used in your work. Save the canceled check or charge card statement as your receipt.

Order online http://www.craftsman-book.com
Free on the Internet! Download any of Craftsman's estimating costbooks for a 30-day free trial! http://costbook.com

10-Day Money Back Guarantee

❍ 36.50 Basic Engineering for Builders
❍ 38.00 Basic Lumber Engineering for Builders
❍ 33.00 Basic Plumbing with Illustrations
❍ 68.50 CD Estimator
❍ 41.75 Construction Forms & Contracts with a CD-ROM for Windows™ and Macintosh.
❍ 42.00 Contractor's Guide to QuickBooks Pro 1999
❍ 44.50 Contractor's Guide to QuickBooks Pro 2000
❍ 45.25 Contractor's Guide to QuickBooks Pro 2001
❍ 46.50 Contractor's Guide to QuickBooks Pro 2002
❍ 39.00 Contractor's Guide to the Building Code Revised
❍ 49.50 Contractor's Plain-English Legal Guide
❍ 34.95 Finish Carpentry: Efficient Techniques for Custom Interiors
❍ 28.50 How to Succeed w/Your Own Construction Business
❍ 47.50 National Construction Estimator with FREE *National Estimator* on a CD-ROM.
❍ 59.50 2002 *National Electrical Code*
❍ 48.50 National Repair & Remodeling Estimator with FREE *National Estimator* on a CD-ROM.
❍ 32.00 Plumber's Handbook Revised
❍ 33.50 Renovating & Restyling Older Homes
❍ 22.00 Roof Framing
❍ 26.50 Rough Framing Carpentry
❍ 22.75 Profits in Buying & Renovating Homes
❍ FREE Full Color Catalog

Prices subject to change without notice

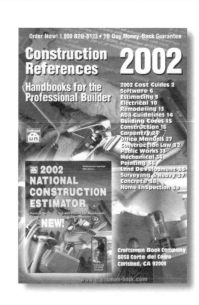

NO POSTAGE
NECESSARY
IF MAILED
IN THE
UNITED STATES

BUSINESS REPLY MAIL

FIRST CLASS MAIL PERMIT NO. 271 CARLSBAD, CA

POSTAGE WILL BE PAID BY ADDRESSEE

Craftsman Book Company
6058 Corte del Cedro
P.O. Box 6500
Carlsbad, CA 92018-9974

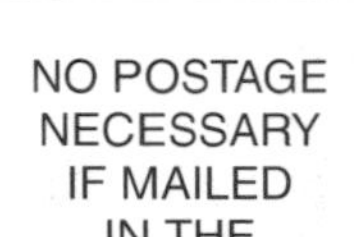

NO POSTAGE
NECESSARY
IF MAILED
IN THE
UNITED STATES

BUSINESS REPLY MAIL

FIRST CLASS MAIL PERMIT NO. 271 CARLSBAD, CA

POSTAGE WILL BE PAID BY ADDRESSEE

Craftsman Book Company
6058 Corte del Cedro
P.O. Box 6500
Carlsbad, CA 92018-9974

NO POSTAGE
NECESSARY
IF MAILED
IN THE
UNITED STATES

BUSINESS REPLY MAIL

FIRST CLASS MAIL PERMIT NO. 271 CARLSBAD, CA

POSTAGE WILL BE PAID BY ADDRESSEE

Craftsman Book Company
6058 Corte del Cedro
P.O. Box 6500
Carlsbad, CA 92018-9974